The WISDOM of ANTS

10 Commandments of Trust

Restore the Secret Power of Trust
That Made America Great
Before It's Too Late

Linnea B. McCord, J.D., M.B.A.

An American Code of Trust

HRD PRESS, INC. • AMHERST, MASSACHUSETTS

Published by: HRD Press, Inc.
                 22 Amherst Road
                 Amherst, MA 01002
                 413-253-3488
                 800-822-2801 (U.S. and Canada)
                 413-253-3490 (fax)
                 www.hrdpress.com

ISBN 978-1-61014-397-4

Editorial services by Sally Farnham
Production services by Jean Miller
Cover design by Eileen Klockars

All truth passes through three stages:
First, it is ridiculed.
Second, it is violently opposed.
Third, it is accepted as being self-evident.

Arthur Schopenhauer

Any intelligent fool can make things bigger, more complex...
It takes a touch of genius—and a lot of courage—to
move in the opposite direction.

E. F. Schumacher

Contents

What Will It Be?   vii

Why This Book Was Written   ix

Part I. The Wisdom of Ants

1   **The Secret Power of Trust**   3
Trust as Competitive Advantage

2   **Through a Different Lens**   17
A "Bystander's" Perspective

3   **Freedom at Risk**   29
Playing with Fire

4   **It's All about Trust**   43
Debunking the Myths about Ethics

5   **Complacency about Trust Is Dangerous**   57
History's Warnings

6   **Why Trust Matters**   75
Freedom Depends on Trust

7   **Trust Is Fragile**   97
Unethical Conduct Destroys Trust

8   **Our Culture of Trust Is Unique**   119
The Secret of Our Survival and Success

9   **Trust Is *Not* Worldwide**   145
National Borders Still Matter

10   **Trust Is Up to All of U.S.**   161
The American Phoenix of Freedom Must Rise

Part II. The 10 Commandments of Trust

11   **Restoring Trust**   183
Not the "10 Suggestions"

12   **Commandment of Trust #1: TRUTH**   189
No Such Thing as Partially Pregnant

13 **Commandment of Trust #2: FAIR**   195
        Forget This at Your Peril

14 **Commandment of Trust #3: LOYALTY**   203
        Two Masters Is One Too Many

15 **Commandment of Trust #4: CARE**   211
        No Going to Sleep at the Wheel

16 **Commandment of Trust #5: ACCOUNT**   217
        The ABCs of Counting the Marbles

17 **Commandment of Trust #6: PROPERTY**   225
        Protecting Fort Knox

18 **Commandment of Trust #7: PEOPLE**   235
        Respecting Our Most Important Asset

19 **Commandment of Trust #8: PROMISES**   243
        Your Word Is Your Bond

20 **Commandment of Trust #9: LEADERSHIP**   249
        Animal Farm Ethics Don't Work

21 **Commandment of Trust #10: ENFORCEMENT**   263
        Today's Loophole, Tomorrow's Noose

Appendix A: 271
10 Commandments of Trust in the United States

Appendix B: 283
10 Commandments of Trust "Go Global"

Appendix C: 287
10 Commandments of Trust in China

Chapter Endnotes   291

References and Resources   337

Index   349

Acknowledgments   397

About the Author   399

What Will It Be?

[Americans, by their conduct and example, will], once and for all answer the question of whether human societies [are] capable of creating good government intentionally by choice or whether they would forever be governed only by accident or force.

— **Alexander Hamilton (1755–1804)**
American Founding Father,
Chief of Staff to General George Washington
1st U.S. secretary of the Treasury, 1789–1795

Why This Book Was Written

In 2001, when Enron suddenly failed, I was astounded to hear some business people, attorneys, academics, and others nonchalantly say that the Enron scandal was just like other American scandals we've had in the past—"no big deal"; just "a few rotten apples." Being an American who had spent a significant number of years living and being educated in a foreign country as well as in the United States, working as a corporate attorney for a multinational Fortune 500 company headquartered in New York and Paris, and teaching law and ethics in that corporation and later full-time in two university business schools, I knew this wasn't true.

What I didn't understand in 2001 was why this was so obvious to me, but not obvious to so many other Americans. Thus began a 13-year odyssey to find out when, why, and how America had gone so dangerously off-track ethically and why it matters [Part 1: The Wisdom of Ants]. This journey led me to discover the 10 Commandments of Trust under ethics-based American Rule of Law (not the current American Rule of Lawyers—and Bureaucrats—we are living under today) [Part 2: The 10 Commandments of Trust].

Because of the massive size and brazenness of the Enron scandal and the other huge scandals that quickly followed, coupled with the incredible complacency of so many Americans, I knew serious pain lay ahead. As discussed in the book, unethical conduct leads to pain—and a lot of it—the only question is when and how it will be felt.

However, it wasn't until 2007, after discovering the staggering misuse of exotic financial products in our financial system, like credit derivatives, mortgage-backed securities, collateralized debt obligations, and such, that I realized Americans were facing economic pain far beyond anything American baby-boomers and later American generations had ever seen in their lifetimes. Internet bloggers and writers warned that a major economic trauma was fast approaching, while mainstream "experts," pundits, academics, and "leaders" said "not too worry"; it's all "under control."

As we now know, the Internet bloggers and writers were right and the mainstream "experts" were wrong. This is why, in addition to traditional "official" academic and legal resources, "non-traditional" information sources are also cited in the book. These "non-traditional" sources proved far more accurate in predicting the economic turmoil and pain of the Financial Crisis of 2008.

As I write this introduction in the last week of 2014, some non-traditional sources are warning of more economic pain and turmoil ahead, while many mainstream "experts," pundits, academics, and "leaders" are again sounding the "all clear" on the financial system and economy. After all, the American stock market has been levitating at an all-time record high, home prices in many parts of the country have risen significantly, and our federal government assures us that our national unemployment rate is back below 6%.

However, beneath the surface, signs of ethical trouble are still simmering in the land. As you will read in the book, during the first decade of the 21st century, it appears that we not only recreated all four financial bubbles of the 1920s, we have added a disturbing fifth financial bubble to the mix. Also, if everything is now so rosy and upbeat, one wonders why the United States and other western governments appear to be implementing *bail-in* regimes to put future financial losses of their "too big to fail" financial institutions on creditors, depositors, and bondholders, instead of taxpayers as was previously done with *bailouts*.

Over the past four decades, we have strayed far from the simple and clear ethical standards of the *10 Commandments of Trust* under *ethics-based* American Rule of Law. We have forgotten (or never learned) that long-term prosperity, peace, stability, and security require ethical conduct. Unethical conduct leads to economic failure, political instability, social disharmony, and insecurity from internal and external threats. It's not complicated.

This book was not written from a political point of view, whether Democrat, Republican, or other. The laws of ethical conduct that create our culture of trust are apolitical—they apply to everyone. Besides, *political thinking* (e.g., creating new ethics theories like situational and relative ethics) is what got us into our current ethics morass. We will need *critical thinking* to get us out of the ethics mess we are in now, if we hope to do so fast enough to keep our freedom.

Nor is this book intended to be an academic or legal tome dispensing investment or legal advice either. As you will also see in the pages of this book, my role as the author is to act only as a *guide, not a guru*, pointing out landmarks and points of interest in our American ethics landscape, as seen through the eyes of an *American bystander* with a *"view from the Moon"* perspective. Because bystanders see the world differently, almost inevitably a bystander's perspective is out-of-step with the popularly held views of the day.

The invaluable gift of our unique brand of self-organizing American freedom is our freedom to *think for ourselves*. We need "all brains on deck" in the United States—and fast. The last time Americans so blindly followed the so-called "experts" was in the 1920s, and as we know, this decade was followed by the extreme economic pain and hardship in the 1930s Great Depression. Think "this time is different"?

To survive and succeed in the 21st century as a free economy, free society, and free nation, we must restore our wise, common sense, self-reliant culture of self-organizing freedom. The *10 Commandments of Trust* under *ethics-based* American Rule of Law are 10 simple and clear ethical standards that must be voluntarily followed, and enforced when necessary, in *all* of our self-organizing civic institutions and voluntary associations, if we wish to keep and maintain our *absolutely essential and non-negotiable culture of trust.* Ethical conduct (doing what's *right*) creates trust. Unethical conduct (doing what's *wrong*) creates distrust. It's as simple as that.

Without our essential culture of trust, Americans cannot maintain a free prosperous economy, a free stable political system, and a free secure and peaceful society and nation *over the long term*. By continuing to tolerate such high levels of unethical conduct in the United States today, Americans are running the risk of losing the most successful experiment in freedom in modern world history. Think that can't happen? Think again.

> *Society in every state is a blessing, but government even in its best state is but a necessary evil; in its worst state an intolerable one; for when we suffer, or are exposed to the same miseries by a government, our calamity is heightened by reflecting that we furnish the means by which we suffer...*
>
> **– Thomas Paine (1737–1809)**
> Founding Father, author of *Common Sense in 1776,* the pamphlet that galvanized Americans to fight the American Revolution

Part I

The Wisdom of Ants

Chapter 1

The Secret Power of Trust
Trust as Competitive Advantage

> *Posterity: you will never know how much it has cost my generation to preserve your freedom. I hope you will make good use of it.*
>
> **– John Quincy Adams (1767–1848)**
> 6th U.S. president 1825–1829

An Amazing Success Story

Kick over an anthill, what will you see? Swarms of ants immediately surging out of their nests to make repairs. They don't call meetings, form task forces, or phone central command for instructions. They act.

Ants have survived and thrived for 100 million years, far surpassing humans who have only been around for about 200,000 years. More than 8,000 species of ants can be found almost anywhere in the world—pretty amazing for a tiny creature that has bad eyesight, cannot hear, and barely has a brain.

An individual ant is extremely strong, capable of lifting 20 to 50 times its own body weight. With that kind of strength, a man could lift a truck over his head. But individual strength is not the secret of the ants' extraordinary success. What sets ants apart from most other living creatures is their ability to self-organize; that is, to act[1]

- automatically,
- voluntarily,
- and cooperatively,
- as a group
- without direction or control
- from any central authority.

Self-organizing ants can harness the collective wisdom of the entire colony to instantly solve problems caused by changed conditions. Scientists call this ability "swarm intelligence." This is what transforms tiny individual ants with limited "brainpower" into a "wise" united collective superpower.

When it rains, ants immediately bind themselves together as a raft to avoid drowning. To overcome a break in their path too wide to cross, ants automatically lock their bodies together to form a bridge for other ants to cross. Since there is no one point of central "top-down" control, there is also no one point of failure.

By "bottom-up" self-organizing, ants have created one of the most sophisticated and complex societies of living creatures found in nature. They specialize by task. The queen lays eggs, while different groups of worker ants find food, keep the nests in good repair, and raise the young. As conditions change, ants automatically switch to whatever task is needed.[2]

In many ways, ant communities resemble human communities. They raise "animals" (aphids) for food, have an elaborate food distribution system, and even go to war. In fact, ant colonies and human communities are so similar, one scientist said, "They do everything [humans do] but watch television."[3]

Argentine ants were transported by humans to every other continent, except Antarctica. In the early 2000s, scientists discovered that teeny-tiny Argentine ants have built a giant super-colony, 3,728 miles long, running along the coastline of France, Portugal, Spain, and Italy. Imagine a single giant ant colony stretching from New York City across the United States to San Diego, then north almost to Seattle.

Millions of *unrelated* queens and billions of *unrelated* ants, working *automatically, cooperatively, and voluntarily as a group without central direction or control* have created the largest and one of the most complex societies of cooperative living creatures on earth.

How did these tiny ants accomplish such a spectacular feat? *By following a few simple laws of behavior.*[4] That's what it takes to self-organize.

This is the wisdom of ants.

The Secret of American Success

Self-organization under Rule of Law has been part of the DNA of American culture since the earliest days of settlement nearly 400 years ago. When early American settlers arrived in the New World there were no familiar homes, farms, or stores—just vast stretches of virgin land, thousands of miles away from any civilization they had ever known.

These early Americans understood that to survive in this New World they would have to peacefully and voluntarily cooperate with one another. To foster this essential cooperation, in 1620 they signed the Mayflower Compact, agreeing to be bound by laws passed by their leaders *with their consent* (discussed in greater detail in Chapter 8). This ushered in a brand new *"bottom-up" self-organizing society under Rule of Law* at a time when English monarchs still ruled "top-down" by "divine right of kings."

English rulers, however, were *more answerable to the people* than European monarchs. In 1215, the Magna Carta put some limitations on the absolute power of English kings and queens. Also, by the time of early American settlements, *Christianity* and *Rule of Law* were well-entrenched in England (later Britain). The first Christian Anglo-Saxon king, King Ethelberht of Kent, established a code of law during his reign from AD 560–616, more than a thousand years earlier.[5]

Large numbers of early American settlers were Protestant Christians escaping religious persecution. Not surprisingly, they patterned their settlements on the "bottom-up" self-directed governance models of their early Protestant churches, instead of the Catholic Church's "top-down" governance model under a Pope.

In the early 1800s, Alexis de Tocqueville, author of *Democracy in America*, described this American propensity for self-organization as follows:

> Americans of all ages, all conditions, and all dispositions constantly form…. not only commercial and manufacturing companies, in which all take part, but associations of a thousand other kinds, religious, moral, …to give entertainments, to found seminaries, to build inns, to construct churches, to diffuse books…; in this manner they found hospitals, prisons, and schools [and] they form a society.[6]

By self-organizing, Americans have been able to unleash the *secret power of trust* to create the most successful free-market capitalist economy and stable democratic constitutional republic in modern world history. Like a self-organizing ant colony, the United States has been both dynamic and stable at the same time; dynamic enough to adapt quickly to constantly changing conditions, yet stable enough to remain *under the same U.S. Constitution and form of government* for more than two centuries.

> *There is nothing wrong with America that the faith, love of freedom, intelligence and energy of her citizens cannot cure.*
>
> **– Dwight D. Eisenhower (1890–1969)**
> Supreme Allied commander, WWII
> 34th U.S. president 1953–1961

Thus far, the United States has remained a united, stable, free country, even through times of extreme national crises that required extraordinary sacrifices by the people. A critical factor of America's longevity has been its ability to remain firmly rooted in the founding principles of our unique brand of constitutional freedom under *ethics-based* American Rule of Law. *This is the life source of our American self-organizing culture of trust.*

However, our ability to continue being a free self-organizing economy, government, and society in the 21st century depends squarely on whether we can keep and maintain this essential culture of trust. *Ethical conduct creates trust. Unethical conduct destroys trust.*

America's self-organizing culture of trust depends on *ethics-based* Rule of Law *that dispenses justice.* Paul Johnson, a well-known British historian, summed up America's attitude toward justice in the dedication of his nearly 1,000-page book on American history titled *A History of the American People*:

> To the people of America—strong, outspoken, intense in their convictions… with a passion for justice no nation has ever matched.[7]

This is the wisdom of ants.

The Wisdom of Ants

It only takes a few simple laws of right and wrong (ethical) conduct to self-organize:

> ➤ To act automatically, voluntarily, and cooperatively, as a group without central direction or control

> ➤ To adapt with lightning speed to changes in the environment and create an extraordinarily successful, complex society

Permanent Turbulence

We live in an age of permanent turbulence marked by chaos, complexity, crisis, and constant change. Advances in technology and the rise of the inter-connected global economy have driven much of this change. In addition, many countries (including the United States) are now so weighed down with debt and leverage (borrowed money), they are vulnerable to sudden painful economic slumps. With the world's economies now so intertwined, a serious economic dislocation in one part of the world will likely be felt in other parts of the world too.

To survive and thrive in this new age of permanent turbulence, individuals, businesses, organizations—and countries—must be able to adapt with lightning *speed* in an environment of never-ending chaos and change. A further complication is this speedy adaptation must be done in ways that are also *sustainable.* This is not easy for any country to do—for long.

> *It is not the strongest of the species that survives, nor the most intelligent... It is the one that is the most adaptable to change.*
>
> **– Charles Darwin (1809–1882)**
> Father of evolutionary biology

The *wisdom of ants* tells us that "bottom-up" self-organizing societies and economies *based on trust* can adapt faster than "top-down" centrally controlled economies, governments, and societies. As well-known management consultant Warren Bennis noted:

Above all, developing trust, [has] become the key source of sustainable competitive advantage.[8]

The Global Economy

The global economy refers to "the speed and ease with which the world's best competitors can enter virtually any market in the world at any time."[9] While other countries ratcheted up their educational standards, American educational standards declined. As soon as high-speed global communications became pervasive, jobs, capital, and expertise took flight across national boundaries.

In today's hyper-competitive global environment, individuals, organizations, and countries must daily ask themselves: "Are we as good as the best in the world?"[10] To survive and succeed in this new environment, countries must be able to produce the world's best products and services at the world's best prices—not an easy task.

Three Billion More Competitors

In the last three decades, three billion more competitors have entered the global marketplace. China, India, Russia (and other former members of the Soviet Union, particularly Eastern Europe) now compete directly with the United States and other western nations. China has transformed itself from an economically depressed country to the second largest economy in the world.

However, for these former communist and socialist economies and countries to continue being competitive and remain stable, harmonious, and secure, they must be able to keep and maintain their "freer" reformed economies. These economies require more trust and less force.

Survival of the Fittest

Nothing better illustrates the perils of this new competitive global environment than the dramatic change in fortunes of General Motors. In the 1950s, GM had more than 50% of the car market in the United States.[11] After the 1973 oil embargo, when the price of oil from OPEC oil-producing countries soared, GM's competitive dominance began to slide.

While GM continued building large, gas-guzzling cars, Japanese carmakers switched to building smaller, more gas-efficient cars in American-based plants. Unlike GM, Japanese carmakers' American-based plants were not unionized. Without GM's wide disparities in pay between executives and workers, these Japanese carmakers could build the same number of cars as GM with half as many workers.

GM's market share continued to erode throughout the 1980s and the 1990s. In 2009, Toyota Motor Co. took away GM's title as the largest car manufacturer in the world that GM had held since 1931. After the Financial Crisis of 2008, GM was forced to declare bankruptcy, even after receiving a multi-billion dollar bailout from the federal government.

However, Toyota's celebration was short-lived. In 2010, there were allegations of deaths and serious injury caused by sudden acceleration in its cars. This led to the recall of millions of vehicles, hundreds of lawsuits, and "the largest criminal penalty ever by an automaker for hiding safety defects from the public."[12] In the late 2000s, Toyota suffered its first loss in its 70-year history.

Indian and Chinese car manufacturers began producing cars costing $5,000 or less. To lower their labor costs, American and Japanese car manufacturers built plants in India and China. Japanese and American carmakers also began experimenting with hybrid cars that ran on electricity or hydrogen fuel cells rather than oil.

In 2011, GM began producing the first subcompact car built in the United States, with a base price of $14,000.[13] To reduce costs, workers would be paid only $14 an hour (not $28 an hour as before) and more robots would be used. That same year, Bill Vlasic, a long-time Detroit automotive reporter, wrote a book titled *Once Upon a Car: The Fall and Resurrection of America's Big Three Auto Makers—GM, Ford and Chrysler.* Toyota's auto sales in the United States rebounded too.

Not long afterward, car sales globally slowed down again. Workers at one Japanese car plant in India rioted, setting a manager on fire and injuring many others.[14] In 2014, GM recalled millions of vehicles amid accusations of safety flaws that may have caused deaths and serious injury.

The endless competitive merry-go-round of "survival of the fittest" continues.

No Jobs Are Safe

Over the past two decades, millions of American manufacturing jobs have been offshored to Asia, former Soviet Union countries (e.g., Russia and Eastern Europe), Mexico, and many other countries. American workers, paid about $49,000 a year, were replaced with Chinese and Indian workers paid approximately $1,200 per year or less.

China became the world's manufacturing center, while America lost nearly three million manufacturing jobs. In the 2000s, China "manufactured 75 percent of the world's toys, 58 percent of the world's clothes, and 29 percent of the world's mobile phones."[15]

Even white-collar service and professional jobs have been offshored to other countries.[16] American college-educated workers were paid about five times more than college-educated workers in India. In addition, Chinese and Indian universities together graduated about 500,000 engineers and scientists a year; American universities only about 60,000 a year.[17]

Tasks like processing insurance claims and home loans, computer programming, and some engineering, architectural, accounting, legal, medical, and dental tasks moved offshore. For example, in 2012, American health care companies began hiring nurses in India and the Philippines to "assess patient needs and determine treatment methods."[18]

American and other western companies moved some research and development centers to India and China. In 2000, China had 100 such foreign research centers; six years later there were 800.[19] GM built a research center in Shanghai, now that China is its largest market. In 2010, Applied Materials became the first major American high technology company to move its chief technology officer to Beijing, the site of its newest and largest research facility.

Reverse Globalization?

Jobs, capital, and factories are on the move again. Rising wages in China and India have driven manufacturing jobs to other Asian and African countries with lower labor costs. Indian companies are even offshoring some service jobs back to the United States.[20]

Some companies have discovered that outsourcing jobs to foreign countries is sometimes more trouble than it's worth.[21] In addition, American companies are facing growing hostility at home for sending jobs overseas when millions of Americans remain unemployed or underemployed. Some manufacturing jobs are returning to the U.S.[22] In 2012, Apple and GE announced they would be bringing some manufacturing back to the United States.

A common belief is that once globalization occurs, it never retreats, but this is not so. As a December 2012 *Fortune* article said: "They forgot to tell us globalization has a reverse gear."[23] What was forgotten was that jobs were sent overseas in an era of relative global prosperity, peace, stability, and security.

Harvard historian Niall Ferguson has pointed out that this retreat of globalization has happened before in history. He said globalization expanded during the Industrial Revolution from 1870, but was stopped by World War I (1914–1918), the Great Depression (1929–1941), and World War II (1941–1945).

Ferguson believes the same five factors that stopped globalization before in history are once present again: "imperial overstretch [this time by the United States instead of Britain], great power rivalries, an unstable alliance system [between countries], rogue regimes sponsoring terror, and the rise of a revolutionary terrorist organization hostile to capitalism."[24]

In an era of increasing instability and uncertainty, investments and jobs will gravitate to countries investors *trust* are safe, secure, and stable, especially in times of hardship and serious crisis. Issues of safety, security, political stability, and legal enforcement (e.g., lack of intellectual property protection) are likely to drive more jobs back to the United States—that is, if we can keep and maintain our essential culture of trust.

Jobs will continue to shift around the world as old jobs are eliminated, new jobs created, and social, political, economic, legal, and security changes continue to occur around the world.

The Molecular Economy

Sometimes technological advances transform our lives. During the Industrial Revolution, a slew of new inventions—the telephone, electricity, and mass-produced cars—changed the American landscape. Millions of Americans left farms and rural life for new factory jobs in the cities.

We are in the midst of another such transformative change. This time around it is being driven by new technologies based on *biology, living cells, and living systems*. Three technological trends are converging to create a new molecular economy: (1) advances in biotech, (2) new developments in nanotechnology, and (3) the development of super-speedy, super-smart computers.[25]

Although the exact path these current technological advances will take cannot always be predicted, what we do know is that rapid technological advances and constant change will be a permanent feature of our 21st century competitive landscape.

The Biotech Revolution

In 2000, the Human Genome Project mapped the entire sequence of human DNA creating a new science called *genomics* (the study of human genes and their functions). One day, we may be able to grow new arms, legs, and organs. Diseases could be cured just by deactivating genes.[26]

Nanotechnology

The most revolutionary changes may come from nanotechnology, the science that uses measurements smaller than a living cell called *nanometers*. Because they are so tiny, nanotechnology products can be seen only through today's most powerful microscopes (e.g., a human hair is about 80,000 nanometers wide). If successful, nanotechnology factories that "fit on top of a kitchen counter" may one day replace today's giant factories.[27]

The science of nanotechnology breaks down substances molecule by molecule, then rearranges them to create completely new substances with different properties and characteristics. Nature already does this. Under intense heat and pressure, over millions of years, coal is transformed into something completely different—a diamond. With nanotechnology, something similar could be accomplished in only hours and days. Scientists have already turned carbon atoms into carbon nanotubes that are "stronger than steel, virtually impervious to heat, and conduct electricity better than copper."[28]

In theory, a nanotech machine could build anything.[29] With nanotechnology, military surveillance equipment could be made as small and agile as a bumblebee.[30] Tiny nanotech surgical tools could be injected into our bodies to locate and kill cancer cells. The possibilities are endless.

Super-Fast, Super-Smart Computers

Today's new sciences generate such an enormous amount of data that much faster supercomputers and extremely sophisticated software are required. This has created a new industry called *bioinformatics.*[31]

Soon, biologically-based bio-chips may replace today's silicon-based technology used in computers.[32] Computers billions of times faster may one day rival the analytical ability of the human brain. Already, today's super-fast, super-smart computers can perform 360 trillion calculations per second. The next generation of supercomputers is expected to perform two to four quadrillion operations a second.[33]

We soon may be processing knowledge much faster and much more accurately, but what about wisdom?

21st Century Success Skills

Creativity, Flexibility, and Innovation

Because of unrelenting change, "survival of the fittest" today requires an ability to adapt ever faster to constantly changing circumstances. To survive and succeed, individuals, organizations, companies, and countries must be creative, flexible, and innovative.

Businesses, organizations, governments, and associations must constantly retool *what they do* and *how they do it* as technological advances, global competition, and other factors constantly render old business models obsolete.

Steel production in the United States is a good example. American steel mills in states like Pennsylvania, New York, and Ohio were hard hit by global competition. Many were offshored to other countries. But fast-rising labor and energy costs in steel-producing countries and much higher global transportation costs (higher oil prices) made it cost-effective to produce steel in the United States again. This time around, however, America's new steel factories were sophisticated and high-tech, aimed at producing higher-profit customized steel products in lower-cost states like Alabama, Mississippi, and Minnesota.[34]

Speed

Ever-increasing global competition, rapid technological advances, and increasing global instability mean individuals, organizations, and countries must respond to changes faster than ever before. Only those able to adapt quickly will survive. *Never-ending, fast-moving, constant change is here to stay.*

Sustainability

The world's population in 1901 was 1.6 billion; by 1960, 3 billion; and is now more than 7 billion. With such a surge in population growth, we can no longer take for granted that we have unlimited resources. Therefore, an essential survival skill for the 21st century is *sustainability*.

Already, 40% of the world's population may face serious water shortages. Natural resources are being depleted and oceans are being over-fished. Unlike in nature, man's industries produce toxic wastes and harmful pollutants. China's air and water pollution are now so serious they jeopardize the population's health and could derail the country's future economic success.

To be sustainable in the 21st century, every country must learn how to use resources wisely so as not to deplete them, or cause permanent environmental damage.

Knowledge Is Not Enough

Creating sustainable economies, political systems, and societies requires *wisdom*, not just knowledge.

Knowledge is defined by the *Oxford Dictionary* as "facts, information, and skills acquired by a person through experience or education; the theoretical or practical understanding of a subject." Individuals with knowledge become experts in a specific subject. Thus, seismologists are experts in earthquakes; botanists are experts in plants; and doctors are experts in medicine.

Obviously, in today's *knowledge-based global economy*, knowledge is essential. Countries must have highly qualified people in science, mathematics, and technology for their businesses, organizations, and economies to survive and succeed.

But knowledge alone is not enough. Navigating complexity, chaos, constant change, and crisis in the 21st century in a creative, speedy, and sustainable manner, requires businesses, organizations, and countries to have much more than mere knowledge; they must have wisdom.

> *Science is organized knowledge. Wisdom is organized life.*
>
> **– Immanuel Kant (1724–1804)**
> German philosopher, central figure of Western philosophy

Wisdom is knowledge, plus experience, plus insight, plus common sense, as a combination of dictionary definitions below shows:

Knowledge:	facts or ideas acquired by study, *plus*
Experience:	practical knowledge or skill from direct observation or participation in events, including the conscious past of a community, a nation, or mankind in general, *plus*
Insight:	the ability to understand the inner nature of things or instinctively know something without rational processes, *plus*
Common Sense:	*the sound, careful, and sensible opinions of ORDINARY people*

Wisdom Is...

Wisdom Is Timeless and Enduring, Not a Passing Fad

Although technologies, economies, political systems, and societies have changed greatly over time, human nature has not. The same wisdom about human nature from the days of the ancient Greeks, thousands of years ago, still applies today.

Knowledge is fleeting and readily accessible, especially with the widespread use of the Internet. Wisdom is much less accessible, develops slowly over longer periods of time and experience, and is much harder to obtain. In today's complex, chaotic world, it will take wisdom, not just knowledge, to produce economically successful and stable, harmonious, secure societies and countries that can survive over the long term.

Knowledge Is Morally Neutral, Wisdom Is Not

Wisdom entails both knowing the difference between right and wrong behavior *and* the ability to do what is right. This has been true since the days of ancient Rome. Cicero, described by the Encyclopedia Britannica as the statesman and scholar who "vainly tried to uphold republican principles in the final civil wars that destroyed the republic of Rome," said: "the function of wisdom is to discriminate between good and evil."[35]

Wisdom Is Not Best Left to Experts

Just because someone is smart or has expertise does not mean that person is also wise. Smart people often fall in love with their own intelligence. Too many experts foolishly believe that, by collecting and organizing information and developing a high degree of knowledge and skill on various subjects, they can find solutions to any problem. Wisdom doesn't rely just on experts; it includes *the common sense of ordinary people*.

In an era of rapid technological advances, it is easy to fall into the trap of believing that expertise (knowledge) is all that matters. Developing sustainable, peaceful, and stable self-organizing human communities that can adapt quickly in sustainable and effective ways requires wisdom, not just knowledge.

Wisdom Includes the Predictability of Human Nature

Wisdom takes into account the lessons of history and the predictability of human nature over thousands of years. Throughout history, the same human failings have led to the destruction of organizations, countries, empires, and civilizations many times.

Ant Wisdom for the United States

The self-organizing *wisdom of ants* can be distilled into three simple concepts:

1. **It Only Takes a Few Simple Laws (Principles).** To self-organize, ants follow a few simple laws of behavior. Take finding the shortest route to food as an example.

   When food supplies run low, specialized foraging worker ants automatically leave the nest, exuding a chemical substance called pheromones for other ants to follow. By trial and error, some ants find food. When they do, they immediately return to the nest, marking the shortest path to the food in both directions with a double-dose of pheromones. This attracts more ants to the shortest route. These additional ants exude more pheromones, attracting even more ants.[36] By following a few simple laws of behavior, ants easily find the shortest route to new food sources.

2. **Swarm Intelligence Works Best.** Ant brains are so tiny they cannot really think for themselves. However, individual ants, acting collectively *as a group* with millions and billions of other ants, have *swarm intelligence*—a kind of "thinking, planning, and calculating" group intelligence.[37]

   Although *each* ant *works independently locally* with other ants, *collectively they respond instantly as a group* to changed circumstances without waiting for instructions from central command. They automatically, voluntarily, and cooperatively organize themselves into complex patterns to adapt immediately to changed conditions.

Because of *swarm intelligence,* ants quickly solve complicated problems. They automatically reroute themselves around obstructions in their path and form separate traffic lanes to minimize congestion. Because they operate "bottom-up" automatically, cooperatively, and voluntarily, as a group, without central direction and control, ants can react instantaneously to changed conditions in a way a "top-down" centralized system cannot.

3. **Don't Kill Each Other.** Argentine ants in Argentina from nearby colonies, even a few miles away from one another, kill each other. As a result, Argentine ants in Argentina still live in small, stunted colonies.

   However, for reasons not yet totally understood, Argentine ants *outside of Argentina* do not kill each other. They work cooperatively together even though they come from nests thousands of miles apart. This is why Argentine ants *outside of Argentina* dominate all other ant species.

The Wisdom and Power of Trust

In human societies, the simple laws of behavior required to create trust are called ethics. Unethical (wrong) behaviors create distrust. If not corrected, distrust will eventually destroy the willingness of a free people to live and work harmoniously and peacefully together.

In other words, without trust, Americans cannot self-organize; that is, we will no longer be able to act automatically, cooperatively, and voluntarily, as a group, without central direction or control. Without trust, we will not be able to adapt quickly to today's constantly changing circumstances, especially in a national emergency or severe crisis.

American wisdom about the essential, non-negotiable ethical standards that create a *culture of trust* has evolved over many centuries, first under British Rule of Law, and later under American Rule of Law. We will only be able to continue self-organizing through our civic institutions and voluntary associations if we follow voluntarily, and enforce when necessary, the simple laws of ethical conduct—*the 10 Commandments of Trust*—under *ethics-based* American Rule of Law.

We cannot self-organize unless we *all* do what is right so that we can trust one another. Only by self-organizing like the ants can we unleash the "swarm intelligence" of the entire population to solve the myriad of challenges and problems that currently threaten our continued survival, success, and freedom. We cannot self-organize if we fight among ourselves.

We will only be able to adapt fast enough to survive and succeed in this new era of chaos, complexity, crisis, and continuous change if we can keep and maintain our all-essential culture of trust.

This is the wisdom of ants.

> *In the 20th century, it was often said that "Knowledge is Power." While knowledge is an essential ingredient of success in today's era of rapidly increasing change, it is not enough. Today, "Trust is Power."*
>
> **– Jim Cathcart**
> Best-selling author of *Relationship Selling*

The Wisdom and Power of Trust

1. **It only takes a few simple rules to create an extraordinarily complex self-organizing society.**

   Genius is the ability to reduce the complicated to the simple.

   C. W. Ceran

2. **Don't kill or hurt one another.**

   United we stand. Divided we fall.

   Aesop's Fables

3. **Voluntarily cooperate with nonrelatives for the greater good of the community.**

   Individual commitment to a group effort—that is what makes a team work, a company work, a society work, a civilization work.

   Vince Lombardi

4. **Self-organized societies can adapt fastest and cope best with constant change.**

   In the long history of humankind (and animal kind, too) those who learned to collaborate and improvise most effectively have prevailed.

   Charles Darwin

Chapter 2

Through a Different Lens
A "Bystander's" Perspective

> *The time is near at hand which must determine whether Americans are to be free men or slaves.*
>
> **– George Washington (1732–1799)**
> American Founding Father, commanding general during the American Revolutionary War, 1st U.S. president, 1789–1797

Seeing the Future

Peter Drucker, a famous 20th century management consultant, could see the future. In the 1960s, when Japan's economy was still recovering from the destruction of World War II, he foresaw that Japan would become a world-class economic power. It did. At the height of Japan's economic boom in the 1980s, when most people believed Japan's economic miracle was unstoppable, he warned that Japan's economy would stagnate.[1] It soon did for more than 20 years.

Drucker did not really see the future. He saw trends that already existed that others *could not* or *would not* see. He was a voracious reader and a student of history and human nature.

In his book *The Adventures of a Bystander*, Drucker said he realized he was a bystander when he was 14 years old. He described a bystander as one who stands off to the side of a theater stage, able to watch the actors on stage and the audience at the same time.[2] In his view, a bystander sees "things neither actor nor audience notices. Above all, a bystander sees differently from the way actors and audience see."[3]

Being a bystander may have saved Drucker's life. He had read Adolf Hitler's book *Mein Kampf,* which clearly outlined Hitler's twisted vision for the future. When Hitler was appointed chancellor in 1933, Drucker left Germany immediately. He didn't wait around wishing and hoping Hitler wouldn't be as bad as his book *Mein Kampf* warned he would be. By doing so, Drucker no doubt escaped the terrible fate of the 12 million people who died in Nazi concentration camps—6 million Jews and 6 million "others."

But Drucker said there is a *downside* to being a bystander. Because bystanders see differently from the way others see, their views are often out-of-step with the popularly held views of the day. A family friend cautioned Drucker that "[t]o watch and think for yourself is highly commendable. But to shock people by shouting strange views from the rooftops is not."[4]

Drucker acknowledged that while this may be wise advice, a bystander has no choice but to say what he sees because "it is [a bystander's] lot to see things differently."[5]

A View from the Moon

Picture yourself standing on the moon looking down at the earth. What can you see? You can see the continents, oceans, rivers, mountains, plains, and surrounding countries—all at the same time. You can see the big picture, all at once.

Now picture yourself standing back here on earth. What can you see? Only what is immediately in front of you. At a formative time of my life and education and a time of great change in America, I was out of the United States watching my own country from afar as though I were standing on the moon.

When I left the United States in 1965, I was a full-fledged acculturated post–World War II patriotic American, steeped in my parents' Great Depression and World War II American culture. However, by the time I returned to the United States after nearly seven years abroad, American culture had shifted so dramatically to an anti-establishment, "if it feels good, do it" baby-boomer culture; it was totally foreign to me. As a result, I have remained a bystander in my own country, watching events through multiple lenses at the same time.

Through one lens, I see the United States with the eyes of a native born-and-bred American, whose family tree goes back many generations in the United States. At the same time, I view the United States through the eyes of recently arrived immigrants, who cherish the freedoms and opportunities they have in America that they did not have in their countries of origin.

In addition, I observe what is happening in the United States through the cultural lens of my American depression and war parents. Perhaps this is why I have been able to see how far we have strayed over the past four decades from the rock-solid ethical standards of depression and war Americans.

Lastly, I am well-versed in the one essential subject often missing from our conversation about ethics—American Rule of Law. The mandatory American ethical standards required to keep and maintain our essential culture of trust have been established under *ethics-based* American Rule of Law.

Because I started law school in Australia first, before restarting law school in the United States, I know something many American lawyers do not know or appreciate. Our American Rule of Law is unique in the world. My Australian constitutional law professor was the first person to point this out to me.

> *Right is right, even if everyone is against it; and wrong is wrong, even if everyone is for it.*
>
> **– William Penn (1644–1718)**
> Founder of Pennsylvania

An American Bystander Is Born

The seeds of this book were sown in 1965 when my family moved from Honolulu, Hawaii, to Sydney, Australia. My dad was the new bureau chief for United Press International (UPI), an international news wire organization headquartered in New York. For the first time in my life, I was identified as an American everywhere I went because of my American accent. Apparently mouth muscles form around 12 years old, so I wasn't able to blend in with an Australian accent, a difficult accent to successfully mimic.

At the age of 14, I began asking a question most Americans rarely think about: *What is different about being an American?* Although I didn't understand why, I could see there were significant differences between Australia and the United States, even though both countries share a common British-based cultural, religious, and legal heritage.

Not in Kansas Anymore

School in New South Wales began in late January or early February and continued until December, summertime in Australia. All high school students, whether in public or private schools, were required to wear school uniforms. My first uniform was a medium grey, belted, cotton dress with navy blue gloves, a navy blue and grey straw hat, white socks, and plain black shoes that reminded me of the shoes Catholic nuns wore. Like Dorothy in *The Wizard of Oz*, I knew I wasn't in Kansas anymore.

There were two state-wide (actually, province-wide) standardized examinations that all high school students in New South Wales were required to take. These exams tested students on specific detailed knowledge on each subject taken in school. Students had to pass the state-wide standardized Fourth Form (10th grade) School Certificate before they were allowed to go on to the Fifth Form (11th grade).

At the end of high school, there was another state-wide standardized exam, the Higher School Certificate. This exam tested students on all subjects taken during the last two years of high school. The closest equivalent in the United States would be the notoriously difficult California bar exam (pre-1990) that new attorneys had to pass before being admitted to practice law.

The Higher School Certificate exam was graded by strangers (definitely not your own teachers from your school). Students were identified only by a number, not by name. As I recall, exam results were published in the newspaper next to your name. This single battery of tests at the end of high school determined if you graduated from high school, if you went to university, which university, what discipline you could study (e.g., law, medicine, architecture, humanities), and who paid for your university tuition (it was free if you scored high enough to get a government Australian Commonwealth scholarship).

A Rude Awakening

Although I had finished half of the ninth grade in the United States, I was initially put back to the beginning of eighth grade (Second Form). Subjects in an Australian school were taught in a different order, making a high school transition from an American to Australian school system particularly difficult. No doubt the head-mistress (principal) was concerned about my ability to catch up fast enough to pass the tenth-grade (Fourth Form) state-wide School Certificate exam.

After spending a few days in the Second Form (eighth grade) class, I went to the headmistress's office to let her know I would be moving up to the Third Form (ninth grade) instead. I will never forget the headmistress's look of utter amazement. Apparently, she had never encountered a 14-year-old student who *automatically assumed* she had *the right* to make that decision for herself.

The headmistress looked at me intently and said firmly, "You can't do that!" I held her gaze and said with a smile "Watch me!" I meant no disrespect. I just *assumed* she would know that I had *the right* to challenge her decision after I had checked it out for myself.

It took some wrangling and my father's intercession, but finally I was moved up to Third Form (the equivalent of ninth grade). American teenagers do not hesitate to question authority because they know they have rights. Having only just arrived in Australia, I did not yet know that my automatic assumption that I had certain *inalienable rights* was American.

My Third Form (ninth grade) Australian history teacher stunned me by announcing to the class that "England won World War II." I looked around the room to see if my classmates were as surprised as I was to hear that. They were not. Of course, when I later understood that England (Britain) had stood alone against Hitler while the rest of Europe fell, I could see that from a British perspective that they won World War II. After all, from where would the Normandy invasion have taken off if England had fallen?

From an American perspective, we won World War II. Americans were the driving force behind the Normandy invasion of Europe that eventually ended the war in Europe. Americans also played a pivotal role in ending the war in the Pacific with Japan. At an early age, I learned firsthand that people from different countries not only have very different cultures, they also have very different perspectives and attitudes.

American Rule of Law Is Unique

Another surprise came when one of my Australian high school teachers announced that students were required to attend religion classes during school time. We could choose to attend Protestant, Catholic, or Jewish religious instruction, but attendance was mandatory.

Again, being an American who knew her *rights* (and forgetting where I was), I asked the teacher how students in a public (government-run) school could be forced to attend classes on religious instruction under the Bill of Rights of the Constitution? She said, "Wrong constitution!" I was flabbergasted. It had never occurred to me that another free western country based on British Rule of Law would have a constitution that did not have a Bill of Rights like the U.S. Constitution.

Later in law school in Australia, I took classes in British legal history, Australian constitutional law, and Australian criminal law. You can imagine my surprise when I discovered that the Australian Constitution, adopted in 1901, was based half on the British legal model with no written constitution and half on the American written constitutional model, yet there was still no American-styled Bill of Rights.

When I restarted law school in Texas after completing one year of law school in Australia, I was in for another surprise. Although both American and Australian legal systems are based on British "judge-made" common law, the way law was taught was very different.

American law school texts were almost entirely excerpts of actual court cases with little explanatory text. Separate texts called hornbooks contained the explanatory text on American law. In contrast, my Australian law texts were mostly explanatory text about the law, not excerpts of actual court cases. No doubt this was because American law can change much more quickly than in other British-based "judge-made" common law legal systems.

I learned first-hand that the Australian legal system, a British *judge-made* common law legal system born of *evolution* from Britain, was very different from the American legal system, born of *revolution* from Britain (discussed later in greater detail). American courts can take into account more than just prior legal precedent when making their decisions (more about this in Chapter 8). Early on, I understood that there was something very different about our American Rule of Law.

American Freedom Is Unique

After graduating from an American law school, I headed to the Middle East to visit my family in Iran and Saudi Arabia. My first stop was Tehran, where my dad was covering the news for UPI. I was expecting a friendly, easy-going welcome when I landed in Tehran, but that's not what happened.

Before my father said hello, he said with a forcefulness and intensity I had never before heard in his voice "DO NOT ask anyone their political opinions or how they feel about their political leaders. There are secret police everywhere and you could get someone tortured or killed!"[6] I was thunderstruck. For an American used to almost unlimited free speech, being told I could not ask Iranians what they thought about their leaders or political system was almost incomprehensible to me.[7]

My father's next UPI assignment was Singapore, where it was, and still is, tricky for foreign journalists to report on the internal affairs of Singapore. In 2011, a British author was sentenced to six weeks in jail, fined $16,090, and deported for suggesting the death penalty in Singapore was given more frequently to poor people than to rich people.[8] At a young age, I was aware how different our American brand of freedom is from other countries.

An Ethics Violation Epidemic

I first began teaching business law and ethics in the late 1970s. My first students were not business school university students. They were the employees, managers, and executives of a company that was part of a giant global Fortune 500 multinational corporation headquartered in New York and Paris. Teaching ethics and law in the company's in-house management development programs was part of my responsibilities as an in-house corporate attorney, and later as a general counsel of one of the companies in the oilfield services division.

When the Enron scandal erupted in 2001, I knew right away that something had gone "bad-wrong" in the United States when it came to ethics. What I did not know then was that the Enron scandal would be just the beginning of multiple nonstop waves of serious ethics violations that continue unabated today, more than a decade later.

We are in the midst of a dangerous ethics violation epidemic. Ethics scandals have touched a wide swath of our self-organizing institutions and associations (further discussed in Chapter 7). Large corporations, high technology companies, Wall Street investment banks, commercial banks, real estate companies, hospitals, drug companies, insurance brokers, defense contractors, and many other businesses have been rocked by serious ethics scandals.

Major ethics scandals have also been uncovered in our federal, state, and local governments, including the military and law enforcement—in the "watchdogs" and "gatekeepers" of our economy and legal system (lawyers, accountants, and judges); in some of our religious and educational institutions, charities, unions, and media; and even in some of our professional sports.

If we don't get our ethics house in order—and fast—we will not only lose our economy, we will also lose our grand multi-century American experiment in freedom.

A Systemic Ethics Breakdown

The financial and economic mess we are in today was not caused by just a breakdown of ethical conduct in business alone. There has been a systemic breakdown in ethics across the board in far too many of the self-governing civic institutions and voluntary associations that are the bedrock of our self-organizing American freedom. Americans have forgotten (or never learned) that when it comes to creating a culture of trust that is actually trusted, there are no loopholes. Our self-governing institutions and associations cannot function without a culture of trust.

Only if "we, the people" awaken from our nearly 40 years of ethical slumber, will the United States have a chance to survive and thrive as a free economy, a free government, and free society in this turbulent new century. Americans must restore what has made the United States so successful over such a long period of time—our ability to self-organize under *ethics-based* American Rule of Law and our *essential culture of trust.*

We must restore the *10 Commandments of Trust* under *ethics-based* American Rule of Law—as the standard of conduct throughout our self-governing civic institutions and voluntary associations (e.g., businesses, governments, charities and nonprofits, schools and universities, unions, and associations). This is the only way to restore our free, prosperous economy and remain a free, peaceful, stable, and secure nation in this new century.

To adapt quickly to constant change and yet remain stable, especially in another major crisis or national emergency, Americans must be able to self-organize. We cannot self-organize without trust.

> *Every government degenerates when trusted to the rulers of the people alone. The people themselves are its only safe depositories.*
>
> **– Thomas Jefferson (1743–1829)**
> American Founding Father,
> 3rd U.S. president, 1801–1809

Make no mistake about it. Without ethics and our culture of trust, not only will our free economy fail, our free political system and free society will fail too—the only question is when.

Eyes Glaze Over

I have been teaching ethics to many different audiences for many years. When I first walk into the room, I can almost see the collective eyes of the audience glaze over as if they were silently screaming, "Oh no, not another sermon on ethics!" No doubt this is because ethics has often been taught as a confusing hodgepodge of philosophical concepts, not tied to practical reality, and without concrete, easy-to-understand standards of ethical conduct to follow.

Like Pavlov's dogs salivating as soon as the dinner bell is rung, many Americans are conditioned to tune out as soon as the word "ethics" is mentioned. Based on past experience, they believe that talking about ethics will be boring and frustrating. They believe they will be just as confused about what's right (ethical) at the end of the session, as when they walked in.

There is another reason many people tune out ethics discussions at work. They resent being lectured on ethics if they can plainly see for themselves that top leaders in their own organizations (often the ones talking the loudest about ethics) are not acting ethically themselves.

Paying lip service to ethics does not create trust. In fact, it does just the opposite: it creates cynicism and distrust. *Right behavior creates trust. Wrong behavior destroys trust.*

A Sea of Ethics Babble

We are drowning in a sea of ethics babble. Go to the web page of almost any online bookseller and you will find a vast array of books on ethics, business ethics, and sister topics like virtues, values, integrity, character, and trust.

In recent decades, American corporations, government entities, nonprofits, and other types of organizations spent billions of dollars on ethics training. They appointed chief ethics officers, made ethics training mandatory, drafted detailed and voluminous codes of ethical conduct, and established anonymous hotlines for ethics complaints. Yet, in spite of all this money and effort spent on ethics, we still have experienced some of the worst ethics scandals in the United States since the 1920s, right before the Great Depression. What went wrong?

When it comes to the topic of ethics in the United States, I am reminded of Samuel Taylor Coleridge's famous poem "The Rime of the Ancient Mariner." Coleridge wrote about sailors lost at sea, dying of thirst, even though they were surrounded on all sides by water. There was "water, water everywhere...but [not] a drop to drink...."

So too, it is with ethics. We have "ethics, ethics, everywhere" and yet we are still suffering from some of the most unethical conduct we have seen in the United States in nearly 100 years. Talking endlessly about ethics does not mean that individuals, organizations, or countries are conducting themselves ethically. *Ethics is about behavior, not talk.*

Many Americans today are confused about (1) what ethics means, (2) why ethics is essential for our survival and success in the 21st century, and (3) what the simple and clear laws of ethical conduct are that we must follow to restore trust in our businesses, governments, and society before it is too late.

We are not talking here about our *personal* standards of ethical conduct in our *personal* lives. We are talking about the *mandatory standards* of ethical conduct in our *public lives* with one another, when we are acting through any of our self-organizing, self-governing institutions and associations (e.g., businesses, governments, professions, religious, educational and charitable associations, and unions).

The *10 Commandments of Trust* is a simple American code of trust we must follow voluntarily, and enforce when necessary under *ethics-based* American Rule of Law, if we wish to survive, thrive, and remain a free nation in the 21st century.

Laws of Gravity

Scientists use simple generalizations like the laws of gravity to describe "recurring facts or events in nature."[9] Similarly, the laws of ethical conduct—the *10 Commandments of Trust*—are simple generalizations that describe the behaviors required to create and maintain our self-organizing culture of trust (see the summaries in Appendix A).

These simple laws of right and wrong hold the United States together as an intact, united, free economy, government, society, and nation as surely as the laws of gravity hold the planets of our solar system in place. Without gravity, the earth would spin off its axis and either burn up by moving too close to the sun, or freeze by moving too far away.

Similarly, without the laws of ethical conduct that create trust in our institutions, associations, economy, and society, our free country will spin out of control into failure, chaos, violence, and anarchy. *Freedom requires trust. Without trust, there is only force. Force leads to dictatorship.*

There is another similarity between the laws of gravity and America's laws of ethical conduct. The earth's orbit around the sun is elliptical, not a perfect circle. As a result, the earth is sometimes closer, sometimes farther away, from the sun than at other times. However, it is always within an absolute minimum and maximum range that does not vary.

Likewise, the laws of ethical conduct in the United States are sometimes enforced more severely, sometimes less severely than at other times. However, to keep and maintain our culture of trust, our adherence to the laws of ethical conduct must always be within a certain minimum and maximum range of behavior.

Our American laws of ethical conduct are like the laws of gravity. Without them, the United States will spin out of control.

Simple Laws of Right and Wrong

Although this is a book about ethics, it is not about the fuzzy, watered-down "you get to make it up as you go along" ethics that has been so often taught in our schools and universities in the past four decades. Instead, this is a book about 10 simple and clear laws of trust under *ethics-based* American Rule of Law.

Discovering these 10 simple laws of ethical conduct was a lot like finding black holes in space. Because the gravitational pull in black holes is so strong, light cannot escape, making them invisible. Scientists only "know" black holes exist through indirect, not direct, evidence.[10]

Similarly, the *10 Commandments of Trust* can only be known through indirect, not direct, evidence. They are not found in any one law book, statute, judicial case, or other legal source. Only after the multiple non-stop waves of serious ethics scandals since the beginning of the 21st century did the *10 Commandments of Trust* become clearly visible through indirect evidence.

Over and over, the public ethics scandals that sparked bad publicity, resignations, government investigations and hearings, civil lawsuits, criminal indictments, or other adverse consequences—both here in the United States and increasingly around the world[11]—involved the same 10 ethical principles of right and wrong behavior. In their shortest and simplest form, they are:

10 Commandments of Trust
1. Tell the truth
2. Be fair
3. Be loyal
4. Be careful
5. Be accountable
6. Observe private property rights
7. Respect people
8. Keep promises
9. Be a *REAL* leader
10. Enforce Commandments 1 through 9

Warning

Although this list of ethical laws of conduct is short and simple, do not be fooled into thinking you are free to make up your own definitions of the behaviors required under each ethical standard. *Remember, this is not about your personal code of ethical conduct.*

What we are talking about here is the *mandatory* code of ethical conduct *required* to keep and maintain the essential culture of trust on which our self-organizing American freedom is based. These are the ethical standards created, defined, and enforced when necessary, under *ethics-based* American Rule of Law.

"We, the People"

This simple American code of right and wrong behavior is why the United States of America has been such an extraordinarily prosperous, politically stable, peaceful (mostly), and secure nation under the same form of government for more than two centuries. Thus far, Americans have been able to self-organize and react with great speed to changes in their environment like the ants.

However, we have now strayed so far from these simple and clear principles of right and wrong behavior, we are running the risk of tipping the country into a destructive downward spiral that leads to a culture of distrust. If that happens, our grand multi-century American experiment in self-organization and freedom will end.

Just memorizing the *10 Commandments of Trust* is not enough, which is why you will not find a more detailed discussion of the *10 Commandments of Trust* until Chapter 11. To use this American code of trust effectively, "we, the people" must first understand how we got ourselves into this ethics mess; why complacency about trust is dangerous; why trust matters; what is unique and different about our American culture of trust under ethics-based American Rule of Law; and why trust is in such short supply today in the United States. Also, in today's era of fuzzy ethics thinking, when it comes to ethics, trust, Rule of Law, and our unique brand of freedom, *national borders still matter.*

To self-organize like the ants, we must behave in a trustworthy manner toward one another. If we do not quickly restore ethical conduct in all our self-governing institutions and associations, we could lose the essential culture of trust that has made the United States the longest-running, enduring constitutional republic in modern world history, and one of the world's most successful economies, governments, and societies.

Without trust, we will not be able to make the necessary changes fast enough to survive the next major crisis or national emergency. The only way for the United States of America to survive and succeed in today's constantly changing, crisis-prone environment is by restoring the essential culture of trust on which our self-organizing freedom rests.

A Guide, Not a Guru

This book was not written as an academic tome or legal treatise. Nor is it intended to be legal advice or the last word on any of the topics covered. In writing this book, the author is acting only as a guide, not a guru, pointing out landmarks and points of interest as seen through American bystander eyes.

One thing is almost certainly true. *This book is likely out of step with many of today's prevailing attitudes.* As Peter Drucker pointed out so eloquently, it is a bystander's "lot [in life] to see things differently" and "to shock people by shouting strange views from the rooftops."[12]

Hopefully, this book will provoke serious thought about the dangerous path we are currently on that can, and will, rob *all of us* of our freedom, if we do not quickly self-correct. The *"U.S.S. America"* is fast approaching a swarm of freedom-threatening icebergs that could, under the right circumstances, sink us as a successful, free, and independent nation.

To navigate the treacherous waters ahead, Americans must stop "fighting over the deck chairs on the *Titanic*" and focus on the icebergs that could sink us all. This is no time to be a political thinker. Our peace, prosperity, stability, security, and freedom depend on us all becoming *ethical American critical thinkers—* and fast.

To restore our prosperity and keep our peace, stability, security, and freedom, we must restore one common standard of right and wrong behavior that applies to all of us when we are acting in any of our civic institutions and voluntary associations, *regardless of political persuasion or any other group affiliation.*

By failing to insist on ethical conduct in all our essential institutions and associations and all our leaders, we are squandering one of our best competitive advantages in today's chaotic, constantly changing, crisis-prone era of turbulence— *the secret power of trust.*

> The genius of the United States is not best or most in its executives or legislatures, nor in its ambassadors or authors or colleges, or churches, or parlors, nor even in its newspapers or inventors, but always most in the common people.
>
> **– Walt Whitman (1819–1892)**
> American poet, essayist, and journalist

Only when we hold everyone to the *same* standard of ethical conduct in our self-governing institutions and associations (our businesses, governments, professions, charities, nonprofits, educational and religious institutions, community and volunteer associations, and unions, to name just a few), including ourselves and all of our leaders, will we be able to restore the culture of trust necessary for us to survive and thrive in the turbulent times of the 21st century.

This is the wisdom of ants.

Chapter 3

Freedom at Risk
Playing with Fire

> *America will never be destroyed from the outside. If we falter and lose our freedom, it will be because we destroyed ourselves.*
>
> **– Abraham Lincoln (1809–1865)**
> 16th U.S. president during the
> American Civil War, 1861–1865

No Country Is Invincible

Most Americans born after World War II cannot imagine the United States failing. They are oblivious to the warning signs of growing stresses in the country and an increasing number of internal and external threats. *Not only can the United States fail, it will fail, as a free nation, if we don't get our ethical house in order, and fast.*

Our economy, political system, and society are reeling from decades of unethical conduct, jeopardizing our country's prosperity, peace, stability, and security. The world is increasingly dangerous and unstable at a time when we are more globally interconnected than at any other time in human history. America's national debt is staggering high at more than $18 trillion, larger than our entire economy. This is unsustainable.

Because of our ethical confusion, Americans could lose one of the greatest experiments in freedom that mankind has ever known, and they don't even know it. Too many have forgotten (or never learned) that, without ethics, we cannot maintain the culture of trust required to remain a free, successful, self-governing economy and nation.

We will only know how much damage we have done to our culture of trust when the next major crisis or national emergency hits, and that might be too late. In spite of the "happy feet" TV pundits, experts, and politicians repeatedly sounding the all-clear on the American economy, serious ethics trouble is brewing in the land.

We are in for a rough ride for many years to come, and it is not just our economy we are risking: it is our freedom and our way of life as well.

From my bystander's perch for over 40 years, I have watched Americans become more and more ethically confused. I first noticed our downward ethical slide in the early 1970s. With each passing decade, I have watched with dismay as our ethics IQ in this country has deteriorated further and further.

Many Americans are now functionally illiterate about the simple and clear ethical standards of conduct (that is, standards of right and wrong behavior) *required* in our self-governing, self-organizing civic institutions and voluntary associations. Many know little about their own country or the rest of the world.[1] *They are unaware that history is littered with the carcasses of countries and societies that mistakenly believed they were invincible.*

> *Liberty lies in the hearts of men and women; when it dies there, no constitution, no law, no court can save it.*
>
> **– Learned Hand (1872–1961)**
> U.S. Federal Appeals Court judge, 1909–1961
> often quoted by the U.S. Supreme Court

We are operating in the ethical danger zone with all lights flashing red.

Disturbing Trends

Top executives of some of our largest corporations are paid princely sums, while worker pay has stagnated and many workers continue to lose their jobs. Wall Street compensation has been so excessive, visions of the French monarchy right before the French Revolution come to mind. In the first decade of the 21st century, income inequality in the United States reached the same level it was right before the onset of the Great Depression.

An unholy alliance between public unions and politicians has produced pension and medical benefits for government workers that have bankrupted some American cities and threaten to bankrupt more. Federal retirement and medical benefits programs like Social Security, Medicare, and Medicaid, as well as federal, state, and city government retirement funds are reported to be seriously underfunded.[2]

Since 2008, the U.S. federal government has opened up the floodgates of federal spending at taxpayers' expense. It paid hundreds of billions of dollars to bail out failed businesses that had rewarded their executives with millions of dollars in compensation for taking excessive risks. Food stamp usage has skyrocketed from 28 million to 48 million people, federal disability claims are the highest in history, and student loans have ballooned to more than $1.2 trillion.

There is a growing sense that no one is watching how the taxpayers' money is being spent. Our federal government recently over-spent more than $1 trillion a year, four years in a row. America is becoming a "top-down" culture of dependency on government, rather than a "bottom-up" self-organizing culture of personal responsibility and self-reliance. This will inevitably fail.

Politicians have been passing laws, thousands of pages long, that they haven't read.[3] These long-winded and complicated statutes, full of mind-numbing legalese, appear to be more for the benefit of special interest groups, not the American people. Our economy, which is supposed to be based on private capital, private property, and freedom, is increasingly weighed down with more and more government control and excessively burdensome and ineffective government statutes and regulations. This will never work.

Massive ethical failures inevitably lead to massive social, political, and economic pain. That is why we call certain behaviors wrong. Wrong behaviors always cause pain; the only question is when and how bad.

From the size, breadth, depth, and scope of the ethics crisis that has exploded onto the public stage in the United States in the 2000s (and still going strong more than a decade later), our ethics reckoning is going to hurt—a lot. The end result of ethical ignorance is misery and hardship for millions of people.

We have lost our ethical way. To restore our culture of trust, we must restore the *10 Commandments of Trust* under *ethics-based* American Rule of Law in our self-governing institutions and associations.

We must also restore the rightful boundaries of our constitutional system, which were specifically designed to restrict the abusive power of a too powerful "top-down" central government. If we do not, the United States will tip over into a culture of distrust. If that happens, a culture of force—martial law or dictatorship—is just around the corner. *Think it can't happen in America? Think again.*

> *Arbitrary power is most easily established on the ruins of liberty abused to licentiousness.*
>
> **– George Washington (1732–1799)**
> U.S. general during American Revolutionary War,
> American Founding Father,
> 1st U.S. president, 1789–1797

Rule of Law, *Not* Rule of Lawyers

American Rule of Law is unique in the world, but just for the record, that's *American Rule of Law*, not the current *American Rule of Lawyers (and Bureaucrats)* version we are operating under today. Don't just blame the lawyers for this development. We did this to ourselves by becoming so ethically confused.

We are now overusing American Rule of Law in ways it was never intended to be used, trying to compensate for the striking drop in our voluntary ethical conduct over the past four decades. *An underdeveloped ethics muscle creates an overdeveloped legal muscle; that is, law on steroids.*[4]

Andrew Fastow, the former Enron Corp. chief financial officer who served six years in prison, pointed out the difference between American Rule of Law (doing what's *right*) and American Rule of Lawyers and Bureaucrats (doing what's *"legal"*). He said initially he didn't think he was doing anything wrong because he was following the "rules." Later he said he realized he was "[using] the rules to subvert the rules."[5]

Under ethics-based *American Rule of Law*, the standard of ethical conduct is not compliance with "the law." The standard is: is it wrong? Right behavior creates trust. Wrong behavior destroys trust. Ethics-based American Rule of Law enforces what is right (ethical) to keep and maintain our essential culture of trust.

American Rule of Lawyers (and Bureaucrats) says it may be wrong (unethical), but is still "legal." Could this be why the legal profession in the United States has such an image problem in the 21st century?[6] When it comes to conduct that seriously damages our essential American culture of trust, there is no such thing as "it's unethical, but legal."

No Loopholes When the Standard Is Trust

The *10 Commandments of Trust* are called *commandments* for a reason. To establish trust *about something important*, there are no loopholes. If you decide not to follow these simple and clear ethical standards today, you do so at your own risk. In our increasingly crisis-drenched and volatile environment, not acting ethically is likely to become about as risky as driving a car 150 miles an hour on an icy highway. You may be able to drive for a while, but your chances of crashing are high, and when you do, the pain will be spectacular.

Enforcement of our ethical standards under ethics-based American Rule of Law can change suddenly. The sources of enforcement are many and varied (e.g., elections, lawsuits, criminal investigations and indictments, bad publicity, Congressional hearings, citizens' action groups, increased taxes).

When unethical conduct threatens our culture of trust, ethics-based American Rule of Law is constitutionally capable of stretching to restore ethics and trust quickly, provided it remains within the minimum and maximum ranges of our established constitutional boundaries. Under ethics-based American Rule of Law, many creative, flexible, innovative, and "deadly" (extremely painful) remedies to restore trust are possible.

Two of our American constitutional rights greatly aid enforcement of American ethical standards—*freedom of speech* and *freedom of the press*. In the United States, publicity alone can, and often does, trigger immediate and painful consequences for unethical behavior in our self-organizing institutions and associations.

No country has the same long-standing, enforceable, constitutional rights and protections that foster the reporting of serious *public ethics* scandals as freely as in the United States. Of course, retaining these constitutional protections depends on teaching each new generation of Americans what is special and different about our uniquely American brand of constitutional freedom and rights.

If history is any guide, *"wrath of God"* enforcement[7] under ethics-based American Rule of Law will soon reappear. You may be an atheist, but ethics-based American Rule of Law is not. (Hint: American Rule of Law dates back to the 1606 Virginia Charter and the 1620 Mayflower Compact, and yes, *both mention Christianity*).[8]

To adapt fast enough to restore our prosperity and keep our peaceful, stable, and secure free society, we must *stop* asking the question: *Is it "legal"?* (excessive statute-and-regulation-dependent American Rule of Lawyers and Bureaucrats) and *start* asking the question: *Is it wrong?* (ethics-based American Rule of Law). Behavior that violates one or more of the principles of the 10 Commandments of Trust is called wrong because it damages our essential culture of trust.

Ethics-based American Rule of Law must enforce what is right and punish what is wrong, if we wish to maintain trust in our self-governing institutions and associations and our American Rule of Law. When it comes to the simple, short, and clear principles of right and wrong behavior required to create trust, there are no loopholes.

To succeed in today's constantly changing, crisis-prone environment, we must restore our self-organizing culture of trust under ethics-based American Rule of Law (which includes our uniquely American constitutional framework and our Judeo-Christian cultural heritage).[9]

Without trust, we will not be able to make the necessary changes fast enough to survive the next major crisis or national emergency, and hold together as a free, peaceful, united, and stable country.

This is the wisdom of ants.

The Secret of American Longevity—So Far

The secret of American longevity and success—*so far*—has been our remarkable ability to survive pain that sometimes feels like the fires of hell and still hold together as a free united nation. Will that happen again when we are faced with the next major crisis or national emergency? Not without ethics and the culture of trust that has enabled us to make painful changes and sacrifices fast enough to adapt quickly to changed circumstances.

It is our ability to self-organize under a culture of trust and ethics-based American Rule of Law that has allowed us to unleash the "swarm intelligence" of the entire population to react quickly in times of danger. By self-organizing, *ordinary* Americans under the leadership of *extraordinary REAL* American leaders[10] have been able to accomplish extraordinary feats many thought impossible at the time. However, we will only be able to do this again if we immediately regain our *ethical intelligence.*

Two generational historians, William Strauss and Neil Howe, have suggested that the United States could already be in the early stages of its fourth *Fourth Turning generational crisis of survival.*[11] These historians describe a Fourth Turning generational crisis as a period of extreme danger and upheaval where it feels like the very survival of the nation is at stake.[12] They said the other Fourth Turning generational crises in American history are (1) the American Revolutionary War, (2) the American Civil War, and (3) the Great Depression and World War II.

After each of these three prior national emergencies, America emerged a united free country with the same form of government (intact since 1789) to become stronger and more prosperous. However, past performance is no guarantee of future success.

Built for Speed and Change

Under our constitutionally limited, but creative and flexible *ethics-based* American Rule of Law (laced with Judeo-Christian values), Americans have been able to adapt quickly in a time of crisis or national emergency. Thus far, because of our self-organization, the United States has been able to morph from a lumbering tortoise that moves slowly in inches to a fleet-footed gazelle that can run long distances at 50 miles per hour to avoid danger. However, this is only possible if we trust one another.

When the United States is operating under the *10 Commandments of Trust* and *ethics-based* American Rule of Law, the country is built for speed and change. But when the country is weighed down by a dizzying array of conflicting and confusing statutes and regulations under American Rule of Lawyers (and Bureaucrats), we can barely move at all. Today, the creativity and flexibility normally inherent in our self-organizing system are being stifled. Unethical conduct is allowed to flourish.

Too much "top-down" government interference and regulation is debilitating. Imagine the United States like the "giant" Gulliver in *Gulliver's Travels*, crisscrossed with so many ropes by the little Lilliputian people, it cannot move at all.

On the other hand, history, human nature, and common sense tell us that too little government oversight does not work either. Human beings are remarkably capable of rationalizing that their behavior is not wrong, especially if they personally benefit from the wrong conduct.[13]

> *My reading of history convinces me that most bad government results from too much government.*
>
> **– Thomas Jefferson (1743–1829)**
> American Founding Father,
> 3rd U.S. president, 1801–1809

What we need in the United States is *"Goldilocks Law"—not too much, not too little—just enough.* This is only possible if we restore the 10 simple and clear standards of ethical conduct—the *10 Commandments of Trust*—in *all* our civic institutions and voluntary associations.

American Rule of Law involves simple, clear ethical standards of right and wrong behavior that everyone can understand and follow. This creates a "bottom-up" self-organizing culture and society.

American Rule of Lawyers (and Bureaucrats) involves a confusing array of incomprehensible and mind-numbing ethical standards written in legal jargon and buried in thousands of pages of statutes and regulations. Standards are so convoluted and confusing, only "experts" can interpret their meaning for the rest of the population. This creates a stunted, stagnant, "top-down" government-controlled economy and society.

American Rule of Lawyers (and Bureaucrats) is *not* what made the United States of America the most successful economy and nation in modern world history. American Rule of Lawyers (and Bureaucrats) robs all of us of our freedom.

The Secret of 21st Century Success

Elements of the *10 Commandments of Trust* have been popping up more frequently around the world.[14] When "top-down" central government-run *communist* and *socialist economies*, like the ones in China, Russia, and India, *failed* to raise the majority of their populations' living standards, countries began experimenting with "freer," more market-oriented economic reforms.[15]

A "freer" more market-oriented economy requires a culture of trust based on *effective* Rule of Law. Force won't work. Investors cannot be forced to invest in a country. They must be enticed.

Therefore, even a country like China, still run "top-down" by a central communist dictatorship government, has been attempting to create its own version of a culture of "trust." That is why elements of the *10 Commandments of Trust* have been surfacing more frequently in China's constitutions, statutes, enforcement actions, scandals, and public discussion.[16]

Sustainable economic success over the long haul requires trust. Investors will invest their money in a country only if they trust their investments are safe. Although stock markets have proliferated around the world, few investors have stopped to think about whether the countries they are investing in have the necessary *ethics-based* Rule of Law to create and maintain the necessary culture of trust. Many don't.

While some countries' economies, political systems, and societies may appear to be successful and stable at one point in time, beneath the surface are often hidden weaknesses and deficiencies. Peaceful, prosperous times can mask serious deficiencies in any country's economy and culture (including our own) until a time of major crisis and severe stress.[17] While economic success is the foundation of any stable and secure society, social unrest, political instability, and threats to security can derail any country as well.

It is easy to write a constitution, pass laws, and set up a court system. What is difficult to do is create an *effective* culture of trust under *effective* Rule of Law that is *actually trusted* by those inside and outside the country.

Creating a culture of trust is about as easy as teaching an elephant to dance on its tip-toes like a ballerina.

Dictatorships will have difficulty establishing the necessary societal safety-valves to prevent competing groups from turning on each other in a major crisis. However, being a democracy is no guarantee of stability in a crisis either. Democracies can degenerate into military dictatorships, or worse, when faced with a crisis that threatens to spin the country into anarchy.

When trust disappears, only force is left. In good times, it is easy to trust. Only in bad times are the bonds of trust in a democratic nation truly tested.

> *Man will ultimately be governed by God or by Tyrants.*
>
> **– Benjamin Franklin (1706–1790)**
> American Founding Father

A Warning Bell Is Ringing

Trust in key American institutions is dangerously low. In 2013, a Gallup poll reported that only 10% of Americans approve of the job Congress is doing.[18] Of all 16 institutions on Gallup's list, Congress has ranked the lowest four years in a row. However, confidence in all 16 American institutions was at the lowest level Gallup had on record.

The 2013 Gallup poll reported that those expressing *"a great deal"* or *"quite a lot"* of confidence in some of our key institutions was below 50%:

- church and organized religion (48%)
- the U.S. Supreme Court (34%), the presidency (36%), and public schools (32%)
- banks (26%)
- newspapers and TV news (23%)
- big business (22%)
- organized labor (20%)
- and in last place Congress (only 10%)

Only three institutions received ratings of "a great deal" and "quite a lot" of confidence above 50%—the *police* at 57%, *small business* at 65%, and the *military* came in first at 76%.[19]

In 2013, the Pew Research Center reported that over a period that included the last two years of President Bush's administration and President Obama's first four years in office, only "...about three-in-ten Americans... said they trust the federal government to do the right thing always or most of the time."[20]

"Majorities across all partisan and demographic groups express little or no trust in government."[21] Distrust in the United States is much too high.

To be self-organizing and remain free, we must restore trust—and fast.

Restoring Trust

To restore our self-organizing free economy, free government, and free society, we must restore

- our free-market capitalist economy *with morality*[22] (by following the simple, clear laws of right and wrong behavior—the *10 Commandments of Trust*); and

- our free democratic constitutional republic with *responsible citizens* and *REAL* leaders who voluntarily conduct themselves ethically; and

- our *ethics-based American Rule of Law* (as opposed to our current statute-and-regulation-dependent American Rule of Lawyers and Bureaucrats) that enforces right behavior and punishes wrong behavior within the boundaries of our uniquely American constitutional framework.

Right behavior is essential to maintain the culture of trust we must have to be a successful free-market capitalist economy and a stable, peaceful, and secure democratic constitutional republic. The *10 Commandments of Trust* is an American code of trust we must voluntarily follow, and enforce when necessary, under *ethics-based* American Rule of Law to survive and thrive in the 21st century.

Right behavior creates and maintains our culture of trust. Wrong behavior damages our culture of trust. It's that simple.

The Race Is On

Which country's model of organization—one based on trust or one based on force—will succeed in the turbulent times of the 21st century? Will freedom win again in this new century as it did in the 20th century? Or will countries with dictatorships and a culture of force be the ones that survive the crisis and turmoil of this new century?[23]

It is not just American baby-boomers and subsequent American generations that have taken their prosperity, peace, and freedom for granted. This is a common attitude in many free countries that have enjoyed peace, stability, and prosperity since the end of World War II.

For Americans, the choice is simple. We only have one question to answer for ourselves: *do we wish to continue being free?* If the answer is yes, then there is only one path for us to follow.

We must restore the *10 Commandments of Trust* under *ethics-based* American Rule of Law throughout our self-governing institutions and associations. This is the only way to keep our unique self-organizing culture of trust that enables us to respond quickly in an age of chaos, crisis, and change.

If we cannot self-correct fast enough, there is only one possible destination for us all—dictatorship and the end of our freedom and self-governance. This is what history warns us. In the 21st century, we are about to find out once again whether a culture of trust (freedom) can still outperform a culture of force (dictatorship).

> *I am a firm believer in the people. If given the truth, they can be depended upon to meet any national crisis. The great point is to bring them the real facts.*
>
> **– Abraham Lincoln (1809–1865)**
> 16th U.S. president during
> U.S. Civil War, 1861–1865

An Ethics Mess

We have dug ourselves a gigantic economic and financial hole, spending trillions and trillions of dollars we don't have and creating an ethics mess in the country of biblical proportions.[24] Some commentators have already written the obituary of the United States as a free, united, strong, independent, and dominant world economic power.[25] One Russian academic predicted the United States would break apart.[26]

Chinese leaders have trumpeted their economic success under the dictatorial rule of the Chinese Communist party.[27] China has already replaced Japan as the world's second largest economy. Will it soon take away America's top spot as the largest economy in the world?[28] The United Nation's International Monetary Fund (IMF) has suggested this could happen as early as 2016.[29]

Is the IMF right? Or will the United States peacefully make the difficult and painful sacrifices necessary to restore our prosperous economy and remain a peaceful, stable, and secure nation in the 21st century? Will China's inability to create and maintain *ethics-based* Rule of Law limit how successful its economy, government, and society will be in the 21st century?

Some say the United States is in a permanent state of decline.[30] For the first time, in 2011, the Triple A rating of the United States for investment safety was downgraded to double A.[31] Questions are being raised about whether the dollar will remain the dominant world currency.

Under current conditions, turning the country around and getting it back on track seems almost like an impossible task. The chances of failure are high and growing. One thing is certain—the longer we put off making the tough choices and hard decisions, the more precarious our situation becomes. *There is no way to fix what financially ails the country without real pain. That is the price for losing our ethical minds.*

Not Much Time

The United States is like a heavyweight champion boxer, punched hard and knocked to the floor of the ring. The referee is counting off the seconds. There is only so much time for the "champ" to get up before the fight will be declared over when the referee finally counts to 10.

The question is: Will the United States be able to get up in time to resume the fight? Or is the country down for the count, unable to get up in time? We can only make the necessary changes and sacrifices fast enough peacefully, if we return to the clear standards of right and wrong behavior on which our culture of trust is based.

We do not have much time. We are on an unsustainable path. Continuing to tolerate such widespread unethical conduct jeopardizes the free economy and society we inherited from those who fought and died so that we could be free.

Our survival and success in the 21st century depend squarely on our ability to be a self-governing, self-organizing government and society *"of the people, by the people, and for the people."* It requires our strict adherence to the principles of freedom of our democratic constitutional republic. It also requires that we restore our free economy based on free-market capitalism (*with morality*) and private property.

We cannot maintain our self-organizing culture of freedom without a culture of trust, and trust can only be created by ethical *conduct. We are on borrowed time and borrowed money—and both are running out fast.*

Let us never forget that government is ourselves and not an alien power over us. The ultimate rulers of our democracy are not a President and senators and congressmen and government officials, but the voters of this country.

– Franklin D. Roosevelt (1882–1945)
32nd U.S. president during the Great Depression and WWII, 1933–1945

"All Brains on Deck"

In our last generational crisis of survival, the Great Depression and World War II, it took *all Americans* from all backgrounds and walks of life, working together, to save our freedom (discussed further in Chapter 10). It will take *all of us* to do that again.

We have only 320 million players on our bench. China has about 1.3 billion people and India about 1.2 billion. For goodness sakes, we don't have any spares. We need "all brains on deck" to unleash the *swarm intelligence* of the entire population. This is the only way we can solve the serious problems we now face fast enough to keep *our* freedom.

It is time for us to stop looking at our differences and focus on what binds us together as a free united country—"one nation, under God, indivisible, with liberty and justice for all" (U.S. Pledge of Allegiance). *United we stand. Divided we fall.* Those words are as true for us today as when they were said in the days of Aesop's Fables more than two thousand years ago. They are as true today as when Abraham Lincoln said "a house divided against itself cannot stand" during the American Civil War in the 1860s.

We are about to find out whether our vaunted American system of freedom can still adapt fast enough to survive and thrive in today's fast-paced, crisis-prone, and constantly changing 21st century global environment. Will the United States remain a peaceful, stable, and secure country, while making the painful adjustments needed to restore fiscal and ethical sanity in our economy, government, and society before it is too late? Will we hold together as a united country through another generational Fourth Turning crisis of survival?

Decades of unethical conduct have weakened the trust Americans have in many of our self-governing, self-organizing institutions. This could lead to disastrous consequences. Whatever problems you think you now have will pale in comparison to the problems we will all have—both here in the United States and around the world—if the United States fails to remain a free, strong, and united country.

If the United States fails as a free nation and a free economy, it will not be because our system of government and Rule of Law failed. It will be because the moral compass, common sense, and critical-thinking abilities of the American people failed.

A person who won't read has no advantage over one who can't read.

– Mark Twain (1835–1910)
American writer and humorist

The United States has succeeded for centuries as a free, stable, secure, and prosperous country *under the same form of government* not because we haven't made mistakes. We have made plenty of them.

We have succeeded because in each freedom-threatening generational crisis of survival we have been able to self-organize and re-invent ourselves. We have been able to wash away what became old, decayed, and corrupt, while maintaining our central, timeless, and unchanging core of American freedom under our unique American Rule of Law and unique constitutional system.

To do so again, Americans must drop any delusions of invincibility and recognize the very serious and very real danger we are in. Consider our ant hill as having already been kicked over. We had better get the repair crews out immediately before the next storm hits. *This is no time to be ethically confused.*

> *The greatness of America lies not in being more enlightened than any other nation, but rather in her ability to repair her faults.*
>
> **– Alexis de Tocqueville (1805–1859)**
> Author, *Democracy in America* (1835)

Freedom Is Work

America's freedom-loving culture of trust is tilting dangerously toward a freedom-busting culture of distrust. Too many Americans are relying on someone else to take responsibility for keeping our freedom. This will never work.

Our unique brand of self-organizing freedom requires active and well-informed citizens. *All of us* must be able to think critically for ourselves, based on objective facts and evidence, not on emotional perceptions, opinions, or political propaganda. We *all* have to do our own homework and educate ourselves sufficiently so that we can be responsible citizens and voters.

Unfortunately, in recent years, our educational institutions have too often failed to effectively teach vital subjects like American history, civics, and critical thinking. As a result, many Americans do not know the basics about what has made the United States so successful for so long.

We cannot hope to restore our free constitutional republic and free capitalist economy fast enough *unless we are ALL willing to do the hard work necessary for freedom*. We must know how our economy and government are supposed to work. We must also stay up-to-date with what is happening in the country and around the world. Most importantly, it means all of us must be able to think critically for ourselves based on *all* of the relevant *facts* and *evidence* needed to make wise decisions.

The essence of self-organization is *personal responsibility*. If you want to see why the United States is in the ethics mess we are in today, look in a mirror. It could not have happened without the complicity of the American people. Only *"we the people"* can restore fiscal and ethical sanity in the country before it is too late.

To continue being free in the 21st century, we must stop waiting for someone to tell us what to do. Instead, we must look around our own environments to see what needs to be done and start doing it—*automatically, voluntarily, and cooperatively as a group without central direction and control*. All of us have the responsibility to self-organize and participate in finding solutions to our most pressing problems to prevent our country from slipping into chaos, violence, and anarchy. *Freedom does not work on auto-pilot.*

"We the people" are responsible for insisting on ethical conduct, not just talk, for ourselves and *all* of our leaders, in *all* of our self-governing, self-organizing institutions and associations. There's just no getting around it. When it comes to ethics, trust, and our freedom, ignorance is not bliss. *An ignorant population that votes will not be free for long.*

If a nation expects to be ignorant and free, in a state of civilization, it expects what never was and never will be.

– Thomas Jefferson (1743–1829)
American Founding Father,
3rd U.S. president, 1801–1809

"Smart" Is Overrated

Americans need to think for themselves and fast. Too many Americans have been blindly following "the experts" and letting "the experts" do their thinking for them. They have forgotten that although some experts may be "smart" (and sometimes even that is debatable), many so-called "smart" experts are missing the most important requirement for the long-term success of an economy, government, and society—*wisdom.*

As described earlier, *wisdom is* knowledge plus experience, insight, and most important of all, *the common sense of the ordinary person.* The last time Americans had such a love affair with the "smart" experts was in the 1920s. As we know, that did not work out too well for the millions of people who suffered terribly during the Great Depression in the 1930s.

We have been told repeatedly in recent years that "smart" people are running our governments, businesses, and other important institutions. That may be true, but "smart" people are also the ones who designed, promoted, and sold the exotic (possibly toxic?) financial products that led to the Financial Crisis of 2008.

Wise people would never have done this. Wise people would have known better than to jeopardize the financial stability of the entire country for their own short-term gain.

This love affair with "smart" people can be traced back to the American baby-boomer generation, raised in an era of rapid technological advances. Many baby-boomers believed they had nothing to learn from their less technology-oriented depression and war-era American parents. Their slogan was "don't trust anyone over 30." They were wrong. They forgot about wisdom.

"Smart" people got us into the ethics mess we are in. We will need *wise* people to help us restore our ethical center quickly enough to keep our freedom in the 21st century.

> *Data are just raw facts. Once data are organized, they become information. Information, when applied, yields knowledge. Knowledge, when studied for patterns and principles, becomes wisdom.*
>
> **– Russell Ackoff[32] (1909–2009)**
> Management consultant and systems thinker
> "Einstein of Problem Solving"

In the words of our three American generational crises of survival presidents:

> *Happiness and moral duty are inseparably connected.*
>
> **– George Washington**
> (American Revolutionary War)
>
> *Important principles may, and must, be inflexible.*
>
> **– Abraham Lincoln**
> (American Civil War)
>
> *Confidence... thrives on honesty, on honor, on the sacredness of obligations, on faithful protection, and on unselfish performance. Without them it cannot live.*
>
> **– Franklin D. Roosevelt**
> (The Great Depression and WWII)

Chapter 4

It's All about Trust
Debunking the Myths about Ethics

Those who stand for nothing fall for anything.

– Alexander Hamilton (1755–1804)
American Founding Father,
1st U.S. secretary of the Treasury

A World without Trust

When the financial crisis slammed into the United States with full force in 2008, giant commercial and investment banks collapsed. Some disappeared, while others were sold at cut-rate prices only after tens of billions of taxpayer dollars were added to close the sale.

Fannie Mae and Freddie Mac both failed. When the federal government took them over, American taxpayers were suddenly saddled with about $5 trillion in potential mortgage liability.

Huge American corporations, even ones in business for more than 100 years, declared bankruptcy. The U.S. federal government doled out hundreds of billions of taxpayer dollars to bail out failed businesses. The U.S. stock market lost more than 50% of its value.

Frightened depositors lined up to withdraw funds from a giant California bank, reminiscent of scenes from the Great Depression. Comparisons to the Great Depression became commonplace.

The U.S. Federal Reserve and the U.S. federal government opened up the spending spigot. Bloomberg reported they "...spent, lent or committed $12.8 trillion, an amount that approaches the value of everything produced in the country [in 2008] to stem the longest recession since the 1930s."[1]

Economic pain did not just strike the United States. Stock markets and home prices in many countries plummeted. Fearing a global financial meltdown, central banks in other countries also slashed interest rates and flooded their economies with massive infusions of cash.

Even Communist China agreed to spend $586 billion to stimulate its economy.[2] The World Bank warned that this global financial crisis might be worse than the one in the 1930s.[3]

In 2008, fear in the United States and around the world was palpable; trust was in very short supply.

A Trillion Is *How Much?*

Americans have become complacent about our federal government's massive over-spending. In 2000, our national federal debt was just under $6 trillion. Since then, we have added about $12 trillion more in debt—about $5 trillion under President George Bush (2000–2008) and about $7 trillion under President Barack Obama (2009–2014).

By the end of 2014, our national debt was over $18 trillion. By any rational, common sense standard, this is an extraordinarily large national debt, growing dangerously fast.

Most people have difficulty comprehending the magnitude of the difference between $1 billion and $1 trillion. *Time* magazine used the following example to help illustrate the difference:[4]

> One *million* seconds = *11½ days*
> One *billion* seconds = *32 years*
> One *trillion* seconds = *32,000 years*

Now can you see why our current national debt of more than $18 trillion, still growing rapidly, is both dangerous and unsustainable?[5] *Distrust is expensive.*

Dangerous Instability

Another threat lurks in the financial system itself. In the 2000s, banks, hedge funds, and other financial institutions used *massive amounts of borrowed money* through exotic new financial products with bizarre names like *collateralized debt obligations, asset-backed bonds, credit derivatives*, and *credit default swaps.*

Don't let these oddball-sounding names put you to sleep. These are the financial products at the heart of the Financial Crisis of 2008. Such exotic (possibly toxic?) investment banker-created bonds were supported and encouraged by our federal politicians through government-sponsored entities like Fannie Mae and Freddie Mac.[6]

These new-fangled financial products were the source of the free-wheeling credit that sent U.S. home prices into the stratosphere in the 2000s in an unprecedented housing mania. During the go-go boom years, these complicated *triple-A rated* financial products were sold to mutual funds, insurance companies, municipalities, and other institutional investors, both in the United States and other countries.

Institutional investors piled into these complicated investment products promising higher returns with seemingly little risk (shouldn't that have been the first warning sign that something was wrong?). The theory was that spreading such complicated derivatives and asset-backed bonds throughout the global financial system would make it more stable. There's only one problem with that theory. That's not how it worked out.

American International Group (AIG) became the poster child for what could go terribly wrong when credit derivatives were misused. The financial debacle at AIG, one of the world's largest insurance companies, involved a special kind of credit derivative called a *credit default swap.*

The U.S. federal government (that is, the American taxpayer) paid about $182 billion to bail out AIG. The American public was told this bailout was absolutely necessary because a bankrupt AIG might set off a chain reaction of defaults that could cause a "catastrophic" global financial crisis.[7] Does this sound like using credit derivatives to disperse risk throughout the global financial system made it more stable? Certainly not.

Hidden Risks

A credit default swap is an agreement in which a third party (like AIG) gets paid a fee to guarantee another against default on "securitized" bonds (e.g., mortgage-backed securities). Although called insurance, credit default swaps were nothing like "real" insurance.

Highly regulated "real" insurance companies were required by regulators to put money aside as "reserves" to ensure they would be able to pay all the claims they were insuring. Lightly regulated credit default swap "guarantors" were not required to set up "reserves" and did not do so.

"Real" insurance can only be purchased by those with an "insurable interest" in the property being insured (e.g., owning a home). As a result, there is a natural limit on the number of "real" insurance contracts that can be bought and sold. This wasn't true for credit default swaps. Virtually an unlimited number of credit default swaps could be (and were) bought and sold in the United States and around the world.

Those buying credit default swaps from AIG had no idea how many other swaps AIG had sold to others, or whether AIG had the funds to pay all the claims it was guaranteeing. In fact, these credit default swaps made AIG appear to be more profitable than it actually was.

The company collected a mountain of extra fees, did not have to set any money aside as "reserves," and was not paying out money for claims (since there were no defaults). Hidden from public view were the enormous financial risks that AIG had undertaken under these swap agreements. When the Financial Crisis of 2008 hit, AIG was soon swamped with so many credit default swap claims, it faced bankruptcy without a federal bailout.

The Scary Unknown

Warren Buffet, one of the world's richest investors, called credit derivatives "financial weapons of mass destruction" in Berkshire Hathaway's 2002 annual report.[8] He said, "I view derivatives as time bombs, both for the parties that deal in them and the economic system."[9]

One of the biggest problems with such exotic (possibly toxic?) financial products like *credit derivatives* is that no one knows for sure how many are floating around in today's highly interconnected global financial markets. One estimate was that the notional value of credit derivatives globally around the time of the Financial Crisis of 2008 was about $600 trillion (in an estimated $65 trillion global economy).[10] A leading derivatives expert, Paul Wilmott, said that the number may be much higher—$1.2 quadrillion; 20 times the size of the global economy.[11]

In 2011, one newspaper suggested that as much as 95% of the $250 trillion in derivatives held by the top 25 American bank holding companies might be in just four financial institutions: JPMorgan Chase, Citigroup, Bank of America, and Goldman Sachs.[12]

No one knows for sure what damage these financial instruments might do in another financial crisis. There is great concern that a default in one country could set off a cascading wave of defaults rippling across the global financial system like a long line of closely stacked dominoes. We are in uncharted territory. This has never happened before in history. *Distrust is dangerous.*

Predictable Failure

While many "experts" in charge of our financial institutions, businesses, and governments claim that no one could have seen this financial calamity coming, that is not true. What is happening today was entirely predictable. Unethical conduct inevitably leads to failure. The only questions are when that failure will occur, and how bad it will be.

How did this happen? In the space of about 40 years, baby-boomer and succeeding American generations forgot (or never learned) that America's prosperity rests squarely on our ability to create and maintain a culture of trust. *Ethical conduct creates trust. Unethical conduct destroys trust.*

Ethical Confusion Reigns

Legend says if you place a frog in boiling water, the frog will immediately jump out because it can feel that the water is dangerously hot. But if you put a frog in cold water, and turn the heat up slowly, it will slowly boil to death because it cannot feel the water becoming fatally hot.

The decline in American ethical standards did not happen overnight. It has occurred over decades—slowly at first; picking up speed over the decades. *Today, our ethical water is extremely hot. If we don't make immediate changes, it could reach the "boiling point" soon.*

Our recent serious ethical lapses will be painful for all Americans, not just the individuals, organizations, and institutions directly involved. So far, that pain has been muted by the U.S. Federal Reserve and the U.S. federal government spending trillions and trillions of dollars and running up a gargantuan debt.

40 Years Can Damage a Culture

Any country's culture can be severely damaged (or destroyed) in just 40 years. Germany after World War II is a good example. After the war, Nazi Germany was split into East and West Germany.[13] At the time of the split, both Germanys shared a common language and culture.

However, by the time the two Germanys were reunited about 40 years later, they had become two completely different countries and cultures. West Germany was a free nation with one of the highest standards of living in the world. East Germany was a repressive dictatorship with an economy that was nearly bankrupt. *Culture matters. Culture is fragile.*

West Germany, placed under the control of free western countries (the United States, Britain, and France), adopted a *"bottom-up" freedom* model: a free-market capitalist economy based on private property and freely elected leaders under a western-styled constitution.

East Germany, under the control of the Communist Soviet Union dictatorship, adopted the Soviet Union's *"top-down" dictatorship* model: a "top-down" central government-controlled-and-run economy where private property was abolished and un-elected leaders used secret police and informants to stifle dissent. When East Germans began to flee to West Germany for a better life, East Germany erected the Berlin Wall. East German border guards shot to kill anyone who tried to escape.

The two Germanys were finally reunited in 1990. Even though West Germany spent at least $1.6 trillion to upgrade the East German economy, 20 years after unification "the eastern German economy [was] still in a sorry state."[14]

Not all cultures succeed. Some cultures fail. Once a country's culture is damaged, it can take a long time to repair the damage.

The Birth of "New Age" Ethics

The "Me" Generation

American baby-boomers grew up in unprecedented peace and prosperity after World War II. American businesses were booming because they had little foreign competition. Most countries were still rebuilding their economies after fighting a war on their own soil.

The post-war American baby-boomer generation grew up taking American freedom and prosperity for granted, believing the United States is invincible. They rejected their depression and war parents' patriotic American values and morality. Instead, their attitude was "if it feels good, do it."[15]

"New Age" Morality

In 1966, Joseph Fletcher's book, *Situation Ethics: The New Morality* took hold on many American college campuses. This began America's lurch into "New Age" morality called *situational ethics*. Under this new ethics theory, the idea that common moral standards of behavior applied equally to *all* Americans in *all* of our institutions and associations was viewed as old-fashioned and out of date.[16]

As diversity later became the watchword across college campuses, another "New Age" theory of ethics—*relative ethics*—became popular.[17] Under this new ethics theory, the United States was no longer viewed as a "melting pot" in which all American citizens adopted a common American culture. Instead, America was described as a "salad bowl" of newly invented cultural subgroups—African-American, Hispanic, Asian-American, etc.[18]

Under relative ethics, each sub-group was free to make up its own ethical standards. Only members of each sub-group were viewed as having the requisite "cultural sensitivity" to determine their group's ethical cultural norms.

Amazingly, American schools and universities began teaching new generations of Americans that the United States was *no longer* a unified country with one set of laws of ethical conduct (laws of trust) that applied equally to *all* Americans in *all* of our institutions and associations. *Is it any wonder Americans have become so ethically confused?*

> *A system of morality which is based on relative emotional values is a mere illusion...which has nothing sound in it and nothing true.*
>
> **– Socrates (469 B.C.–399 B.C.)**
> One of the founders of the philosophy
> of western civilization

The Greed Generation

These "New Age," non-uniform standards of ethical conduct under *situational* and *relative* ethics fit perfectly with the attitudes of the 1980s "Greed Generation." This was the decade when top corporate players in *leveraged buy-outs* walked away with huge payoffs while ordinary rank-and-file workers often lost their jobs.

In 1988, CEO F. Ross Johnson was paid $53 million in the giant $25 billion leveraged buyout of R.J.R. Nabisco. According to *Bloomberg Businessweek*, dealmaker Kohlberg Kravis Roberts & Co. was paid about $414 million in fees.[19] *The age of mega-pay for only a few had arrived.*

The 1980s era of high-flying junk bonds led to numerous insider trading scandals and thousands of failed savings and loans (with losses estimated to be between $160 billion and $500 billion[20]). Michael Milken, dubbed the junk bond king, landed in jail. The investment bank where he worked, Drexel Burnham Lambert, went out of business.

Michael Milken was sentenced to 10 years in prison, but served only 2½ years in a minimum-security, white-collar prison. Even after paying a record $600 million fine, he still had a fortune estimated to be worth several hundred million dollars.[21] Leniency in his case had the unintended consequence of sending the wrong message—that white-collar crime did pay if huge amounts of money were involved.

"Greed is good," made famous by Gordon Gekko in the 1989 movie *Wall Street,* became the new American mantra. A *"winner-take-all" attitude* took root in the United States. The "new morality" was pay those at the top fabulous sums of money, while everyone else's income fell further and further behind.

This attitude has not only permeated our big businesses, it has spread to other self-organizing civic institutions and voluntary associations.[22] Americans are ignoring the warnings of history that great disparities in income, wealth, and privileges, left unaddressed for too long, can lead to trouble in any country— even one like the United States that has been stable and successful for so long.

The Death of Critical Thinking

Another reason Americans have become so ethically confused is because too often our schools and universities have been teaching political thinking, not critical thinking.

Political thinking is indoctrination, defined by dictionary.com as "teaching someone to accept a set of beliefs without questioning them." Political thinkers use propaganda, defined by multiple dictionaries as presenting information in a biased or inaccurate way to promote a political agenda.

Political thinkers do not tolerate dissent. This is why many American universities passed speech codes trying to dictate what could and could not be said on college campuses (contrary to the free speech protections guaranteed in the Bill of Rights of the U.S. Constitution).[23]

> *The philosophy of the school room in one generation will be the philosophy of government in the next.*[24]
>
> **– Abraham Lincoln (1809–1865)**
> 16th U.S. president during the
> American Civil War, 1861–1865

Critical thinking is the exact opposite. The goal of critical thinking is to produce independent thinkers who think for themselves. Critical thinkers objectively and rationally analyze *data, facts, information, and evidence* on their own.

They consider all sides of an issue from multiple perspectives without prejudgment. Critical thinkers reach a conclusion only after thoroughly and objectively analyzing *all relevant facts and evidence*, both favorable and unfavorable.

They are voracious readers and students of history and human nature. Because critical thinkers are independent thinkers, they cannot easily be manipulated and controlled by others.

Analysis based on critical thinking *does not* devolve into character assassination and personal attacks, as often occurs when a political thinker's views are challenged. Those engaged in critical thinking welcome differing perspectives, so long as they are not based solely on bare opinion or political belief.

Critical thinkers focus on the credibility and reliability of *facts and evidence*, not the presumed credibility of the speaker. Winning the argument is not the goal of critical thinkers.

What matters is that *all relevant facts, evidence, and information needed to make wise, informed decisions* are discovered, discussed, and analyzed before a decision or choice is made. Critical thinkers always take into account the lessons of *history* and predictability of *human nature*.

Political thinking has no place in a free society. Political thinking is the province of dictatorships that want to maintain control over their populations. A free society like ours depends on knowledgeable and well-informed citizens and voters.

Our schools and universities must *educate, not indoctrinate*, each new generation of Americans. It is essential that our schools and universities teach why free-market capitalism—*with morality*—is essential for our continued survival, success, and freedom in the 21st century.

They must also teach each new generation of Americans what is special and different about our unique brand of freedom, based on the Declaration of Independence, the U.S. Constitution, and the Bill of Rights (discussed in greater detail in Chapter 8). *Political thinking, especially about ethics, is a threat to our freedom.*

Critical thinkers generally "see" future trends. They are more likely to be better prepared to cope with crisis and emergencies. Political thinkers are almost always "unpleasantly surprised" by "unexpected" events.

The only way for us to solve our ethics problems in the United States today is by using critical thinking. Political thinking is what got us into this ethics mess in the first place.

Clearing Up Our Ethical Confusion

Political thinking about ethics has led to massive ethical confusion in the United States. Words like *character, values, integrity, virtue, morality,* and *ethics* have been used indiscriminately as though they are interchangeable definitions for ethics. Using dictionary definitions and critical thinking, we can easily see why this is not so:

Character: **moral** excellence and firmness

Values: a principle or quality intrinsically valuable or desirable (such as **morality**)

Virtue: **moral** excellence

Integrity: firm adherence to **moral** values

Ethics: a voluntary code of conduct of **moral** behavior

As you can see, it is impossible to define *character, values, virtue, integrity,* and *ethics* without first defining *morality.* Using words like *character, values, virtue,* and *integrity* to describe *ethics*, without first defining *morality* (the difference between right and wrong), leads to circular reasoning, confusion, and sometimes downright silliness.

Here's an example. An administrator of a prominent American business school was asked to describe a business school's responsibility to teach ethics to its students. He responded that it was the business school's responsibility to teach students how to protect their integrity at work, but *not* to teach students right from wrong.

Let's take a closer look at this statement. Since *integrity* is defined as the firm adherence to *moral* values, how can a business school teach students how to protect their integrity at work without first teaching them the difference between right and wrong? The answer is, it can't.

It is impossible to teach ethics without first teaching the difference between right and wrong behavior—that is, morality.

> *In matters of style, swim with the current; in matters of principle, stand like a rock.*
>
> **– Thomas Jefferson (1743–1826)**
> American Founding Father,
> 3rd U.S. president, 1801–1809

Three Legs of the Same Stool

Under America's essential self-organizing culture of trust, *morality, ethics,* and *law* are intimately intertwined:

Morality: *Knowing* the difference between right and wrong behavior

Ethics: *A voluntary code of conduct* that recognizes the difference between right and wrong behavior

Law: The *enforcement mechanism* that enforces the code of conduct that recognizes the difference between right and wrong

Ethics and law are concerned with right and wrong behavior—that is, morality. *Right* behavior creates the culture of trust we must have for our successful *capitalist* free-market economy (as it is supposed to be) and our free, peaceful, politically stable and secure government and society under a free democratic *republic. Wrong* behavior does just the opposite.

By looking through the lens of *ethics-based* American Rule of Law (behavior that is enforced), it is possible to discern the code of conduct (ethics) that describes the American morality (concepts of right and wrong) required to create and maintain our all-essential culture of trust.

That is, when it comes to describing the mandatory ethical standards of our American culture of trust, *morality, ethics,* and *law* are three legs of the same stool. *Right behavior creates trust. Wrong behavior creates distrust.*

Ethics-based American Rule of Law is infused with specific deep-seated principles of right and wrong behavior. Over centuries, Judeo-Christian values have become embedded in the social, political, economic, legal, and cultural fabric of the United States (discussed in greater detail in Chapter 8).

Misunderstanding the close connection between morality, ethics, and law in the United States and the importance of our Judeo-Christian cultural heritage is not harmless error. These are critical pillars of our free economy, free society, and free nation.

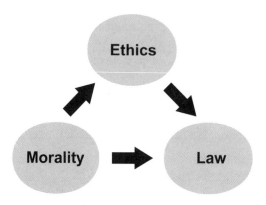

Law is order, and good law is good order.

- **Aristotle (384 B.C.–322 B.C.)**
Greek philosopher, often called the
"Father of Ethics"

The Missing Link

The ethical conduct required to maintain our essential culture of trust *cannot be taught without morality*—that is, without knowing the difference between right and wrong behavior.

While studying right and wrong conduct from multiple perspectives such as philosophy, management, and religion is certainly helpful and appropriate, these ethical perspectives should be taught *in addition to, not instead of*, the mandatory principles of right and wrong conduct that can and *must* be enforced under *ethics-based* American Rule of Law.

Joseph Wharton understood this intimate connection between law, ethics, and morality in the United States. This is why, when he created the first business curriculum at the college level at the University of Pennsylvania in 1881, law was one of the five required courses.[25]

It is impossible to teach the ethical conduct required to create and maintain our essential American culture of trust without reference to ethics-based American Rule of Law.

Debunking the Myths about Ethics

Principles of morality and ethics, established and enforced under *ethics-based* American Rule of Law, are *not personal*. Individuals and organizations are not free to align their behaviors in keeping with their own values or personal beliefs about what constitutes right and wrong behavior.

The *public* ethics standards *required* in all of our self-organizing institutions and associations are defined under *ethics-based* American Rule of Law. Contrary to popular belief, the laws of ethical conduct required to create and maintain our essential culture of trust in the United States are

NOT situational,
NOT relative,
NOT unclear,
NOT hard to teach, and
NOT optional.

Like the 10 Commandments in the Bible, there are certain *bright-line principles of right and wrong behavior—the 10 Commandments of Trust*—that we *must all* follow in *all* of our civic institutions and voluntary associations. This is the only way to keep the *essential culture of trust* required to maintain our free economy, free society, and free nation.

> *Facts are stubborn things; and whatever may be our wishes, our inclination, or the dictates of our passions, they cannot alter the state of facts and evidence.*[26]
>
> **– John Adams (1735–1826)**
> American Founding Father,
> 2nd U.S. president, 1797–1801

Public Ethics vs. *Private* Ethics

There is some overlap between private and public ethics standards because behaviors that create trust in our institutions and associations also create trust among individuals.

However, in the United States, individuals only have some control about whether they act in keeping with their own beliefs and values in the arena of *private ethics* in their personal lives, *not* when *public ethics* standards are involved.

The American *public ethics* standards that create the culture of trust required in our civic institutions and voluntary associations are *mandatory*. Failure to follow them can, and often does, lead to serious and painful consequences under *ethics-based* American Rule of Law.

Public ethics standards apply automatically whenever we are acting through our self-organizing institutions or associations, like our businesses, government entities, nonprofits, charities, unions, associations, and the like.

Individuals in our self-organizing institutions and associations are not free to set their own personal ethical standards based on their own character, integrity, or values. They may only set ethical standards *higher, never lower*, than the *public ethics* standards established under *ethics-based* American Rule of Law.

Because of our long-standing, well-entrenched *free press* and *free speech* rights, serious unethical conduct rarely remains hidden in the United States for long. As noted by U.S. Supreme Court Justice Louis Brandeis, "If the broad light of day could be let in upon men's actions, it would purify them as the sun disinfects."[27]

Enforcement of *public ethics* standards under *ethics-based* American Rule of Law can take many forms. Sometimes these standards are enforced by bad publicity and a scandal that leads to a resignation or changed institutional policy.

At other times, an ethics scandal might lead to something more serious, such as a Congressional hearing, civil lawsuit, or criminal action. Executives, employees, and others may end up in prison. Individuals and/or their institutions may be required to pay huge financial penalties.

> *[P]ublic virtue is the only foundation of republics. There must be a positive passion for the public good [and] the public interest...in the minds of the people, or there can be no republican government, nor any real liberty: and this public passion must be superior to all private passions.*
>
> **– John Adams (1735–1826)**
> American Founding Father,
> 2nd U.S. president, 1797–1801

Think "It's Unethical, But Legal"?

Confusion over this distinction between *private ethics* and *public ethics* has misled executives, employees, and individuals in many of our self-governing organizations into believing their behavior can be "unethical, but legal." In the context of a *public ethics* scandal that seriously damages our culture of trust, this is not the case.

In the *public ethics* sphere, behavior is deemed wrong because it damages the culture of trust we must have to support our free economy, free political system, and our free society. In this context, when someone does something wrong (unethical), *ethics-based* American Rule of Law *must* enforce public ethics standards to restore trust quickly and do justice to keep the peace.

Therefore, serious unethical conduct that violates *public ethics* standards is, by definition, also "illegal" (or about to be), under the right circumstances. Americans often confuse *failure to currently enforce* public ethics standards under *ethics-based* American Rule of Law with behavior that is "legal."

When it comes to the *public ethics* standards required to keep and maintain our culture of trust, a better phrase to remember is: *If it's unethical, it's probably "illegal" (or about to be) and even if it's not, it's likely to be painful and/or expensive in some way.*

Enforcement Whiplash

For long stretches of time, enforcement of ethical standards in the United States may appear to be lax or dormant. This often occurs during extended periods of peace and prosperity. *But in a crisis, enforcement of ethical standards in the United States can, and often does, radically change from little or no enforcement to extreme and severe enforcement.*

Within the boundaries of our constitutional parameters, *ethics-based* American Rule of Law is capable of inventing new, powerful ways to quickly restore trust in our free markets and free society. For example, during the savings and loan scandals, a statute passed in 1970 to eradicate organized crime (the Mafia)—the Racketeer Influenced and Corrupt Organizations (RICO) statute—was used to sue investment banker and junk-bond king, Michael Milken.[28]

Once an ethical violator lands on the government's "serious unethical conduct" list, government prosecutors can be relentless. Richard Scrushy, former CEO of HealthSouth, was acquitted in his first trial for accounting fraud under the Sarbanes-Oxley Act of 2002. However, he was later convicted and sent to prison on a charge of bribery.[29] Walter Forbes, the former CEO of Cendant Corp., was finally convicted and sent to prison for accounting fraud after three trials.[30]

A crisis is not always needed to spark creative legal enforcement of American ethical standards. Sometimes public dissatisfaction over unethical conduct builds up over time until finally, as though a dam has broken, public anger triggers enforcement.

For decades, tobacco companies successfully defended themselves against lawsuits seeking damages for cigarette-induced deaths. In 1994, seven CEOs of the largest tobacco companies swore under oath in a televised Congressional hearing that "nicotine is not addictive." Public opinion swiftly changed. In 1998, American tobacco companies paid more than $200 billion to settle claims from 46 states.[31]

When acting in any of our civic institutions and voluntary associations, it is wise to remember that in the United States, *the loophole you love today may be a noose around your neck tomorrow.*

Think Trust

"Are you ethical?" If asked this question, without hesitation your immediate response would be a resounding "yes." Instinctively, we all know that doing something unethical (wrong) at work is unacceptable, even if we have no idea which wrong behaviors are included in the definition of unethical.

Since "experts" disagree on what ethics means and what behaviors are unethical, it is easy to rationalize that wrong behavior is "ethical," especially if we benefit from the unethical treatment of others. In recent decades, defining ethics became a lot like defining pornography—we don't know what it means, but we "know it when we see it." Thus, defining what is right and wrong behavior in terms of "ethics" does not give us much helpful guidance.

But if you are asked a different question: *"If you do that (behavior), will you be trusted?"* Right away you know whether your behavior is right or wrong. You don't need an ethics "expert" or anyone else to tell you what behaviors instill trust and which ones destroy trust. Each and every one of us knows automatically who we trust and who we don't.

Trust is a primitive and basic human emotional state that may be biologically based. Using advanced MRI brain scans, researchers say they have located the specific part of the brain where trust resides.[32] Technology and societies may have changed dramatically over thousands of years, but the standards of behavior that create trust between human beings have not. *The laws of trust are timeless, immutable, clear, and absolute.*

Compare: "Is it ethical to lie?" with "If you lie *about something important*, will you be trusted?" You may be able to fudge the answer to the first question, but the answer to the second question about trust is clear. Lying *about something important* destroys trust.

So if you want to know if your behavior is wrong in the context of *public* ethics, the question you should ask yourself is *not Is my behavior ethical?* A better question to ask yourself is *If I do this, will I be trusted?* By framing the definition of right behavior using trust, not ethics, as the standard, the laws of ethical conduct are simple, clear, and nonnegotiable. We either trust someone or something, or we don't.

When it comes to something important that could seriously damage our country's culture of trust, trust is black and white, not shades of grey. *When trust is the standard, there are no loopholes.*

The purpose of ethical conduct

=

To create TRUST

Chapter 5

Complacency about Trust
Is Dangerous
History's Warnings

> *The things that will destroy America are prosperity-at-any-price, peace-at-any-price, safety-first instead of duty-first, the love of soft living, and the get-rich-quick theory of life.*
>
> **– Theodore Roosevelt (1858–1919)**
> 26th U.S. president, 1901–1909

Ostriches Don't Survive

It is an oft-repeated myth that ostriches bury their heads in the sand when they see danger, but ostriches do not do that, humans do. Ostriches are the fastest-running birds on earth, capable of running at speeds of more than 40 miles per hour. When danger approaches, they run.

Humans are the ones who sometimes bury their heads in denial, foolishly believing that danger will magically disappear on its own. The ancient Greeks had a name for such false beliefs and optimism—*hubris.*

A free people who cannot face the reality of their current situation will not be free for long.

> *By failing to prepare, you are preparing to fail.*
>
> **– Benjamin Franklin (1706–1790)**
> American Founding Father

Delusional Blind Optimism

Wisdom has been passed down from generation to generation through myths, fables, and true stories that describe *timeless, immutable,* and *universal* traits of *human nature.* No matter how technologically advanced a civilization becomes, flaws in human nature can, and often have, led to unexpected disasters.

The ancient Greeks, more than two thousand years ago, wondered why some extraordinarily successful people made terrible decisions and ended up destroying themselves. They said such reckless behavior was caused by a flawed human character trait called *hubris.*

Hubris is an emotional state of blindness that causes some extremely successful people to believe they are invincible. In such an emotional state of mind, they no longer can realistically evaluate their own weaknesses or accurately assess the dangers around them.

Individuals, organizations, or countries that suffer from hubris become overconfident, arrogant, and complacent. They seriously *overestimate their abilities and underestimate the risks* they are facing, with predictable and often disastrous consequences.

No Such Thing as "Too Big to Fail"

The sinking of the *Titanic* has fascinated people for more than 100 years. This tragic event is a stark reminder of the terrible consequences of hubris, warning us there is no such thing as "too big to fail." In today's age of "too big to fail" businesses and other entities, we would be wise to remember that what happened to the mighty "unsinkable" *Titanic* can happen to a mighty company, a mighty organization, and even a mighty country.

When the *Titanic* made its maiden voyage across the Atlantic in April 1912, she was "the largest movable object constructed up to that time."[1] It took 3,000 men two years to build this gargantuan ship.

Equipped with the latest safety technology, she had 16 "watertight" compartments. Because the ship was designed to float even if four of these compartments flooded, the press called her "unsinkable."

Her specially manufactured, double-bottom steel hull was tightly fastened with more than three million iron rivets.[2] The captain, with more than 40 years of sailing experience, had an unblemished safety record. When asked if the *Titanic* could sink, he said, "modern shipbuilding had gone beyond that."[3]

Freak weather conditions in 1912, not seen before or since, caused an unusually large number of icebergs to travel further south into Atlantic shipping lanes.[4] Shortly after leaving port, the *Titanic* began receiving multiple warnings of numerous icebergs ahead. In spite of these warnings, the ship did not reduce her speed. *Complacency reigned.*

Just before midnight on April 14th, the *Titanic* struck an iceberg. Seawater immediately began flooding the lower decks, but because of the *Titanic's* immense size, passengers on the top decks remained blissfully unaware of the extreme danger they were now in. Some passengers mistakenly believed they would be safer remaining on the giant ship. Early lifeboats left the *Titanic* only half-full.

Passengers were unaware that there were not enough lifeboats to rescue all onboard. Nor did they know that the ship had a design defect; the walls of the ship's 16 "watertight" compartments did not go all the way to the ceiling. As soon as water filled up one compartment, it immediately spilled over into the adjoining compartments. It didn't take long for more than four compartments to flood, making the ship's sinking inevitable.

In only 2 hours and 40 minutes, the mighty "unsinkable" *Titanic* sank in the icy waters off the coast of Newfoundland. Almost 1,500 people died; only 712 people survived. Rich and poor, old and young, men and women perished together.

When it comes to ships, individuals, businesses, organizations, and even countries, there is no such thing as "too big to fail."

Our Ethics Rivets

The *Titanic* sank in waters more than two miles deep, so a visual inspection of the ship was not possible until 1985. Up until that time, most experts believed the ship had sunk because the iceberg had ripped a large gash in the ship's hull. That wasn't true. There was no such gash—only numerous small holes dotting the 300-foot section of the hull that had struck the iceberg.

Upon further testing, it was discovered that the *Titanic's* iron rivets had been made with too much slag. This would have made them brittle in the super-cold Atlantic waters.[5] The force of striking the iceberg would have sheared off the tops of the rivets, causing them to pop out. The hull's steel plates would have separated, allowing tons of seawater to rush in and sink the "unsinkable" ship.[6] In the end, the world's largest ship sank because rivets, measured only in inches, were defective.

Ethics and trust are the rivets that hold the American ship-of-state together as a united country in a time of extreme crisis. Because our ethics rivets have been strong, the United States has been able to remain a united nation *under the same form of free constitutional government* for more than two hundred years, a rare feat in modern world history.

However, repeated success breeds complacency. History warns us that any country can fail—even a free country like the United States that has been so stable and successful for so long. *This is no time to be complacent about ethics and trust.*

> - **Ethical standards and conduct** are the rivets that hold our companies, our organizations, our institutions—indeed our country—together, by creating our essential culture of trust.
>
> - **Without ethics,** what happened to the mighty *Titanic* can happen to a mighty company, a mighty organization, a mighty institution—even a mighty country.
>
> - **Have you ever stopped to consider** how many ethical holes already exist in the hull of the American ship-of-state that, if combined with one or more adverse conditions, could sink the "unsinkable *U.S.S. America*"?

History Doesn't Rhyme, It Repeats

A popular slogan often used today is "history doesn't repeat, it rhymes," as though human beings don't make the same mistakes twice. Two American generational historians disagree.

They say history does repeat—over and over—in four successive periods (turnings) of approximately 20 years each. William Strauss and Neil Howe, in their groundbreaking 1997 book, *The Fourth Turning*, described these four repetitive cycles in history as follows:[7]

- **The High (First Turning):** A period of great optimism after the country survived a Fourth Turning crisis like the Great Depression and World War II. Because it took collective action to survive these twin emergencies, public cooperation and faith in civic institutions and collective action are extremely high. Individualism is weak (e.g., post-World War II; from about 1946 to about 1964).

- **The Awakening (Second Turning):** The post-crisis generation, raised only in peace and prosperity, grows up taking freedom and prosperity for granted. With no knowledge or experience of the hardships and sacrifices of the Fourth Turning crisis years, they rebel against the restrictiveness of their parents' generation (e.g., the Consciousness [Hippie] Revolution; from about 1964 to about 1984).

- **The Unraveling (Third Turning):** A time of infighting and disagreement as those without any experience of the hardships and sacrifices of the Fourth Turning crisis take charge of our businesses, organizations, and institutions. Faith in collective action and civic institutions is at an all-time low. Individualism is "celebrated," even at the expense of the country's common good (e.g., the Culture Wars; from about 1984 to about 2005).

- **The Crisis (Fourth Turning):** The return of another Fourth Turning crisis era when again it feels like the survival of the country is at stake (e.g., the American Revolution 1775–1783, the Civil War 1861–1865, and the Great Depression and World War II 1929–1945).

Strauss and Howe said these four generational *turnings* are like seasons. Some are milder, some more severe; some shorter, some longer; but they always come in the same order. A Fourth Turning *Crisis* is always followed by a new *High*, a new *Awakening*, a new *Unraveling*, and again, another Fourth Turning *Crisis*.

In 1997, these generational historians predicted that if history is our guide, the next Fourth Turning generational crisis of survival in the United States would begin around 2005 (or a few years before or after).[8]

They said the prelude to a Fourth Turning crisis era starts with a catalyst—"a startling event (or sequence of events) that produce[s] a sudden shift in mood."[9] The September 11, 2001, Islamic terrorist attack on the World Trade Center in New York certainly qualifies as such a startling event.

Strauss and Howe also predicted that the baby-boomer generation, born in a period of wealth and economic prosperity (1946 to 1964), was "sure to drive the system over the edge, without the experience of the past decline to provide financial and economic sobriety."[10] After the financial crisis of 2008, and our national debt higher than $18 trillion (and still growing fast), this prediction also appears to be coming true.

If these generational historians are correct, we are already in the early stages of America's next Fourth Turning crisis of survival.

A Slow, Devastating Leak

America's last Fourth Turning generational crisis of survival was the Great Depression and World War II. While most know the Great Depression began with the 1929 stock market crash, few realize that prosperity in the United States did not disappear overnight. The onset of the Great Depression was "...more like the slow leak in an automobile tire than a sudden blowout." [11]

In the early years after the 1929 stock market crash, the economic downturn was still called "the depression" with a lowercase "d." The constant refrain in these early years was *"prosperity is just around the corner."* Although stock prices dropped 40% in 1929, they recovered enough in the spring of 1930 for President Hoover to declare "the depression" over.

In the summer of 1930, stock prices resumed their downward slide. By July 1932, stock prices had dropped about 89%.[12] Thousands of banks failed. Because there was no federal bank deposit insurance, the savings of millions of Americans were wiped out. Only after the full scale of the country's economic trauma became clearly visible, did "the depression" with a lowercase "d" become "the Great Depression" with capital letters.

America's national unemployment rate reached 25% and stayed high for most of the decade. Farmers lost their farms when farm prices fell. Soup kitchens had to be set up to feed hungry people. Homeless people lived in cardboard boxes on the outskirts of many American cities. When cities ran out of cash, they paid their workers with coupons redeemable at certain stores.[13]

A page of history is worth a pound of logic.

– Oliver Wendell Holmes, Jr. (1841–1935)
U.S. Supreme Court justice, 1902–1932

The Greatest Generation

The United States survived its last Fourth Turning crisis (the Great Depression and World War II) because of the selfless and heroic sacrifices of Americans called the "Greatest Generation."[14] In a time of extraordinary crisis, this generation of Americans acted for the greater good of the country, not their own selfish gain or advantage. They endured 16 years of extreme hardship and deprivation.

Depression and war Americans emerged from this terrible time of crisis valuing "personal responsibility, duty, honor ...faith," country, loyalty, honesty, hard work, and discipline at a visceral level few Americans today can appreciate.[15]

Members of America's "Greatest Generation" recognized the difference between right and wrong with a clear-sightedness foreign to succeeding generations of Americans.

Bonds of community and mutual cooperation forged under the extreme duress of 1930s and 1940s hardships remained with depression and war Americans for the rest of their lives. These Americans, most of whom are already gone, would be appalled to see today's prevalent loophole mentality in America. They would be deeply saddened to see so many Americans looking for ways to skirt doing what's right and seriously harming their fellow citizens. Unfortunately, members of the "Greatest Generation" have not been running our companies, our organizations, our institutions, and our governments for a long time—and it shows.

Because of the very real and painful experiences of the Great Depression and World War II, this "Greatest Generation" of Americans never took our peace, prosperity, or freedom for granted. They saw first-hand how quickly circumstances changed and how wrong "smart" people were at accurately predicting future events.

Two examples stand out:

- In 1929, Irving Fisher, a nationally recognized economist from Yale, boldly stated that stock prices in the United States had reached "a permanently high plateau."[16] Within months, the American stock market crashed, leading to the onset of the Great Depression.

- British Prime Minister Neville Chamberlain signed a peace treaty in 1938 with Germany's dictator Adolf Hitler announcing, "I believe it is peace for our time... peace with honour."[17] The next year, Hitler invaded Poland, marking the beginning of World War II.

Could it happen again? Of course it can. Few members of America's "Greatest Generation" are alive today to warn us that history has a way of repeating itself. Sadly, generational wisdom is lost when one generation dies and another one takes its place.

Complacency Reigns

Now, more than two generations of Americans later, these life-altering threats to our peace, prosperity, and freedom have faded into the mists of history. Most Americans have lived in a prosperous, peaceful, free nation for so long, they have become complacent. They no longer seem to understand that behaving ethically is an *absolute necessity* for our continued peace, prosperity, stability, and security. Many foolishly believe our gifts of freedom are guaranteed. They are wrong.

Too many Americans are ignoring the rampant unethical conduct they see all around them. They rationalize "it's always been like this" and that the constant barrage of improprieties we are seeing in the United States today are nothing new. Besides, they believe the United States can never fail; we are too strong, too powerful, and have been too stable and successful, for that to ever happen.

While optimism and confidence are positive traits, blind optimism and hubris are not, especially in today's highly volatile, unstable, and unpredictable world.

Few Americans today appear to be paying attention to history's warnings that complacency and hubris are not only dangerous, they can sometimes be fatal.

> *Those who do not learn from history are doomed to repeat it.*
>
> **– George Santayana (1863–1952)**
> American philosopher

The Siren Song of Get Rich Quick

In ancient Greek mythology, the Sirens were half-human, half-bird creatures that lived on a remote island. They sang such hauntingly beautiful songs that sailors on passing ships became entranced and steered their ships closer to the island to hear them. Eventually, their ships crashed on the jagged coral reefs surrounding the island, killing all on board.

The Siren song of *get rich quick with little or no effort* has lured human beings to their financial destruction many times throughout history. These financial *get rich quick manias* have followed a similar pattern, whether they involved tulips (Holland in the 1630s), company stock (South Sea Company in England in the 1720s), or Internet stocks (United States in the 1990s).[18]

When the Siren song of "easy riches" is playing loudly, human beings are lulled into believing that skyrocketing asset prices will go up forever. *Hubris and complacency blind those in a financial bubble from seeing the reckless risks they are taking until it is too late.*

Eerie Similarities from the Past

For most baby-boomers and later American generations, the 1920s was viewed as an aberrant time in American history that could never happen again. After all, in the 1930s, federal statutes were passed to prevent a recurrence of the reckless behaviors that had created the 1920s financial bubbles.

For example, the Banking Act of 1933 (Glass-Steagall Act) prevented American banks from loaning huge sums of money for risky speculative investments as they had done in the 1920s. The activities of commercial depository banks (with some federal insured deposit guarantees) were separated from the much riskier activities of investment banks (with investor funds that were not federally insured). Financial institutions (e.g., commercial banks, investment banks, brokerage firms, and insurance companies) were prevented from combining their operations to create gargantuan "too big to fail" institutions.

But in 1999 and 2000, "smart" people from giant financial institutions, citing global competitive pressures, successfully lobbied "smart" people in the federal government to make changes to our federal laws that virtually guaranteed a repeat of the 1920s financial mania. *Hubris was once again afoot in the United States.*

In 1999, the Glass-Steagall Act was repealed. In addition, in 2000, the Commodities Futures Modernization Act was passed, limiting the federal government's ability to regulate credit derivatives—new risky financial products that could be used to extend massive amounts of credit. *The stage was now set for a repeat of the 1920s "get rich quick" financial mania.*

The Roaring Twenties

The 1920s was a decade of extreme optimism. "Smart" people believed the American economy had entered "a permanent plateau of prosperity." After the devastating losses of World War I, "smart" people also believed world peace would be permanent too. However, the 1920s decade was soon followed by one of the worst economic collapses in U.S. history and a cataclysmic world war on a scale never before seen in world history.

The booming economy of the 1920s was fueled by *extremely lax lending standards,* allowing individuals and businesses to *borrow* enormous sums of money. A credit and debt binge created four speculative bubbles: *a consumer debt boom, a real estate boom, a stock boom,* and *a mergers and acquisitions boom.*

When all four bubbles burst, there was a massive destruction of wealth during the Great Depression. Tens of millions of Americans lost their homes, their farms, their businesses, their jobs, their investments, and their life savings.

In the 1930s, Americans painfully rediscovered a simple economic truth that never changes. Using lots of *borrowed money* (*leverage*) for investments, not savings, magnifies profits when prices are rising. But when prices fall—and they always do after a financial mania—using lots of borrowed money magnifies losses too.

Borrowing too much money for speculative investments creates only "phantom" wealth that suddenly disappears when the multiple bubbles in a financial mania burst.

"The Roaring 2000s"[19]

In the first decade of the 21st century, millions of Americans again fell under the siren song of "get rich quick." Instead of making money by saving and investing over the long term, many Americans again believed that they could "get rich quick" by borrowing extreme amounts of money to speculate in risky investments.

There was a massive explosion of credit fueled by many new risky ways to borrow lots of money. Lending standards were extremely lax.

An over-extension of risky credit by "smart" people created four speculative financial bubbles: *a consumer debt boom, a real estate boom, a stock boom,* and a *mergers and acquisitions boom.* Sound familiar? Only this time around, we added a dangerous new twist—a national debt bubble of more than $18 trillion that is still growing fast.

In Both Decades

Individuals and businesses succumbed to the siren song of instant riches with little or no effort. In both the 1920s and the 2000s, there was

1. too much debt and leverage,
2. wide disparities in income and wealth,
3. rampant cheating, and
4. complacency about risk.

	1920s	2000s
1. Too much debt and leverage: *Consumer debt boom*	Installment debt	Home equity loans Credit cards Payday loans Student loans
Real estate boom	Interest-only loans	Mortgage-backed bonds Subprime loans Liar loans N.I.N.J.A. loans Adjustable loans with low teaser rates
Stock market boom	Buying stock on margin	Hedge funds Private equity funds
Mergers and acquisitions boom	Investment trusts	Private equity funds Hedge funds
2. Wide disparities in income and wealth	A small percentage of Americans became fabulously rich, while the incomes of most Americans stagnated	A small percentage of Americans became fabulously rich, while the incomes of most Americans stagnated
3. Rampant cheating	Conflicts of interest, self-dealing, fraud, etc.	Conflicts of interest, self-dealing, fraud, etc.
4. Complacency about risk	Excessive leverage (borrowed money) and risk-taking	Excessive leverage (borrowed money) and risk-taking

1. Too Much Debt and Leverage

Consumer Debt Boom

1920s: Mass production and technological advances produced a deluge of new products in the United States—cars, radios, refrigerators, washing machines, and many others. There was only one problem. Most Americans didn't have enough income to buy them. The solution was to create *installment debt contracts*. With only a small cash payment down, Americans could buy these new consumer products, agreeing to pay the balance over time with interest.

A "buy now, pay later" culture of instant gratification soon replaced traditional American habits of thriftiness and saving money. In this decade, "[o]ver 85% of the furniture, 80% of phonographs, 75% of washing machines, and the greater part of household goods sold in the United States were bought on credit."[20] By the end of the decade, Americans were heavily in debt from purchasing so many new products.

2000s: Americans again did not have enough income to buy all the goods and services available. To take care of this problem, risky new ways to finance purchases were used (e.g., numerous credit cards, payday loans, home equity loans, and lines of credit). Lending standards were extremely lax. Traditional American notions of thrift and frugality were soon replaced by an attitude of instant gratification.

With such huge amounts of borrowed money available, millions of Americans went on a spending spree. They bought expensive "fairy-tale" weddings, luxury vacations, and gigantic homes they couldn't really afford. They also borrowed heavily to pay for fast-rising college tuition and sky-high uninsured medical costs.

Many Americans maxed out multiple *credit cards*. Military personnel and low-income households used *payday loans* with yearly interest rates of 400% (or more) if not immediately repaid. By 2006, total consumer debt in the United States reached a record level of $2.17 trillion.[21] This high level of individual debt is particularly worrisome since 70% of the American economy's Gross Domestic Product (GDP) is consumer spending.

Millions of Americans borrowed huge amounts of money through loans on their homes. In 2005 alone, Americans borrowed almost $600 billion through *home equity loans* and *lines of credit* with high fees and high interest charges.[22] A *Wall Street Journal* article described a typical example, summarized below:

> A 51-year-old Southern California homeowner bought her home in 1985 for $105,000, with a fixed mortgage of less than $600 a month for thirty years. Twenty-two years later, she owed $625,000 and would be paying her new mortgage long past her retirement date. She had only been able to pay her much more expensive adjustable monthly mortgage by constantly re-refinancing her house, which she could do so long as home prices continued to go up. But when home prices fell, she quickly fell into default and likely will lose her home.[23]

Real Estate Boom

1920s: Americans did not have enough income to buy land, so *interest-only* loans were invented. With only a small cash down payment, buyers could buy land, agreeing to pay high interest rates until the loan was repaid. Extremely lax lending standards sparked a speculative land boom in many parts of the country.[24]

So long as land prices kept going up, buyers could immediately "flip" (resell) the land at a profit and re-pay their expensive loans. When the speculative land bubble burst in 1926, land prices fell, and land buyers quickly defaulted on their loans.

2000s: Extremely lax credit standards fueled another real estate bubble. Home prices in many parts of the United States rose higher and faster than ever before. New outlandish risky mortgages were used: "liar loans" (credit information not documented and verified), N.I.N.J.A. loans (loans given to people with no income, no job, and no assets), and "piggyback" loans (loans for 100% or more of the purchase price).

Mortgages were routinely given to borrowers with bad credit histories (subprime loans). "Flip That House" became a popular TV show, indicating speculative excesses in buying real estate were back in style. In 2003, Americans owed $6.8 trillion for mortgage loans against their homes.[25] By 2007, they owed $10.6 trillion.[26] *For the first time in history, home prices around the world rose at the same time.*

Stock Market Boom

1920s: In 1927, stocks could be bought using *margin loans* at brokerage companies. With only 5% cash down, 95% of the stock price could be borrowed from banks through brokerage firms.[27] This set off a speculative stock boom. Stock prices zoomed upward in 1928 and 1929. Stock market fever gripped the nation as never before.

So long as stock prices continued going up, those buying stock using these highly leveraged, expensive margin loans could immediately "flip" (re-sell) their stock at a profit and repay their expensive loans. But when the stock market crashed in 1929, investors with margin loans quickly defaulted.

2000s: After the repeal of the Glass-Steagall Act in 1999, banks were again free to loan huge amounts of money to investors to speculate in stocks and other securities. This time around, extreme borrowing was often done through *hedge funds* and *private equity funds* (formerly called leveraged-buyouts in the 1980s).

Hedge funds were private pools of investment money available only to "sophisticated" investors (that is, investors presumed to have the requisite knowledge and experience to understand what they were investing in). Unlike mutual funds, hedge funds had little regulatory oversight. They could invest in virtually anything.

Wealthy individuals and institutional investors (e.g., pension funds, insurance companies, endowments, municipalities) snapped up these risky new funds that were promising much higher returns. Many of these institutional investors were still trying to recover from huge losses incurred in the 2000–2002 stock meltdown. According to the FBI, hedge funds quadrupled between 1996 and 2006, from about 2,100 to about 8,800, becoming 20–50% of the daily trading volume on the New York Stock Exchange.[28]

Although hedge funds promised higher returns, they were much riskier than mutual funds. Hedge funds used massive amounts of borrowed money to make their investments, commonly 25% cash and 75% borrowed money. Hedge fund managers had huge incentives to do this because the more they borrowed, the higher their fees.

Hedge fund managers became billionaires. In 2007, the top hedge fund manager was paid $3.7 billion.[29] In 2009, even after the Financial Crisis of 2008, the highest-paid hedge fund manager made $4 billion.[30] In 2011, the highest-paid fund manager was paid $3 billion even though "[i]t was a terrible year on the whole for hedge funds."[31]

In its December 2012 issue, *The Economist* noted that "[o]ver the past ten years, hedge-fund managers have underperformed not just the stock market, but inflation as well."[32] Further, it said that because of their fees of 2% and 20% of profits, "[i]t is...easy to think of people who have become billionaires by managing hedge funds; it is far harder to think of any of their clients who have got[ten] as rich."[33]

Brooksley Born, an experienced securities attorney in charge of the federal agency trying to regulate credit derivatives (the Commodity Futures Trading Commission), had been sounding the alarm on credit derivatives long before 1998.[34] That's the year when failed risky investments in just *one* hedge fund, *Long-Term Capital Markets* (LTCM), run by "smart" people (Nobel prize winners), threatened to disrupt the entire financial system.

Nevertheless, it was *after* both Born's repeated warnings and the near-catastrophe of the LTCM hedge fund that "smart" people still undid the 1930s federal statutory protections of the Glass-Steagall Act in 1999, and passed new legislation in 2000 to prevent the federal government from regulating credit derivatives. *Why?*

Mergers and Acquisitions Boom

1920s: Wall Street investment banks invented *investment trusts*—private pools of money that used excessive amounts of borrowed money (leverage) to fund mergers and acquisitions deals. Since stock prices rose for almost the entire 1920s decade, increased stock value, not cash, was used to fund successive investment trusts.

Securities sold to the public through these investment trusts grew extremely fast from 1927 to 1929. However, businesses, investors, and banks ignored the enormous risks they were taking by using such huge amounts of borrowed money, *not savings*, to fund their mergers and acquisitions deals.

By 1929, investment trusts, using *excessive amounts of borrowed money*, had become extraordinarily complex holding companies. One of the largest ones, United Founders Company, was a complex web of 13 interlocking companies by the time it declared bankruptcy in 1929.[35] Its stock value, in 1929 estimated at about $700 million, rested only on $500 in cash from an investment made in the early 1920s.[36]

2000s: After the repeal of the Glass-Steagall Act in 1999, private equity firms began buying gigantic multi-billion dollar multinational public companies. A worldwide boom in mergers and acquisitions began around 2003.

Private equity funds used extreme amounts of borrowed money to fund buyouts (like hedge funds and 1980s leveraged buy-outs).[37] They borrowed heavily from banks and other large institutional investors like pension funds, insurance companies, and hedge funds.

Like hedge fund managers, private equity managers had huge financial incentives to use extreme amounts of borrowed money. The more they borrowed, the higher their fees. Also, private equity managers had special tax breaks. Although they paid ordinary income tax of 35% on their management fee of 1–2%, their 20% fee for future fund profit was taxed at the much lower 15% capital gains tax rate. Top private equity deal-makers became billionaires too.[38]

Many executives at targeted companies had huge financial incentives to sell their companies. They stood to make millions of dollars under *change-of-control clauses in their employment contracts* if their companies were sold.[39]

The New York Times reported that between 2005 and 2007, there were 1,287 leveraged buyout (that is, private equity) deals with a total value of $787 billion.[40] These deals used extremely lax credit terms, which became known as *"covenant-lite"* terms.

This buyout spending binge culminated in the largest buyout in U.S. history at the time—a $45 billion deal to take over the Texas utility operator TXU Corp. (later renamed Energy Future Holdings). Loaded down with debt, seven years later (in 2014), this company declared bankruptcy.

2. Wide Disparities in Income

1920s: Extremely easy access to credit drove real estate and stock prices higher. But rising asset prices during this decade masked a troubling reality— only a small percentage of Americans were becoming fabulously wealthy, while the incomes of most Americans stagnated. "In 1929, the top 1 percent of the people owned 44.2 percent of household wealth; at the other end of the scale, 87 percent of the people owned only about 8 percent of the wealth."[41]

2000s: From 1947 to 1968, during the post-war economic boom, family income inequality in the United States declined.[42] During this time, the wages of ordinary working Americans rose much faster than the incomes of those at the top of the income scale. However, in the 1970s and especially in the 1980s, this trend began to reverse. The incomes of a small percentage of highly-paid Americans began to rise much faster than the incomes of the rest of America's working population, which stagnated.[43]

By 2005, income disparities in America were again as wide as they had been in 1928, right before the Great Depression.[44] Those at the top of the pay ladder were paid about 440 times more than the average person in the bottom half earned.[45]

In Both Decades: The gap between a small percentage of very rich Americans and everyone else grew dramatically wider in both decades. This growing income disparity was hidden by the widespread and excessive use of credit.

Freewheeling lax credit encouraged people to speculate in risky investments, with the hopes of getting rich quick. When the financial bubbles in both decades burst, it caused painful hardships for millions of people.

3. Rampant Cheating

1920s: As often occurs in an era of perceived prosperity common in a financial mania, enforcement of ethics standards was lax. Conflicts of interest, self-dealing, corruption, and outright fraud were rampant, including *Ponzi* schemes and *"pump and dump"* stock schemes.

A *Ponzi scheme* involved an operator who promised investors extremely high investment returns. Instead of making the promised investments, the scam operator paid off earlier investors (to keep the scam going) and used the money to pay for his extravagant lifestyle. Investors rarely recovered much of their lost money.

"Pump and dump" stock schemes involved insiders who organized a group of investors to buy stock at the same time to artificially drive up the price of the stock. Once the desired price was reached, they all dumped their stock in concert on unsuspecting buyers, who suffered the losses when the stock price inevitably dropped.

CEOs at some top banks and companies were paid enormous salaries in the 1920s. In 1929, the CEO of Bethlehem Steel was given a $1.6 million bonus ($20 million in 2010 dollars).[46] That same year the President of National City Bank was paid more than $1 million in salary and bonus.[47]

2000s: In another era of perceived prosperity and lax enforcement, conflicts of interest, self-dealing, corruption, and outright fraud were again rampant.[48] The stock market crashed in 2000, and again in 2008, causing huge companies to suddenly go bankrupt, leading to numerous civil and criminal trials. Serious ethical violations were uncovered across a wide spectrum of our essential civic institutions and voluntary organizations (for further discussion see Chapter 7).

Multi-million dollar compensation packages for Wall Street and commercial bankers, fund managers, and CEOs of many of our giant companies became commonplace. Outsized pay, perks, and benefits were also given to top executives in other key institutions and associations, including nonprofits, unions, government, churches, and many others.[49]

4. Complacency about Risk

1920s: Warnings of excessive risk-taking were ignored. Edward Merrill, a founder of Merrill Lynch, advised his clients in March 1929 to get out of the stock market. Roger W. Babson issued a similar warning in September of 1929.[50]

Their warnings were drowned out by the "happy talk" of "smart" cheerleading Wall Street "experts," journalists, economists from prestigious universities, and senior government officials.[51] *Of course, these "smart" people turned out to be totally wrong.*

2000s: Credit derivatives, asset-backed bonds, and mortgage-backed bonds were so complicated, most investors had no idea how risky they were. They relied only on the Triple A ratings of these risky financial products, taking on faith that these math-driven financial products would "work" in a serious market downturn. *As demonstrated by the Financial Crisis of 2008, these "smart" people were wrong again.*

Will today's "smart" financial "experts" and their "smart" cheering squads of politicians, government officials, economists, and journalists, still reassuring us throughout 2014 that "prosperity is just around the corner," turn out to be just as wrong as the "smart" experts were in the 1920s and 1930s, and again in 2008?

What Went Wrong

To understand the huge risks now built in to our financial system, you need to know what changed when massive amounts of risky new financial products were misused in the 2000s.

In the "old" days, lending institutions carried loans on their books for the life of the loan. Because any loan losses would immediately reduce their profits, lenders carefully scrutinized their borrowers to be sure they could pay the money back.

Home loans generally required a 10% cash down payment; 20% down for more expensive homes. Qualifying for a mortgage loan was an onerous process. Borrowers were required to provide stacks of back-up documentation to verify their ability to re-pay their loans.

In the 2000s, as soon as loans were made, they were immediately re-sold, bundled, packaged, and repackaged into trusts to create *mortgage-backed bonds* and *collateralized debt obligations* that were immediately resold to investors. This led many financial institutions to believe that they wouldn't be financially liable if these loans went bad.

Suddenly, almost anyone could borrow huge amounts of money easily, without proof they could repay the loans. (Of course, let's not forget that this lax borrowing was also being pushed by U.S. federal politicians and officials through such entities as Fannie Mae and Freddie Mac).

Relying only on complicated math formulas, using faulty assumptions built into the models, Wall Street math wizards sliced and diced these bundled loans into multiple layers of risk. The riskiest loans, supposedly at the bottom of the risk pyramid, were given the lowest investment ratings by the ratings agencies. In theory, only the least risky bundled loans at the top of the risk pyramid would receive the coveted "Triple A" rating. This top rating was critical because large institutional investors like pension funds, municipalities, and insurance companies were only allowed to invest in Triple A-rated investments.

Such math-driven justifications for assigning risk may have sounded good in theory, but reality proved to be very different.[52] After the Financial Crisis of 2008, massive taxpayer-funded bailouts were required to prevent many "too big to fail" investment banks, commercial banks, brokerage firms, and insurance companies from failing because of the massive misuse of these exotic (possibly toxic?) financial products.

A Painful Ethics Lesson

Many financial institutions appear to have been lulled into believing that while making risky loans to unqualified buyers may have been unethical, it was perfectly "legal." After all, financial executives were paid huge bonuses to make such risky, unverified loans. There's only one problem with that line of reasoning. That's not how *ethics-based* American Rule of Law works.

Already, some of America's largest commercial banks and Wall Street investment banks have paid billions of dollars to settle government and private claims brought against them for making and reselling bad loans as Triple A-rated bonds. The ratings agencies are also being sued for the Triple A ratings they gave some of these bundled loan products. Bank of America's $4.5 billion investment in Countrywide Financial Corp., made in 2008, had already cost the company an estimated $40 billion in losses and costs by 2012.[53]

In 2011, federal regulators filed a lawsuit against 17 financial institutions for almost $200 billion worth of asset-backed bonds sold to Fannie Mae and Freddie Mac that went bad.[54] In December 2012, *The New York Times* reported that "[r]egulators, prosecutors, investors and insurers have filed dozens of new claims against Bank of America, JPMorgan Chase, Wells Fargo, Citigroup and others, related to more than $1 trillion worth of securities backed by residential mortgages."[55]

Investors, insurers, and municipalities sued financial institutions for damages caused by the mortgage mess, the financial crisis, and other major scandals. A 2013 headline in *The Wall Street Journal* said: "Banks Looking at $100 Billion [Legal] Tab."[56]

In the fall of 2013, JPMorgan agreed to settle claims for $13 billion. In 2014, Bank of America agreed to an almost $17 billion settlement, "the largest [settlement] ever reached between the U.S. and a single company."[57] This pushed up the amount Bank of America had spent on settlements stemming from the financial crisis to nearly $80 billion. By August of 2014, *Time* magazine reported that "the six largest banks by assets have paid more than $123.5 billion in settlements over faulty mortgages..."[58]

Ethical violations in the United States, if serious enough, can bankrupt any individual, business, organization, association, or government entity. Ethical violations can also send those acting unethically in our civic institutions and voluntary associations to prison.

Not knowing the simple and clear underlying ethical principles of ethics-based American Rule of Law—the 10 Commandments of Trust—can be both expensive and painful.

This Time It's Different?

Many Americans again seem to believe that "this time it's different," a common reaction in a financial mania. They take on faith that "smart" people in the United States will somehow be able to prevent another economic calamity on the scale of the Great Depression that occurred after the 1920s financial mania.

While it is true that in some ways "this time is different" from the 1920s and 1930s, some of those differences are not reassuring:

- **At War:** In the 1920s, we were at peace. We were not involved in extremely expensive, difficult, and long-running wars, like the ones in Iraq and Afghanistan, or the expensive military action in Libya.

- **The World's Largest Debtor Nation:** In the 1920s and 1930s, we were the world's largest creditor nation, not the world's largest debtor nation we are today. David Walker, a former Comptroller General of the U.S. Government Accountability Office (the Congressional "watchdog" agency that investigates how the federal government is spending tax dollars) has warned that we are headed for a *"fiscal train wreck."*[59]

Instead of four bubbles bursting as in the 1920s, the United States is *facing the possibility of an additional fifth bubble* bursting—the *federal government debt bubble involving trillions of dollars.*

- **An Unsustainable Path:** If something isn't changed soon, Medicare and Social Security payments (discussed in greater detail in Chapter 10) to 77 million baby-boomers and interest payments on our mammoth debt will be so high, they will consume most of our federal government's yearly budget. This would crowd out spending on other essential government services, including defense.

  "Like a ticking time bomb, our national debt is an explosion waiting to happen."[60] That was said in 2007, when our national debt was "only" around $9 trillion, not the more than $18 trillion it is today.

- **A Negative Savings Rate:** With free-flowing credit, Americans became extreme spenders, not savers. Even in 2005 and 2006, when unemployment was low, Americans saved very little.[61] Without savings, most Americans will be in financial trouble fast if they lose a job or someone in their family gets sick.

Of course, there are also differences today. We have Social Security retirement and disability programs, bank deposit insurance, unemployment insurance, and food stamp programs. However, with our national debt larger than $18 trillion and still growing rapidly, and many more trillions of dollars of unfunded retirement and medical benefit promises, is it really realistic for Americans to believe our government-sponsored social safety nets can shield us from economic pain for very long?

Could hubris be again at work in the United States, blinding us to the reality of our current fiscal situation? Are we over-estimating our governments' abilities and underestimating the dangers surrounding us all?

We've Been Warned

We have already received plenty of warnings about serious economic, financial, and other turbulence ahead. The Chief of the United Nations' International Monetary Fund (IMF) issued a warning on 1930s-style threats to the global economy.[62]

For many Americans, the first decade of the 21st century was a "lost" decade financially, just as it was for millions of Americans in the 1930s.[63] Eleven of the largest bankruptcies in American history occurred in the 2000s.[64]

Americans are poised to re-learn a painful economic lesson learned in the 1930s—that prosperity based on excessive borrowing isn't prosperity at all. Borrowed money is debt, and debt must be repaid with interest. During a financial mania, excessive borrowing for investment creates only "phantom" wealth that quickly disappears when the financial "bubbles" burst.

Of course, when stock and real estate markets in the United States zoomed back up in 2013 and continued to hover around new highs in 2014, voices of caution were again drowned out. However, logic, common sense, wisdom, and critical thinking warn us that the financial and ethical risks we are taking in the United States are extremely serious.

Wouldn't it be wiser for us to be prepared for the worst and pleasantly surprised, than to only be prepared for the best and unpleasantly surprised, when the price of being wrong could mean the loss of our freedom?

Chapter 6

Why Trust Matters
Freedom Depends on Trust

> *Man perfected by society is the best of all animals; he is the most terrible of all when he lives without law and without justice.*
>
> **– Aristotle (384 B.C.–322 B.C.)**
> Greek philosopher; Father of science
> and ethics in western civilization

Trust and Oxygen

Trust is like oxygen. Although we would die without oxygen, we take it for granted because there has always been enough oxygen in our air for us to breathe properly. Because oxygen is a colorless, odorless, invisible gas, we would only know oxygen is running low when we have difficulty breathing.

Most Americans take trust for granted, too. Since the end of World War II, there has always been enough trust in America for us to maintain a prosperous, stable, peaceful, secure, and free economy, government, and society.

Like oxygen, trust is invisible. *We would only know trust is running low in the country when signs of distress begin appearing in our economy, political system, and society—like now?*

Distrust and Carbon Monoxide

Distrust acts like carbon monoxide, a colorless, odorless, tasteless gas that displaces oxygen. In sufficient amounts, it is fatal. Similarly, when distrust seeps into a human community—whether a business, government, union, charity, nonprofit, or even a country—it displaces trust.

The only cure for distrust is trust, but once distrust takes hold, restoring trust is not easy to do. *Distrust, like carbon monoxide, spreads quickly. If trust is lost, distress soon follows. If trust cannot be restored quickly, force is just around the corner.*

A 2007 Gallup poll revealed that only 2 in 5 Americans trusted banks; five years later, only 1 in 5 Americans did.[1] In 2008, frightened depositors lined up in front of IndyMac Bank, a $32 billion California savings and loan. To restore trust quickly, the U.S. Federal Deposit Insurance Corporation (FDIC) raised the federal bank deposit guarantee from $100,000 to $250,000—first temporarily, then permanently.

In the Financial Crisis of 2008, giant Wall Street investment banks, commercial banks, and corporations suddenly disappeared. JPMorgan Chase bought Bear Stearns with $29 billion of American taxpayer money and also took over Washington Mutual Bank. Bank of America bought Merrill Lynch (later receiving a $45 billion taxpayer bailout).

Lehman Brothers, with more than $600 billion in assets, went bankrupt. Wells Fargo took over Wachovia Bank. The federal government took over IndyMac Bank. Huge retailers like Circuit City and Linens 'N Things declared bankruptcy. General Motors, after receiving billions of dollars in federal taxpayer bailout money, declared bankruptcy too.

Trust and Freedom

Rarely do free people stop to think about what the only alternative to freedom is—*force*. Nor do free people often consider that over thousands of years of human history, *freedom has been the exception, not the rule.* Put simply, our choice is stark. We can either:

- choose to *voluntarily follow and enforce* the ethical conduct required to maintain our essential *"bottom-up" self-organizing culture of trust* and be *free, or*

- choose to continue tolerating unethical conduct and be increasingly *ruled involuntarily under a "top-down" culture of force* that curtails or eliminates our freedoms, and eventually will lead to martial law and *dictatorship.*

Trust is the glue that holds our free economy, our free political system, and our free society together, especially in a time of extreme crisis. To keep our freedom, we must keep and maintain our culture of trust. *Without trust, freedom is impossible.*

Most Americans alive today find it difficult, if not impossible, to imagine a recurrence of national emergencies on the scale of the Great Depression or World War II. However, anything that has happened before in history can certainly happen again.

Just because the United States has succeeded as a free country for more than two hundred years does not mean it is guaranteed to remain a free country in the 21st century.

Without morality, ethics, and trust, the United States will fail as a free country— the only question is when.

A Difficult Juggling Act

Every country in the world is trying to juggle the same four "success balls" at the same time:

- **Economic Success:** The economy provides basic necessities for the people—food, shelter, water, etc., as well as schools, jobs, roads, and basic sanitation.

- **Social Harmony:** People live and work peacefully together.

- **Political Stability:** The government is predictable and stable.

- **Security:** The government can protect its people from internal and external security threats.

Juggling all four "success balls" at the same time is extremely difficult for any country to do over the long term. To succeed *over centuries*, not decades, requires a country to have the right economic, political, cultural, social, and legal framework. Countries that succeed over the long term have mastered the art of juggling all four "success balls" with the skill and timing of an expert juggler. They can spin each "success ball" *just enough*, at *just the right time*, to keep each ball from falling (failing) most of the time.

If one or more of these "success balls" falls (fails), and cannot be restored fast enough, it can destabilize *any* country (including the United States). These "success balls" are interdependent. If one "ball" falls (fails), it increases the likelihood that one or more of the other "success balls" will also fall (fail).

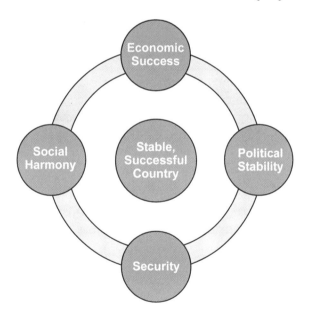

Angry, hungry people protest, and sometimes riot. If protests are large enough and last too long, they can eventually topple an existing government. If governments become unstable and unpredictable, investors and tourists will flee, causing further economic harm. As the economic situation worsens, and the plight of a country's citizens becomes more desperate, violence and anarchy are likely to follow.

To restore order, force will be used. If trust can be quickly re-established, the use of force will only be temporary. If trust fails, martial law, a military coup, or some other form of dictatorship will become permanent.

Trust *or* Force?

In the 20th century, countries experimented with *three basic ways* to organize and run their economies and governments:

- a *culture of trust* in both the economy and government based on Rule *of* Law and freedom (as contrasted with Rule *by* Law discussed further in Chapter 9),

- a *culture of force* in both the economy and government based on Rule of Force and dictatorship, or

- a *hybrid culture of "trust" and force* in the economy and government, attempting to mix elements of both.

	All Trust	All Force	Part "Trust" Part Force (Hybrid #1)	Part "Trust" Part Force (Hybrid #2)
Economy	Trust	Force	Force	"Trust"
Government	Trust	Force	"Trust"	Force

- **All-Trust:** *A culture of trust in both the government and economy.* An example is the United States (when it is operating as it should)—a capitalist free-market economy and government that is a democratic constitutional republic. Citizens freely elect their political representatives.

    Citizens' rights are protected from the arbitrariness of abusive government power by Rule *of* Law. The guiding principle of a country run on the "all trust" model (as it is supposed to work) is maximizing the "bottom-up" freedom of its citizens.

- **All-Force:** *A culture of force in both the government and economy.* The best examples are the former Soviet Union (Communist) before it disintegrated in 1991, and Communist China from the time of the revolution in 1949 until about the late 1970s.

    In an all-force model, both the economy and government are controlled and run "top-down" by force under a centrally controlled dictatorship. Leaders are not elected by the citizens and citizens are not protected from the arbitrariness of government power.

    The economy and government depend on *Rule of Force*, not Rule of Law and a culture of trust. Citizens have little or no freedom in either the economy or government. Private property doesn't exist. All economic resources belong to the State and are operated and distributed only through the central government.

- **Part "Trust," Part Force (Hybrid #1):** *A culture of "trust" in the government and a culture of force in the economy.* An example is India after it became independent from Britain in 1947, until it adopted economic reforms several decades later. The democratically elected socialist Indian government, operating under a socialist constitution, initially adopted a government-controlled, state-run economy like the one in the former Soviet Union.

- **Part Force, Part "Trust" (Hybrid #2):** *A culture of force in the government and a culture of "trust" in the economy.* An example is China today. The central Communist Chinese government is a dictatorship. Leaders are not elected by the people.

    But since the late 1970s, the central communist dictatorship has been attempting to create a "freer," western-styled, more "market-oriented" economy, and has attempted to create its own version of a culture of "trust" (with Chinese characteristics).

> *Force is the vital principle and immediate parent of despotism.*
>
> **– Thomas Jefferson (1743–1826)**
> American Founding Father,
> 3rd U.S. president, 1801–1809

In the 20th century, the American *all-trust* model succeeded. The Chinese and Russian (former Soviet Union) *all-force* models both failed. The Indian hybrid culture of "trust" in the government and force in the economy (Hybrid #1) also failed. It is too soon to tell whether the Communist Chinese hybrid culture of "trust" in the economy and force in the government (Hybrid #2) will succeed over the long term, especially in a time of extreme crisis or national emergency.

*Cultures of trust around the world are **not** the same.*

All-Trust Worked

With the massive intrusion of the U.S. federal government into the private business sector on a scale not seen since the Great Depression, it is sometimes hard to remember that the United States is supposed to be a *"bottom-up, all-trust" model.* Our free economy, free political system, and free society are supposed to be based on a "bottom-up" self-governing culture of trust, not a "top-down" culture of increasing government intrusion and force.

Trust in the Economy

The hallmarks of the American free-market economy (when it is operating as it should) are *private capital* and *private property rights.* In a capitalist free market economy, *private individuals* and *private entities, not* governments, are viewed as the ones best able to make the right decisions to create a prosperous, successful economy.

Free markets depend on trust. Investors must trust that the stock exchanges are transparent and fair, not rigged in favor of a few investors. They must trust that contract, property, and other rights will be fairly and predictably enforced by independent judges and courts. Investors must trust that their investments will not be confiscated by arbitrary government action.

Trust in the Government

The United States is a *democratic constitutional republic.* Americans elect *representatives* to act on their behalf. It is supposed to be a *"bottom-up,"* not a *"top-down,"* system of government: *"of* the people, *by* the people and *for* the people" based on a culture of trust.

Citizens must trust that elections are fair, transparent, and accurate. They must trust that elected politicians will fairly represent all citizens, not just special interests, or a privileged few. They must trust that their elected political representatives always put the interests of the citizens first, above their own self-interests. They must also trust that the legal system dispenses justice fairly and impartially to everyone, so that disputes between citizens can be resolved peacefully.

"Bottom-Up" Self-Organization Is the Key

Our "bottom-up" American free-market capitalist economy and our "bottom-up" free democratic constitutional republican government depend on *self-organization* through a multitude of well-established civic institutions and voluntary associations (businesses, governments, professions, unions, charities, nonprofits, educational and religious institutions, and associations, etc.).

This economic and governance model requires an independent judiciary, which follows predictable Rule *of* Law within the boundaries of our uniquely American constitutional framework.

This is the wisdom of ants.

Success—So Far

Over more than two centuries, our free economic, social, political, and legal systems have produced a remarkably successful and resilient country.

We survived a devastating Civil War in the 1860s in which 620,000 American soldiers died, *with the same political system and Rule of Law intact*—a remarkable achievement in world history. In the 20th century, we survived the twin calamities of the Great Depression and World War II to become the most successful economy and country in modern world history. *Thus far, the United States has been like a Timex watch that "takes a licking, but keeps on ticking."*

However, our continued survival and success as a free economy and a free nation in this new century will depend on our ability to keep and maintain our successful self-organizing culture of trust. *To be a free self-organizing nation, we must trust one another, and trust cannot be created without morality and ethics.*

> *The instrument by which it [government] must act are either the authority of the laws or force. If the first be destroyed, the last must be substituted; and where this becomes the ordinary instrument of government there is an end to liberty!*
>
> **– Alexander Hamilton (1755–1804)**
> American Founding Father,
> 1st U.S. secretary of the Treasury, 1789–1795

All-Force Failed

After the *communist revolutions* in *Russia* in 1917 and in *China* in 1949, both countries organized their economies and political systems using the all-force model. Both economies were "top-down" government-run and controlled by their central communist governments. Both political systems were ruthless "top-down" communist dictatorships. This "top-down" all-force model was the exact opposite of our free, "bottom-up," self-organizing American economy and government model based on trust.

Force in the Government

Communist dictators in China and the Soviet Union ruled with an iron fist. Their central communist governments controlled their populations with harsh and brutal force and terror, not trust. Free and fair elections were nonexistent. Dissent against the government was not tolerated. Dissidents were often killed or sent to prison labor camps.

Citizens had none of the freedoms Americans take for granted, such as freedom of the press, religion, and assembly. They had no right to a fair trial, due process, or protection from arbitrary government intrusions into their lives.

Force in the Economy

All facets of the economies in both countries were owned and operated by the central communist governments under multi-year economic plans they designed and implemented. These economies were based on a culture of force, not trust.

The communist belief was that *central governments, not private individuals or entities,* are best able to make the right decisions to create a prosperous, successful economy. There was no private property. All property and labor belonged to the State. Economic resources were distributed only through government-controlled entities. Tens of millions of people died of starvation in the man-made famines created by these "top-down," centrally-controlled, communist dictatorship-run economies in both countries.[2]

"Top-Down" Government Control Is the Key

Both communist dictatorships were based on the "all-force" model that used "top-down" rigid control. There were very few civic institutions, no voluntary associations, and certainly no independent courts following well-established Rule of Law.

Failure

The Soviet Union broke apart in the 1990s, and beginning in the late 1970s, the Communist Chinese dictatorship was forced to switch to a "freer," more "market-oriented" economy. Both all-force regimes were abysmal economic failures. *Both failed to raise the living standards of the majority of their people.*

Part Trust, Part Force (Hybrid #1) Failed

After becoming independent from British rule in 1947, *India* tried a mixture of force in the economy and "trust" in the government (Hybrid #1: Part "Trust," Part Force). As a former British colony, India inherited some democratic principles and British Rule of Law traditions.

The new Indian government, although chosen by free elections, adopted a *democratic socialist constitution* in 1950. India's version of a culture of "trust" was based on *Hindu* values, not Judeo-Christian values as in America. This produced a very different kind of culture of "trust." The Hindu religion is an ancient religion based on a rigorous caste system. A person's place in society is determined by birth, not individual ability or talent.

Instead of adopting a "bottom-up" western-styled free-market capitalist economy, the newly elected socialist Indian government opted to adopt the Soviet Union's "top-down" centrally controlled, government-run economy. The Indian central government planned and controlled the Indian economy under multi-year plans like the government-run economy of the former Soviet Union.

The Indian "top-down" centrally-planned-and-controlled economy failed miserably too. More than three decades after independence from colonial rule, India was still a desperately poor country.[3] *Like the communist all-force model, India's Hybrid #1 model also failed.*

> *The inherent vice of capitalism is the uneven division of blessings, while the inherent virtue of socialism is the equal division of misery.*
>
> *It is said that democracy is the worst form of government except all of the others that have been tried.*
>
> **– Winston Churchill (1874–1965)**
> British prime minister during WWII, 1940–1945

More Trust Is Tried

China, Russia, and India

China, Russia, and India painfully discovered that "top-down" government-controlled, state-run economies don't work—whether run by non-elected leaders in a communist dictatorship or by elected leaders in a socialist democracy. *"Top-down" government-controlled economies do not create prosperity for the majority of the population.*

The economic failure in the Soviet Union was so severe, the Soviet Union in 1991 disintegrated, becoming the much smaller Russian Federation. Eventually, China, Russia, and India instituted reforms in their economies aiming to make them "freer" and more market-oriented. All three countries experimented with ways to create their own versions of a culture of "trust" in their economies. These "freer" economies, dependent on more foreign investor capital, required more trust, less force.

Global capital now rockets across national boundaries in an instant. To attract foreign investment capital, countries must have social, political, economic, and legal environments that global investors trust. Investors inside and outside the country must trust their investments are safe. Countries must be seen not only as economically successful, but as peaceful, stable, and secure, as well.

Russians, once under the absolute control of Josef Stalin, one of the most cruel and oppressive dictators in history, now elect their prime minister (although recently mass protests erupted over possible election fraud[4]).

China adopted a new slogan: "to get rich is glorious," a huge departure from the attitude of prior Chinese Communist dictators.[5] Although China instituted economic reforms to create a "freer," more market-oriented economy, its central government has remained a dictatorship, still firmly under the control of the Chinese Communist Party (Hybrid #2: Part "Trust," Part Force).

Even so, because of instant global communications, Communist China has found it necessary to adopt some of the trappings of a "freer" society to avoid bad publicity that could frighten away foreign investors. In the era of Facebook, Twitter, and Google, the Chinese central government is no longer as free to act with the same raw force of its founding communist dictator, Mao Tse-tung. Too many mass protests and social dislocations could drive away the foreign investments, technology, and customers that China still needs.

China adopted a written constitution in 1982. It has passed statutes and regulations, attempting to create its own version of a culture of "trust" and Rule of Law "with Chinese characteristics" (although it has been suggested that China may be backtracking on its effort to establish effective Rule of Law[6]).

It was only after China, Russia, and India abandoned their "top-down" central government-controlled economies and adopted "freer," more market-oriented economies that living standards in all three countries improved. Only after instituting economic reforms did China become the world's manufacturing floor, India a central outsourcing hub for the world's services, and Russia a dominant player in the world's energy business.

The Rest of the World

After "top-down" government-controlled economies based on force failed, the only economies that seemed to "work" were ones with significantly more freedom. Freedom and "trust" gained momentum in the economies of many other countries, too. Euphoria was in the air.

After the fall of the Soviet Union in 1991, Eastern European countries like Hungary and Czechoslovakia were freed from their Russian Communist masters. The former Soviet Union had invaded both countries: Hungary in 1956 and Czechoslovakia in 1968. Once they became independent, these countries experimented with "freer," more market-oriented western economies and increased political freedom. The freedom "bug" even reached the tiny secluded Himalayan monarchy of Bhutan, which became a democracy in 2008.

For a while, it seemed that freedom was on the march around the world. However, since 2007, progress toward freedom in one-fifth of the world's countries has either slowed down or reversed.[7] *Countries are discovering that not only is freedom hard to get, it is even harder to keep over the long term, especially in a time of hardship and crisis.*

Freedom Is Like Ballet

Picture a ballerina leaping through the air, twirling on her toes, and bouncing to the floor with her legs split in opposite directions lying perfectly flat against the floor. A professional ballerina makes ballet dancing look effortless.

What the audience doesn't see are the years and years of grueling 8-hour-a-day practice sessions, painful blisters, and bloody toes. A prima ballerina endures many hardships and sacrifices to become, and remain, such an accomplished dancer. Ballet looks easy—it's not.

Like ballet, free countries that have created a culture of trust over a long period of time (measured in centuries, not decades) make freedom look easy too. It is easy to draft a constitution, pass statutes, hold elections, establish a stock market, and create courts and other civic institutions. What is hard to do is make freedom and trust actually work over the long term, through both good and bad times.

Freedom is especially difficult to maintain when an economy sours, there are not enough jobs to go around, and internal and external security threats threaten a country's stability. *Maintaining the essential culture of trust for a free economy and/or free society looks easy. It's not.*

Trust Is Hard

Almost every country in the world today has a written constitution, whether it is actually a free country or not. By 2007, 63% of the world's countries had democratically elected governments, up from about 40% twenty years earlier.[8] But the number of nations with written constitutions and elected governments is misleading.

As many countries have learned, once the euphoria and newness of being "free" wears off, keeping and maintaining a free country and/or a free economy is extremely difficult to do. Ethnic and religious frictions, corruption, unfair treatment, and wide income disparities between too few "haves" and too many "have-nots" can cause tensions to boil over in any society. If serious enough and left unaddressed for too long, these tensions can destabilize any country—including a long-standing free country like the United States.

Freedom is an intoxicating concept, but the reality of the responsibilities and difficulties that come with freedom are sometimes overwhelming. Many free countries have lapsed into dictatorships after a promising beginning. Adolf Hitler's rise to power in the 1930s is an example.

After crushing hyperinflation in the 1920s (it took a wheelbarrow of German currency to buy a loaf of bread), the democratically elected Weimar Republic established after World War I lost the public's trust. In the 1932 elections, desperate German voters, suffering greatly in the Great Depression, turned to strongman Adolf Hitler.

Because Hitler had received about 30% of the votes, elected German President Hindenburg appointed Hitler chancellor of Germany in 1933. Once in office, Hitler quickly hijacked Germany's democracy, replacing it with one of the most savage dictatorships in world history, the Nazi Third Reich. While pledging peace by treaty to lull western nations into complacency, Hitler prepared for all-out war. He started World War II in 1939 when Nazi Germany invaded Poland.

With the recent financial crises in the European Union, concerns are growing about whether some deeply indebted European countries will survive as democracies. In 2010, the head of the European Commission warned that democracies in Greece, Portugal, and Spain could be overthrown by a military coup or popular uprisings if members of the European Union did not approve a bailout plan worth hundreds of billions of dollars.[9] These three countries have a history of military coups and have only been democracies since the 1970s.

It is hard to keep and maintain the culture of trust required for freedom to succeed over the long term, especially in times of economic turmoil and hardship. *Freedom is never guaranteed and should never be taken for granted—in any country, including the United States.*

Freedom Sometimes Masks Force

Just because constitutions and elections have proliferated around the world does not mean nations that have both are actually free. Sadly, democratic processes are often used by elected leaders as a smokescreen to solidify their dictatorial power and control, not to increase the freedom and prosperity of the people.

Venezuela's democratically elected president, Hugo Chavez, was one of the latest examples of freedom masking force. Like most Latin American countries, Venezuela had a small, rich elite, while the majority of the population was poor. By promising to shower the poor with government benefits, Chavez won enough votes to change Venezuela's constitution, effectively giving himself lifetime tenure. Had he not died in office, he would have been president of Venezuela for 20 years if he had served out his latest term of office.

During his long tenure in office, Chavez imposed a government takeover of private property, in furtherance of his "socialism for the 21st century" vision. He stifled dissent and closed down newspapers that opposed him. He even neutered election results by getting the power to rule by decree from the outgoing legislators before newly elected opposition representatives took office. He used the excuse that he needed the additional powers to help flood victims.[10] These are the actions of a dictatorship, not a free country.

> *Democracy and socialism have nothing in common but one word, equality. But notice the difference: while democracy seeks equality in liberty, socialism seeks equality in restraint and servitude.*
>
> **– Alexis de Tocqueville (1805–1859)**
> Author of *Democracy in America* (1835, 1840)

Greed Is *Never* Good

Greed is listed as one of the seven deadly sins in the Bible. Major world religions refer to greed as "the mother of all sins."[11] Greed is never good.

In ancient Greek mythology, as a reward for showing kindness to a stranger, the gods gave King Midas the power to turn everything he touched into gold. Because the King loved money, at first he was delighted with his newfound "golden" power. Only when the food and drink he touched also instantly turned into gold, did the king realize his "golden power" was a curse, not a blessing. The final straw was when he turned his beloved daughter into gold when she hugged him. In the end, King Midas begged for his "gift" to be taken away, which the gods granted.

What Is *Not* Greed

The Merriam-Webster Dictionary defines greed as "a selfish and excessive desire for more of something (as money) than is needed." Not a very helpful definition.

Nineteenth century entrepreneurs like Andrew Carnegie, John D. Rockefeller, and J. P. Morgan amassed fabulous fortunes far beyond what they needed. So have modern-day high-tech superstars like Bill Gates at Microsoft and Steve Jobs at Apple. These hard-charging, sharp-elbowed entrepreneurs created huge, sensationally successful new American industries. Because of them, and many others like them, the American economy has been dynamic, innovative, and prosperous—at times, the envy of the world.

Greed should never be confused with the drive to excel in a competitive environment and reap the rewards of one's own ideas and hard work. This type of constructive behavior is essential in a competitive free-market capitalist system, like ours is supposed to be. If we want a prosperous and successful economy and country, this behavior must continue to be highly valued in the United States. The "American Dream" is that anyone with talent, who is willing to work hard to create a successful business or enterprise, can go from "rags to riches."

The essential philosophy of our American capitalist market economy (when it is operating as it should) is: *you create it, you own it, you get to keep it.* If you take away the incentives for people to excel by working hard, investing their own money, and taking risks in the private sector, it will doom any economy to failure. Human nature is predictable.

One business professor illustrated the point using student grades. He told his students that to promote equality, on future tests "A" students and "F" students would be given a grade of "C," regardless of how they performed on the tests. He astutely observed that it wouldn't take long before all students were performing at the "F" level. After all, why would anyone study when there was no reward for doing so, and students were given "C" grades regardless of how they performed? They wouldn't.

This is why communist and socialist "top-down" government-run economies eventually fail. Their economic systems violate a cardinal rule of human nature. People only consistently work hard *productively*, if they are allowed to personally reap the benefits from their labors.

Cuba is the latest in a long line of examples of failed communist central government-controlled-and-run economies. Cuba became a communist dictatorship in 1959. By the 2000s, almost the entire Cuban workforce depended on the government for a job.

Cuban government workers did too little, and what they did do, didn't help create a successful economy. Finally, the Cuban government's interference had harmed so much of the private sector, there were not enough workers in the private sector earning enough income to send the taxes needed to pay the government workers.

In 2010, the Cuban government announced it was laying off 500,000 government workers, with a goal of laying off a total of 1 million workers (about 20% of Cuba's workforce).[12] Displaced workers were told they would have to find new jobs by re-creating the private sector. This is the inevitable and predictable result of too much "top-down" central-government control and ownership in an economy.

Too much "top-down" central government interference will similarly damage the economy of a free country as well. The bottom line is that redistributing wealth from productive to unproductive people eventually destroys wealth in *any* economy, whether in a free country or a dictatorship. Human nature never changes.

What *Is* Greed

Greed is the *wrongful* acquisition of wealth. Under *ethics-based* American Rule of Law, there is a right way to make money and a wrong way. *Violations of one or more* of the *10 Commandments of Trust* that seriously damage our essential culture of trust is the *wrong way* to make money. If this type of wrong behavior is not stopped, eventually the United States will experience severe economic and social pain that could lead to greater political instability and increased security threats.

Greed is *wrongful* self-enrichment, often prevalent in a financial mania, when corruption, fraud, and conflicts of interest are rampant because of lax enforcement. Greed is not found only in businesses. It can also be found in our other self-governing institutions and associations, including governments, nonprofits, charities, and unions, etc.

Greed is a recipe for serious trouble in any society, but it is especially harmful in a free country like the United States that depends on self-organizing institutions and a culture of trust. Greed leads to envy and envy can quickly turn into distrust.[13] If distrust becomes widespread, it will corrode the bonds of trust necessary to maintain a peaceful, cooperative, free economy, government, and society, especially in a major crisis or national emergency. *Without trust, a free country will not be free for long.*

A Giving Culture

America's super-rich have a long history of donating part of their fortunes to help others, both here in the United States and around the world. Successful American capitalists of the late 19th and early 20th centuries gave huge sums of money to better the lives of others.

Steel baron Andrew Carnegie, the richest man in the world, donated money to build America's public libraries. Oil tycoon John D. Rockefeller established the Rockefeller Foundation "to promote the well-being of mankind throughout the world".[14] Auto manufacturing kingpin Henry Ford established the Ford Foundation in 1936 to "strengthen democratic values, reduce poverty and injustice and advance human achievement."[15]

> *Surplus wealth is a sacred trust which its possessor is bound to administer in his lifetime for the good of the community.*[16]
>
> **– Andrew Carnegie (1835–1919)**
> "Robber Baron" steel magnate

In modern times, multi-billionaires Bill Gates and Warren Buffet, among the top-five richest people in the world, pledged the vast bulk of their fortunes to charitable causes in the United States and around the world. They challenged other billionaires to do the same. As of April 2012, 81 billionaires have committed to giving at least half of their fortunes to charity.[17]

American celebrities have been generous with their fortunes too. Talk show host Oprah Winfrey topped the list of celebrity giving in 2007, "spending $50.2 million on education, health care, and advocacy for women and children worldwide."[18] As of June 23, 2012, the 20 largest U.S. corporate foundations have given about $1.8 billion to charitable causes.[19] When Category 5 hurricane Katrina devastated New Orleans in 2005, billionaires donated millions of dollars to aid hurricane victims.[20]

It is not only America's super-rich who donate their time and resources to help others in need. Ordinary Americans do too. For example, after super-storm Sandy devastated much of the coastlines of New Jersey and Long Island, New York, total strangers volunteered to help. One stranger agreed to pay for the entire cost of rebuilding a family's home.[21]

Like self-organizing ants, Americans have a long history of voluntarily, cooperatively, and automatically acting as a group, without central direction and control, to do whatever is necessary to help others who need help.

This is the wisdom of ants.

Dangerous Disparities in Wealth

Wide disparities in wealth and income between minority "haves" and majority "have-nots" have been the raw material of violent revolutions throughout history. A yawning gap between too few "haves" and too many "have-nots" led to the overthrow of rulers and governments in France (e.g., the French Revolution of 1789), Russia (e.g., the Russian Communist Revolution of 1917), and China (e.g., the Chinese Communist Revolution of 1949), to name just a few. Such wide disparities in wealth are potentially destabilizing in *any* country, even a free country like the United States.

During good economic times and extended periods of peace and stability, the damage greed has done to the bonds of trust in a free country is not readily apparent. However, resentments between the "haves" and the "have-nots" can quickly flare up in a major crisis or national emergency. This jeopardizes a free people's ability to peacefully and voluntarily cooperate as a group, to quickly make whatever changes and sacrifices are necessary "for the greater good" of the country.

To successfully survive a major crisis or national emergency intact, quick, effective, cooperative action is vital. This can only be done in a free country if there is an effective culture of trust.

> *The best political community is formed by citizens of the middle class.*
>
> **– Aristotle (384 B.C.–322 B.C.)**
> Greek philosopher, Father of science
> and ethics in western civilization

The problem of too few "haves" and too many "have-nots" is not just an issue in the United States. Income inequality has been rapidly rising in other countries as well. According to *Forbes' 28th Annual World's Billionaire Issue* released online on March 3, 2014, the United States was the country with the most billionaires at 492, China came in second with 152, and Russia third with 111. Regionally, Europe had 468 billionaires and Asia-Pacific had 444. The concentration of wealth in the world's top 20 billionaires increased $838.6 billion (net worth), up from $714.5 billion in 2013.

In 2014, a *Los Angeles Times* article said a new report suggests that the 85 richest people in the world may own as much as the bottom half of the world's population.[22] *Huge disparities like this, left unaddressed, will eventually threaten the economy, social cohesion, political stability, and security in any country.*

Huge disparities between the "haves" and "have-nots" exploded into mass protests and political instability in North Africa and the Middle East in early 2011. Long-term dictatorships in Tunisia (President Zine al-Abidine Ben Ali, 23 years) and Egypt (President Hosni Mubarak, 30 years) were toppled. The presidents of both countries (and their families) had amassed billions of dollars in personal wealth while in power, while most of their populations lived on very little (e.g., 40% of Egypt's population lived on $2 a day).

Any country with wide disparities between only a small percentage of "haves" and a much larger majority of "have-nots" is not stable. Failure to address the causes of such imbalances can eventually jeopardize the peace, stability, security, and prosperity of any nation—including the United States.

Distrust Leads to Distress

When distrust takes hold, distress soon follows. If the distress is serious enough, a country will no longer be able to juggle all four "success balls" in the air at the same time. Eventually, one or more of these "success balls" will become one or more "failure balls."

- **Economic failure** (e.g., recession, unemployment, hyperinflation, depression)
- **Social disharmony** (e.g., mass protests, riots, civil war, violence)
- **Political instability** (e.g., military coup, revolution, revolving-door elections)
- **Insecurity** (e.g., terrorism, rampant crime, war, cybercrime, piracy)

Like the four "success balls," a failure in one area significantly increases the likelihood of a failure in one or more of the other areas. For example, if a country's economy runs into trouble or a large segment of the population believes elections are rigged, mass protests, riots, or violence may result. This could destabilize the government, further weakening the economy and compromising the country's ability to protect itself from internal and external security threats.

Economic Pain

The Financial Crisis of 2008 threw millions of Americans out of work. The 4.6% unemployment rate in 2006 climbed to 9% in 2009. If under-employed and discouraged workers (those who stopped looking for work) were included, the real unemployment rate was likely much higher (and still is?).

Millions of Americans lost their homes in foreclosures. State governments laid off workers and raised taxes. In two years, 279 banks failed and the Federal Deposit Insurance Corporation placed more than 800 banks on its problem list. Washington Mutual Bank, the largest bank failure in U.S. history, had 2,200 branches and $188 billion in deposits.[23]

The gap between the "haves" and the "have-nots" in the United States (and around the world) has widened dramatically. This is not stable.

Social Disharmony

Social disharmony can take many forms—from peaceful mass protests to violent riots, civil war, or rampant crime. If people no longer trust that they can get their concerns resolved by peaceful means, the situation can turn ugly quickly. When civility breaks down, bloodshed soon follows.

In Iraq, members of different branches of Islam, the Sunnis and the Shiites, resorted to mass executions, torture, and beheadings against one another. In Rwanda, 800,000 people, mostly from the Tutsi tribe, were massacred in 100 days by members of the Hutu tribe. When the Yugoslavian dictatorship fell, a civil war between the Christian Serbs and Muslim Bosnians killed more than 100,000 people. Fighting in Darfur (Sudan) between the African Christians (and animists) and Arab Muslims killed about 450,000 people.

Social tensions can flare up in any country, especially when economic problems grow, jobs disappear, and people are hungry.

Signs of distress in the United States are growing—a lone gunman in a shoot-out at the Pentagon,[24] a man flying a small plane into the Austin offices of the IRS,[25] a college professor who shot and killed three colleagues when she wasn't granted tenure,[26] and numerous reports of individuals killing their families before committing suicide.[27]

The suicide rate among middle-aged Americans has risen.[28] Thieves are stealing fire hydrants, manhole covers off the streets, and copper wiring.[29] Flash mobs of young people are converging on stores and stealing items off the shelves.[30]

In 2012, there were several random mass shootings: 12 people shot and killed at a Colorado movie theater by a lone gunman; another gunman shot and killed at least six people at a Sikh Temple in Wisconsin; and a 20-year-old gunman in Connecticut shot and killed 26 people at an elementary school, including 20 young children.

Signs of social distress have been growing around the world: food riots in Somalia, Bangladesh, and Egypt; riots over austerity measures in France, England, Italy, Greece, Iceland, Latvia, Russia, and Spain.[31] In Greece, riots turned violent in 2011.

Food and job shortages led to violence in India. At one protest, police fired into a crowd, killing 30 people.[32] Although the Indian government has been trying to eliminate the long-standing Hindu tradition that orders society by caste from Brahmin to the untouchables, it has not always been successful. Violent clashes involving Hindus, Muslims, and Sikhs have periodically flared up in some parts of the country.

Mass protests and riots across China have become more prevalent. The authoritarian Communist Chinese central government's power and legitimacy depends on its ability to provide increased material wealth to the masses. If an economic slowdown in the West causes massive unemployment in China, it could trigger widespread civil unrest and possibly even political instability.[33]

While 90% of China's 1.3 billion people are ethnic Han, more than 100 million people in China are ethnic minorities. Deadly riots broke out in Tibet in 2008, killing at least 19 people. Riots in 2010 between the Han Chinese and ethnic Uighurs in the far western region of China left more than 200 people dead.

Social tensions in the United States and around the world are growing.

Political Instability

The United States has been politically stable for so long, the possibility of the U.S. government becoming unstable seems remote. Clashes over election results in the 2000 presidential election, the 2004 governor's election in Washington, and the 2008 U.S. Senate election in Minnesota led to lawsuits, not violence.

Thus far, American Rule of Law in the United States has been so deeply ingrained in the American psyche, as soon as our courts ruled on these disputed elections, candidates, voters, and citizens peacefully accepted the court's verdict. If our faith, acceptance, and trust in our free elections under *ethics-based* American Rule of Law should ever falter, future election disputes could lead to fatal violence, as it did recently in Kenya.

Kenya, like India, inherited some traditions of British Rule of Law after gaining independence from Britain after World War II. For many years, Kenya was believed to be one of the most law-abiding and politically stable countries in Africa. But *effective* Rule of Law requires trust, and trust is fragile. If leaders behave unethically, it doesn't take long for trust to turn into distrust, and for violence to replace a trip to the courthouse.

After gaining its independence, Kenya became a very poor country, but its politicians were some of the highest paid in the world.[34] A United Nations' investigation report said that Kenyan police death squads had killed 500 people. After a Kenyan whistleblower was killed, and powerful people not prosecuted, many Kenyans lost faith in Kenya's Rule of Law.

In 2007, violence erupted over fears that the national elections were rigged. One tribe locked members of another tribe in a church and set it on fire.[35] By the time the violence subsided, at least 1,000 people were killed and 260,000 people displaced.

When Rule of Law fails, the only institution strong enough to restore order is often the military. Thailand, a constitutional monarchy since 1932, has had at least 11 successful military coups (and 7 more attempted) since that time. In 1997, it adopted its 17th constitution since 1932.

In 2006, the Thai military took over the government when it became public that the prime minister's family would make huge profits from the sale of a publicly owned Thai communications company. Over the next four years, the ousted prime minister's rural, mostly "have-not" supporters engaged in mass protests that eventually turned violent; 121 people died and 800 were wounded. A state of emergency was declared.[36]

Later, the smaller, wealthier group of Thais from the cities took to the streets. When their protests disrupted elections, another state of emergency was declared in January 2014, along with another military coup.[37]

Political instability is rising around the world.

Insecurity

Countries face many types of insecurity. Invasion by another country is one worry, as when Iraq invaded Kuwait. A country's security can also be threatened by rampant crime, internal and external terrorist threats, cyber-attacks on essential computer networks, and attacks on vital shipping lanes like the ones used to transport oil around the world. In just the first half of 2010, there were 196 attacks on shipping around Africa, Asia, South America, India, and the Middle East.[38]

Militant Islamic terrorist attacks are not new, but what is new is that they are now targeting large numbers of civilian populations: 3,000 dead in the World Trade Center attack in 2001 in the United States; more than 200 killed by a bomb at a popular foreign tourist spot in Bali, Indonesia in 2002; almost 150 killed by terrorist bombs on Spanish trains in 2004 and on a London bus and train in 2005; 170 dead when Islamic terrorists attacked civilians using automatic weapons on the downtown streets of Mumbai, India, in 2008; and at least 68 people killed in an attack on a Kenyan shopping mall in 2013.

Powerful, violent Mexican drug cartels threaten Mexico's security, even after the Mexican government mobilized 45,000 military troops to fight these hyper-violent drug cartels. In recent years, more than 50,000 people have died in Mexico in drug-related violence.

Beheadings and kidnappings became routine in some parts of Mexico. In Acapulco, the beheaded bodies of more than 15 people were placed in the street near a popular shopping center. In 2012, another 49 mutilated bodies—head, hands, and feet missing—were dumped on the side of the road.[39]

Mexico's culture of corruption has hampered its ability to stamp out these violent cartels. Drug cartels routinely bribe corrupt politicians, judges, law enforcement officials, and the police.[40] Even more disturbing, these cartels are now using more sophisticated military weapons.

Drug-related violence has spilled over into American cities. Beheadings, believed to be the work of Mexican drug cartels, have occurred in the United States.[41] American drug enforcement officials fear that Mexican drug cartels, willing to pay staggering sums in bribes, are expanding their operations in Europe, Africa, and elsewhere.

Insecurity is rising around the world.

> *History does not long entrust the care of freedom to the weak or the timid.*
>
> **– Dwight D. Eisenhower (1890–1969)**
> Supreme Allied commander, WWII
> 34th U.S. president, 1953–1961

Will Trust Still Win?

To survive and succeed over the long term, countries must be economically successful *and* be able to maintain peaceful, stable, and secure societies and governments. This is a tall order at any time, but especially difficult to do in today's environment of constant, unpredictable, and speeded-up change and crisis.

According to *The Wall Street Journal* and Heritage Foundation's 2011 *Index of Freedom*, countries with the freest economies, not economies based on government control and force, have created a much higher standard of living for their citizens.[42]

Free countries are more stable and prosperous than countries based on force, like socialist and communist centrally planned economies and government dictatorships. Economies dominated by government interference and force, such as Zimbabwe and Venezuela, have fared significantly worse than countries with free governments like those in the United States, Australia, New Zealand, Hong Kong, and Singapore.

Of course, Hong Kong may not be ranked as free for long. In 2014, thousands in Hong Kong protested China's changes to Hong Kong's political system. Although retaining the right to vote directly for their leaders, Hong Kong voters were told they could only choose from a pool of candidates approved by China.

In 10 years of rule under President Hugo Chavez, Venezuela's experiment with "socialism for the 21st century" led to water shortages and blackouts in a country "with the largest conventional oil reserves outside the Middle East and one of the world's mightiest hydroelectric systems."[43]

Zimbabwe's dictator Robert Mugabe, through gross mismanagement, turned a once stable and prosperous country (formerly called Rhodesia) into a hyper-inflationary financial disaster. Like India and Kenya, Zimbabwe inherited some traditions of British Rule of Law.

After the Zimbabwe government confiscated land from white farmers and gave it to inexperienced black farmers, there were severe food shortages in a country once known as the breadbasket of southern Africa. In 2009, Zimbabwe issued a currency note of $100 trillion.[44] Its economy was on the verge of total collapse. *Think the wrong government policies can't destroy an economy and a country? Think again.*

China vs. United States

China

China believes its hybrid approach—a "freer" market economy, coupled with its communist dictatorship government (Hybrid #2: Part "Trust," Part Force)—is better than America's all-trust freedom model.

China is an ancient civilization that can trace its roots back 5,000 years. Except for a brief interlude in the 20th century, the Chinese government has always been a dictatorship. China's current communist government dictatorship only dates back to 1949. Getting effective justice in China's legal system is still extremely difficult.[45]

Even though in a communist country, where everyone is supposed to be equal, in 2012 fewer than 1% of Chinese households controlled 70% of the country's private financial wealth.[46] Chinese state-owned or related entities still own about half the wealth (outside of agriculture). China is one of the largest foreign buyers of America's federal national debt.

United States

America's current self-organizing civilization based on *ethics-based* Rule of Law dates back about 400 years (although the roots of our Rule of Law can be traced back about a thousand years earlier in England). The United States has been an independent nation under the same U.S. Constitution, with few amendments, since 1789. It has always been a free country with well-established and effective Rule of Law—at least so far.

Businesses are owned and run privately, not by the government (at least that's how it's supposed to work). With America's outrageously high national debt of more than $18 trillion, and our recent economic and financial malaise, America's freedom model is looking ragged.

The American free enterprise economy, free government, and free society created enormous wealth and prosperity for the majority of its citizens in the 20th century. Will this hold true in the 21st century?

Will trust still win in the 21st century?

- Freedom depends on trust.

- Trust depends on ethical conduct.

- Ethical conduct depends on morality.

- Morality depends on knowing right from wrong.

- Knowing right from wrong depends on knowing the *10 Commandments of Trust* under ethics-based American Rule of Law and our uniquely American brand of freedom.

Chapter 7

Trust Is Fragile

Unethical Conduct Destroys Trust

> *The toughest thing about the power of trust is that it's very difficult to build and very easy to destroy.*
>
> **– Thomas J. Watson (1874–1956)**
> Founder and former president of IBM

The Ethical Danger Zone

How much unethical conduct does it take to tip a culture of trust into a culture of distrust? No one knows for sure. What we do know is trust is fragile. American institutions have been strong and stable over centuries, and can therefore withstand *some* unethical conduct. *Even so, there is a limit.*

Americans are too complacent about the unethical conduct they see all around them today. Many have forgotten (or never learned) about the terrible consequences that inevitably flow from tolerating too much unethical conduct: economic misery, social unrest, political instability, and insecurity.

One thing is clear. *From the number, size, scale, scope, and breadth of the ethics scandals we have seen since the beginning of the 21st century, we are clearly operating in the ethical danger zone.*

A Tsunami of Scandals

We have seen *public* ethics scandals in the United States before. In the 1970s, President Nixon resigned and several high-ranking members of his staff and Cabinet went to prison for the Watergate scandal. In the 1980s, a rash of insider trading scandals sent many high-profile white-collar criminals to prison. In the 1990s, President Clinton was impeached in another presidential scandal, but remained in office, and there was a string of corporate accounting scandals at several giant American corporations.

However, since 2000, instead of the intermittent scandals we have seen since the end of World War II, we have experienced a much more dangerous and potentially destabilizing *tsunami of public ethics scandals.* A tsunami involves *multiple* waves of water zooming toward land at jet speeds of 600 miles per hour after a geological event like an earthquake.

It is not necessarily the height of each wave that makes a tsunami so destructive. It is the *volume* of water striking the shore that does the most damage, as wave after wave after wave hits the shore. The worst tsunami in recorded history occurred in 2004, after a gigantic 9.1 (on the Richter scale) underwater earthquake struck off the coast of Indonesia. By the time the waters of that tsunami receded, more than 200,000 people in at least eleven countries were dead.

An *ethics scandal tsunami* generally occurs at the end of a financial mania, when euphoria over rising prices and instant riches suddenly turns into panic and fear. *The larger and more numerous the speculative bubbles in a financial mania, the larger and more destructive the ethics scandal tsunami that follows.*

A Still-Unfolding Crisis

Since the beginning of the 21st century, as one wave of *public ethics* scandals receded, another one, often larger and more destructive, took its place. Even more unsettling, these multiple waves of ethical wrongdoing still show no sign yet of abating, more than a decade later. *The ethics mess we are in today is alarming.*

> *To educate a man in mind and not in morals is to educate a menace to society.*
>
> **– Theodore Roosevelt (1858–1919)**
> 26th U.S. president, 1901–1909

Abuses of trust are now splashed across the country and the world at Internet speed. As a result, today's ethics scandal tsunami is much more damaging to our culture of trust than the multiple scandals uncovered in the 1930s Great Depression.

As one senior FBI official noted: "Corruption, whether in the form of crooked officials [or] financial fraudsters...is tearing at the fabric of U.S. society and is the country's No. 1 criminal threat...."[1] *If we wish to remain a free people in the 21st century, "we, the people" must recognize the very real ethics danger we are in— now.*

The *public ethics* scandals described in this chapter are just *some* of the many waves of public ethics scandals reported in various media outlets in recent years. Some verdicts, settlements, and events described in this chapter may not yet be final.

Nonetheless, these continuous waves of ethics scandals, over more than a decade, highlight the very real likelihood that our essential culture of trust has been seriously weakened.

> *When the taste for physical gratifications among them has grown more rapidly than their education... the time will come when men are carried away and lose all self-restraint.... It is not necessary to do violence to such a people in order to strip them of the rights they enjoy; they themselves willingly loosen their hold... they neglect their chief business which is to remain their own masters.* [2]
>
> **– Alexis de Tocqueville (1805–1859)**
> Author, *Democracy in America,* Vol. 2 (1840)

Business Scandals

Ethics scandals in business not only damage the businesses involved; they damage the public's faith in free-market capitalism—the engine of America's extraordinary economic success and prosperity.

History has repeatedly shown that centrally controlled socialist and communist "top-down" economies based on force do not work for long. But a "bottom-up" free-market capitalist economy based on private property and private capital will not work for long either, *without morality, ethics, and trust.*

It Started with Enron

Enron Corp. was the darling of the business press throughout the 1990s. Only when it suddenly imploded into bankruptcy in 2001 did the public learn that Enron's success was built on rampant accounting fraud and self-dealing. The jobs, pensions, and investments of thousands of people were wiped out.

Enron's $2 billion accounting fraud scandal sent 15 Enron executives to prison. Former CEO Jeff Skilling received the longest sentence of 24 years, reduced on appeal to 14 years. With $65 billion in assets, Enron was the largest bankruptcy in American history, but it didn't hold that title for long.

WorldCom's bankruptcy, with assets of $103 billion, quickly followed. Four WorldCom executives pleaded guilty in an $11 billion accounting fraud scandal. Former CEO, Bernie Ebbers, was sentenced up to 25 years in prison.

Giant investment and commercial banks like JPMorgan Chase, Lehman Brothers, Citigroup Inc., Bank of America, and others, paid more than $13 billion to settle legal claims they had helped Enron and WorldCom conceal their precarious financial condition from investors and regulators.[3] In 2008, WorldCom's bankruptcy was dwarfed by the bankruptcy of Lehman Brothers, with assets of more than $600 billion.

Looting

Father and son executives (former CEO and former CFO) at Adelphia Communications Co., one of the largest cable companies in the United States, were convicted of misappropriating $2.3 billion of company assets. They were accused of using company money to buy company stock in their own names, build a $13 million golf course, and pay $52 million in personal cash advances.[4] Former CEO

John Rigas was sentenced to 15 years in prison. His son received a 20-year prison sentence.

The former CEO of Tyco International, Dennis Kozlowski, was convicted of misappropriating $600 million of the company's money (e.g., $30 million on a personal New York residence, $1 million for his wife's 40th birthday party held in Sardinia, off the coast of Italy, and many millions of dollars more for unauthorized pay and bonuses for himself and the company's CFO).[5] Both the former CEO and CFO were sentenced to 8 to 25 years in state prison. In 2007, Tyco shareholders received a settlement of nearly $3 billion.

Rampant Accounting Fraud

Rampant accounting fraud was uncovered in some high-technology companies. A former CEO of Peregrine Systems, Inc. was sentenced to 8 years in prison for accounting fraud.[6] Qwest Communications International paid a civil penalty of $250 million to settle SEC claims the company "fraudulently recognized over $3.8 billion in revenue and excluded $231 million in expenses...."[7]

A former CEO of Computer Associates International was sent to prison for 12 years and fined $8 million for a $2.2 billion accounting fraud scheme.[8] Ten former Homestore.com executives pleaded guilty or were convicted of accounting fraud; its former CEO received a 15-year prison sentence.[9] The company paid $70 million to settle accounting fraud claims.

Even well-established corporate giants were tarnished by widely publicized financial misdeeds. Cendant Corporation, the giant conglomerate that owned Ramada Hotels and Avis rental cars, paid shareholders $2.83 billion to settle accounting fraud claims. A former CEO and chairman of the board went to prison for more than 12 years.[10] Waste Management paid $457 million for accounting irregularities.[11] AOL/Time Warner paid a $510 million fine and $2.4 billion to settle lawsuits over improper accounting.[12]

Fifteen former HealthSouth employees (including all five of the company's former CFOs), who worked for one of the nation's largest providers of rehabilitative healthcare, pleaded guilty to criminal fraud. Its former CEO, acquitted on accounting fraud charges under the Sarbanes-Oxley Act of 2002, was later sent to prison for 7 years after being convicted for bribery.

Fannie Mae and Freddie Mac, the two largest financiers of home mortgages in the United States, became embroiled in massive accounting fraud scandals. In 2003, Freddie Mac paid a record civil fine of $125 million for an alleged $5 billion accounting fraud. The U.S. Office of Federal Housing Enterprise Oversight reported that the company's flawed accounting was the result of management misconduct.[13]

In 2007, Freddie Mac paid $50 million to settle charges by the U.S. Securities and Exchange Commission (SEC) that it fraudulently misstated its earnings over a four-year period.[14] In 2004, Fannie Mae paid a $400 million fine, one of the largest civil accounting fraud fines in U.S. history, for an estimated $11 billion accounting fraud scandal.[15] Taxpayers have paid more than $169 billion to bail out these entities.

Not Just a Few Rotten Apples

Ethics scandals have touched a wide array of American industries including energy, healthcare, insurance, and defense, to name just a few.

Two of the largest hospital chains in America, Hospital Corporation of America, Inc. and Tenet Healthcare, paid more than $3 billion to settle claims of ethical breaches that included allegations of false reports, kickbacks to doctors for referring Medicare patients, and unnecessary surgeries.[16]

The third largest drugstore chain, Rite Aid Corp., admitted to overstating profits by more than $1 billion over a three-year period.[17] Its former CEO was sentenced to eight years in prison.[18] Merck & Co., Inc., one of the largest pharmaceutical companies in the world, paid one of the largest healthcare fraud settlements in U.S. history—$670 million to settle Medicaid fraud claims.[19]

Giant insurance broker Marsh & McLennan paid $850 million to settle allegations it had taken kickbacks from insurance companies for referring business to them.[20] It also paid $400 million to settle claims it placed clients with insurance companies that paid the broker additional fees.[21] American International Group, one of the largest insurance companies in the world, paid $1.6 billion to settle similar kickback claims.[22]

Chevron Corp., America's second largest oil company, paid $30 million to settle government charges it paid illegal kickbacks to Saddam Hussein's regime in Iraq.[23] The former CEO of ImClone Systems, Inc., a biotech firm, was given a seven-year prison sentence for insider trading. He sold his company stock before the Federal Drug Administration's disapproval of one of the company's drugs became public.[24]

The second largest defense contractor in the United States, the Boeing Company, was involved in two major ethics scandals. Boeing was accused of hiring a former Lockheed Martin Corp. employee who brought with him thousands of pages of Lockheed documents that Boeing then used in competitive Pentagon bids.[25] The Pentagon revoked $1 billion of Boeing government contracts and gave them to Lockheed.

In another case, a former Boeing CFO and a former Air Force official received prison sentences. The former CFO offered a $250,000 a year job at Boeing to the Air Force official, which she accepted while still overseeing government contracts Boeing was bidding on. Boeing was fined $615 million, the largest penalty ever levied against a military contractor.[26]

Even an ethics stalwart like Johnson & Johnson (J&J) found itself in ethical hot water. J&J became famous for "doing the right thing" after cyanide-laced Tylenol capsules killed several people in 1982. The company immediately recalled 31 million bottles of Tylenol at a cost of $100 million.[27]

In the 2000s, J&J paid $751 million to settle taxpayer health care fraud claims and $70 million to settle foreign bribery charges.[28] It also paid expensive fines, settlements, and penalties over allegations it failed to disclose all the risks of its drug, Risperdal: a $327 million civil penalty in South Carolina, a $158 million settlement in Texas, and a $1.1 billion penalty in Arkansas.[29]

Backdating Stock Options

Stock options are given to many executives as part of their compensation. These options grant executives the right to buy company stock at a specified price on a specific date. However, some companies backdated their executives' stock options to an earlier date when the company's stock price was at its lowest level. By doing this, executives automatically got a boost in pay when they exercised their stock options.

The Securities and Exchange Commission (SEC) filed civil charges against 24 companies and 66 individuals for failing to pay the necessary taxes or failing to disclose this backdating practice to their shareholders. Backdating-related offenses have resulted in at least 15 criminal convictions.[30]

United Healthcare, one of the largest healthcare organizations in the United States, paid $895 million to settle backdating claims. As part of the settlement, a former CEO forfeited more than $400 million in compensation.[31]

Broadcom Corp., one of the world's largest semiconductor companies, agreed to pay $160 million to settle claims that by backdating stock options the company misstated its financial picture by $2 billion over a five-year period.[32] Comverse Technology Inc., a giant software-consulting firm, paid $225 million to settle similar backdating claims.[33]

Widespread Corporate Fraud

By 2008, the Department of Justice Corporate Fraud Task Force (formed in 2002) reported that there were nearly 1,300 convictions for corporate fraud.[34] *The American Lawyer,* with its own corporate fraud database that tracked 124 investigations, said that most of the 440 indicted defendants from a wide cross-section of businesses either pled guilty or were convicted after a trial.[35]

Just before the 10th anniversary of the 2001 Enron scandal, a *Wall Street Journal* article headline said it all: *"Ten Years Later, Enron Pales in Comparison."*[36]

Wall Street Scandals

Serious ethics scandals involving Wall Street investment banks harm the public's trust in American capital markets. While Wall Street investment bankers, hedge fund and private equity managers, and their firms became extremely wealthy, many individual investors, employees, retirees, pension funds, insurance companies, and state and local governments suffered painful losses.

Initial Public Offerings (IPOs)

The IPO process to sell stock to the public for the first time was established by the 1933 Securities Act, passed during the Great Depression to protect investors. IPOs were the financial rocket fuel used to fund the Internet stock boom in the second half of the 1990s. When that bubble burst in 2000–2002, investors lost trillions of dollars.

Wall Street firms had been improperly handing out IPO stock for "hot" new companies to top corporate executives, hoping they would steer their companies' future investment banking business to their Wall Street firms. Wall Street firms called this practice IPO "spinning." A judge called it a "sophisticated form of bribery."[37]

JPMorgan paid $65 million to settle IPO spinning claims.[38] Credit Suisse First Boston, a member of the Credit Suisse Group, paid a $100 million fine.[39] Goldman Sachs and Morgan Stanley paid $40 million each to settle such claims.[40]

Stock Analysts

Stock analysts are supposed to make their stock recommendations based on independent and unbiased research. Overly optimistic stock reports by Wall Street stock analysts contributed to the dramatic run-up in Internet stock prices in the late 1990s. Wall Street executives were accused of pressuring in-house stock analysts to give high ratings to stocks of companies that could send future banking business to them.

Ten Wall Street firms, including Goldman Sachs, Morgan Stanley, JPMorgan Chase & Co., Lehman Brothers, Merrill Lynch, Salomon Smith Barney, and others paid $1.4 billion to settle federal and state claims that their analysts' stock recommendations were tainted.[41]

Mutual Funds

Although mutual funds have been around since 1924, most of the phenomenal growth in mutual funds has occurred since 1980. By 2004, thousands of mutual funds controlled more than $8 trillion worth of investments.[42] For almost 80 years (1924 to 2002) the American mutual fund industry was free of major scandals.

But in 2003, New York's Attorney General Eliot Spitzer accused the mutual fund industry of serious unethical conduct. Allegations of impropriety included charging excessive fees, failing to tell investors they were being paid by others to recommend certain funds (e.g., in-house brokers were paid more to recommend "in-house" funds over other financial products), and allowing some customers to trade frequently at the expense of other long-term, buy-and-hold clients.[43]

Twelve of America's top 15 mutual funds were included in his investigation. They included such well-known names as Morgan Stanley, Bank of America, Prudential Securities, Inc., Putnam Investments, and Pacific Investment Management Co. (PIMCO).

There were 10 guilty pleas to criminal charges and payouts of more than $3 billion: "$1.5 billion in restitution to investors, $966 million in civil penalties and $945 million in anticipated reductions in mutual fund fees...."[44] This scandal did not enhance investors' trust in Wall Street.

Hedge Funds and Private Equity

To recoup earlier investment losses, institutional investors began investing in more lightly regulated and riskier investment vehicles like hedge funds and private equity investments. Institutional investors included financial institutions like pension funds, insurance companies, municipalities, university endowments, and foundations. Hedge funds grew to $1 trillion in assets. Private equity fund participation in mergers and acquisitions deals grew from 5% to 25%.[45]

When the Bayou Management hedge fund collapsed in 2005, investors lost about $400 million. That's when investors discovered that the fund had been overstating its assets and earnings almost from its inception in 1997. The hedge fund's co-founder was sentenced to 22 years in prison and ordered to forfeit $300 million.[46]

Refco Inc., a giant U.S. futures and commodities broker, was taken public by a private equity firm in a successful IPO that raised $600 million. Its former top officers were accused of fraudulently hiding $430 million in debt from auditors and investors for years. The former CEO was sent to prison for 16 years, the former president 10 years, and the ex-finance chief 20 years.[47]

Rampant Insider Trading

In general, insider trading occurs when an investor buys stock and other securities using material information not yet publicly available. Between 2009 and 2012, the Manhattan U.S. Attorney's office charged 72 people with insider trading crimes; 68 have either pleaded guilty or been convicted at trial.[48] According to a top U.S. securities regulator, insider trading is no longer a sporadic event based on opportunity as in the 1980s, but may have become "a central tenet of [the] business models" of hedge funds.[49]

A former Morgan Stanley financial analyst and her husband, a former hedge fund analyst at the ING Group, were sentenced to 18 months in prison for trading on inside, nonpublic information about companies about to be acquired.[50]

A former Goldman Sachs Group, Inc. employee pleaded guilty to an insider-trading scheme involving material nonpublic information about pending Merrill Lynch & Co. deals.[51] A "star" ex–Merrill Lynch analyst was sentenced to more than 3 years in prison for participating in that scheme.[52]

In 2009, Raj Rajaratnam, the billionaire hedge fund founder of the giant hedge fund Galleon Group, was sentenced to 11 years in prison and ordered to pay a $92 million fine for insider trading.[53]

Auction Rate Securities

State and local governments, colleges, universities, hospitals, and other types of nonprofits loaded up on auction rate securities because Wall Street firms assured them these investments were as safe and liquid as cash.[54] But in 2008, the auction rate securities market collapsed. Investors were stunned to discover they could not withdraw their funds. Wall Street investment firms had failed to disclose that the only ones buying these securities at the auctions were the Wall Street firms themselves, not independent third party buyers.

To settle with regulators, giant Wall Street investment firms and large commercial banks agreed to repurchase more than $60 billion of auction rate securities from their clients. This was the largest return of funds to investors in history.[55] A former Credit Suisse Group broker pleaded guilty to criminal charges and another one was convicted after a trial.[56]

MF Global

MF Global's CEO, Jon Corzine, was a former Goldman Sachs CEO, a former U.S. senator, and a former New Jersey governor. After making bad investments, MF Global, a major global commodities brokerage firm, declared bankruptcy in 2011. Investors were shocked to learn an estimated $1.7 billion of investor money that was supposed to have been held in separate, segregated individual accounts, was missing.[57] It wasn't until 2014 that investors finally learned that they would be made whole.

After so many Wall Street scandals, it is no surprise that "[a]nimosity toward Wall Street is at its highest level in at least 40 years."[58]

Ponzi Scandals

In recent years, thousands of investors have lost more than $16.5 billion in Ponzi schemes.[59] The FBI is investigating more Ponzi schemes than at any time in FBI history—about 500 open investigations involving hundreds of millions of dollars of losses.[60]

These schemes have inflicted widespread damage on a wide variety of people and institutions, including multimillionaires, blue-collar workers, and large institutions like Carnegie Mellon University and the Iowa Public Employees Retirement System.[61]

The largest Ponzi scheme in American history was perpetrated by a former chairman of the NASDAQ stock exchange, Bernie Madoff. Cash losses from that scheme are estimated to be about $21 billion.[62] Madoff was sentenced to 150 years in prison and ordered to pay $170 billion.

Another multibillion-dollar Ponzi scheme involved billionaire Allen Stanford. He sold Certificates of Deposit (CDs) in an Antigua bank through a company with offices in the United States, the Caribbean, and Latin America. Most of the billions of dollars raised by these CD sales is now missing. In March of 2012, Mr. Stanford was convicted of running a $7 billion Ponzi scheme and sentenced to 110 years in prison.[63]

Other examples of Ponzi schemes include a $428 million fraud targeting senior citizens and their retirement savings (the Ponzi scheme operator pleaded guilty to criminal charges);[64] a $20 million fraud perpetrated on fellow Mormons by a former Mormon bishop (the perpetrator was sentenced to 12½ years in prison);[65] and a $413 million Ponzi scheme that defrauded investors (the Ponzi operator received a 25-year prison sentence).[66]

Real Estate Scandals

Predatory Lending Practices

After one of the largest housing bubbles in U.S. history burst in the 2000s, there were allegations of predatory lending.

Household International, a giant consumer credit company for middle-income consumers, paid $484 million in restitution for failing to disclose excessive fees, prepayment penalties, and high interest rates to borrowers refinancing their homes.[67] This is believed to be "the largest consumer restitution award in U.S. history" in a state or federal consumer case.[68]

Ameriquest Capital Corp., the largest home lender to those with bad credit, was accused of lying about a borrower's income, inflating appraisals, and charging hidden fees. When sued, the company agreed to pay $295 million in restitution to borrowers.[69]

Countrywide Home Loans, the nation's largest mortgage company, was accused of putting borrowers into mortgages they could not afford and not warning them that their loan payments would escalate quickly. After Bank of America took over Countrywide, it paid the largest predatory lending settlement in U.S. history—$8.6 billion in home loan and foreclosure relief.[70]

Rampant Mortgage and Foreclosure Fraud

As early as 2004, before the worst of the housing bubble was in full-swing, the FBI warned Congress that mortgage fraud was rampant.[71] Fraudulent schemes have cost lenders and mortgage companies hundreds of millions of dollars. The U.S. Justice Department set up more than 40 mortgage fraud task forces nationwide, and the FBI had 1,600 ongoing investigations into alleged mortgage fraud.[72]

In 2011, eight northern California real estate agents pleaded guilty to criminal charges of rigging bids at public foreclosure auctions to short-change lenders and homeowners.[73]

Watchdog Scandals

"Watchdog" or "gatekeeper" professionals (e.g., accountants, attorneys, and judges) play a pivotal role in maintaining the integrity of our economy, capital markets, and Rule of Law. Accountants have a duty to protect the public's interest when performing audits on public companies. Attorneys and judges, as officers of the court, have a responsibility to uphold the law.

Accountants

One commentator suggested that some accountants have morphed from "watchdog to lapdog."[74] In 1989 only about 21.6% of the big accounting firms' revenue was from consulting fees; by 2002 it was more than 40% of their revenue.[75] As more of their income came from consulting rather than auditing fees, audit work suffered:

- Deloitte & Touche paid $210 million to settle a lawsuit alleging accounting fraud in connection with the failure of Adelphia Communications.[76]

- Arthur Andersen agreed to pay $217 million to settle claims by creditors and trustees of the Baptist Foundation of Arizona. The charity declared bankruptcy after Andersen had certified the soundness of its financial statements.[77]

- PricewaterhouseCoopers agreed to pay $225 million to settle securities and accounting fraud claims stemming from the Tyco International scandal, "one of the largest recoveries on record from an outside auditor."[78]

- Xerox shareholders and the SEC accused the giant accounting firm KPMG of using accounting tricks to help Xerox hide its real financial performance from the public. To settle shareholder claims, Xerox paid $670 million and KPMG paid $80 million. KPMG also paid $22.5 million to the SEC, the largest payment ever made to the SEC by an audit firm.[79]

Some large accounting firms were accused of helping wealthy Americans evade hundreds of millions of dollars in U.S. taxes. A former BDO Seidman partner was convicted and sentenced to 18 months in prison for tax shelter crimes.[80] BDO Seidman agreed to pay $50 million as part of a deferred prosecution agreement for helping "U.S. citizens evade about $1.3 billion in income taxes from 1997 to 2003."[81]

Four current or former Ernst & Young partners were convicted of designing and marketing fraudulent tax shelters for high net worth individuals with incomes of more than $10 or $20 million.[82] Two former employees of KPMG and a former top tax lawyer were also convicted of similar tax shelter crimes. KPMG paid $456 million to the federal government to settle charges related to flawed tax shelters.[83]

Attorneys

Jenkens & Gilchrist, a well-known Dallas law firm, closed its doors after three of its attorneys were indicted for creating fraudulent tax shelters. The firm paid a $76 million fine.[84] Two of their attorneys pleaded guilty.[85]

Four top partners at Milberg Weiss, one of the most successful plaintiffs' securities class-action law firms in the United States, were accused of perpetrating a fraud on the legal system itself. They were indicted for paying illegal kickbacks to individuals to act as lead plaintiffs in their class action lawsuits. These lawsuits cost corporations an estimated $45 billion, while the firm's attorneys reaped more than $1 billion in legal fees.[86]

After pleading guilty, all four were given prison sentences ranging from six months to 2½ years and criminal restitution fines from $250,000 to $10 million. The law firm agreed to pay $75 million.

In a separate case, a prominent plaintiff's attorney, who made tens of millions of dollars in legal fees from asbestos and tobacco litigation as the lead attorney, was accused of bribing a state judge. The bribe was allegedly paid in exchange for a favorable ruling on the attorney's $26.5 million in legal fees for Hurricane Katrina lawsuits. The lead attorney was sentenced to 5 years in prison.[87]

A former high-profile Georgia attorney was sentenced to 20 years in prison for running a $35 million Ponzi scheme.[88] A former Florida attorney was sentenced to 50 years in prison for a $1.2 billion Ponzi scheme.[89] A prominent New York attorney was sentenced to 20 years in prison for selling fictitious promissory notes to hedge funds and misappropriating client funds, causing more than $400 million in investor losses.[90]

Judges

Scandals involving judges go to the heart of our legal system. Judges who cannot be trusted seriously undermine the public's faith in the American legal system.

Two judges pleaded guilty to criminal charges for accepting more than $2.6 million in kickbacks to sentence teenagers in their courts to two privately run youth detention centers.[91] A sitting Jackson, Mississippi, Supreme Court judge was sentenced to 18 months in prison for accepting a bribe from an attorney to get higher attorneys' fees.[92] An ex–Brooklyn State Supreme Court judge pleaded guilty to bribery and was sentenced to 3 years in prison for attempting to get paid $250,000 for a favorable legal ruling. [93]

Government Scandals

Since the turn of the 21st century, a steady stream of federal, state, and local government scandals has eroded trust in our elected officials, whether Democrat or Republican. To have *effective* American Rule of Law *that actually creates trust* requires all government ethics scandals to be viewed through a common lens of right and wrong conduct, not by political party or group affiliation.

Numerous politicians, government employees, and government contractors have been caught in public ethics scandals such as conflicts of interest, self-dealing, financial mismanagement, and corruption.

Federal

Congress: A former *Republican* member of the U.S. House of Representatives, Randy "Duke" Cunningham, was sent to prison for 8 years for steering $70 million in government contracts to military contractors in exchange for almost $2.4 million in gifts (e.g., cars and furniture, $200,000 for a down payment on a condominium, and receiving $700,000 more than the market value of his house when he sold it).[94] The third highest-ranking officer in the Central Intelligence Agency (CIA) also pleaded guilty to steering military contracts to a close friend in exchange for a high-paying job and expensive vacations.[95]

A former *Democrat* U.S. Representative from Louisiana, William Jefferson, was sent to prison for 13 years for accepting bribes to help get business deals in Nigeria and elsewhere in Africa. The FBI discovered $90,000 in cash in his home freezer. [96]

Lobbyists: A lobbyist grossly inflated the cost of his services and expenses to Native American Indian clients. He received a $5 million kickback out of $15 million paid. The lobbyist was given a longer prison sentence than the prosecutors requested. The judge said the longer four-year sentence was given because of the damage the lobbyist had done to the public's trust in the federal government.[97] Twenty people either pleaded guilty or were convicted, including a former U.S. congressman, federal officials, and lobbyists.

Military: The American military has been the one branch of the federal government more trusted than any other branch of government. Even so, trust in the military has been hurt by recent scandals. Three Army officers, including a colonel and two lieutenant colonels, were convicted of accepting $1 million in bribes for steering $8 million in contracts to a civilian supplier.[98] Prison sentences for them ranged from 42 months to 5 years.

In a separate investigation, career soldiers confessed to accepting bribes in exchange for defense contracts in Iraq and Kuwait.[99] The ringleader of this bribery scheme, a former Army major, received a 17-year prison sentence. Five other U.S. military officers were indicted. Three army officers pleaded guilty. At least 36 people were convicted for bribery-related offenses in reconstruction contracts.[100]

Border Patrol: Fears are growing that Mexican drug smugglers are creating a culture of corruption along the U.S.–Mexico border. From 2004 to 2006, 200 public officials were criminally charged with helping move narcotics and illegal immigrants across the border.[101]

Government officials charged with such offenses included local police and law enforcement officials, an FBI supervisor, school district officials, prison guards, immigration examiners, motor vehicle clerks, and members of the American military. Most have pleaded guilty or been convicted at trial.[102]

About 84 U.S. Customs and Border Protection officers have been arrested on corruption charges, and 62 have been convicted.[103] In 2007, a former Customs and Border Protection officer was sentenced to 57 months in prison for accepting more than $70,000 in bribes for allowing hundreds of immigrants to cross the U.S. border illegally.[104]

Is it any wonder Americans' trust in the federal government is so low?[105]

State

Governors: Louisiana, Connecticut, Alabama, and Illinois governors have been sent to prison for crimes ranging from rigging state licenses, bribes, corruption, and misusing state funds:

- *Louisiana*: A former governor was sentenced to 10 years in prison for racketeering, extortion, and fraud for rigging the casino licensing process.[106]

- *Connecticut:* An ex-governor, convicted of corruption and favoritism in awarding state contracts, was sentenced to one year in prison.[107]

- *Alabama:* A former governor was convicted of taking a $500,000 bribe from a former ex-CEO of a giant healthcare company. The bribe was in exchange for appointing the ex-CEO to the state hospital licensing board that regulated the former CEO's company. The ex-Alabama governor was sentenced to 7 years in prison.[108]

- *Illinois:* An ex-governor was given a 6½-year prison sentence for using public money for campaign work and accepting money and gifts in exchange for state business. The next governor was convicted of trying to sell or trade the state Senate seat vacated when Barack Obama became the U.S. president. He was sentenced to 14 years in prison.[109]

State Senators: Former state senators in Maryland, Tennessee, Oklahoma, Florida, New York, and Wisconsin went to prison for a variety of charges, including misusing money entrusted to them, lying under oath, bribery, and corruption:

- *Maryland:* A former senator received a 7-year prison sentence for accepting bribes in exchange for state contracts. His wife was sentenced to 1 year in prison for receiving almost $200,000 for a fictitious state job. Nine others were convicted in this corruption scheme involving millions of dollars of state government contracts.[110]

- *Tennessee:* A former senator was convicted for accepting $800,000 in bribes from two companies to promote their interests (while he was acting as a state lawmaker).[111]

- *Oklahoma:* A former senator was convicted of perjury and other charges for illegally funneling about $245,000 through phony transactions to a political campaign for the U.S. House of Representatives.[112]

- *Florida:* A former senator was convicted of taking a bribe for a favorable vote on the county's purchase of a former soccer complex.[113]

- *New York:* A former senator was sentenced to a year in prison for soliciting and accepting bribes in exchange for public works contracts.[114]

- *Wisconsin:* A former senator was sentenced to six months in prison for using state employees to run his political campaign for attorney-general.[115]

Other State Lawmakers: Lawmakers were sent to prison for ethics scandals involving misuse of charitable funds, stealing from Native American tribes, and taking bribes:

- *North Carolina:* A former lawmaker was sentenced to 6 to 8 years in prison for mishandling charitable contributions and fraudulently obtaining a $150,000 loan.[116] He was the fourth member of the state house to be convicted or to plead guilty to a crime.[117]

- *Texas:* A former state representative was sentenced to 78 months in federal prison for a scheme to steal more than $2 million from the Kickapoo tribe and casino.[118]

- *Alaska:* A former Speaker of the House was sentenced to six years in federal prison for accepting bribes to influence favorable legislation.[119] So far, there are 10 criminal convictions in the ongoing public corruption investigation in Alaska.[120]

- *New York:* Former assembly members were convicted or pleaded guilty on a variety of criminal charges that included bribery, diverting more than $100,000 of union money to pay for personal expenses, and extortion.[121]

Public Officials: "Pay to play" scandals in state pension plans were uncovered:

- *New Mexico:* Two ex–state treasurers were sentenced to 3 years and 40 months respectively for taking kickbacks to funnel state pension business to certain money managers.[122]

- *New York:* An ex–state comptroller was sentenced to 1 to 4 years in prison for accepting bribes from a financial company in exchange for a state contract to manage $250 million of New York's $126 billion public pension plan. Eight people have pleaded guilty, including a former New York deputy comptroller and a former chief investment officer of the New York pension fund.[123] At least a dozen people and financial firms have paid $170 million in civil penalties.

Public Employees: As states face an estimated $2 trillion in unfunded liabilities for public pensions, investigations of pension abuses have increased. One such abuse is "pension spiking." Public employees have been given dramatic boosts in their annual compensation (e.g., overtime) right before retirement, greatly increasing their lifetime pension payouts.

One newspaper reported that if a $74,000-a-year police officer made $125,000 in overtime payments during his last year of employment, he would receive $1.2 million more in pension payments based on a $200,000 annual salary.[124]

Local

Mayors: Mayors in cities from Alabama, Michigan, California, and Maryland have been convicted of various crimes, including obstruction of justice, perjury, bribery, corruption, and defrauding city residents by illegally funneling city work to themselves and their families:

- *Alabama:* A former mayor of Birmingham was given a 15-year prison sentence for accepting $230,000 in bribes in exchange for $7.1 million in county bond business.[125]

- *Michigan:* A former mayor of Detroit, was sentenced to 28 years in prison for public corruption charges. He "had steered millions to himself, family, and friends" as Detroit careened towards bankruptcy.[126]

- *California*: Several former California mayors have gone to prison for unethical conduct. A former Compton mayor was convicted of using city credit cards to pay for personal expenses.[127] A former Lynwood mayor was sentenced to 16 years in prison for using extremely high-priced no-bid city contracts to send city work to a company controlled by him and his family.[128] A former interim mayor of San Diego was convicted of taking bribes from a strip club operator to obtain favorable legislation.[129]

- *Maryland:* An ex-mayor of Baltimore was forced to resign after being convicted of stealing gift cards intended for the city's poor.[130]

City Officials: Many local city officials have been caught in unethical activities. Their misconduct includes fraudulently issuing tax refunds, corruption, bribery, vote-rigging, lying about pension finances, embezzling city funds, and misappropriating federal funds:

- *District of Columbia:* The District of Columbia was hit with the costliest corruption scandal in its history. A former middle manager from the D.C. tax office was sentenced to 17½ years in prison for stealing $48.1 million through fraudulent tax refunds over nearly two decades. She had forged paperwork authorizing tax refund checks to friends, relatives, and herself. For participating in the fraud, 10 others received prison sentences.[131]

- *Pennsylvania:* A former Philadelphia city treasurer was convicted of fraud and conspiracy for accepting gifts and cash from those bidding on city contracts.[132] He was sentenced to 10 years in prison.

- *Ohio:* In 2007, two county election workers in Ohio were sentenced to 18 months in prison for rigging a recount of 2004 presidential election ballots.[133]

- *California:* A former Los Angeles Commissioner was accused of accepting a $100,000 bribe from a Taiwanese shipping company for additional space at the port of Los Angeles. He was convicted of bribery, conflicts of interest, perjury, and theft by embezzlement and sentenced to 5 years in state prison.[134] A former city treasurer of Southgate, California, was sentenced to 10 years in federal prison for taking more than $20 million from the small, working-class city.[135] Former city manager, Robert Rizzo, of Bell, California, was given a 12-year prison term and ordered to pay nearly $9 million in restitution for misappropriating public funds. He paid himself and other top city officials outrageously high salaries and gave loans to fellow employees.

- *Illinois:* A former Chicago water department official pleaded guilty to taking $400,000 in bribes in exchange for awarding city trucking business. So far, 11 former city employees have been convicted in this Chicago corruption probe.[136]

Employees: Lower-level city workers have also been caught in corruption scandals that have led to criminal convictions. As part of a huge public corruption inquiry in El Paso, Texas, a former County Commissioner pleaded guilty to accepting bribes. A former chief of staff for an El Paso County judge pleaded guilty to bribery and conspiracy to commit fraud, including attempting to rig the district court system. His testimony has implicated 17 city, county, and school officials, and business employees.[137]

Law Enforcement: When law enforcement officers are the criminals, our culture of trust is in serious trouble:

- *New York:* A former New York Police Commissioner was indicted on charges he did not report more than $200,000 in rental income or disclose a $250,000 loan when being vetted by White House officials for a cabinet position. He pleaded guilty to eight felonies, including tax fraud and lying to the federal government. [138]

- *California:* A former Sheriff of Orange County, California, was charged with misusing his office to enrich himself and others. He was convicted and sentenced to 5½ years in prison.[139] His Deputy Sheriff received a 1-year prison sentence for lying to a grand jury and the unauthorized use of a county helicopter.[140] Several ex–Los Angeles police officers were sentenced to prison for conducting bogus raids of drug dealers that netted them about $1 million in drugs and cash.[141]

More Scandals

Religion

Our religious institutions and religious leaders have had their share of ethics scandals too:

- The Catholic Church in the United States was rocked by child abuse scandals and alleged cover-ups that led to the bankruptcy of some U.S. parishes.[142] In Los Angeles alone, the Catholic Church paid $660 million to 500 sexual abuse victims as far back as the 1940s. It was the largest sex abuse settlement in the United States.[143]

- When the Baptist Foundation of Arizona declared bankruptcy, investors lost nearly $600 million, making it the largest charity collapse in American history. In 2006, the foundation's former president and its ex-legal counsel were found guilty of fraud.[144]

- A former president of Oral Roberts University resigned amid allegations that he misused university funds to remodel his home multiple times, fly his daughter to the Bahamas on the university's jet, and buy his wife luxury cars.[145]

- Church leaders of Greater Ministries International were accused of running a Ponzi scheme that took nearly $500 million from 18,000 people. The leader of the Ponzi scheme received 27 years in prison and his wife was sentenced to 12 years and 7 months.[146]

- Two men were convicted of running a Ponzi scheme that defrauded 21 African-American churches in Michigan. They were both sentenced up to 20 years in prison.[147]

- In 2001, a man pleaded guilty in a Ponzi scheme that bilked hundreds of millions of dollars from members of the Islamic faith.[148]

- An orthodox Jewish rabbi pleaded guilty to helping donors avoid paying federal income taxes on millions of dollars donated by secretly refunding most of the donors' money. He received a 2-year sentence for tax fraud. His assistant and four other associates also pleaded guilty.[149]

In a separate case in 2012, a rabbi was given a 46-month prison sentence for conspiring to launder about $900,000 from criminal activities. He was one of five rabbis arrested. All five pleaded guilty.[150]

Charities and Nonprofits

The former CEO of the local chapter of the largest charity in the United States retired in 2001 after 27 years with the United Way. In 2004, he was sentenced to 27 months in prison for defrauding the charity out of $500,000 by using the charity's money to pay for personal expenses and being paid for annual leave he had already taken. He also took $94,000 from the charity's pension plan.[151]

Two University of Illinois trustees resigned over an admissions scandal. They had used a separate admissions process for applicants from families of elected officials, trustees, and donors, even if they didn't qualify to be admitted to the university.[152]

Six schools agreed to reimburse students $3.27 million for inflated loan prices that resulted from revenue-sharing agreements with student loan companies.[153] Another university paid $1.1 million for a financial aid director who promoted a student loan company (in which he had a financial interest) to the university's students.[154]

Unions

The former president of Service Employees International Union (SEIU), one of the largest unions in the country, resigned after being sued for restitution of more than $1.1 million. He was accused of using union money in his family's businesses and to pay personal expenses at resorts and restaurants. He was indicted in federal court on charges of embezzlement, tax evasion, and other offenses.[155] In 2013, he was sentenced to 33 months in federal prison.

In another case, a union official of two labor unions (a local division of the International Brotherhood of Electrical Workers [IBEW] and the largest municipal labor council) was accused of using union funds to pay personal expenses (e.g., personal credit card bills, country club dues, and payments on a personal residence). He was also accused of accepting thousands of dollars, vehicles, and other personal benefits from contractors in exchange for allowing them to employ fewer union members. He was sentenced to 10 years in prison and ordered to forfeit more than $3 million from his alleged criminal conduct.[156] In 2013, he was sentenced to 33 months in federal prison.

Ethics Scandal Waves Keep Coming

A bankruptcy court examiner in the Lehman Brothers bankruptcy issued "a scathing report."[157] It contained "fresh allegations" alleging that "Lehman executives manipulated its balance sheet, withheld information from the board, and inflated the value of toxic real estate assets."[158] It also alleged that Lehman management and its auditor Ernst & Young ignored warnings of accounting irregularities raised in May of 2008 by a Lehman senior vice-president.[159] Lawsuits and allegations are flying.

New waves of ethics scandals are still coming:[160]

- **Libor Scandal:** A scandal erupted over whether some banks knowingly submitted false data to calculate the London Interbank Offered Rate (LIBOR) that influences "the value of hundreds of trillions of financial contracts around the world."[161] Barclays PLC admitted liability and paid about $450 million in fines. A subsidiary of UBS pleaded guilty to felony wire fraud in December 2012 and agreed to pay $1.5 billion in fines.[162]

- **Peregrine Financial Group Inc.:** The former CEO of this collapsed brokerage firm admitted to defrauding and embezzling more than $100 million over nearly 20 years.[163] In 2013, the FBI reported that he was sentenced to 50 years in federal prison for stealing $215 million in customer funds.

- **Iraq:** The rebuilding of Iraq's security forces and infrastructure was "the largest reconstruction project of its kind in U.S. history."[164] Of the $51 billion in American taxpayer dollars authorized for the project, federal auditors found that billions of dollars were lost to fraud and waste. Because record-keeping was so poor, the exact amount of misspent taxpayer money will never be known.

- **California Schools:** Twenty-three California schools were stripped of a key state ranking because of cheating and other irregularities when administering state standardized tests. *The Los Angeles Times* reported "...that the violations ranged from failing to cover bulletin boards to helping students correct errors or coaching them with actual test questions."[165]

A Cheating Epidemic

David Callahan wrote a provocative book called *The Cheating Culture* describing how pervasive cheating was in 2004 in the United States. Almost a decade later, cheating appears to be even more widespread.[166] You know we are in real ethics trouble when a common complaint heard today is that those who are playing by the rules feel like fools when everywhere they turn they see people cheating and getting away with it.

Taxes

Rich Americans evaded taxes by hiding their money in offshore accounts. Swiss banking giant UBS was forced to reveal thousands of names of American depositors. Approximately 14,500 wealthy Americans came forward in 2009 to avoid criminal prosecution for tax evasion. UBS paid $780 million to settle claims it had defrauded the IRS by setting up sham offshore entities for about $20 billion.[167]

Education

High school administrators were accused of falsifying grades and records to give unqualified students a high school diploma[168] and changing or deleting grades to help students get into colleges and universities.[169] Eleven Atlanta high school teachers, testing coordinators, and other administrators were convicted on racketeering charges for helping students to cheat on standardized tests used to evaluate teacher performance.[170] An ex-director of a New York college was found guilty of accepting money to change grades and fabricate degrees.[171]

If teachers and administrators cheat, it should come as no surprise that many of our high school and college students believe cheating is acceptable.[172] Texas students at a top high school were recently caught cheating.[173] In 2012, students at a top New York high school were also caught cheating on final exams.[174]

Two community college students were expelled for forging their college transcripts from other colleges.[175] The Graduate Management Admission Test required for admission to business school was cancelled for 84 students because of cheating.[176] Fifteen cadets from the Air Force Academy were expelled and three others resigned for cheating.[177] Thirty-four students at Duke University business school faced discipline for cheating on a take-home exam, the most widespread instance of cheating in the business school's history.[178]

Media

A *New York Times* reporter lost his job for making up comments and scenes in his articles.[179] Two authors who wrote memoirs that received national attention have admitted they wrote about events and facts that did not happen.[180]

Sports

Several prominent athletes were caught in steroids scandals. A former Olympic track star[181] and a former Olympic cyclist[182] were convicted of a crime related to using steroids. In 2012, the seven-time winner of the world Tour de France bike race was stripped of his titles over accusations of steroid use.[183] An MLB baseball home-run star was convicted of obstruction of justice for lying to federal officials about his use of steroids.[184]

An NBA basketball referee pleaded guilty to betting on games he was officiating.[185] An NFL football star was sent to prison for 23 months for an illegal dog-fighting-gambling operation and lying about his participation.[186]

Résumés

Several high-profile people resigned from their positions after accusations of lying about their educational qualifications became public: a former president of the U.S. Olympic Committee was accused of lying about having a graduate and doctorate degree,[187] a former dean of admissions of the Massachusetts Institute of Technology was accused of lying about three academic degrees,[188] a former head football coach at Notre Dame was accused of lying about his education at NYU,[189] and an ex-CEO of Radio Shack was accused of lying about having a college degree.[190]

Cab Drivers

In 2010, New York City "revealed… that about 3,000 [cab drivers] had overcharged 1.8 million riders over two years, costing passengers a total of $8.3 million."[191] Drivers often charged their city passengers the much higher long-distance rates reserved only for trips outside the city.

Just as night follows day, when cheating becomes the "new" normal, a painful ethics reckoning inevitably will follow—the only question is when and how bad it will be.

A Culture of Distrust?

Our self-organizing American brand of freedom depends on the trustworthiness of our public and private institutions and organizations and associations.[192] Rampant cheating threatens the foundation of our free economy, free political system, and free society by damaging public trust in our capital markets, our governments, and other essential social, political, economic, and legal self-governing institutions.

Our ethics scandal tsunami cannot be resolved easily or overnight. While swift, powerful enforcement against wrongdoers is essential to restore trust quickly, "top-down" enforcement alone is not enough. To restore our culture of trust, we must regenerate "bottom-up" voluntary ethical conduct throughout our economy, political system, and society.

Growing distrust in our essential self-governing, self-organizing institutions and associations on which our freedom and prosperity are based, is a dangerous development. Without faith, trust, and our ability to self-organize, we will not be able to survive the next major crisis or national emergency as an intact, united, free nation.

Chapter 8

Our Culture of Trust Is Unique
The Secret of Our Survival and Success

> *At the dawn of a new century, indeed a new millennium, the United States is now the oldest enduring republic in world history, with a set of political institutions and traditions that have stood the test of time.*
>
> **– Joseph J. Ellis (1943–)**
> American historian

A Blizzard of Flags

On September 11, 2001, Islamic terrorists hijacked four jetliners. They deliberately crashed two of the planes into the World Trade Center in New York, reducing both 110-story buildings to rubble. About 3,000 people died; 400 of them were firefighters and police officers who died trying to rescue others.

The terrorists crashed the third plane into the Pentagon building outside of Washington, D.C., killing almost 200 people. Passengers on the fourth plane revolted, crashing it into a Pennsylvania field, killing all onboard.

Almost overnight, Americans began flying American flags everywhere—on their cars, in their offices, and outside their homes—as a show of national solidarity in the face of an extraordinary crisis. For many Americans, this was the first time they had seen such an automatic and spontaneous outpouring of American patriotism and unity.

This ability of Americans to change and unify "overnight" often catches non-Americans off-guard. However, this quick-changing behavior is vintage American—a by-product of centuries of self-government and self-organization under *ethics-based* American Rule of Law and our unique brand of constitutional freedom.

For a time, Americans put aside their petty political bickering and name-calling and rallied around the flag and country in a way not seen since the patriotic days of World War II. Unfortunately, that intense resolve of unity has dissipated, as the immediate threat of more terrorist attacks appeared to diminish.

A Self-Organizing Culture of Trust

Our self-organizing culture of trust under *ethics-based* American Rule of Law is a key factor of American stability and success over centuries (not decades). *To keep our freedom in the 21st century, Americans must rediscover the essential, nonnegotiable components of our unique American self-organizing culture of trust.*

In recent decades, American education has too often failed to teach what is unique and different about the United States. As retired U.S. Supreme Court Justice David Souter recently observed, the United States will not remain a free, self-governing republic unless American civics classes are taught more effectively in our schools.[1]

This lack of knowledge jeopardizes our continued survival and success as a free, independent, self-organizing nation based on a culture of trust.

American Exceptionalism

The term "American exceptionalism" is often misunderstood. In the context of our self-organizing culture of trust, it refers to *our uniquely American system of government and brand of freedom that has created the most enduring, self-governing constitutional republic in modern world history.*

That statement may surprise many Americans, including many of our leaders, who do not appear to understand or appreciate what is special and different about our unique brand of self-organizing American freedom. Our Founding Fathers risked their lives and everything they owned to create a brand of freedom never seen before in the world.

Today's financial and economic crises, and an increasingly volatile, unpredictable, and unstable world, virtually guarantee Americans will soon be called upon again to quickly unite as one nation and one people. To continue being free, Americans *must* understand how our unique brand of freedom, under ethics-based American Rule of Law and our unique constitutional framework, *must* work.

The United States has remained a successful, self-governing experiment in modern world history because these unique American concepts of freedom have been applied and implemented in uniquely American ways.

The American Paradox

The Merriam-Webster Dictionary defines a paradox as "one having contradictory qualities." The American experiment in freedom has survived and succeeded for so long—*so far*—because Americans have had the ability to delicately balance two opposing ideas at the same time, namely

- the *wisdom of knowing what we must always change* to adapt quickly to a continuously changing environment, and

- the *wisdom of knowing what we must never change*—the timeless principles of our freedom—that have held us together as a united nation under the same government for centuries, even through extreme crisis.

It is easy for a country to be successful in times of economic prosperity and peace. What sets countries apart is whether they can hold together *under the same form of government* through a major crisis or national emergency. That is when most countries fall apart.

Alexis de Tocqueville, a French aristocrat who lost relatives to the guillotine during the French Revolution, traveled extensively in the United States in the early 1800s. He wanted to find out why the American Revolution had turned out so differently from the French Revolution. Unlike the American Revolution, the French Revolution devolved into mass beheadings, dictatorship under Emperor Napoleon, and eventually to a return of the French monarchy.

De Tocqueville wrote *Democracy in America,* documenting his insights about America and the American people (as seen through his French bystander eyes). He had this to say about the American paradox:

> Two things in America are astonishing: the changeableness of most human behavior and the strange stability of certain principles.

De Toqueville's sentiments were echoed in President Carter's 1977 inaugural address when he said: "[w]e must adjust to changing times and still hold to unchanging principles."[2] The United States has survived for more than two centuries under the same form of government because of our remarkable ability to adapt to ever-changing circumstances, while remaining firmly rooted to the immutable principles of freedom on which this nation was founded.

Americans have *so far* been able to distinguish what we must *always change* to adapt to constantly changing conditions from what we must *never change*—the timeless principles of our unique approach to freedom.

The American paradox is a key reason why our self-governing experiment in freedom has survived centuries, not just decades, *under the same U.S. Constitution and form of government.* Like the self-organizing ants, the United States has been able to be strong and stable, yet still flexible enough to adapt to constantly changing conditions.

This is the wisdom of ants.

A Common Belief System

The United States of America has held together as a united nation under the same government for so long because Americans have forged a common belief in American freedom. Unfortunately, many Americans today take our American rights and freedoms for granted, unaware how different our brand of freedom is from any other country in the world.

Margaret Thatcher, the former Prime Minister of Britain, summed up the difference between Americans and Europeans by saying: "Europe was created by history. America was created by philosophy." The United States of America is a product of a specific belief system about freedom, self-governance, and *ethics-based* Rule of Law reflected in three uniquely American documents:

- Declaration of Independence, 1776
- U.S. Constitution, written in 1787, effective in 1789
- Bill of Rights, the first 10 amendments to the U.S. Constitution, 1791

These American documents, unique in their language and content at the time they were drafted, have been applied and enforced over the centuries in a uniquely American way. We are a government "*of* the people, *by* the people, and *for* the people." John Marshall, the Chief Justice of the U.S. Supreme Court from 1801 to 1835, described the new American government as follows:

> [t]he government of the Union, [then] is emphatically and truly a government of the people. In form and substance it emanates from them. Its powers are granted by them, and are to be exercised directly on them and for their benefit. [3]

Our firm adherence to the unifying principles of the Declaration of Independence, the U.S. Constitution, and the Bill of Rights is what has provided the over-arching unifying framework of our self-organizing success *under the same form of government* for more than 200 years. *A common belief system is a powerful unifying force.*

It is easy for newcomers to the United States to quickly assimilate into American society. *To become an American* only requires adopting this common belief in freedom found in these three seminal American documents. No particular background or membership in the "right" social class is required.

Being an American requires taking the Oath of Allegiance, renouncing allegiance to any other country, and agreeing *to uphold the U.S. Constitution against all enemies, foreign and domestic.*[4] Most importantly, being an American means having a *fervent devotion to follow our American Rule of Law.*

This is why the issue of illegal immigration is so problematic. The question that must be answered is *How can one become an American by violating our immigration laws when the hallmark of being an American is and must always be a fervent devotion to follow our American Rule of Law?*[5]

New Americans *must* share this fervent devotion to follow our American Rule of Law because without Rule of Law, the only thing left is Rule of Force, under which we would all lose our freedom.

Unicultural, Not Multicultural

To say that the United States is unicultural, not multicultural, is viewed as heresy in some circles, especially on many American college campuses. However, what proponents of multiculturalism fail to appreciate is that one of America's greatest strengths is that we are a *diverse, unicultural, not* multicultural, society.

What binds us together as a united people is our shared belief in our unique brand of American freedom and constitutional rights found in the Declaration of Independence, the U.S. Constitution, and the Bill of Rights. This *common belief system* has provided the essential over-arching, unifying, unicultural umbrella, under which Americans have been free to express their multiple differences.

Emphasizing differences between groups of people, without a common belief system and shared cultural and ethical norms, will inevitably lead to chaos and violence, especially in times of stress, in *any* country—including the United States. Unfortunately, many of our own educational institutions, under the banner of "multiculturalism," have failed to teach newcomers and succeeding American generations about our *essential unicultural American cultural heritage.*

Multiculturalism causes trouble in any country, as Britain, France, and Germany are the latest to discover. In 2011, after touting multiculturalism for years, the leaders of all three countries publicly declared that multiculturalism doesn't work.[6] *Blind adherence to the tenets of multiculturalism is political thinking, not critical thinking.*

Critical thinkers know that without a common unifying culture, terrible violence has erupted between different groups of people in country after country around the world. Not having a common shared overarching unifying cultural bond led one African tribe to go on a murderous rampage against members of another tribe in Rwanda,[7] members of one Iraqi Muslim sect to kill and torture members of another Iraqi Muslim sect,[8] and Christian Serbians to slaughter Bosnian Muslims upon the break-up of Yugoslavia.[9]

The official motto of the Great Seal of the United States is *"e pluribus unum"* which means "out of many, one." This signifies that although Americans come from many and varied backgrounds, we are united by our common belief in our uniquely American brand of constitutional freedom.

Americans pledge their allegiance "to the flag of...the Republic, *one nation, under God, indivisible*...." Our unifying overarching common belief system under ethics-based American Rule of Law and our uniquely American constitutional system is the foundation of our successful American self-organizing culture of trust.

Americans Are Made, Not Born

America's unique approach to self-governance is different from other countries. Our common American heritage and culture were forged *on purpose* through deliberate, painstaking education. Noah Webster, of *Webster's Dictionary* fame, created the books used by American schools to teach young Americans *what it meant to be an American.* His books "...did more than teach children to read, write, and speak American. They taught children to live, breathe and think American...."[10]

Historically, the United States has held together as a unified nation, even in a major crisis or national emergency, because newcomers to the United States quickly became Americans. As new Americans, they renounced their allegiance to their mother countries (as required by the American Oath of Allegiance discussed further in Chapter 9). They adopted the United States of America as their new mother country, with its own unique American culture of trust, Rule of Law, and culture of freedom.

These new Americans did not come to the United States seeking to impose the culture and language of their countries of origin on the United States. After all, they left their home countries precisely because they did not have the same rights, freedoms, and opportunities in their home countries that are available in the United States under our American Rule of Law.

If the United States is to remain free, all newcomers *must* continue to *become Americans* and adopt our common *unicultural* culture of freedom. Because Americans have been *unicultural and diverse, not multicultural,* unrelated groups of Americans have been able to self-organize under the common unifying bond of our uniquely American brand of freedom and culture of trust.

If Americans ever lose this common bond of freedom and trust under *ethics-based* American Rule of Law and our unique constitutional framework, the United

States will end up like Argentine ants in Argentina. Because those ants kill each other, they still live in small, stunted colonies.

Thus far, Americans have been able to mimic the unrelated Argentine ants in the European super-colony and cooperate voluntarily and automatically with one another based on trust, even in a major crisis or national emergency.

This is the wisdom of ants.

The Wisdom of Our Founding Fathers

The United States was the first country in history founded on the moral principle that "all men are created equal" with inalienable rights to "life, liberty, and the pursuit of happiness" (as stated in the Declaration of Independence). Although it took a bloody civil war and almost two centuries to make American freedoms apply to all Americans, the power of this overriding belief in freedom spurred America, imperfect from the beginning, to continually strive to make this freedom dream a reality for all.

America was the first country where the rights of its citizens *came directly from God*, not through a human ruler like a king, emperor, or czar. Such inalienable rights that come directly from God can *never* be taken away by *any* leader or man-made government, including any American leader or American government. The Declaration of Independence clearly states that the government established to secure these rights derives "their just powers from the consent of the governed...."[11]

Unlike the French Revolution of 1789, the Russian Revolution in 1917, and the Chinese Revolution in 1949, the American Revolution did not seek to overthrow everything. Americans created a new self-governing society never before seen in the world, but continued to use well-established principles of British Rule of Law developed over many centuries.[12]

The Declaration of Independence, the U.S. Constitution, and the Bill of Rights created a uniquely American culture of freedom and trust under *ethics-based* American Rule of Law. For the first time, leaders were chosen because of their ability, not because they were rich or could trace their roots to a pedigreed family. America became known as the "land of opportunity" because anyone—regardless of birth, background, or wealth—had a chance to succeed.

> *Don't interfere with anything in the Constitution. That must be maintained, for it is the only safeguard of our liberties.*
>
> **– Abraham Lincoln (1809–1865)**
> 16th U.S. president during the
> American Civil War 1861–1865

Our North Star

For thousands of years, sailors found their way home by locating the North Star in the sky, even when they were in the middle of the ocean with no land in sight. The U.S. Constitution has been our North Star guide for succeeding American generations on how our self-governing nation *must* operate.

America's Founding Fathers were intelligent, educated, well-read men who studied the many different forms of government tried throughout history. This is why they set up a constitutional government based on *general principles and beliefs.*

The U.S. Constitution *contains several key essential features that **must** be maintained to keep our unique American brand of freedom:*

1. **A Representative Republic:** For a time, ancient Rome was a *direct democracy;* that is, the Roman people *participated directly* in their government, not through representatives. It failed. Rome degenerated into a dictatorship under an emperor.

   America's Founding Fathers deliberately rejected this form of democracy. Instead, the United States is a *democratic constitutional republic with elected representatives* to act on behalf of the people in the government. James Madison explained the difference between a *democracy* and a *republic*:

   > ...[i]n a democracy the people meet and exercise the government in person; in a republic, they assemble and administer it by their representatives and agents. A democracy, consequently, will be confined to a small spot. A republic may be extended over a large region.[13]

   To maintain representative harmony in the country, the American president is elected by an *electoral college*, not by which a presidential candidate wins the most votes overall in the election.

2. **Reverence for the Constitution:** Americans have successfully lived under the same U.S. Constitution for more than 200 years "because they haven't regarded it simply as statute law that could be changed easily and often whenever the whim hit them."[14] The framers of the U.S. Constitution made sure that it would be very difficult to make changes to the U.S. Constitution— on purpose.

   > *But the Constitution which at any time exists, till changed by an explicit and authentic act of the whole people, is sacredly obligatory upon all.*
   >
   > **– George Washington (1732–1799)**
   > American Founding Father,
   > 1st U.S. president 1789–1797

   Unlike America, other countries have routinely rewritten or replaced their constitutions: Greece and Sweden in 1975, the People's Republic of

China and Canada in 1982, the Netherlands in 1983, Brazil in 1988, and Portugal in 1989, among many others; France has had 15 different constitutions.[15] Venezuela has had 26 constitutions.[16]

The United States has been operating under *the same* U.S. Constitution since 1789. The first 10 amendments (the Bill of Rights) were added in 1791. Over the next 200 years, only 17 amendments were added. As a comparison, India's latest constitution, adopted in 1950, already has more than 90 amendments.

The U.S. has only had *one* Constitution since 1789 with very few changes. *It has endured and stood the test of time.*

3. **Distrust of Power:** In the famous words of Lord Acton, "[p]ower tends to corrupt and absolute power tends to corrupt absolutely." The framers of the U.S. Constitution understood this fundamental truth. The first American constitution, the Articles of Confederation, only gave the federal government weak powers. It didn't work.

   Our current U.S. Constitution, effective since 1789, gave the central federal government substantially more power. But because of our Founding Fathers' wise distrust of human nature (e.g., when people have too much power), the U.S. Constitution has *key limitations on federal power* (e.g., *checks and balances, federalism*, and the *Bill of Rights*).

   These limitations are especially relevant today, now that the power and reach of the federal government has expanded so enormously. Our Founding Fathers wisely distrusted placing too much power in anyone's hands. Throughout history, abusive government power has often been created slowly, under the guise of what initially appeared to be a good cause.

   > *The truth is that all men having power ought to be mistrusted.*
   >
   > **– James Madison (1751–1836)**
   > American Founding Father,
   > 4th U.S. president 1809–1817

4. **Checks and Balances:** A fundamental concept of our self-governing system is *divided power*. Under the U.S. Constitution, the *legislative, executive,* and *judicial* branches of government are each separate and independent, with certain powers to review the actions of one another.

   The purpose of checks and balances in the U.S. Constitution is to ensure that no one branch of the federal government—the executive (president), legislative (Congress), or judicial (U.S. Supreme Court)—becomes too powerful. President George Washington in his 1796 Farewell Address to the nation upon leaving the presidency warned Americans to be very vigilant:

   > It is important...that the habits of thinking in a free Country should inspire caution in those entrusted with its administration, to confine themselves within their respective Constitutional Spheres; avoiding in the exercise of the Powers of one department to encroach upon another.

Each of these three branches of the federal government *must not encroach on the powers of the other branches* of the federal government. Washington warned that if Americans are not vigilant, the federal government could consolidate its power into one branch of government, which would pave the way for a cruel and oppressive ruler with absolute power.[17]

Since the *Marbury vs. Madison* case in 1803, the U.S. Supreme Court has had the power to challenge the constitutionality of any laws passed by Congress, or any executive action taken by the president. British courts did not have similar power.[18]

There is also a check on the power of the U.S. Supreme Court. The U.S. Congress can pass a federal statute (if signed by the president) that overturns U.S. Supreme Court decisions. For example, the 1991 Civil Rights Act, in part, specifically overruled several U.S. Supreme Court decisions on employment law. Power is further divided by the requirement that the president's nominations for U.S. Supreme Court judges must be confirmed by the U.S. Senate.

Unlike judges in many countries, American judges are not rubber-stamps for government actions. American federal judges have lifetime tenure. When cases warrant, they are free to reject the actions of the American government, and they do:

- In 2009, a New York federal judge rejected the Securities and Exchange Commission's (SEC) $33 million dollar settlement with Bank of America Corp. The bank was accused of misleading shareholders about the $3.6 billion bonuses paid to Merrill Lynch & Company employees before their companies merged. The federal judge said the settlement was too low for a $3.6 billion claim. The case later settled for $150 million.[19]

- A federal appeals court threw out a new Securities and Exchange Commission (SEC) rule giving investors more power to oust corporate directors. The SEC had failed to "adequately analyze the costs to U.S. companies of fighting contested board elections" and "failed [to prove] its claim the rule would improve shareholder value and board performance."[20]

> *The dignity and stability of government in all its branches, the morals of the people, and every blessing of society depend so much upon an upright and skillful administration of justice, that the judicial power ought to be distinct from both the legislative and executive, and independent upon both, so that it may be a check upon both, and both should be checks upon that.*
>
> **– John Adams (1735–1826)**
> American Founding Father,
> 2nd U.S. president 1797–1801

5. **Federalism:** Federalism is another fundamental American concept. *The purpose of American federalism is to prevent power from being concentrated in the U.S. federal government, away from the people and the states.*

Under the U.S. Constitution, the federal government is granted *only certain specific enumerated powers.* The 10th amendment of the Bill of Rights specifically states that *all other powers remain with the states or with the people.*

This is the reverse of the Canadian system of federalism that says powers not specifically granted to the provinces remained with the central government.[21] In America, there are 50 U.S. state constitutions and 50 state legislatures competing for power with the U.S. federal government under the U.S. Constitution. Under the 10th Amendment of the U.S. Constitution (the Bill of Rights), "The powers not delegated to the United States by the Constitution, nor prohibited by it to the States, are reserved to the States respectively, or to the people."

> *The proposed Constitution, so far from implying an abolition of the State governments, makes them constituent parts of the national sovereignty...and leaves in their possession certain exclusive and very important portions of sovereign power.*
>
> **– Alexander Hamilton (1755–1804)**
> American Founding Father,
> 1st U.S. secretary of the Treasury, 1789–1795

Since the Great Depression and World War II, the power and size of the U.S. government has expanded so greatly, tensions are growing between the federal government and the states. This tension is a natural outgrowth of the federalism system established by the Founding Fathers in the U.S. Constitution.

When the U.S. Supreme Court issued an unpopular decision on eminent domain in the *Kelo* case, the states were quick to react. The *Kelo* case significantly expanded the government's power to take a private citizen's property forcibly by eminent domain. Within five years of that decision, most states restricted the government's power of eminent domain.[22]

In 2009, four states passed sovereignty resolutions based on the 10th amendment of the Bill of Rights to remind the federal government it has only *limited power* under the U.S. Constitution.[23] Fifteen states sued the EPA to stop it from issuing regulations without scientific proof that greenhouse gases threaten human health.[24]

Americans must constantly monitor how much power is being centralized in Washington, D.C., and why. When Bill Clinton was elected president in 1992, presidential candidates spent just under $200 million. In 2012, both presidential candidates spent an estimated $1 billion each on their campaigns.

We can no longer rule out the strong possibility that the voices of "ordinary" American citizens and taxpayers are being drowned out by big-money special interest groups with their own agendas. That's not a Democrat or Republican issue. That's an American issue.

*To remain free, states and the people must restore their rightful powers under the U.S. Constitution. The U.S. federal government **must** return to performing **only** those specific enumerated powers listed in the U.S. Constitution.*

> *Government big enough to supply everything you need is big enough to take everything you have. The course of history shows us that as a government grows, liberty decreases.*
>
> **– Thomas Jefferson (1743–1829)**
> American Founding Father
> 3rd U.S. president 1801–1809

6. **Protecting the Individual:** Rights granted under the U.S. Bill of Rights in 1791 are, in language and application, uniquely American. After the American Revolution, American Rule of Law developed very differently from Rule of Law in Britain and other former British colonies.

   For example, Canada's version of citizens' rights, called Canada's Charter of Rights and Freedoms, was only included *for the first time in its constitution in 1982*. The Australian Constitution, effective in 1901, based on both the British and American models of government, did not include an American-styled Bill of Rights.

   In 1789, significantly more power was given to the federal government under today's U.S. Constitution than it had under the original Articles of Confederation. To be sure the rights of individuals were protected, the American Bill of Rights (the first 10 amendments to the U.S. Constitution) were added in 1791.

   The purpose of the Bill of Rights is *to guarantee certain protections of American citizens against the power of the U.S. federal government.*

   These guarantees include freedom of the press, speech, assembly, and religion; the right to petition the government for redress of grievances; and the right to keep and bear arms. Individual Americans are also protected from unreasonable searches and seizures by the government.

   Americans are not required to incriminate themselves in a criminal proceeding. We have a right to due process and a right to speedy public trial before an impartial jury, the right to be informed of the charges against us and to confront witnesses, the right to subpoena favorable witnesses, and the right to an attorney and trial by jury.

   Americans are protected from excessive bail or fines or cruel or unusual punishments. As noted earlier, under the 10th Amendment, powers not specifically delegated to the federal government are reserved for the states or the American people.

   James Madison understood "it was not enough for the new Constitution to have the support of the majority… it had to have the universal allegiance of 'the great mass of people.'"[25] The Bill of Rights is one reason Americans have held their constitution in such reverence.

> *Without Freedom of Thought there can be no such Thing as Wisdom; and no such Thing as Public Liberty, without Freedom of Speech.*
>
> **– Benjamin Franklin (1706–1790)**
> American Founding Father

Our Founding Fathers also understood how important it was to prevent an oppressive political majority from trampling on the individual rights of the minority.[26] Today, we must be just as careful to ensure that the rights and needs of the majority are not crushed by the "tyranny of minorities." The key word is balance—not too much, not too little—just enough. Our Founding Fathers wisely understood that whoever held power for too long, no matter who it was, would abuse it.

The beauty of *ethics-based* American Rule of Law has been its ability to swing in one direction for a while, then in another direction, yet still remain within the constitutional boundaries of the U.S. Constitution. So far, American Rule of Law has been able to maintain this all-important balance of power required for a stable, peaceful, prosperous, and secure nation over centuries.

An Absolutely Essential Ingredient

No subject has been more politicized and inaccurately portrayed than the role of religion in the success of the American experiment in self-organization and self-government. In certain circles, while it is acceptable to identify Saudi Arabia as a Muslim country, Israel as a Jewish country, or Thailand as a Buddhist country, it is taboo to identify the United States as a country with a longstanding Christian heritage.

This denial of our American Christian heritage appears to be based on a mistaken notion that recognizing the influence of Christianity in the United States (and in particular Protestant Christianity) somehow jeopardizes the religious freedom of non-Christians. In fact, just the opposite is true.

Religious freedom is an entrenched cultural value in the United States precisely because so many of our early settlers were Protestant Christians escaping religious persecution in Europe.[27]

> *Liberty cannot be established without morality, nor morality without faith.*
>
> **– Alexis de Tocqueville (1805–1859)**
> Author, *Democracy in America* (1835, 1840)

The relationship of religion and government in the United States is very different from that in Britain and other European nations. In those countries, the Christian religion (either Catholic or Protestant) was adopted as *the official religion of the country.* This is not possible in the United States. The 1st Amendment to the U.S. Constitution says: "Congress shall make no law respecting an establishment of religion, or prohibiting the free exercise thereof...."

Thus, religion in America has never been, and can never be, a "top-down" central government-mandated official religion, as it is in many other countries. In keeping with our principles of self-governance and freedom, religion in America is, and always has been, a voluntary, self-organizing "bottom-up" affair. However, that doesn't mean that Christianity, and in particular Protestant Christianity, hasn't played a very important role in the country's success over hundreds of years. It has.[28]

The dominant cultural influence of Christianity and the Bible in western civilization first began in Europe around 400 A.D., when the last Roman emperor Constantine made Christianity the official religion of the Roman empire.

In 1983, the U.S. Congress acknowledged a long-standing cultural influence of the Bible in the United States by declaring that year to be the "year of the Bible" stating:

> The Bible, The Word of God, has made a unique contribution in shaping the United States as a distinctive and blessed nation.... Deeply held religious convictions springing from the Holy Scriptures led to the early settlement of our Nation.... Biblical teaching inspired concepts of civil government that are contained in our Declaration of Independence and the Constitution of the United States.[29]

Most Americans identify themselves as Christians. In 2004, ABC News reported that 83% of Americans called themselves Christian, 13% non-believers, and 4% non-Christians (Jewish, Muslim, Buddhist, and the like).[30] In a 2007 Gallup poll, 82% of Americans said that they identified with the Christian religion.[31] According to the last census, 75% of Americans describe themselves as Christians, with Protestant Christians still greatly outnumbering Catholic Christians.[32]

Our unique brand of freedom, culture of trust, and *ethics-based* American Rule of Law are infused with concepts of right and wrong behavior based on our Judeo-Christian heritage, with a decidedly Protestant Christian cultural accent. Why does this matter? *It matters because different religious heritages in different countries have created vastly different cultures, governments, economies, legal systems, and societies.*

Countries based on Christianity are decidedly different from those based on Islam. Christian countries favor freedom of religion and religious tolerance. The same is not true in many Islam-based countries today. In 2011, a Christian pastor in Iran was facing the death penalty for allegedly converting from Islam to Christianity (*apostasy*).[33] That would be impossible under the U.S. Constitution.

Our Protestant British Legal Heritage

Although fashionable in certain circles to ignore or deny the influence of our Judeo-Christian religious heritage (and in particular our Protestant Christian heritage), this ignores historical fact. Europe and England were Catholic until the Protestant Reformation in the early 1500s. England officially became Protestant when King Henry VIII declared the Church of England the official religion of the country in 1534.

British "judge-made" common law is a product of two different court systems that developed in England over time. One was secular (non-religious), called *law* courts, which could only award money damages. However, because justice sometimes required something other than money damages, a second court system developed in England through its religious-based Chancery courts.

These English religious-based courts had the power to create more flexible equitable remedies other than money damages in order to reach a just result. Most judges in the Chancery courts in England initially were Christian ministers (presumably Protestant after Henry VIII). They had wide discretion to render "fair" decisions to overcome the unfairness of the law courts.[34]

We inherited these Judeo-Christian ethical principles and values (with a Protestant Christian cultural emphasis) by adopting the principles of British Rule of Law, first as a British colony, and later as an independent nation. In the United States, British law (secular courts) and equity (originally religious courts) principles are merged into one single American court system under our American Rule of Law.

> It is impossible to rightly govern a nation without God and the Bible.
>
> **– George Washington (1732–1799)**
> American Founding Father,
> 1st U.S. president 1789–1797

Our Protestant Christian Cultural Heritage

To understand how heavily influenced we have been by our Protestant Christian cultural heritage, take a look at our U.S. presidents. Our *first Catholic president in U.S. history* was John F. Kennedy in 1960. Even then, concerns were raised in the presidential campaign about whether a Catholic president would be too heavily influenced by the Catholic Church's Pope in Rome.

Our Protestant Christian heritage has deeply influenced our American *self-governing, self-organizing American culture of trust.* As already noted, early American self-governing settlements were often patterned on the "bottom-up" self-governance models of early Protestant churches. Because so many of our Protestant forefathers were fleeing religious persecution in Europe, freedom of religion was enshrined in the U.S. Constitution and American culture.

As the name itself implies, Protestants have a long-standing culture of protesting against what is wrong. After all, Protestants came into being protesting what they thought was wrong in the Catholic Church. That culture of protest is alive and well in the United States today. Also, although Catholics rely on church officials to read and interpret the Bible for them, Protestants read and interpret the Bible for themselves. Similarly, Americans do not rely only on official "interpreters" to tell them what the plain language of the U.S. Constitution says and means.

Finally, the Protestant work ethic has been the backbone of the development of our free-market capitalist economy. Protestants believed in "sacrifice, labor, discipline and hard work by the individual....and [t]hrift, sobriety and industriousness."[35]

> *By our form of government, the Christian religion is the established religion; and all sects and denominations of Christians are placed upon the same equal footing, and are equally entitled to protection in their religious liberty.*[36]
>
> **– Samuel Chase (1741–1811)**
> American Founding Father,
> U.S. Supreme Court justice 1796–1811

God's Law Is "In" the Law, Not "Over" the Law

Although American Rule of Law is steeped in Judeo-Christian religious principles, it is still *civilian law OVER God's law*. That is, one's own interpretation of the Bible or any other religious text (God's Law) *never* takes precedence over our *civilian* American Rule of Law. The "law of the land" in America is the U.S. Constitution and our *civilian* American common law, not the Bible. *American Rule of Law fosters "bottom-up" freedom.*

In contrast, Saudi Arabian "Rule of Law" is *God's law OVER* independent *civilian law*. The most extreme implementation of Sharia law under the Koran is wahhabism in Saudi Arabia. Wahhabism is defined as "… an austere form of Islam that insists on a literal interpretation of the Quran [Koran]. Strict Wahhabis believe that all those who don't practice their form of Islam are heathens and enemies…."[37]

Saudi Arabian "Rule of Law" is *God's law OVER* independent *civilian law.* Saudi Arabia's law of the land is literally Islamic Sharia law. Court judges, although trained attorneys, are Muslim clerics who interpret Islamic Sharia law (God's Law according to the Quran [Koran] and the Sunnah (the sayings, practices, and teachings of the Prophet Mohammed) for the rest of the country's population. "Precedents and analogy applied by Muslim scholars are used to address new issues."[38] *Islamic Sharia Law fosters "top-down" dictatorial control, not "bottom-up" freedom. This control extends to both the public and private lives of the people.*

Under Sharia law in Saudi Arabia, witchcraft or apostasy (that is, abandoning the Muslim religion) might result in a beheading.[39] Wife-beating and rape might hardly be punished at all.[40] Those who commit adultery when married might be stoned to death. Recently in Saudi Arabia, Raif Badawi was charged with blasphemy (insulting God the Prophet or the religion, Islam) and given a sentence of 1,000 lashes and 10 years in prison for criticizing Islamic clerics.[41]

Imagine designating the Bible as "the law of the land" in the United States instead of our U.S. Constitution and our *civilian* American Rule of Law. Also imagine that all American judges, although attorneys, were required to also be Protestant scholars, steeped in a literal reading of the Bible. Further imagine that these Biblical scholar American judges were given the power to interpret the Bible (not the U.S. Constitution and our *civilian* American common law) as the "law of the land" for the rest of the American population.

Can you now see *why a Sharia law system of God's law OVER civilian law is diametrically opposite and incompatible with our American civilian Rule of Law? Our American Rule of Law, although steeped in Judeo-Christian principles, is still always civilian law OVER God's law.*

"Freedom Of," *Not* "Freedom From"

Freedom *of* religion guaranteed in the Bill of Rights does not mean, nor was it ever intended to mean, freedom *from* religion. In fact, several key Founding Fathers clearly understood that unless Americans remained a religious people, our self-governing experiment would fail.

The Bill of Rights expressly prohibits the federal government from establishing any religion as the official religion for the country, as occurred in England. Americans have the right to freely exercise their religion without federal government interference.

But this did not mean that our Founding Fathers were neutral about religion. The issue is not whether the Founding Fathers were themselves religious—some were, and some were less so.[42]

What our Founding Fathers recognized was that *religion was an absolutely necessary support for the republican form of government* they were establishing. Why? Because our form of government depends on a culture of trust, which can only exist if Americans have the highest degree of morality and ethical conduct.

They understood that religion is essential to keep and maintain the ethical standards that Americans must voluntarily follow (and enforce when necessary) for our experiment in self-governing freedom to work.

> *Statesmen may plan and speculate for liberty but it is religion and morality alone that can establish the principles upon which freedom can securely stand... We have no government armed with power capable of contending with human passions unbridled by morality and religion. Avarice, ambition, revenge or gallantry would break the strongest cords of our Constitution as a whale goes through a net. Our Constitution is designed only for a moral and religious people. It is wholly inadequate for any other.*
>
> – John Adams (1735–1826)
> American Founding Father,
> 2nd U.S. president 1797–1801

Our Founding Fathers understood that America's experiment in freedom required a population that lived within certain clear moral boundaries; they understood that this could only be done over the long term by a religious people.

In their view, the government's role was to support and encourage religious belief in the population. Thus, in 1787, they passed the Northwest Ordinance that, in addition to protecting the free exercise of religion in the colonies, also encouraged schools and education because "Religion, morality, and knowledge [are] necessary to good government and the happiness of mankind...."[43]

From the outset, liberty in America included the responsibility of behaving morally in accordance with Judeo-Christian ethical principles and values, now embedded in our American Rule of Law.

If atheist countries "worked," the two atheist communist countries that abolished religion—Russia (as part of the Communist Soviet Union) and Communist China—would not now be trying to bring religion back. The Russian Orthodox Church is enjoying a resurgence in the new Russian Federation.[44] The Chinese Communist government has reinstituted teaching Confucianism in China.[45] Although Confucianism is not a religion, it is a clear code of moral conduct. China now even permits some Christian religious practice, provided it is under their strict government control.

A Covenant with God

The Mayflower Compact of 1620 begins "In the name of God, amen," saying that the settlers had undertaken to establish the first Virginia colony, "for the Glory of God, and *Advancement of the Christian faith.*" They *covenanted with* God to follow the laws passed from time to time with their consent. Because Americans have had such a fierce reverence for following the law, for most of our history we have been able to resolve our disputes peacefully.

Our Rights Come from God

The Declaration of Independence refers to God, not once, not twice, but four times: "*the laws of Nature and Nature's God*" when explaining our right to dissolve our bonds with the British; our inalienable rights to life, liberty, and the pursuit of happiness are "*endowed by [our] Creator*"; an appeal is made to "*the Supreme Judge of the world* for the rectitude of our intentions"; and ending with a mutual pledge "in firm reliance *on the protection of Divine Providence.*"

God in Our Songs

American patriotic songs are filled with references to God:

- *The Spar-Spangled Banner*, the American national anthem: "Praise the Power that hath made and preserved us a nation... And this be our motto: "In *God* is our trust."

- *The Battle Hymn of the Republic*, the Northern states' anthem during the U.S. Civil War in the 1860s: "Mine eyes have seen the coming of the glory of the *Lord*," and "In the beauty of the lilies *Christ* was born across the sea," and "*God* is marching on."

- *America*: "with Freedom's *holy light,* Protect us by *thy might Great God, our King."*

- *America the Beautiful*: "America, America, *God shed His grace* on thee."

State References to God

The U.S. Constitution did not mention God, but that's not surprising. The U.S. Constitution envisioned a federal government with *limited* power to do only certain enumerated things. Since most of the authority and powers remained with the states and the people, references to Christianity are found in the states.

The Christian religion was a major influence in the development of American civic institutions of self-government in the original 13 colonies.[46] The Virginia Charter of 1606 was granted by the English King *"to propagate the Christian religion."*

Within the 13 colonies (later states), governments could use state tax dollars to support churches, and some did (e.g., Massachusetts and Connecticut).

Article 22 of the 1776 Delaware Constitution read:

> Every person who shall be chosen a member of either house, or appointed to any office or place of trust, before taking his seat, or entering upon the execution of his office, shall take the following oath [and declare]......: I, [_____] do profess faith in God the Father, and in Jesus Christ His only Son, and in the Holy Ghost, one God, blessed for evermore; and I do acknowledge the holy scriptures of the Old and New Testament to be given by divine inspiration. [47]

A Pennsylvania Act in 1705-06 "required that to serve as a civil magistrate, a person had to 'also *profess to believe in Jesus Christ, the savior of the world.'* "[48] There was a similar required Christian declaration for legislators under the Pennsylvania Constitution (1776).[49] Other state constitutions required their legislators to be Protestant, such as New Jersey (1776), Georgia (1777), New Hampshire (1784), and North Carolina (1776–1876).[50]

American state constitutions also acknowledge our religious heritage. They include repeated references to God, mostly in their preambles, such as "grateful to *Almighty God*," or "grateful to the *Supreme Being*," or referring to *"the Sovereign Ruler of the Universe"* or *"Our Creator."*[51]

More References to God

The official motto of the United States is "In God We Trust." Members of Congress take an oath to "support and defend the Constitution of the United States against all enemies, foreign and domestic" that ends with *"so help me God."* George Washington began the tradition of adding "so help me God" at the end of the president's oath of office (and kissed the Bible).[52] Succeeding U.S. presidents have also added "so help me God."

America's first president, George Washington, in his first inaugural address, referred to "that Almighty Being, who rules over the universe... that His benediction may consecrate to the liberties and happiness of the people of the United States a Government instituted by themselves..." and he said that "[n]o people can be bound to acknowledge and adore the Invisible Hand which conducts the affairs of men more than those of the United States...."[53]

> *That wise Men have in all Ages thought Government Necessary for the Good of Mankind; and, that wise Governments have always thought Religion necessary for the well ordering and well-being of Society, and accordingly have been ever careful to encourage and protect the Ministers of it, paying them the highest publick Honours, that their Doctrines might thereby meet with the greater Respect among the common People.*
>
> **– Benjamin Franklin (1706–1790)**
> American Founding Father

Since 1789, paid chaplains have opened sessions of the U.S. Congress with a prayer. Our dollar bills and coins say "In *God* We Trust," the official motto of the United States. Christian inscriptions can often be found on our public buildings: "*The New Testament according to the Lord and Savior Jesus Christ*" is on the walls of the Capitol Dome.[54] Inscribed on Thomas Jefferson's memorial is:

> God who gave us life gave us liberty. Can the liberties of a nation be secure when we have removed a conviction that these liberties are the gift of God? Indeed I tremble for my country when I reflect that God is just, that his justice cannot sleep forever.[55]

Americans are more religious than Europeans because they have never had a national religion imposed on them by the federal government. Nevertheless, our Founding Fathers believed that the government does have an important role in fostering a religious sensibility in the American people.

It is a delicate dance to maintain balance: "just enough" government support to foster a religious people (a "bottom-up" self-organizing approach) and not "too much" government interference into religious matters that is destructive (a "top-down" dictatorial approach).

> *I have lived, Sir, a long time, and the longer I live, the more convincing proofs I see of this truth—that God governs in the affairs of men. And if a sparrow cannot fall to the Ground without his Notice, is it probable that an Empire can rise without his Aid?*
>
> **– Benjamin Franklin (1706–1790)**
> American Founding Father

No Atheists in Foxholes

Our last generational crisis of survival, World War II, ended in 1945. Beginning in 1947, and picking up speed in the 1960s and ensuing decades, American courts began to restrict Christian and religious expression in many of our institutions. For example, nondenominational prayer was not permitted in public schools.[56] This post–World War II secular trend was in contrast to the long-standing acceptance of Christian principles as the foundation of the country's culture and institutions since its founding in the 1600s.[57]

As they say, "there are no atheists in foxholes."[58] In a time of uncertainty and crisis, Americans have relied upon their belief in God to help weather tough times that have sometimes felt like "the fires of hell." Through the words of our three crisis American presidents, it is obvious religious belief runs deep in American history, society, culture, and institutions—especially in a time of extreme crisis.

George Washington

George Washington made history by voluntarily relinquishing power at the end of his second term as president. In his Farewell Address in 1796, Washington warned that:

> Of all the dispositions and habits which lead to political prosperity, religion and morality are indispensable supports.... And let us with caution indulge the supposition, that morality can be maintained without religion. Whatever may be conceded to the influence of refined education on minds of peculiar structure—reason and experience both forbid us to expect that national morality can prevail in exclusion of moral principle....[59]

Abraham Lincoln

During the American Civil War in 1863, President Lincoln issued a Proclamation for a day of national prayer and humiliation to "confess our national sins, and to pray for clemency and forgiveness" stating:

> ...whereas it is the duty of nations as well as of men, to own their dependence upon the overruling power of God, ...[a]nd insomuch as we know that, by His divine law, nations like individuals are subjected to punishments... like this civil war because although we have grown in wealth and power, as no other nation has ever grown...we have forgotten God. We have forgotten the gracious hand which preserved us in peace, ...and we have vainly imagined, ...that all these blessings were produced by some superior wisdom and virtue of our own. Intoxicated with unbroken success, we have become too self-sufficient to feel the necessity of redeeming and preserving grace, too proud to pray to the God that made us![60]

Franklin D. Roosevelt

On June 6, 1944, as the Allied forces were crossing the channel in the Normandy invasion to defeat Hitler's Nazi Germany, President Roosevelt led the country in prayer:

> Almighty God: Our sons...this day have set upon a mighty endeavor, a struggle to preserve our Republic, our religion, and our civilization, and set free a suffering humanity... [t]hey fight not for the lust of conquest. They fight to end conquest. They fight to liberate. They fight to let justice arise, and tolerance and good will among all Thy people... Some will never return. Embrace these, Father, and receive them, Thy heroic servants, into Thy Kingdom...help us, Almighty God, to rededicate ourselves in renewed faith in Thee in this hour of great sacrifice.[61]

An Outsider's Perspective

Alexis de Tocqueville, the French aristocrat bystander who traveled across America in the early 1800s, explained the role of religion in the United States as follows:

> Religion in America...must be regarded as the foremost of the political institutions of that country ... [because]... the whole nation and ...every rank of society [holds] it to be indispensable to the maintenance of republican institutions....[62]

> *I sought for the key to the greatness and genius of America in her harbors...; in her fertile fields and boundless forests; in her rich mines and vast world commerce; in her public school system and institutions of learning. I sought it in her democratic Congress and in her matchless Constitution... Not until I went into the churches of America and heard her pulpits flame with righteousness did I understand the secret of her genius and power. America is great because America is good, and if America ever ceases to be good, America will cease to be great.[63]*
>
> **– Alexis de Tocqueville (1805–1859)**
> Author, *Democracy in America* (1835, 1840)

De Tocqueville described the important influence of the Christian religion in the United States with these words:

> Moreover, all the sects in the United States belong to the great unity of Christendom, and Christian morality is everywhere the same....Besides, in the United States the sovereign authority is religious....America is still the place where the Christian religion has kept the greatest real power over men's souls; and nothing better demonstrates how useful and natural it is to man, since the country where it now has the widest sway is both the most enlightened and the freest....[64]

Law with an American Accent

Two characteristics of *ethics-based* American Rule of Law deserve special mention: the *"just kidding" clause* and *"wrath of God" enforcement.* Of course, these are not real American legal theories—just tongue-in-cheek descriptions highlighting how flexible American law can be, even while remaining *firmly rooted* within the boundaries of our uniquely American constitutional framework.

Thus far, *ethics-based* American Rule of Law has been flexible enough to allow the United States to bend and sway when necessary, like bamboo in the wind, but never break—at least, not yet. This is how Americans have been able to adapt quickly to changed circumstances, especially in an era of crisis.

The "Just Kidding" Clause

The "just kidding" clause is an essential feature of *ethics-based* American Rule of Law that often surfaces in a time of crisis *to restore financial solvency and economic common sense quickly* to our businesses, governments, and other essential institutions and associations.

I was first introduced to this unique feature of American law by my Australian constitutional law professor in 1970. He said that the U.S. Supreme Court was the only court of last resort that can take into account social, political, and economic factors, not just legal precedent, when making its decisions. As a result, American law can, and often does, "change on a dime" to accommodate changed circumstances.

Behavior that is ruled constitutional in the United States can later be ruled unconstitutional when conditions change. In 1896, the "separate but equal" doctrine that made racial segregation possible was ruled constitutional by the U.S. Supreme Court in the *Plessy v. Ferguson* case. However, that same "separate but equal" doctrine was declared unconstitutional in 1954 in the *Brown v. the Board of Education* case.

Those saying "it's unethical, but legal" are playing Russian roulette. "Legal" can fast become "illegal" in the United States when circumstances change, especially in times of financial distress. During the Great Depression, because of economic necessity, the U.S. federal government could no longer pay customers in gold as required by contract. The U.S. Supreme Court said "just kidding" and allowed the federal government to pay in dollars instead of gold.[65]

In recent times, economic necessity has led to painful reductions of promised benefits for retirees of both private and public employers. When the bankruptcy court approved United Airlines' termination of its severely underfunded pension plan in 2005, it was transferred to the federal Pension Benefit Guaranty Corporation (PBGC), also seriously underfunded. An airline pilot's $12,000-a-month pension might be reduced to only $2,000 a month.[66]

Central Falls, Rhode Island, declared bankruptcy when it could not pay the pension and medical benefits for its retired unionized government workers. A federal bankruptcy judge voided the pensions of public employees, including firefighters and police, and ordered retirees to pay 20% of their own medical coverage, effective immediately.[67] "Central Falls slashed one in three of its retirees' pension checks by more than half, ...with the majority of the city's former public-safety workers set to lose tens of thousands of dollars a year...."[68]

Colorado and Minnesota have made cuts in their public workers' pensions for *existing retirees* by reducing their automatic cost-of-living increases. Courts in both states dismissed challenges to those cuts.[69] Even without bankruptcy, when state governments run out of money, they may have no choice but to default. This occurred in Pritchard, Alabama. After several years of nonpayment, the city's retirees received much lower pension benefits.[70]

The U.S. Congressional Budget Office estimates that unfunded liabilities for state and local pensions for unionized government state workers may be between $2 and $3 trillion.[71] Even though state budgets improved by 2013, many of their long-term financial problems are unchanged.[72]

California is likely to be the next battleground over cuts to pensions and medical benefits promised to its government workers. By June 2012, 18,000 California state worker retirees were receiving pensions of more than $100,000 a year.[73] In 2010, California's unfunded liability for its pension, medical, and other benefit promises to its unionized government workers and retirees was estimated to be about $500 billion.[74]

The California cities of Vallejo and Stockton filed for bankruptcy. Police captains in Vallejo were paid about $300,000 a year and firefighters averaged $171,000 a year. Both groups could retire at age 50 with about 90% of their salaries and lifetime medical benefits for the rest of their lives and their spouses' lives.[75] A Stockton, California, police chief, who retired from the city at the age of 52, had an annual pension of more than $204,000. He was "the third of four chiefs who stayed in the position for less than three years and retired with an average of 92% of their final salaries."[76]

The federal bankruptcy court in the Vallejo case said "just kidding"—the city could void the pension and medical benefit agreements with its public worker unions.[77] Thus far, only medical benefits have been cut.[78] CalPERS, California's giant state pension fund, said pension obligations for state workers cannot be voided by bankruptcy under California law.[79]

But when CalPERS tried to force another bankrupt city, San Bernardino, to make its contributions to CalPERS, a federal bankruptcy judge refused to allow the CalPERS lawsuit.[80] This fight has shifted to Stockton, one of the largest cities in American history to declare bankruptcy. In October 2014, a federal bankruptcy judge said "just kidding" again, ruling that Stockton has the power to cut its pension obligations.[81] Moody's Investor Service has warned that Stockton and other bankrupt California cities could face bankruptcy again if they fail to cut their public pension costs.

"Wrath of God" Enforcement

"Wrath of God" enforcement is an essential feature of *ethics-based* American Rule of Law. It is generally used in cases of egregious unethical conduct *to restore trust quickly* in our essential self-organizing institutions and associations.

Under *ethics-based* American Rule of Law, there are many creative ways to constitutionally inflict serious pain against wrongdoers for their wrong (unethical) behavior. "Wrath of God" enforcement under *ethics-based* American Rule of Law can sometimes feel like God's wrath in the biblical story of Sodom and Gomorrah in Genesis. God rained down fire and brimstone, destroying both towns, for the peoples' failure to keep God's laws.

Two of the best recent examples of "Wrath of God" enforcement under ethics-based American Rule of Law (discussed earlier) are Bernie Madoff's 150 years in prison and an order to personally repay $170 billion; and the criminal conviction for obstruction of justice that essentially drove Arthur Andersen, one of the largest accounting firms in the United States, out of business (even though that conviction was subsequently overturned).

Spirit of the Law

It's not just the *letter of the law* that matters in the United States. The *spirit of the law* is important too. U.S. Supreme Court Justice Earl Warren noted: "it is the spirit and not the form of law that keeps justice alive."

When considering the source of the "spirit of the law" in the United States, keep in mind that the U.S. Supreme Court recognized that the United States was a Christian country in 1892 and again in 1931.[82] As late as 1954, the Supreme Court declared that "[w]e are a religious people whose institutions presuppose a Supreme Being."[83]

Court sessions in the U.S. Supreme Court begin with "God save the United States and this honorable court." Moses holding the 10 Commandments is front and center on the eastern portico of the U.S. Supreme Court building in Washington, D.C.

Harmful Consequences

Moving away from our Judeo-Christian heritage under *ethics-based* American Rule of Law has been harmful to millions of Americans and the country.[84] One example is the dramatically higher interest rates charged in recent decades. One bank credit card offered to those with bad credit was charging an interest rate of 79.9%.[85] The annual interest rate per year (APR) on a payday loan can be as high as 650% if loans are not immediately repaid.[86]

Historically, the maximum interest rate banks and credit card companies were allowed to charge customers was restricted by state *usury* laws, based on biblical admonitions against charging an excessive rate of interest (e.g., more than 12%).[87] After the oil embargo in 1973 led to soaring oil prices and interest rates, federal intervention weakened state usury laws. However, once that economic crisis passed, without the enforcement of state usury laws, interest rates on credit cards and other forms of credit have remained high.

High rates of interest mean that heavily indebted Americans will find it difficult (if not impossible) to get out of debt. This will create economic and social tensions that eventually could threaten our political stability and security. History warns us that countries with large gaps between the "haves" and the "have-nots" are not stable for long.

> ...[W]ise Governments have always thought Religion necessary for the well ordering and well-being of Society, and accordingly have been ever careful to encourage and protect the Ministers of it, paying them the highest [Public Honors], that their Doctrines might thereby meet with the greater Respect among the common People.
>
> **– Benjamin Franklin (1706–1790)**
> American Founding Father

More than the Sum of Its Parts

Comparisons have been made between the United States of America and the European Union (EU), which has sometimes been called "the United States of Europe." However, there are many significant differences between American and European experiments in unity.

The EU

The European Union is made up of 25 separate countries (with different national cultures and languages), with 491 million people, that is attempting to create a single integrated economic market under some type of political unity.

The EU's common currency, the Euro, is little more than a decade old. As the current global financial crisis in Europe is demonstrating, it is difficult for the EU to speak with one voice or take immediate common action, making it clear that the European Union still remains less than the sum of its parts.[88]

The United States

The United States was formed a little more than two centuries ago under a shared culture of trust that now binds all 50 state governments to the federal government under the same culture of freedom and *ethics-based* American Rule of Law in a single country. Because of this, the United States of America is more than the sum of its parts. The United States has been operating under the same constitution since 1789 and the U.S. dollar can trace its origins back to 1792.

> *The Bible is the rock on which this Republic rests.*
>
> **– Andrew Jackson (1767–1845)**
> General, Battle of New Orleans, War of 1812
> 7th U.S. president 1829–1837

Over two centuries, the United States has demonstrated that it can react as a single unified nation, with one voice, under a single overarching American culture of freedom and *ethics-based* American Rule of Law. The question we have to ask ourselves today is will we be able to do so again in this new century?

If we cannot, our American experiment in freedom will end up in the dustbin of history—a shining light of freedom that burned brightly for a little over two centuries until like Rome, it self-destructed because of the arrogance, ignorance, and complacency of its citizens.

> *Hold fast to the Bible. To the influence of this Book we are indebted for all the progress made in true civilization and to this we must look as our guide in the future.*
>
> **– Ulysses S. Grant (1822–1885)**
> Commanding general, U.S. Civil War
> 18th U.S. president 1869–1877

U.S. RULE OF LAW AND CULTURE OF TRUST = UNIQUE IN MODERN WORLD HISTORY

- Longest-running enduring constitutional democratic republic in modern world history

- 1620 Mayflower Compact: covenant with God to follow laws passed with the consent of the people

- 1787 – oldest written constitution

- Unicultural and diverse, not multicultural
  - ➢ Declaration of Independence
  - ➢ U.S. Constitution
  - ➢ Bill of Rights

- Distrust of power
  - ➢ Checks and balances
  - ➢ Federalism
  - ➢ Protection of the individual

- Ethics-based American Rule of Law
  - ➢ U.S. Supreme Court "Just Kidding" Clause
  - ➢ "Wrath of God" Enforcement
  - ➢ Spirit of the Law, Not Just Letter of the Law

Chapter 9

Trust Is *Not* Worldwide
National Borders Still Matter

> *Without commonly shared and widely entrenched moral values and obligations, neither the law, nor democratic government, nor even the market economy will function properly.*
>
> **– Václav Havel (1936–2011)**
> President of Czechoslovakia,
> later the Czech Republic

Outsourcing Our Prisons to Turkey

A 1978 movie, *Midnight Express,* catalogued the nightmare experiences of a young American tourist, Billy Hayes, caught smuggling drugs in Turkey. In a trial he didn't understand, Hayes was sentenced to four years in prison and put in a dirty, freezing jail cell. When he took blankets from a nearby open cell to keep warm, the prison guards beat him so severely he was unconscious for days.

Shortly before his scheduled release, a higher Turkish court resentenced him to at least 30 years in prison. Hayes realized he would only be free again if he took the "midnight express," a prison term for escape. After years of terrible abuse, he finally did.

Whether or not this movie accurately depicts Turkish justice and prisons, it highlights a key point often forgotten in today's "globalized" world. *Concepts of justice and Rule of Law, if they exist at all, are dramatically different in different countries. National borders still matter—a lot.*

Ask yourself a question: why don't we outsource our prisons to Turkey? The answer is: we can't. American citizens are guaranteed certain specific and enforceable rights under the Bill of Rights in the U.S. Constitution, especially when it comes to the criminal justice system.[1] As nonsensical as that question may sound, it illustrates some key facts often overlooked by *politically thinking* "experts."

- There is no one world government that protects the same rights and freedoms for all the people in the world and to which all of the world's people owe their allegiance (*global citizenship*).

- There is no universally accepted uniform standard of ethical conduct that applies and is enforced equally in all countries (*global ethics*).

- There is no global court with the power to enforce the same standards of ethical conduct under universally accepted and uniform legal and ethical principles and procedures that are applied and enforced equally in all countries (*global Rule of Law*).

In sum, there is no such thing as "global citizenship," "global ethics," or "global Rule of Law."

Joined at the Hip

Countries are more interdependent today than ever before. Americans buy Chinese goods. China buys U.S. treasuries, subsidizing America's national debt. Any downturn in the American economy would be felt in Germany and Mexico. German companies sell parts to Chinese companies that depend on sales in the United States; 80% of Mexico's exports go to the United States.

When fires and drought in Russia in 2010 prevented wheat exports, local food prices soared in other countries. Deadly infectious diseases like bird flu, ebola, and drug-resistant tuberculosis do not respect national borders. A global flu pandemic in 1918–1919 killed approximately 50 million people worldwide.[2] With today's advanced transportation systems daily shuttling millions of people around the world, the death toll in another global pandemic could be much higher.

Key elements of the global financial system are now so intertwined, a financial crisis in one country would be felt in many other countries. Trillions of dollars of credit derivatives and asset-backed bonds have been bought and sold around the world.

When American taxpayers paid $100 billion to bail out American International Group (AIG), $58 billion went to banks headquartered outside the United States (including $36 billion to French and German banks).[3] If Greece defaults on its national debt, German, French, and British banks that loaned Greece billions of euros will be hurt.

Advances in technology have enabled criminal cartels and terrorists to operate across national borders. In 2010, more than 100 people were arrested in the United States for using computer viruses to steal millions of dollars from American and British bank accounts.[4] A nuclear weapon can be transported in something as small as a suitcase.

Although in many ways countries are joined at the hip like conjoined twins, that doesn't mean we are all operating under the same ethical and legal standards, implemented in the same way. We are not.

The Dis-United Nations

Some "smart" people in the West have been repeating the United Nations' "human rights" mantra, as though there is one universal code of right and wrong behavior enforced in countries throughout the world. There isn't.

Besides, Americans do not have wishy-washy, often unenforced "human rights" listed in the 1948 United Nations' Charter of Human Rights. Americans have *specific, clear, enforceable rights* under our Declaration of Independence

(1776), the U.S. Constitution, and the Bill of Rights that dates back to 1791. American constitutional rights are *enforceable* in the United States under centuries-old *ethics-based* American Rule of Law by an effective independent judiciary—at least, so far.

Talking about vague United Nations' *"human rights"* as though they applied in the United States is yet *another example of political thinking, not critical thinking.*

No Accountability

After the destruction and devastation of World War II, 51 countries formed the United Nations (UN) with the lofty goals of maintaining international peace and security, raising living standards, and promoting "human rights."[5]

Today the UN has 192 member countries. However, the UN is still only a voluntary, loose association of separate and distinct independent countries with *very different* moral, ethical, and legal standards within their own borders.

Even if a member UN country kills or tortures its own people, it still has the same one vote on the UN's Human Rights Council that free UN member countries (that respect their citizens' rights and freedoms) have. The United States pays about 22% of the UN's rapidly escalating annual budget, which more than doubled "from $2.6 billion in 2001–2002 to $5.4 billion in 2010–2011."[6]

United Nations officials are not answerable to the citizens of UN member nations. UN officials are rarely held accountable, even for corruption or gross mismanagement of funds. Prison sentences are even rarer. A good example of this lack of accountability is the UN's Oil-for-Food scandal.

The UN's Oil-for-Food Scandal

The UN Security Council imposed economic sanctions on Iraq after Iraqi President Saddam Hussein invaded Kuwait in 1990. Later, to allegedly alleviate the suffering of the Iraqi people, the UN allowed Iraq to sell oil to buy food, medicines, and other humanitarian goods.

When Hussein was removed from power, the UN's gross mismanagement of this program came to light. Instead of supervision, the UN had given Hussein unfettered control over who could buy Iraq's oil and who was allowed to sell Iraq humanitarian goods. Hussein was able to personally siphon off $1.8 billion in bribes and kickbacks from thousands of firms participating in this program.[7]

Questions were raised about whether UN executives, UN administrators, and perhaps even high-ranking politicians in member UN countries had personally profited from Hussein's abuse of this program.[8]

In 2005, a UN committee headed by Paul Volcker (former chair of the U.S. Federal Reserve) issued a report detailing gross misconduct in the UN's Oil-for-Food program. Most UN member countries ignored the report (e.g., Russia, China, Cyprus, Yemen, Egypt, Vietnam, Malaysia, and the United Arab Emirates). Almost all of the successful prosecutions or civil enforcement actions against those involved in this scandal took place only in the United States.[9] *Accountability at the UN remains an elusive goal.*

Limited Effectiveness

The existence of the UN did not prevent more than 4 million people dying in the Congo because of disease and constant war. Even though the UN has spent billions of dollars and sent 18,000 UN peacekeeping troops to protect Congo civilians, UN troop presence failed to prevent 150 people from being massacred in 2008 near a UN base or prevent hundreds of women from being gang-raped in 2010.[10] As the president of an international crisis organization noted: the UN has "had strikingly little success at fulfilling its primary objective to protect civilians."[11]

The Myth of Global Citizenship

Although countries today are interconnected in many ways, that does not mean we are all now citizens of a one-world government. We are not. No single global government, association, or entity can, or does, protect and enforce the same rights, privileges, and freedoms equally for all people around the world.

Americans are *not* citizens of any global government. We are citizens of the United States of America. *The American government* is obligated to protect the rights and freedoms of all American citizens as defined in our Declaration of Independence, the U.S. Constitution, and the Bill of Rights.

These *clear* and *specific constitutional American rights* are *enforced* by effective independent American courts. In exchange for the U.S. government's protection of *these clear and specific American rights*, American citizens owe their allegiance to the United States of America *and to no other country* or global entity claiming supreme authority.

Read the oath on the following page carefully. Does this sound like dual citizenship is acceptable under *ethics-based* American Rule of Law—*especially in a time of war?*

Many countries have constitutions that mimic the language of the U.S. Constitution, but that does not mean their citizens have the same American freedoms and rights granted under the U.S. Constitution. They do not.

For example, Article 35 of the Chinese constitution reads a lot like our American first amendment rights under our Bill of Rights—freedom of speech, assembly, association, and freedom of the press.[12] But American constitutional rights protect *individual* Americans from the abusive power of the U.S. federal government. Article 35 constitutional "rights" in China do not.

Chinese courts have interpreted Article 35 "rights" as being subordinate to China's "national interests." These "national interests" are often *dictated to the courts* by directives of the Chinese Communist central government.[13] Unlike our American constitutional rights, Chinese Article 35 "rights" do not protect individual Chinese citizens from the abusive power of the central Chinese Communist government. This is why in 2011, Freedom House ranked the United States as "free," and China as "not free."[14]

A citizen's rights, privileges, and freedoms, *if they exist at all*, are still country specific. They can still only be determined *on an individual country-by-country basis.*

"I hereby declare, on oath:

- that I absolutely and entirely renounce and abjure all allegiance and fidelity to any foreign prince, potentate, state or sovereignty, of whom or which I have heretofore been a subject or citizen;

- that I will support and defend the Constitution and laws of the United States of America against all enemies, foreign and domestic;

- that I will bear true faith and allegiance to the same;

- that I will bear arms on behalf of the United States when required by the law;

- that I will perform noncombatant service in the armed forces of the United States when required by the law;

- that I will perform work of national importance under civilian direction when required by the law; and

- that I take this obligation freely without any mental reservation or purpose of evasion; so help me God." [15]

The Myth of Global Ethics

No Universal "Human Rights" Standards

The United Nations' *Universal Declaration of Human Rights* was adopted in 1948. It uses words like "the inherent dignity" and "equal and inalienable rights" of all members of the "human family" on which "the foundation of freedom, justice and peace in the world" depend.

In fact, some UN "human rights" sound like American rights: the right to life and liberty, equality and equal protection before the law, no cruel and unusual punishment, no arbitrary arrests, a presumption of innocence in a public criminal trial and freedom of thought, conscience, and religion, and freedom of assembly and association. However, as a practical matter, the UN's Human Rights and the United States' Bill of Rights have almost nothing in common. For example, the latest "human right" granted by the UN is the "right" to have access to the Internet.[16]

For citizens in many UN countries, the UN's Universal Declaration of Human Rights is only an empty symbolic gesture, not a practical reality. Eight out of ten of the worst dictatorships in the world that regularly abuse their own citizens' "human rights" are UN members.[17]

The sobering reality is that UN member countries can pick and choose which, if any, of these "human rights" they will grant their citizens, and even if they do, that does not mean these "rights" are enforced.[18] Many UN countries do not have freely elected governments, let alone the necessary independent judiciary and centuries of effective Rule of Law, to effectively enforce such citizens' "rights."

For example, although Article 16(2) of the UN's Declaration clearly states that "[m]arriage shall be entered into only with the free and full consent of the intending spouses," individuals in many UN member countries are still stoned to death for choosing their own spouses.[19] There are no consequences for UN members that "disobey" the UN's Universal Declaration of Human Rights.

In contrast, our *specific, well-defined, entrenched, and deliberately hard to change American rights* under the Declaration of Independence, the U.S. Constitution, and the Bill of Rights can and are *enforced* by effective independent American courts—*at least so far*.

China, a permanent member of the UN Security Council, sentenced "human rights" activist, Liu Xiaobo, to 11 years in prison. His "crime" was promoting free elections and freedom of assembly in China—activities listed as "human rights" by the United Nations.

When Liu was awarded the 2010 Nobel Peace Prize, China organized a boycott of the award ceremony in Norway. Eighteen countries (China, Russia, Kazakhstan, Colombia, Tunisia, Saudi Arabia, Pakistan, Iraq, Iran, Vietnam, Afghanistan, Venezuela, Argentina, Algeria, Egypt, Sudan, Cuba, Morocco, and the Philippines) refused to attend. Does this sound like all member UN countries operate under and enforce UN "human rights"? Obviously not.

> *The moment we engage in confederations, or alliances with any nation, we may from that time date the downfall of our republic.*
>
> **– Andrew Jackson (1767–1845)**
> General, Battle of New Orleans, War of 1812
> 7th U.S. president 1829–1837

No Common Definition of Global Ethics

Individuals and organizations use the term "global ethics" as though there is widespread agreement on what it means. There isn't.

In fact, there are so many different and conflicting definitions of global ethics, using this term only adds to our ethical confusion. The term "global ethics" does not provide clear guidance on what "right" behavior is.

One ethics "expert" has defined "global ethics" by enumerating specific wrong behaviors: e.g., taking bribes, lying about a firm's financial condition, selling harmful products, outsourcing jobs to low-wage countries, and operating in countries that violate "human rights."[20]

Another ethics "expert" defines "global ethics" in terms of four levels of social responsibility on a pyramid. At the bottom rung of the pyramid is *economic responsibility* (a firm must be profitable); the next level up is *legal responsibility* (a firm must obey the law); the next rung up is *ethical responsibility* (a firm must be ethical); and at the top of the pyramid is *philanthropic responsibility* (a firm must be a good global corporate citizen).[21]

Some define "global ethics" in terms of *universal human values,* but there is no agreement on what values are included in that definition. The Institute for Global Ethics includes *honesty, responsibility, respect, fairness,* and *compassion* in defining universal human values.[22] However, in a speech given by a retiring chairman of a Chinese state-owned bank, universal human values included *freedom, democracy, and "human rights."*[23]

Talking about "global ethics," "universal human values," and "human rights" does not provide clear universal guidance as to what behaviors are "right" (ethical). In fact, it does just the opposite. It creates ethical confusion.

The Myth of Global Rule of Law

The Ethics World Is Not Flat

In his 2006 book *The World Is Flat,* Thomas Friedman argued "the world is flat" because countries in the modern global economy compete directly with one another on the price of goods and services. In an era of global peace, prosperity, stability, and security, it was easy to believe that the only thing that mattered in global competition was the price and quality of goods and services.

However, in the rush to think "globally," an all-important reality has been ignored. Although we may have global communications, global travel, and global capital markets, when it comes to morality, ethics, a culture of trust, and *effective* Rule of Law, *the world is definitely not flat.*

In 2000, a well-respected Peruvian economist, Hernando de Soto, wrote a book called *The Mystery of Capital.* He sought to find out why capitalism has succeeded only in the West (e.g., United States, Western Europe, and Japan) and failed everywhere else.

He pointed out that people in non-Western countries work just as hard, if not harder, than people in the West, and often save more money than their Western counterparts, too. In spite of this, people in non-Western countries have not been able to turn their savings into capital that grows wealth.

De Soto concluded that this was because non-Western countries are *missing the essential ingredient for producing wealth* in a free-market (capitalist) economy—*effective Rule of Law.*[24] As de Soto noted, to be able to borrow money to buy property, goods, and services, countries *must have* an established system of *clear title to property and effective contract law.*

De Soto said that although non-Western countries have been trying to copy the laws of Western countries since the 19th century, they have not been successful. *Creating and maintaining effective Rule of Law that is actually trusted, both inside and outside a country, is extremely difficult to do.*

Rule of Law in countries with Westernized legal systems is far superior to Rule of Law, if it exists at all, in non-Westernized countries. According to the World Justice Project's 2010 Rule of Law Index, the United States, Canada, Japan (and now Singapore and South Korea) scored significantly higher than all other countries on its *10 criteria for effective Rule of Law*:

> limited government powers; absence of corruption; clear, publicized and stable laws; order and security; fundamental rights; open government; regulatory enforcement; access to civil justice; effective criminal justice; and informal justice[25]

In many countries, rampant corruption and unfair or under-developed legal systems prevent individuals and other investors from profiting from their investments.[26]

Foreign investment in emerging markets exploded from about $20 billion in the early 1990s to about $164 billion by the turn of the 21st century.[27] Stock exchanges are now found in Shanghai, Moscow, and Bombay, not just New York, London, Frankfurt, and Tokyo.

However, many investors have given little thought about whether countries have the necessary Rule of Law to keep and maintain trust in their "freer" market economies and stock exchanges over the long term, especially in a major crisis. Many do not.

Effective Rule of Law and a *culture of trust* are required to create and maintain the successful, stable, peaceful, and secure societies, economies, and political systems that foreign and local investors and consumers can, and will, trust over the long term.

The UN International Criminal Court (ICC)

The UN established a permanent international criminal court in Holland in 2002 to prosecute individuals who commit genocide, war crimes, and "crimes against humanity" from countries without effective national courts. Its first conviction wasn't until 2012. Liberia's former president, Charles Taylor, was convicted of killing, raping, and torturing more than 50,000 people during a civil war in Sierra Leone from 1991–2001. He was sentenced to 50 years in prison.

Although more than 100 countries have ratified the treaty establishing the ICC, several key countries, like the United States, China, Russia, and India, have not. Subjecting U.S. citizens to foreign criminal jurisdiction like the ICC would violate specific constitutional protections in criminal cases guaranteed Americans in the Bill of Rights.[28] Also, countries are justifiably concerned that their citizens could be subjected to politically motivated "show trials" at the ICC.

The ICC has sometimes done more harm than good. After atrocities were reported in Darfur, Sudan, in the long-standing conflict between the Arab Muslim dominated government and Christian (or animist) African rebels (that has already killed hundreds of thousands), the ICC indicted Sudan's president, Omar Hassan al-Bashir, for rape, murder, and torture, and issued a warrant for his arrest.

The Sudanese government responded by kicking out foreign aid workers who had been providing food, water, and medicine for the millions of people displaced by the fighting. Chad and Kenya, both UN member countries that have ratified the ICC treaty, refused to enforce the ICC's arrest warrant when al-Bashir visited their countries.[29]

Effective Rule of Law is still only country specific.

National Borders Still Matter

All Cultures Are *Not* Alike

Today, surface similarities in countries mask deep cultural differences. Culture is the accumulated wisdom of a country, including how a country's government, economy, and society are structured and operate. It includes the beliefs and attitudes of people that make them distinctive from people in other countries.[30]

A country's culture is a product of its own unique history, experiences, religious heritage, and beliefs and attitudes acquired over a substantial period of time. Culture determines which countries are rich and stable, while others remain poor and unstable.[31]

In today's era of global communications and global investment, trade, and transportation, it is easy to forget how vastly different cultures in different countries still are. *Cultural standards of right and wrong behavior (ethics) differ markedly in different countries. Different cultures produce very different countries and very different results.*

Different religious heritages have created wildly different economies, societies, political and legal systems, and nations. British, Western European, Canadian, Australian, and American societies based on Judeo-Christian principles favor freedom and democracy. On the other hand, many of the world's Islam-dominated countries are either "not free at all" or only "partially free."[32]

Here are a few more examples highlighting how deep-seated cultural differences in countries still are:

- *Middle East:* A Saudi Arabian woman who was gang-raped was sentenced to 200 lashes in 2007. Her sentence was "reduced" on appeal to *only* 90 lashes and 6 months in prison.[33] In Afghanistan in 2009, the husband of a beautiful 18-year-old woman was given permission to cut off her ears and nose after she ran away from home to escape being beaten.[34]

- *India:* Honor killings still occur in India, especially when an educated woman tries to choose a husband outside of her family's caste. For choosing their spouse, a young couple was tortured and beaten to death by the girl's family.[35]

- *China:* Applicants for state jobs must produce their official state file with proof of their grades, test results, and college degrees. Corrupt local officials sold the files of some college graduates from poor families to other applicants who were seeking state jobs. Without their files, these graduates from poor families can only get menial jobs. This leaves their parents, who went heavily into debt to pay for their education, unable to repay their loans.[36]

- *Africa:* In many African countries, homosexuality is a crime.[37] In some African countries, when a parent dies of unknown causes, the family accuses the children of witchcraft. The children are beaten until they confess, then abandoned to live on the streets.[38] President Jacob Zuma of South Africa has 6 wives and 21 children by at least 10 different women.[39]

- *Europe:* Different cultures in European countries have produced profoundly different economic results. Greece, Portugal, Italy, Ireland, and Spain have government debt levels far exceeding that of other EU countries, like Germany. Tax evasion is common practice in Greece, estimated to cost the Greek government $30 billion a year in lost taxes.[40]

- *Islamic Countries:* Finance in Judeo-Christian countries based on the Bible is very different from finance in Islamic countries based on the Koran. The Koran forbids interest payments of any kind. Islamic financing only involves sharing profits and losses, not paying interest on the borrowed money. In countries that follow Judeo-Christian principles *as they are supposed to be implemented*, interest can be charged, so long as it is not excessive (usurious).

Rule of Law Is *Not* the Same

Even in Western countries, Rule of Law is not the same. Although Americans and Europeans both value privacy, because of Europe's terrible experiences with Nazi Germany's secret police during World War II, European privacy laws are much stricter.

Investors have painfully discovered that getting your investment money out of a country when something goes wrong is not always easy. During the boom years, investors lined up to buy apartments in the world's tallest building in Dubai. They paid as much as 80% of the purchase price as a down payment. When the real estate market crashed, work on the building stopped. However, not only were investors not able to get their money out, they were still being charged for their construction loans.[41]

Japan has a European-styled statute-based *civil law* legal system. Remarkably, Japanese prosecutors have a 99% conviction rate in criminal trials, almost always based on confessions. Criminal suspects in Japan can be questioned for 23 days *at a time,* without an attorney present, before they are charged or released.[42] Suspects are often held in cramped holding cells. They are not allowed contact with the outside world. Sometimes they are not given adequate food or breaks.

Mexico also has a European-styled statute-based *civil law* legal system. Trial proceedings in Mexico have generally been held behind closed doors, not in an open public court. This created a culture of bribes and corruption in the police force and legal system. Mexican drug cartel members have often been arrested, but are rarely prosecuted. In 2008, Mexico's Congress passed a law making public trials mandatory nationwide by 2016.[43]

India has a British-based judge-made *common law* legal system, but is plagued by terrible backlogs. In 1997, there were 20 million backlogged civil and criminal cases; by 2006, 30 million. Resolving a dispute over terminating an employee may take 20 years.[44] In 2007, the World Bank ranked India 173 out of 175 countries on contract enforcement effectiveness.[45] One Indian collection agency hired by one of India's largest banks to collect an unpaid debt beat a college student so badly he spent 10 days in the hospital.[46]

Different Freedom, No Freedom

"Free" Speech?

According to *Time* magazine "[f]ree-speech protections in the U.S. are stronger than in any other place on earth at perhaps any time in history...."[47] American protections of freedom of speech have been enshrined in the Bill of Rights of the

U.S. Constitution for more than 200 years. Because of our free speech and free press protections, it is much easier to report ethics scandals in the United States than in other countries.

Western Countries: Free speech in other British-based *common law* legal systems is not the same as American free speech. Without the same American Bill of Rights free speech constitutional protections, it is much easier to sue individuals and companies for *defamation* in other British-based common law countries.

Companies often stifle public criticism by filing defamation claims in British courts, a hotspot for "libel tourism." For example, an Israeli company making lie detectors threatened to sue a Swedish professor in a British court after the professor wrote an article questioning whether lie detectors work.[48] The publisher withdrew the article.

The Australian High Court ruled *Barron's* magazine, an American-based Dow Jones news organization, could be sued in Australia for defamation for statements made about an Australian businessman on a New Jersey web server that was available only to subscribers.[49] Dow Jones paid $440,000 to settle the lawsuit.

Some American states (e.g., New York, Illinois, California, and Florida) have passed libel tourism laws to prevent enforcement of such foreign defamation judgments within their jurisdictions.[50] Other American states are considering similar measures.

Europeans can suppress speech through *national "speech codes"* in ways not possible in the United States. For example, in Croatia, it is a crime to spread racism and xenophobia. A Canadian newspaper ad listing Biblical passages opposing homosexuality was called a "human rights" offense and prevented from being published by the Saskatchewan Human Rights Commission.[51]

Similar types of speech codes on American college campuses were repeatedly struck down in American courts as contrary to our constitutional free speech protections under the 1st Amendment of the Bill of Rights.[52]

Non-Western Countries: Protesting university students can be kicked out of the university and are sometimes sent to prison. A young Iranian-Canadian blogger in Iran was sentenced to 19 years in prison for "cooperating with hostile governments" and "setting up websites deemed to be 'vulgar and obscene.'"[53]

Chinese government authorities routinely censor the Internet to prevent "inappropriate content" from entering the country. Graduates of top Chinese universities have been given long prison sentences (e.g., 8 years) for discussing democracy, government corruption, and rural poverty.[54] The father of a Chinese boy poisoned by milk laced with melamine was sentenced to 2½ years in prison in China for creating a website to warn other parents of the danger.[55]

"Free" Press?

Most Americans do not know how uncommon free press protections are in much of the world.[56] *The New York Times* was required to publicly apologize and pay a settlement to Singaporean leaders for an editorial it published in Singapore saying there was "dynastic politics" in Singapore's leadership.[57] Venezuela's President Hugo Chavez shut down radio and TV stations that criticized him.[58]

Physical Violence and Death: Sixty-six journalists were killed around the world in 2011 alone.[59] In 2014, 52 journalists were killed. Because of powerful drug cartels, Mexico is one of the most dangerous countries for journalists today. At least 80 journalists have been killed in Mexico since 2000. These killings are rarely investigated or prosecuted.[60]

A Russian journalist investigating "human rights" abuses by Russian soldiers was shot and killed in the elevator of her apartment building. She was the fifth journalist from the same Russian newspaper killed in 10 years.[61] An outspoken Russian newspaper editor was beaten so severely in front of his home, he "suffered brain damage that left him unable to talk. Three of his fingers and a leg had to be amputated."[62] An American journalist for *Forbes* magazine in Moscow was gunned down on a Moscow street in 2004.

Prison: More than 70 journalists were imprisoned in Iran after mass protests over the presidential election in 2009.[63] Prison sentences for editors and journalists in China ranged from 8 years to life for such things as sending the Chinese government's instructions on what to say about the Tiananmen Square massacre to a foreign website; reporting on land disputes or the SARS epidemic; or writing a letter about official misconduct to a Chinese newspaper.[64]

"Freedom" of Religion?

Freedom of religion is listed as a "human right" in the United Nations' Universal Declaration of Human Rights. A 2009 report said that nearly 70% of the world's 6.8 billion people still do not have the freedom to practice their religion as they choose.[65]

China: According to the Chinese constitution, freedom of religion is respected in China. In reality, religion is permitted only when it is controlled by the Chinese Communist government. About 30 million Christians in China must worship through state-run churches. Catholic bishops in China are chosen by the Chinese Communist party, not the Pope. Illegally printing and distributing thousands of Bibles led to a three-year prison sentence.[66] Thousands of members of the spiritual group Falun Gong have been given long prison sentences or died in police custody.[67]

Islamic Countries: Blasphemy charges in some Muslim countries are used to stifle comment and debate about Islam. A student journalist in Afghanistan was sentenced to death (later "reduced" to 20 years) for downloading an Internet article on women's rights that didn't agree with Islam's view of the role of women.

After Muslims attacked Christians in Egypt, an Egyptian law student wrote on an Internet blog that Muslims appeared to the world to be "full of brutality, barbarism and inhumanity"; he was sentenced to four years in prison.[68]

A Christian mother of five was given the death penalty in Pakistan for blasphemy against the Prophet Mohammed.[69] In Iran, 300,000 followers of the Baha'i faith are not allowed to hold a government job, attend university, or practice their religion. Seven leaders were imprisoned on espionage charges, which could lead to execution.[70]

Some Islamic countries have a religious police force, in addition to their regular police force, to enforce Islamic religious practices (e.g., closing stores five times a day for prayers, separation of men and women, and modest dressing). In some Islamic countries, conversion from Islam to another religion (apostasy) can lead to execution.[71]

Attempts to Limit Free Speech in Western Countries: A Dutch filmmaker, Theo van Gogh, was murdered in Amsterdam, Holland, for making a film about violence against women in Islamic societies. When a Danish cartoon depicted Mohammed as a terrorist, Syrians set the Norwegian and Danish embassies in Damascus on fire. A Danish cartoonist who drew cartoons of Mohammed only escaped an attempted assassination at his home by hiding in a "panic room" in his house.[72]

"Freedom" of Assembly?

Freedom House, an independent watchdog organization, reported that freedom of association declined from 2004 to 2007. Forty-three countries (more than 20% of the world's total) had lower scores for freedom of association, especially in such authoritarian regimes as Russia, Zimbabwe, Venezuela, and Iran.[73]

In China, two men who led protests of thousands of laid-off workers over unpaid wages by a bankrupt Chinese manufacturing company were sentenced to 7- and 4-year prison terms.[74] Russians have the right of free assembly under their constitution, but protestors must get government permission first.[75] In Moscow, gay and lesbian protestors are regularly denied permission to protest, while ultranationalist skinheads are not.[76]

"Freedom" to Petition the Government for Grievances?

The right to petition the central government for grievances has a long history in China and is guaranteed in the Chinese constitution. However, citizens who travel to Beijing to petition the government for grievances, like unpaid wages or illegal land sales, sometimes end up in makeshift "black jails."

In such "jails," often underground rooms beneath hotels, they may be held for months before being forcibly returned home.[77] Those filing complaints against local governments may sometimes find themselves involuntarily committed to a mental hospital for years.[78]

Rule *by* Law Is *Not* Rule *of* Law

Bureaucratic Harassment

In many countries, those in power use the law and government bureaucracies not for justice, but as a weapon against those who try to interfere with their power. This is Rule *by* Law, *not* Rule *of* Law. It can occur even in countries that elect their leaders.

Groups targeted for Rule *by* Law government harassment include those try-ing to monitor "human rights," evaluate how judges and the police are behaving, or challenge the power of political elites. In years past, such agitators would have been hauled off to prison camps.

In today's era of instant communications, such heavy-handed enforcement could scare off foreign investors and tourists. Instead, disfavored groups are har-assed by government misuse of the law to stifle opposition (e.g., repeated tax investigations, building code violations, and laws that prohibit foreign funding).

Corrupt Police, Non-Independent Judicial System

Some countries have the trappings of an independent legal system but that does not mean their courts and law enforcement are actually immune from political pressure. In some countries, the police and courts are not there to protect the people at all. They only protect the wealthy and the politically well-connected elites. This is also Rule *by* Law, *not* Rule *of* Law.

Russia: The police force is supposed to protect the public from crime and cor-ruption, but the Russian police often only protects powerful business and politi-cal elites. Nearly two-thirds of the Russian people fear and distrust the police because "[t]hey shoot, beat and torture civilians, confiscate businesses, and take hostages."[79]

According to an American attorney who has advised foreign companies for decades on how to do business in Russia, "corrupt law enforcement is the single biggest risk to doing business in Russia."[80]

The Russian legal system does not appear to be independent of political pres-sure. When Mikhail Khodorkovsky, former billionaire CEO of Yukos Oil, chal-lenged President Vladimir Putin's power, he was convicted of fraud and tax eva-sion in 2003 and sentenced to 8 years in a Siberian prison. His company was bankrupted and its assets transferred to other Kremlin insiders. Shortly before his release, Khodorkovsky was charged with new embezzlement and money laun-dering charges and sentenced to 6 more years in prison. Most Western commen-tators view these additional charges and conviction as politically motivated and improper.[81]

One American investor, whose grandfather was the general secretary of the American Communist party, said, "Russia is becoming criminalized at an expo-nential rate. I wish I had not gone there."[82] After exposing that at least $1 billion in assets were being stripped from Russia's largest company, Gazprom, that American investor was denied re-entry into Russia in 2005. The Russian police raided his office. He was accused of receiving a $230 million fraudulent tax refund. The Russian attorney he hired to fight this charge was arrested and died in prison in 2009.[83]

China: In China, the judiciary often acts like an extension of the Communist Chi-nese government, rather than an independent court system. After a Chinese company was refused permission to purchase a stake in Rio Tinto, an Anglo-Australian mining company, Rio Tinto employees in China were detained by the

Chinese government in July, 2009. Seven months later, in February 2010, they were indicted on charges of bribery and stealing commercial secrets.[84]

The accused had limited access to legal assistance during their trial, and they were unfamiliar with the court procedures used at their trial. The part of the trial pertaining to the charge of stealing commercial secrets was held behind closed doors and the defendants were not allowed legal representation. All four executives were convicted, receiving prison sentences ranging from 7 to 14 years.

Indonesia: Paid middlemen in Indonesia called "markuses" get legal cases dropped by giving money to corrupt police officers, prosecutors, or judges.[85]

Inching Toward Harmony

While there is no common standard of global ethics universally accepted, elements of the *10 Commandments of Trust* have been surfacing in many countries around the world in civil lawsuits, criminal cases, government actions, constitutions, statutes, public discussion, and foreign media coverage. This is not surprising. Countries experimenting with "freer," more market-oriented economies must be able to create a culture of trust that investors and consumers trust (*see* Appendix B: *The 10 Commandments of Trust "Go Global"*).

Elements of the *10 Commandments of Trust* in some form can even be found in a totalitarian communist dictatorship like the People's Republic of China. It speaks volumes about how important the *10 Commandments of Trust* have become around the world that China is trying to use these same ethical principles to attempt to create their own version of a culture of "trust" (*see* Appendix C: *The 10 Commandments of Trust in China*).

To survive and thrive in the 21st century, countries must be able to keep and maintain a successful culture of trust, a very difficult task for any country to do over the long term.

Chapter 10

Trust Is Up to All of U.S.

The American Phoenix of Freedom Must Rise

> [T]he propitious smiles of Heaven can never be expected on a nation that disregards the eternal rules of order and right, which Heaven itself has ordained...
>
> **– George Washington (1732–1799)**
> American Founding Father,
> 1ˢᵗ U.S. president, 1789–1797
> First Inaugural Address, April 20, 1789

Code Blue

When a patient's heart stops beating, oxygen to the brain is cut off. If not treated within minutes, the patient will suffer irreversible brain damage or death. To warn the medical staff of the imminent emergency, a "code blue" announcement is made over the hospital's loudspeakers. With so little time to react, the chance of failure is high.

Recent indexes warn us that *economic freedom, respect for property rights*, and *global competitiveness* have declined significantly in the United States, while *corruption* has increased. *If we had a code blue loudspeaker for ethics and trust in the United States, it would be sounding an imminent code blue emergency.*

Economic Freedom and Property Rights

As China, India, and Russia learned the hard way, only greater economic freedom leads to higher living standards for the majority of people. *Today, the United States is going in the wrong direction.*

The Heritage Foundation's annual *Index of Economic Freedom* measures specific freedoms in 183 countries, under four main categories: (1) *Rule of Law* (property rights, freedom from corruption); (2) *Limited Government* (fiscal freedom, government spending); (3) *Regulatory Efficiency* (business freedom, labor freedom, monetary freedom); and (4) *Open Markets* (trade freedom, investment freedom, financial freedom).[1]

On overall economic freedom, the United States ranked 3ʳᵈ in the world in 2000. According to the 2014 Index, the United States was only ranked 12ᵗʰ in the world, and only ranked as "mostly free," no longer "free." Only Hong Kong, Singapore, and Australia were listed as "free" in the 2014 Index.

Corruption

According to Transparency International's *Corruption Perceptions Index*, corruption has been rising in the United States. In 2010, the United States even dropped out of the rankings of the top 20 least corrupt nations in the world, ranking only 22nd out of 178 countries.[2] According to the 2013 Index,[3] the United States regained a spot in the top 20 least corrupt nations, but ranked only 19th. New Zealand, Australia, Canada, the United Kingdom, Japan, Germany, Hong Kong, and Singapore were all ranked as less corrupt than the United States. In the 2014 Index, the United States was ranked 17th.

Global Competitiveness

America was ranked #1 in the 2008–2009 global competitiveness report of the World Economic Forum.[4] In the 2012–2013 report, the United States had slipped to 7th. In the 2014–2015 report, the United States was ranked 3rd, behind Switzerland and Singapore.

> *When the people fear the government, there is tyranny. When the government fears the people, there is liberty.*
>
> **– Thomas Jefferson (1743–1826)**
> American Founding Father
> 3rd U.S. president, 1801–1809

Our Ethics Rubber-Band

Picture a rubber-band stretched between two hands pulling in opposite directions. A thick and strong rubber-band can be stretched longer than one that is thin and weak. However, no matter how thick and strong a rubber-band is, if stretched too long, it will eventually reach a critical breaking point.

When that happens, either the rubber-band will break or it will snap back suddenly to its original shape, causing great pain to the fingers on the opposite hand. The longer a rubber-band has been stretched, the greater the pain to the fingers on the opposing hand. Although pinpointing the precise breaking point of a rubber-band is difficult, before it reaches a critical breaking point, signs of stress are clearly visible.

After more than 200 years, our American *public ethics* rubber-band is thick and strong. However, over the past 40 years, we have continuously stretched our public ethics rubber-band by tolerating more and more unethical conduct in our self-governing institutions and associations. Today, our public ethics rubber-band is stretched to the breaking point. Signs of stress are everywhere—in our economy, our society, and our political system.

If we cannot restore morality and trust fast enough, the bonds of trust that have held us together for more than 200 years may not hold in the next national emergency or major crisis. The threats to our freedom are real and growing. We don't have much time to self-correct. What will we choose? Will it be:

- *Restoring ethical conduct*, a culture of trust, "bottom-up" self-organization, freedom, and success? *or*

- *Continuing down the path of unethical conduct*, a culture of distrust, "top-down" government control, the loss of our freedom, and failure?

Our ethics rubber-band in the United States has been pulled way too tight for too long. It cannot be stretched much further. Something is going to give—sooner, rather than later.

A thing moderately good is not so good as it ought to be. Moderation in temper is always a virtue, but moderation in principle is always a vice.

– Thomas Paine (1737–1809)
American Founding Father
Author of "Common Sense," 1776

Freedom Is Only for Grown-Ups

Adolescence is a transitional stage between childhood and adulthood that generally begins around age 13. Legally, we are an adult at 18 years of age for such things as signing a binding contract, getting married, or joining the military. Practically, we only become an adult when we *take on the responsibilities of a mature, independent adult*, not before.

Becoming a "real" grown-up is about behavior, not age. In today's era of crisis and turmoil, it will take a nation of self-organizing American *grown-up citizens* to act swiftly enough to restore our prosperous free-market economy, and keep our peace, stability, security, and freedom.

Grown-up citizens prepare in advance for the possibility of a future crisis or national emergency. They understand it is better to be prepared for the worst and pleasantly surprised, rather than prepared only for the best-case scenario and unpleasantly surprised. Adolescent citizens believe America is invincible and that our freedom, stability, prosperity, peace, and security are guaranteed without any effort on their part. Responsible, ethical, and critically thinking grown-up American citizens know this is not true.

Grown-up citizens understand that governments cannot spend more money than they take in—for long—and that continuing to do so will inevitably lead to a financial and economic crisis. The only question is when and how bad it will be. Grown-up citizens insist that their elected politicians be grown-ups too.

Grown-up voters look for grown-up *REAL* American leaders who are deeply committed to our uniquely American brand of freedom and can be trusted to "do the right thing" for the country and for *all* Americans. Grown-up citizens face reality as it is with courage, fortitude, determination, perseverance, and hard work. They know that with every passing day, a bad situation, left alone, will only get worse.

> *I predict future happiness for Americans if they can prevent the government from wasting the labors of the people under the pretense of taking care of them.*
>
> **– Thomas Jefferson (1743–1826)**
> American Founding Father
> 3rd U.S. president, 1801–1809

Adolescents prefer to live in a state of permanent denial. Adolescents ignore financial and economic reality, preferring to believe in "magical thinking"—that the money to pay for our government over-spending will be found somewhere, somehow, by someone. Adolescent citizens assume this can happen without real financial damage and harm to the economy and country. It cannot.

Grown-up citizens choose their elected leaders, not because they *say* all the right things, but because the leaders actually *do* the right things. Grown-up citizens double-check to make sure that what their leaders are telling them matches what those leaders are actually doing. Adolescent citizens swoon over a leader like he or she is a rock star and take everything that a leader says at face value. They do not do their own independent critical thinking, research, and analysis.

Grown-up citizens understand that *we* will only succeed together as one nation and one people. To survive crisis and economic hardship in an era of global instability and insecurity, we must *all* be concerned for the "common good" of the country and our fellow Americans, as well as our own self-interest. After searing economic pain and life-threatening war, Depression and World War II Americans understood this. United *we* stand. Divided *we* fall.

Freedom is only for grown-up citizens. Freedom in the hands of adolescent citizens leads to distrust, instability, insecurity, and failure. Adolescent citizens will not be free for long.

Freedom Has a Price

It has taken a little over 40 years to yank the United States off the ethical moorings of absolute standards of right and wrong that depression and war Americans clearly understood. If we wish to keep our free economy, free political system, and free society in the 21st century, we must re-learn what it means to be an *ethical critical-thinking American.*

We must understand our *true rights* as outlined in the Declaration of Independence, the U.S. Constitution, and the Bill of Rights, and what is unique about our American system of government and brand of freedom. Above all, we must remember that "being an American" entails *responsibilities*, not just rights.

As Thomas Jefferson warned, "the price of freedom is eternal vigilance." *Our Founding Fathers understood that not only is freedom hard to get, it is even harder to keep.*

> *There is no nation on earth powerful enough to accomplish our overthrow. Our destruction, should it come at all, will be from another quarter. From the inattention of the people to the concerns of their government, from their carelessness and negligence.*
>
> **– Daniel Webster (1782–1852)**
> U.S. senator from Massachusetts
> just before the U.S. Civil War

Responsibilities, Not Just Rights

American citizenship entails responsibilities, not just "rights." Our *responsibilities* as American citizens are spelled out clearly in the Oath of Allegiance every new American citizen is required to take. Our *rights* as American citizens are the irrevocable God-given and constitutional American *rights* spelled out in the Declaration of Independence, the U.S. Constitution, and the Bill of Rights.

Since the passage of the Civil Rights Act of 1964, Americans have talked almost nonstop about their "rights": the "rights" of African-Americans, American Indians, women, the disabled, homosexuals, children, the poor, students, the elderly, illegal immigrants, and even atheists. Almost daily, more "rights" are added, such as the "right" to an education, the "right" to health care, the "right" to housing, and the "right" to retire and receive Social Security and Medicare benefits. *The list goes on and on.*

As President Kennedy pointed out, the United States of America was founded on the revolutionary belief "that the rights of man come not from the generosity of the state, but from the hand of God...."[5] *Our God-given irrevocable American rights should never be confused with government benefits called "entitlements."*

> *Our great modern Republic. May those who seek the blessings of its institutions and the protection of its flag remember the obligations they impose.*
>
> **– Ulysses S. Grant (1822–1885)**
> U.S. commanding general during the U.S. Civil War
> 18th U.S. president, 1869–1877

The Merriam-Webster Dictionary defines an *entitlement* as "a government program that provides benefits to members of a specified group." Entitlements are *revocable privileges*, not *rights.* When the money runs out, entitlements (privileges) will be reduced or ended, either voluntarily to avoid a crisis, or involuntarily after a crisis. No amount of political maneuvering, foot-stomping, or protesting can change this simple economic fact of life—for long. *What cannot be paid, will not be paid.*

To remain a peaceful, stable society, cuts in government entitlements must be made ethically in accordance with the *10 Commandments of Trust.* For example, changes must be made fairly, truthfully, and carefully. They must be made without any conflicts of interest. Decisions must be made in the best interests of *all* the American people (that is, the common good) by trustworthy ethical *REAL* leaders, who put the interests of the people they represent *above their own self-interests.*

Restoring fiscal responsibility in an era of scarce resources without debilitating civil unrest and major political upheavals is extremely difficult for any country to do. This is when the social, political, and economic systems of countries are most likely to suffer serious breakdowns.

The question is, can the United States make the necessary painful changes and still remain an intact, united, free country under the same form of government in the 21st century as it has done for more than 200 years? *Not without quickly restoring morality, ethics, and our self-organizing culture of trust throughout our economy, society, and government.*

> *The American Republic will endure until the day Congress discovers that it can bribe the public with the public's money.*
>
> **– Alexis de Toqueville (1805–1859)**
> Author, *Democracy in America* (1830)

Facing Reality

Our massive national federal debt is now more than $18 trillion. American military leaders have warned such a huge federal debt not only threatens our national economy, it threatens our national security.[6] Among the largest items of federal expenditure are *Social Security, Medicare and (Medicaid), defense,* and *interest on the national debt.*[7] In addition, the Affordable Care Act (Obamacare) is expected to add nearly $2 trillion in federal spending by 2024.[8]

Social Security, Medicare/Medicaid

Two of the largest items of federal spending are Social Security and Medicare (and Medicaid). When Social Security was established in the 1930s, Americans died right around the time they became eligible to collect benefits at 65 years of age. Today we live at least 20 years longer.

Until 2010, the federal government collected substantially more in payroll taxes than it paid out in benefits. Now, the huge baby-boomer generation that had been providing Social Security's massive surplus tax revenues is rapidly qualifying for benefits. The first wave of 77 million baby-boomers turned 65 in January 2011. An estimated 10,000 American baby-boomers a day will qualify to receive benefits for 19 years.[9]

Beginning in 2010, our federal government began borrowing billions of dollars *to pay current* Social Security benefits. In 2010, it was $29 billion;[10] in 2011 and 2012, it borrowed more than $45 billion;[11] in 2013, it borrowed an estimated $79 billion.[12] According to *A Summary of the 2014 Annual Reports,* which can be found at Social Security's official website, the federal government will need to borrow about $77 billion each year from 2014 until 2018 (and much more thereafter).

If the Social Security trust fund is "solvent" as some have claimed, why is our federal government borrowing tens of billions of dollars to make current payments to Social Security beneficiaries? The reality is that our federal politicians spent the baby-boomers' surplus Social Security tax revenues (that had been collected over decades) on other federal spending.

Social Security's mis-named "trust fund," estimated to be about $2.6 trillion, is really composed only of government IOUs backed "by the full faith and credit of the U.S. government"[13] (already more than $18 trillion in debt). A recent Social Security Trustees' Report estimated the combined deficit for both Social Security and Medicare programs may be $66 trillion.[14]

> *Government is not reason; it is not eloquent; it is force. Like fire, it is a dangerous servant and a fearful master.*
>
> **– George Washington (1732–1799)**
> Founding Father,
> 1st U.S. president, 1789–1797

Interest on Our National Debt

Short-term interest rates, close to zero for years, have nowhere to go but up. With our gargantuan national debt of more than $18 trillion, any increase in interest rates will cause our interest payments on such an extremely high debt to shoot up very quickly. According to the Congressional Budget Office, yearly interest payments on our federal national debt could be as high as $916 billion by 2020.[15] Obviously, this would crowd out other essential government spending, including spending for defense.[16]

Defense

Cutting defense may seem like a "no brainer" to some (and certainly some cuts will be required), but in an era of increasing global instability and unrest, we must be careful how and what we cut. When deciding what cuts to defense are warranted, we must use critical thinking, not political thinking. *Countries that ignore obvious warnings of danger will not survive as free and independent countries for long.*

If we are attacked, we must be able to defend ourselves. Foreign hackers can now wreak havoc on any country via the Internet. The Pentagon has warned that our next "Pearl Harbor" attack could come from a foreign country taking down our electric grids and our important computer systems rather than through physical combat.[17]

In March 2011, 24,000 sensitive files on a new weapons system were stolen from an American defense contractor's computers, probably by a "foreign intelligence service."[18] A Pentagon report accused China of cyber-spying on the United States.[19]

China, with more than 1.3 billion people, has been building a large, well-equipped, and advanced military.[20] It now has missiles that can destroy American aircraft carriers. Recently, China has been asserting control of shipping lanes for oil in the South China Sea, causing tensions with its neighbors—Japan, Vietnam, and the Philippines. In December 2011, China's President Hu Jintao reportedly told the Chinese navy to speed up its modernization and "prepare for warfare."[21]

> *[I]f we desire to secure peace, one of the most powerful instruments of our rising prosperity, it must be known, that we are at all times ready for War.*
>
> **– George Washington (1732–1799)**
> Founding Father,
> 1st U.S. president, 1789–1797

Too Much Global Debt

Governments of many other nations have been borrowing extraordinary amounts of money too. With so many countries trying to rescue their economies by borrowing money, the next in line to default could be the countries themselves. The United States, Japan, and Western European countries are all carrying huge national debts.

> *You cannot escape the responsibility of tomorrow by evading it today.*
>
> **– Abraham Lincoln (1809–1865)**
> 16th U.S. president during the
> American Civil War, 1861–1865

Tick, Tick, Tick

We are drowning in debt and on an unsustainable path. By not facing the reality of how serious our debt problems are, we are running the risk that our American experiment in freedom will not survive in the 21st century. *If we do not self-correct, the United States could end up a failed experiment in freedom.*

To remain a free people in the 21st century, we must accept the reality that our national federal debt is far too large and will not go away by itself. Such high levels of government debt are "ticking time bombs" that, if not dealt with in time, threaten our long-term prosperity, peace, stability, and security.[22]

If we wish to keep our freedom, the age of entitlement is over. The age of responsibility is upon us all.

> *The most perfect political community is one in which the middle class is in control, and outnumbers both of the other classes.*
>
> **– Aristotle (384 B.C.–322 B.C.)**
> Greek philosopher; Father of science
> and ethics in western civilization

Icebergs Ahead

What makes an iceberg so dangerous to ships is that only about one-eighth of its total size is visible on the water's surface. Seven-eighths of an iceberg is hidden below the waterline.

In 2014, 92 million Americans were out of the work force, the highest percentage in the past 35 years (including those retired and those who cannot find work and have stopped looking). In 2013, almost 48 million Americans were collecting food stamps, up from about 27 million in 2007. The number of people on federal disability has skyrocketed. There is growing concern that our governments are not carefully monitoring who is receiving public benefits at taxpayers' expense.

Food stamp fraud may already be costing American taxpayers an estimated $750 million a year.[23] Newspapers reported that a $2 million lottery winner was receiving food stamps and the owner of a $1.2 million home was receiving public housing vouchers and food stamps.[24] A September 2011 Gallup poll revealed Americans believed that more than half of every dollar of federal spending is wasted.[25]

Our aging infrastructure must be replaced to prevent our roads, utilities, bridges, and power grids from failing. Repairs and upgrades for our essential infrastructure have been estimated to be about $2.2 trillion over a five-year period.[26] Where will the money come from? Many cities and states cannot pay the retirement and medical benefits promised to unionized government workers. In addition, over the past decade, the United States has spent an estimated $3.3 trillion fighting the war on terror.[27]

We have had crippling storms, devastating tornadoes, severe droughts, massive flooding, and raging wildfires in the United States. Recently, 12 weather disasters caused more than $1 billion in damage each, a new record high.[28]

Fires in Russia, floods in Australia, and drought in China have destroyed a substantial portion of the world's food supplies. With each natural disaster, there is an increasing possibility of a global food shortage. Increasing instability in the euro zone and questions about the future of the euro could spark another financial and banking crisis that could be worse than the one in the United States in 2008.[29]

Instability and violence are increasing in the Middle East, threatening to disrupt the world's oil supplies. In 2012, China announced a new pact with Saudi Arabia to provide Saudi Arabia with nuclear weapons technology as a counter to Iran's continued development of nuclear weapons capability.

The Muslim Brotherhood took control in Egypt via elections after removing its long-term dictator. Although some in the West claimed the Muslim Brotherhood is "moderate," its motto is hardly reassuring: "Allah is our objective; the Prophet is our leader; the Quran [Koran] is our law; Jihad is our way; dying in the way of Allah is our highest hope." When the elected Muslim Brotherhood president proposed to give himself nearly dictatorial powers, millions protested. In November 2012, the Egyptian army stepped in and took control of the government.

In 2014, an ultra-brutal militant terrorist organization called ISIS took control of large swaths of Iraq. Its stated intent is to set up a Sunni caliphate under strict Islamic law. An all-out Sunni-Shiite Muslim tribal war in the Middle East appears to be more and more likely.

We must be prepared for the possibility of not only one major crisis, but multiple crises at the same time, both here in the United States and around the world.

A Nation of Mutts

The word "diversity" has been so politicized in the United States that just mentioning the term evokes strong emotions, both positive and negative. Using dictionary definitions, *diversity* means "variety," and *variety* refers to "differences within a similar grouping."

We know from Biology 101 that diversity (that is, variety) is a good thing. When living things breed outside of their own gene pool, they are healthier and stronger, and can adapt faster to changes in their environment than those that only breed within their gene pool.

Applying this biological concept of diversity to the United States: "What would you rather be? A mutt or an in-bred poodle?" Biology 101 says a mutt, and the United States is a nation of mutts. One in 12 marriages in the United States is now interracial.[30]

> *In our personal ambitions we are individualists. But in our seeking for economic and political progress as a nation, we all go up or else all go down as one people.*
>
> **– Franklin D. Roosevelt (1882–1945)**
> 32nd U.S. president during the Great
> Depression and WWII, 1933–1945

However, diversity is only a positive if we can keep and maintain our *overarching common American culture of trust* under *ethics-based* American Rule of Law. If we cannot, instead of our diversity being one of our greatest strengths, it will be one of our greatest weaknesses, especially in the next major crisis or national emergency.

United *We* Stand

America's survival and success in every major crisis and national emergency has depended on the extraordinary feats of diverse groups of ordinary people under the leadership of extraordinary *REAL* leaders they trusted. The United States was forged as a free nation by people from different backgrounds who *united* to overcome seemingly insurmountable odds.

During our last national emergency, World War II, Americans did not fight and die for our freedom as hyphenated-Americans: African-Americans, Native-Americans, Japanese-Americans, Caucasian-Americans, and such. They fought and died as *Americans,* united around a love of country and the preservation of our uniquely American brand of freedom, with courage, fortitude, determination, selflessness, and faith.

Of the 16.1 million Americans who served in the military during World War II, about 1 million were members of minority groups. Because of the outstanding service of the Tuskegee Airmen, the Navajo Code Talkers, and Japanese-Americans during World War II, the U.S. military was finally desegregated after the end of World War II in 1948.

Many World War II American soldiers came from poor, disadvantaged backgrounds full of hardships. Women did their part too, taking on the roles of the men shipped overseas to fight. The net result is that *diverse* patriotic Americans, at great personal sacrifice, did whatever was needed to protect *our* nation and *our* freedom and preserve *our* way of life.

> *We must, indeed, all hang together or, most assuredly, we shall all hang separately.*
>
> **– Benjamin Franklin (1706–1790)**
> American Founding Father

The Tuskegee Airmen

The American military in the 1920s said African-Americans could not fly military planes.[31] Benjamin O. Davis, Sr., was the third African-American to attend the army's military academy, West Point. His son, Benjamin O. Davis, Jr., the fourth African-American to attend West Point, wanted to fly.

In the early 1930s, Ben Davis, Jr., braved discriminatory treatment at West Point that would have broken an ordinary man. His fellow cadets refused to share a room with him and only spoke to him when it was absolutely necessary. Ben, Jr., ate his meals in silence. Instead of breaking him, this unfair treatment forged in him a white-hot determination to succeed—and he did.

In 1941, black and white soldiers were still separated in a racially segregated U.S. military. African-Americans were mostly assigned non-skilled jobs. Some American states still had segregated public facilities (e.g., public bathrooms, public drinking fountains, and restaurants) marked "Colored" and "White." In July 1941, an experimental African-American pilot program was established on a segregated military base in Tuskegee, Alabama.[32]

American bombers had been suffering high casualty rates in bombing raids over Europe because their fighter escorts left formation to fight enemy aircraft. When the Tuskegee Airmen were assigned to escort American bombers, Colonel Benjamin O. Davis insisted that his fighter planes not break formation. This dramatically reduced the number of American bombers who did not make it home.

The Tuskegee Airmen painted the tails of their planes bright red, earning the nickname Red Tails. They "downed 111 enemy planes and destroyed or damaged 273 on the ground."[33] The Red Tails had one of the best records of any flying air fighter group in World War II, receiving 96 Distinguished Flying Crosses. After the war, Colonel Davis was promoted to General Davis.

The Navajo Code Talkers

Native American tribes in the United States were forcibly marched long distances onto reservations. Navajo children were separated from their families and sent to English-only schools, where they were severely punished if caught speaking their native language.

Luckily, no matter how hard these schools tried to stomp out the Navajo language, they failed. Had they succeeded, American troops in World War II might not have won some of the toughest battles in the Pacific (e.g., Guadalcanal and Iwo Jima).

Navajo is an unwritten language believed to be derived from Chinese Tibetan languages. U.S. Marines recruited Navajo Code Talkers to develop a special code that could not be broken by the Japanese enemy. They succeeded. Because of the Navajo Code Talkers, American troops could radio essential military information without fear that intercepted messages could be decoded by the Japanese (e.g., enemy troop movements, bomber air support, troop re-supply, etc.).

Navajo Code Talkers could code and decode messages with extraordinary speed and accuracy. At Iwo Jima, six Navajo Code Talkers in one marine division sent and received over 800 error-free messages in the first two days of fighting.[34]

The 100th/442nd

After the Japanese bombed Pearl Harbor on December 7, 1941, President Roosevelt signed an executive order that put 120,000 Japanese-Americans into internment camps in western states. Many lost their businesses, homes, and almost everything they owned. Nevertheless, many of their sons volunteered to fight in World War II. They fought in the U.S. Army side by side with the sons of Japanese immigrants from Hawaii, whose families had not been interned.

To avoid confusion, most Japanese-American soldiers were sent to Europe to fight. Raised in the Japanese tradition of not bringing shame on their families, Japanese-American soldiers refused to retreat. Their units suffered such high casualties, they became known as the "Purple Heart Battalion."[35] The Japanese-American 100th and 442nd Regimental Combat Teams became the most highly decorated units of their size and length of service in U.S. history.[36]

Audie Murphy

Audie Murphy, the most decorated American combat soldier in World War II,[37] came from a poor white tenant farming family. Audie was the 7th of 12 children. His father, who could barely read or write, abandoned the family when Audie was only 11 years old. Audie had to drop out of school in the 5th grade to help support the family, picking cotton for $1 a day.

Audie became an expert hunter, able to shoot straight even while moving. The game he shot was often the only food his family had to eat. Audie's mother died when he was only 16 years old.

As soon as World War II broke out, Audie immediately volunteered to fight. The Marines rejected him because he was so skinny and small. When the Army accepted him, Murphy insisted on combat duty.

Because of Audie's well-honed hunting and trapping skills, he excelled in the infantry. He intuitively seemed to sense where the enemy was, even when the enemy could not be seen. He was also courageous under fire. In one instance, after ordering his men to fall back, he jumped on a burning tank. With its .50 caliber machine gun, he single-handedly held off advancing German infantry and tanks, even after being wounded.

Rosie the Riveter

With men fighting overseas, women filled the factories at home to make the ships, planes, tanks, and guns needed for war. Many jobs, like working in explosives factories, were very dangerous.

These women came from all kinds of backgrounds and ethnicities. Some were experienced factory workers. Others had never worked outside the home before. They worked long hours, six days a week, with little vacation time.

Women also joined the Armed Forces, serving at home and overseas. The American war effort could not have succeeded without the heroic efforts and sacrifices of these American women.[38]

> *A house divided against itself cannot stand.*
>
> **– Abraham Lincoln (1809–1865)**
> 16th U.S. president during the
> American Civil War, 1861–1865

When it comes to our freedom, the only color that matters is red, white, and blue.

Crisis = Danger + Opportunity

A crisis is a "critical event or point of decision which, if not handled in an appropriate and timely manner (or if not handled at all), may turn into a disaster or catastrophe."[39] Some have suggested that the Mandarin word for crisis consists of two Chinese characters: one symbolizing danger, the other opportunity. *Whether this is accurate or not, the notion of crisis entailing both danger and opportunity is true.*

> *Courage is resistance to fear, mastery of fear, not absence of fear.*
>
> **– Mark Twain (1835–1910)**
> American writer and humorist

A crisis is *dangerous* because a positive outcome is not guaranteed. If our American democratic institutions fail, something truly terrible could follow. The rise of Hitler and Nazi Germany was sparked by the 1931 failure of the Viennese Creditanstalt Bank, setting off a banking crisis that "sent economic shock waves across Europe."[40]

On the other hand, a crisis can be positive if it sparks the much-needed changes necessary for future survival and success.

It will take *all* of us self-organizing (working together automatically, cooperatively, and voluntarily without central direction and control) to adapt fast enough in this new century to survive, succeed, and keep our freedom. To do this, our American post–World War II *"me"* generations must become like the crisis-surviving depression and war American *"we"* generations once again.

If we can no longer self-organize in the 21st century, our American experiment in freedom will end up in the dustbin in history—an experiment in freedom that burned brightly for two centuries, before sputtering out in failure.

> *Freedom is never more than one generation away from extinction. We didn't pass it to our children in the bloodstream. It must be fought for, protected, and handed on for them to do the same.*
>
> **– Ronald Reagan (1911–2004)**
> 40th U.S. president, 1981–1989

The Light of Liberty

Alexander Hamilton said that Americans would, by their conduct and example, "once and for all answer the question of whether human societies [are] capable of creating good government intentionally by choice or whether they would forever be governed only by accident or force."[41] Our Founding Fathers believed that, if Americans could not hold onto their freedom under the extraordinarily favorable conditions existing in the United States, freedom could not last for long anywhere in the world.

We will only be able to fashion flexible, creative, and innovative solutions to adapt fast enough to changed conditions in this new century, if we

1. restore trust by conducting ourselves ethically in our self-organizing institutions and associations,

2. fiercely protect our uniquely American constitutional brand of freedom,

3. understand the vital role our Judeo-Christian cultural heritage plays in our continued survival and success,

4. restore free-market capitalism based on morality, ethics, and trust, and

5. insist that our ethical standards be enforced when necessary under *ethics-based* American Rule of Law (not our current American Rule of Lawyers and Bureaucrats).

> *It is a common observation that our cause is the cause of all mankind, and that we are fighting for their liberty in defending our own.*
>
> **– Benjamin Franklin (1706–1790)**
> American Founding Father

If the light of liberty goes out in America, it will likely go out in the world for a very long time. We must keep the light of liberty on.

The Race So Far

In the early 2000s, most American pundits scoffed at the notion that there were signs of economic trouble ahead. The European Union (EU) seemed strong and stable; China's economy appeared to be invincible; and the Indian, Russian, and Brazilian economies looked as though they were on ever-increasing trajectories of success.

A constant refrain repeated in the popular press was that these vast, vibrant, new emerging market economies would soon eclipse their western counterparts, including the United States. Dictatorships in Middle Eastern countries were still firmly in control.

Fast forward to the second decade of the 21st century. The global picture has changed dramatically. The Financial Crisis of 2008 has shaken the European and American financial systems to the core. There was talk of total financial collapse without massive trillion-dollar bailouts at taxpayer expense.

Now the floodgates of government spending have been opened so wide, there are growing fears the next round of debt defaults could involve sovereign nations themselves. At the end of 2011, commentators were wondering aloud whether the euro zone would break up and whether the euro would survive.[42] Media reports suggested that "[e]ven powerhouse Germany may be faltering."[43]

The Chinese economic miracle is showing signs of stress. A giant housing bubble, massive over-borrowing, and bad loans at the local level threaten China's continued economic success.[44] With China's economy still heavily dependent on exports, a global economic slowdown that throws millions of Chinese out of work could lead to civil unrest.[45] One newspaper subheading summed up China's possible new economic reality: "[u]nbridled optimism about the world's No. 2 economy is giving way to fears of an impending collapse."[46]

China is making its neighbors nervous. In 2012, China issued new passports to its citizens with a map showing China in control of parts of the world long viewed as belonging to other countries.[47] China has promised to back up these new territorial claims with military force.

Russia, India, and Brazil are facing increased economic, social, and political headwinds. Corruption is a major problem in all three countries.[48] Money was pulled out of their stock markets.[49] Foreign investors began to flee Russia. Trust in the Russian economy and political system evaporated as conditions inside the country deteriorated.[50] In 2012, power grids in India failed, cutting off power to about 600 million people.[51]

Our federal government's financial situation is becoming more and more precarious. For four years, our federal government spent more than $1 trillion more than it collected. Our national federal debt is now more than $18 trillion.

The U.S. Federal Reserve Bank has poured $85 billion a month (more than $1 trillion a year) of "created" money into the U.S. economy. The federal government continues to churn out complex statutes and regulations at a furious pace, forgetting that too much government regulation is just as bad for our economy as too little regulation.

Concerns are growing about the increasing instability and violence in the Middle East. Syria's bloody civil war has killed an estimated 100,000 people. The rise of a brutal radical Islamic terrorist group like ISIS that resorts to mass murder and beheadings of non-believers is deeply disturbing. Religious intolerance and restrictions on freedom of religion continue to grow in many parts of the world.[52]

My dream is of a place and a time where America will once again be seen as the last best hope of earth.

– Abraham Lincoln (1809–1865)
16th U.S. president during the
American Civil War, 1861–1865

More changes are underway. The winners in the global competitive race remain in a constant state of flux in an increasingly unstable, unpredictable, and volatile world.

The Gift of Freedom

The problems we face in America are daunting and serious. If our culture of trust holds, we will have the advantage of greater stability in a crisis. So far—the United States has been remarkably stable, operating under the same Constitution and form of government since 1789.

China's current government structure dates back only to 1949, Russia's to 1991, and India's to 1950. Brazil was a military dictatorship until 1985. While America's longevity is a positive factor, if we don't get our financial house in order fast enough, investors could eventually lose trust in the U.S. treasury bonds that fund our debt.

Today, Americans are more polarized than at any time in post–World War II history.[53] Some believe the common moral, ethical, legal, and cultural foundations of the United States have deteriorated so much, we will not be able to unite and change fast enough to avert a catastrophe. *Certainly history warns us that this is one possible scenario. It cannot be ruled out.*

Another scenario is also possible. Americans have been willing to fight and die for freedom since the days of Patrick Henry's 1775 speech: "give me liberty or give me death." *If Americans today still feel the same way about freedom, what painful sacrifices might we be willing to make to keep our freedom?*

> *There is a certain enthusiasm in liberty that makes human nature rise above itself, in acts of bravery and heroism.*
>
> **– Alexander Hamilton (1755–1804)**
> American Founding Father
> 1st U.S. secretary of the Treasury, 1789–1795

The Winds of Change

To make the necessary and painful sacrifices required to restore our fiscal and economic health in time to save our freedom requires a rock-solid culture of trust. Will we change fast enough to restore the secret power of trust that made America great—*before it is too late*?

There are incipient signs our Judeo-Christian heritage is seeping back into mainstream American culture. In September 2012, a *Wall Street Journal* article "Hollywood's New Bible Stories" announced the return of Bible themes to mainstream Hollywood movies.[54] In 2013, millions watched the Bible mini-series on TV. In 2014 alone, there were four movies with Biblical themes: *Son of God*, *Exodus*, *Heaven Is for Real*, and *Noah*. Comedian Jeff Foxworthy is hosting a new TV game show on the Bible. A new TV mini-series on the Bible's 10 Commandments has been announced.[55]

Tim Tebow, formerly a National Football League (NFL) quarterback, became famous for dropping to one knee in prayer on the field to thank his "Lord and Savior Jesus Christ." Even after he left the NFL, it was reported that he still had 2.2 million Twitter followers. In 2013 he topped Forbes' list of America's most influential athletes.[56] A national basketball star, Jeremy Lin, was quoted saying, "I just give all the praise to God."[57]

In 2012, a Gallup poll indicated that nearly 80% of Americans still identified themselves as Christians.[58] Atheists in the United States make up only about 1–5% of the population. A *Scientific American* study reported that atheists are the least popular group because they are not trusted.[59]

Other positive changes in the United States may be afoot. We have new sources of oil and gas because of technological advances in oil-shale drilling. In 2012, the largest number of Americans in 75 years identified themselves not as Democrats or Republicans, but as Independents.[60] American teens and young people are helping others in record numbers at a level not seen since the 1940s.[61] Seniors are volunteering to help others in need in these tough times.[62]

There are nascent signs of positive change at the *state level*. States cannot "print" money. There is a limit on how much they can borrow and tax. Rhode Island passed a sweeping new law overhauling its government workers' pensions and medical benefits. In 2012, voters in two California cities—San Diego and San Jose, the nation's 8th and 10th largest cities—overwhelmingly voted in favor of cutting the pensions of public government unionized workers. High-spending, high-taxing, high-regulation states like New York, Illinois, and California lost people as Americans "voted with their feet" for better opportunities in other states.[63]

At the *federal level*, there are still too many "top-down" federally controlled and federally mandated solutions based more on force than trust. The *wisdom of ants* warns us that such "top-down" centralized federal control will not work in today's fast-changing environment. If we wish to find solutions fast enough to survive, succeed, and keep our freedom, we must seek out more "bottom-up" self-reliant and self-organizing solutions in our states, local communities, and the private sector.

A hopeful sign of potential positive change at the federal level was *a December 2013 Gallup poll indicating 72% of Americans now fear big government more than big business or big labor.*[64]

Out of the Ashes

Ants have successfully adapted to changes in their environment over 100 million years because of their self-organizing wisdom. We are about to find out whether Americans are still capable of maintaining the *wisdom of ants'* self-organizing freedom responsible for our long-standing survival and success. *If we cannot, our grand American experiment in freedom will go the way of the dinosaurs.*

Dinosaurs ruled the world for millions of years but became extinct when they could not adapt fast enough to sudden changes in their environment. It will happen to us, too, if we can no longer self-organize (act voluntarily, automatically, and cooperatively as a group without central direction and control) under *ethics-based* American Rule of Law and our essential culture of trust. *So what will our future be?*

Will the United States once again surprise the world with how fast we can self-organize and self-correct to get our economy and country back on track? The answer depends on whether the *American phoenix of freedom* can rise again for the fourth time in our history. *This will only be possible if our bonds of trust hold.*

The phoenix is a beautiful mythical bird with iridescent feathers of green, red, blue, and gold. It lives forever, but the price of its immortality is high. To remain immortal, the phoenix must periodically set itself on fire, burning away the old and decayed feathers to restore its plumage to its former brilliant beauty. *Only after a painful self-inflicted fire can a new beautiful phoenix rise again out of the ashes.*

Like the legendary phoenix, the United States has survived three prior generational crisis fires in which the very existence of the country was at stake: the

American Revolution, the U.S. Civil War, and the Great Depression and World War II. Out of the ashes of each of these three national emergencies, a rejuvenated American phoenix of freedom has risen to survive and thrive again. *Will we survive the fourth? Not without morality, ethics, and trust.*

> *Intellectually I know that America is no better than any other country; emotionally I know she is better than every other country.*
>
> **– Sinclair Lewis (1885–1951)**
> American novelist and playwright

For the past four decades, we have squandered our self-organizing gift of freedom. We will pay a high price for our ethical lapses. To survive and succeed in the 21st century, "we, the people" must insist that all of us must be held to the *same uniform ethical standards* when we are acting in our self-governing civic institutions and voluntary associations.

Only by following the *10 Commandments of Trust*, under *ethics-based* American Rule of Law (laced with Judeo-Christian values and within the boundaries of our uniquely American constitutional brand of freedom), will we be able to restore our prosperous economy and maintain our peaceful, stable, and secure nation. *While some have suggested prosperity is just around the corner, our public ethics barometer says otherwise.*

Because of the size, scale, and breadth of our ethical failings, restoring trust and our financial solvency will not be easy or painless. Sometimes it may even feel like the fires of hell once again. The generational historians say that *if* we survive the next generational crisis of survival, the United States could once again become an extraordinarily strong, successful, and dominant free economy and free nation in the 21st century.[65]

One thing is certain: restoring our culture of trust is our only chance of surviving and thriving as a free nation in the tumultuous century ahead. We have been able to adapt over centuries to changing circumstances *with the same form of government intact* because we have trusted one another enough to be able to self-organize. *The secret of American longevity and success—so far—has been our ability to follow the wisdom of ants.*

> *[T]he preservation of the sacred fire of liberty, and the... republican model of government, are... finally, staked on the experiment entrusted to the hands of the American people.*
>
> **– George Washington (1732–1799)**
> American Founding Father; general
> during American Revolutionary War;
> 1st U.S. president, 1789–1797

Our future is up to U.S.

Part II

The 10 Commandments of Trust

Chapter 11

Restoring Trust
Not the "10 Suggestions"

> *Every kind of peaceful cooperation among men is primarily based on mutual trust and only secondarily on institutions such as courts of justice and police.*
>
> **– Albert Einstein (1879–1955)**
> Nobel Prize-winning physicist

Only a Snapshot Picture

In *Part 2* of this book, we switch gears from *why* trust matters to the nuts and bolts of *how* the 10 simple ethical principles—the *10 Commandments of Trust*—have been applied and interpreted under American Rule of Law.

For ease of understanding, *some* of the existing general subcategories for each of 10 general ethical principles have been provided in each of the following chapters. At the end of each of chapter, you will find a short summary of each ethical principle, along with just *some* of many *diverse types of law* that might be used in an American court to try to enforce that ethical principle.

Although the ethical principles remain constant, how they are applied and interpreted under American Rule of Law can, and sometimes does change over time, as social, political, and economic factors in the country change. *Therefore, think of these general subcategory descriptions under each ethical principle as only a snapshot picture in time, subject to change.*

Also, keep in mind that under our American Rule of Law, these 10 general ethical principles are often enforced outside of American courts. For example, issues of unfairness may be addressed by other means such as changes in tax policy, bad publicity that triggers a Congressional investigation and public hearing, or elections that elect new political leaders.

To create an *effective* culture of trust, these 10 ethical principles must be applied under *ethics-based* American Rule of Law, not our current American Rule of Lawyers and Bureaucrats, with long-winded and incomprehensible statutes that generate thousands more pages of convoluted regulations.

Ethics-based American Rule of Law includes our unique brand of constitutional freedom, embodied in the Declaration of Independence, the U.S. Constitution, and the Bill of Rights. It also means relying on Judeo-Christian values, with a decidedly self-organizing Protestant Christian cultural accent.

Simple Is Always Better

When it comes to codes of right and wrong behavior that have stood the test of time, simple works, complicated does not.

The Bible's 10 Commandments and the first 10 amendments in the U.S. Constitution (the Bill of Rights) are each less than 500 words, yet both have provided clear guidance on "right" conduct over centuries. The U.S. Constitution is only 6 pages long; 10 pages if all 27 amendments are included.

Similarly, the 10 Commandments of Trust is a short and simple code of right and wrong behavior—an American code of trust (see Appendix A for the short summaries of these commandments of trust).

Law on Steroids

The number, length, and complexity of American statutes have grown at an extreme pace in recent decades. The exponential increase in the number of pages in the U.S. federal tax code is a great example:[1]

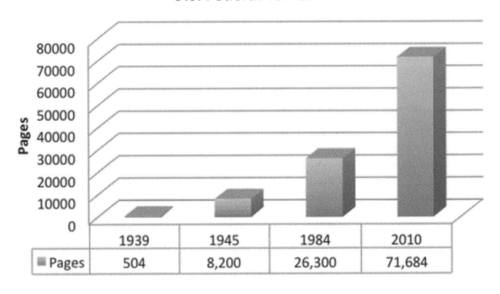

U.S. Federal Tax Code

Pages	1939	1945	1984	2010
Pages	504	8,200	26,300	71,684

In 2013, the U.S. Income Tax Code was 73,954 pages long. Members of the U.S. Congress have been passing bills, thousands of pages long, full of legal doublespeak that are difficult for "ordinary" Americans to understand. In addition, when these excessively long and complex bills became law, they generated thousands of pages of regulations, full of legal gobbledygook, drafted by unelected bureaucrats.

Almost two-thirds of likely American voters do not believe Congress has read these bills before they are passed.[2] One member of Congress admitted this is true, saying that even if they did read them, they wouldn't be able to understand them either without consulting "expert" attorneys.[3] *This is law on steroids.*

> *The more corrupt the republic, the more numerous the laws.*
>
> **– Tacitus (A.D. 56 – A.D. 117)**
> Senator and historian, Roman Empire

Two recent examples of *law on steroids* are:

- **Health Care "Reform,"** a 2,700-page bill that became about 900 pages as a statute, innocuously labeled the *Patient Protection and Affordable Care Act*[4] (sometimes called "Obamacare"). Just one 6-page section of this new statute generated *429 pages* of new regulations.[5] By 2013, there were already 13,000 pages of new regulations, with many more regulations yet to be written.[6]

- **Financial "Reform,"** a 2,300-page bill that became about 900 pages as a statute with another helpful-sounding title—the *Wall Street Reform and Consumer Protection Act* (also called the "Dodd-Frank Act"). A *Wall Street Journal* editorial pointed out that it took one law firm 150 pages to describe the new bureaucracies created by this statute; another firm needed 26 pages to show the timeline for implementing this law over 12 years.[7] Under this statute, 11 federal agencies must pass at least 243 new formal rules.[8] By November 2012 there were already 9,000 pages of rules and regulations, with thousands more pages of regulations yet to be drafted.[9]

U.S. Finance Reform Laws

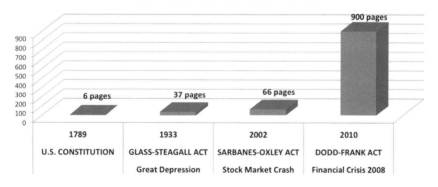

Complying with such complicated statutes and regulations is not only expensive and time consuming, it stifles our most important gift of freedom—our *wisdom of ants* self-organizing "swarm intelligence." Law on steroids prevents our "bottom-up" self-organizing civic institutions and voluntary associations from operating as they should under our culture of trust and *ethics-based* American Rule of Law.

The flexibility, creativity, and speed normally inherent in our self-organizing culture of trust are hobbled by these long, complicated statutes and regulations. These mind-numbingly long statutes and regulations create multiple layers of intrusive, expensive, and ineffective government bureaucracies that impede our ability to adapt quickly in today's fast-moving, fast-changing, chaotic, and complex environment.

Our current *law on steroids,* that is, *American Rule of Lawyers and Bureaucrats*, produces statutes and regulations so long and complicated only "experts" can understand and interpret them for the rest of us.[10] *Law on steroids allows unethical conduct to flourish and robs us all of our freedom.*

Conversely, the *10 Commandments of Trust* under *ethics-based* American Rule of Law is a simple code of general ethical principles that "ordinary" people can understand (see Appendix A).

It will be of little avail to the people that the laws are made by men of their own choice if the laws be so voluminous that they cannot be read, or so incoherent that they cannot be understood.

– James Madison (1751–1836)
American Founding Father,
4th U.S. president, 1809 – 1817

Too Many Crimes

The more ethically confused we have become, the more we have relied on the criminal law to fill the void. Originally, there were three federal crimes in the U.S. Constitution—treason, piracy, and counterfeiting. Now we have more than 4,000 crimes in our federal statutes, and as many as 3,000 crimes in our federal regulations.[11]

Since the 1980s, federal crimes have increased by one-third.[12] According to one law professor's analysis, "as of the end of 1996, over one-quarter of all federal criminal provisions enacted since the Civil War were passed in a 16-year period from 1980–1996."[13]

Today's long and complicated statutes favor the wealthy who can afford expensive attorneys. They also favor those who are politically well-connected because of big-budget lobbying efforts and large campaign contributions to politicians. This is not the government "*of* the people, *by* the people and *for* the people" envisioned by our forefathers. *Law on steroids* relies too much on "top-down" enforcement and compliance and too little on "bottom-up" voluntary "right" conduct.

Instead of enhancing our culture of trust, law on steroids destroys trust by creating a culture of loopholes, favoritism, and special treatment.

Where you find the laws most numerous, there you will find also the greatest injustice.

– Arcesilaus (316 B.C.–241 B.C.)
Greek philosopher

Restoring Right and Wrong

In order to eliminate our current ineffective "top-down," centralized, bureaucratic, and corrupt *law on steroids*, we must restore our "bottom-up" self-organizing ethical American culture of trust. This can be accomplished by restoring the the *10 Commandments of Trust*, based on 10 simple and clear ethical principles of right and wrong behavior in all of our self-organizing institutions and associations.

Although the overarching principles of 10 Commandments are the same for everyone, sometimes there are differences in details. For example, *full disclosure* falls under Commandment of Trust No. 1: Tell the Truth. Hiding key facts *about something important* destroys trust, whether it is done by businesses, governments, nonprofits, charities, unions, or other self-governing institutions or associations. However, the requirements of what constitutes *full disclosure* for selling stock in a public company under the Securities and Exchange Commission (SEC) may be different from the IRS requirements of *full disclosure* when soliciting charitable donations.

To restore prosperity and keep our peaceful, stable, and secure free society, we must *stop* asking the question*: Is it legal?* (*statute-and-regulation-dependent American Rule of Lawyers and Bureaucrats law on steroids*) and *start* asking the question: *Is it wrong?* (*ethics-based American Rule of Law*). Behavior that violates one or more of the ethical principles of the 10 Commandments of Trust is wrong because it destroys the American culture of trust essential for our continued survival and success as a free economy, society, and nation.

In order to keep our culture of trust that has created our successful economy, and our peaceful, stable, and secure country, we must do what is right (ethical). As noted earlier, although the details of how each ethical principle of trust is implemented may vary over time, the simple, short statements of the ethical principles of trust themselves do not change. *Right behavior creates trust. Wrong behavior destroys trust.*

Without a culture of trust under ethics-based American Rule of Law, the only alternative is Rule of Force and the loss of our freedom.

> *The eternal difference between right and wrong does not fluctuate, it is immutable.*
>
> **– Patrick Henry (1736–1799)**
> American Founding Father

Chapter 12

Commandment of Trust #1: Truth
No Such Thing as Partially Pregnant

#1. Tell the Truth

Tolerating lies *about something important* undermines trust in our free capital markets and economy, free political system, and free society. This is true whether the lying that damages trust is through fraudulent investment scams, deceptive advertising of products, fraudulent voting in elections, lying in a court of law, deceiving charitable donors about where their money is spent, or politicians lying to voters.

Failing to disclose important information or only disclosing part of the information may also be a lie. Failure to tell the truth may be done innocently (misrepresentation) or with intent to deceive (fraud). As you might expect, the consequences for intentional deception are much more severe.

> *Honesty is the first chapter in the book of wisdom.*
>
> **– Thomas Jefferson (1743–1826)**
> American Founding Father
> 3rd U.S. president, 1801–1809

When it comes to something important that can damage or destroy our essential culture of trust, you must do your homework. Failing to tell the truth *about something important* damages credibility and can lead to serious and painful consequences—even prison.

Lying is not a victimless crime. Lying that damages our essential culture of trust hurts us all.

Lying Under Oath

A former Detroit police deputy was fired while investigating whether the mayor had misused city resources to cover up an affair with his chief of staff. In the former police officer's lawsuit against the city, the mayor and his chief of staff both denied *under oath* that they were having an affair.

When text messages later proved they had both lied in their court testimony, the mayor was sentenced to four months in jail and ordered to pay $1 million in restitution. His chief of staff was sentenced to 120 days in jail. The city paid close to $9 million in settlements (when legal costs were included).[1]

It is a crime (*perjury*) to deliberately give false or misleading testimony under oath about something important that could affect the outcome of an official proceeding—whether orally (e.g., in court, a deposition, or Congressional hearing) or in writing (e.g., an affidavit). Lying about evidence, destroying evidence, and tampering with witnesses in a judicial proceeding are also crimes (*obstruction of justice*).

If witnesses lie in official legal proceedings or produce documents that are not true and accurate, miscarriages of justice will cause the public to lose trust in our American Rule of Law. Without Rule of Law, we will lose our freedom. Only Rule of Force (dictatorship) would be left.

Before you swear under oath (or give an affirmation) as oral or written testimony *in an official legal proceeding*, whether you believe in God or not, imagine yourself placing one hand on the Bible and raising the other hand to swear to "tell the truth, the whole truth and nothing but the truth, so help you God." This oath is a warning to believers and nonbelievers alike that failing to take the oath (or affirmation) seriously can result in grave and painful consequences.

> *Let it simply be asked, Where is the security for property, for reputation, for life, if the sense of religious obligation desert the oaths which are the instruments of investigation in Courts of Justice?*
>
> **– George Washington (1732–1799)**
> American Founding Father
> 1st U.S. president, 1789–1797
> Farewell Address, 1796

Lying to the Government

After the federal government had opened an accounting fraud investigation of Computer Associates (CA), a large software company, the company's board of directors hired attorneys from an outside law firm to investigate. These outside attorneys interviewed the company's top four corporate executives and reported their findings to the federal government.

All four former CA executives were indicted for accounting fraud *and lying to the federal government*. The former CEO received a 12-year prison sentence and was ordered to pay $800 million in restitution. The former head of sales received a 7-year prison sentence; the former general counsel, 2 years, and the former chief financial officer (who had cooperated with the government) received a prison sentence of 7 months in prison and 7 months of home detention.[2]

It is a *federal crime* to lie about something important to a federal official in an official investigation, whether by concealing or covering up information or making false statements orally or in writing.[3] An oath is not required and the setting can be informal.

Federal: A former New York police commissioner was sent to prison, in part, for lying to White House officials when applying for the job as head of the Department of Homeland Security.[4] A well-known billionaire CEO was indicted for insider trading, but sent to prison instead for lying to federal officials and tampering with evidence at her trial.[5] Lying is an easier case to prove than insider trading.

State and Local: When a mother and father lied about their son being carried off in a balloon to create interest in a reality TV show, the ensuing search-and-rescue effort cost taxpayers $50,000. The parents were sentenced to several months in jail.

After a mother was found not guilty of murdering her daughter, the judge ordered her to pay $217,000 for repeatedly lying to state and local authorities, while they were searching for her missing child.[6]

Intent to Deceive

> The founder, former CEO, and chairman of the board of a giant mortgage company, Taylor, Bean & Whitaker (TBW), was indicted for criminal fraud in "one of the largest bank fraud schemes in history." Employees and executives at TBW and a large regional bank were accused of improperly diverting money from the bank to cover TBW's growing losses and fund the CEO's expensive lifestyle (private plane, mansions, and luxury cars). In addition, false financial information was given to the government and TBW's investors.
>
> In 2009, TBW and the bank failed, resulting in $3 billion in losses. Six TBW and bank employees pled guilty and received prison sentences ranging from 3 months to 8 years. After a trial, the former CEO was sentenced to 30 years in prison.[7]

Common law judge-made *fraud* under American Rule of Law is deceptively simple. Generally it requires (1) an *intent to deceive,* (2) about something *material* (relevant and important enough that it could change the outcome of a decision), (3) that another person *actually relies upon,* and *(4) reasonably relies* upon, and (5) is *injured.*

Fraud can be *civil* (e.g., compensatory and sometimes punitive money damages) and *criminal* (e.g., prison, fines, penalties, restitution).

The *types of fraud* are as varied as human imagination: a teacher accepting $200–$500 payments from high school students to change their grades (*theft by deception*); an immigrant lying on a visa application (*immigration fraud*); a financier running scams to defraud investors out of their money (*investment fraud*); a mortgage candidate lying about incomes when applying for a home loan (*mortgage fraud*); a telemarketer creating hundreds of bogus charities to collect hundreds of thousands of dollars in donations (*telemarketing fraud*); an election official forging ballots in a federal, state, or local election (*voter fraud*); an art dealer selling a fake Picasso painting for $2 million (*art fraud*); an official lying to obtain federal government money intended to stimulate the economy (*government stimulus fraud*).

There is also *health care fraud, insurance fraud, bankruptcy fraud, credit card fraud, banking fraud, identity theft,* and *affinity fraud.*[8] *Rampant fraud in the United States is estimated to cost our economy $500 billion to $1 trillion a year.*[9]

Other recent examples of fraud allegations have included:

- **Mortgage Securities:** The Federal Housing Finance Agency (FHFA) sued 17 giant U.S. banks to recover $196 billion alleging that the banks misled Fannie Mae and Freddie Mac "about the soundness of the mortgages underlying the securities."[10]

- **Charities:** The Federal Trade Commission (FTC) (in cooperation with law enforcement officials in 49 states) launched "Operation False Charity." It brought 76 law enforcement actions against 32 fundraising companies, 22 nonprofits, and 31 individuals for allegedly making deceptive claims about their charities.[11]

- **Disability Claims:** In October 2011, prosecutors indicted two doctors, seven retirees, and two others alleging fraudulent disability claims. The Railroad Retirement Board had declared almost all of the full-time railroad employees disabled, potentially costing taxpayers $1 billion.[12] Adding disability pay to their retirement pay could result in retired railroad workers (who could retire at age 50) being paid more in retirement than when working full-time.

Moderation in temper is always a virtue; But moderation in principle is always a vice.

– Thomas Paine (1737–1809)
American Founding Father
Author of "Common Sense," 1776

Trust in our businesses, governments, nonprofits, charities, unions, and other civic institutions and voluntary associations is the backbone of our unique American self-organizing culture and freedom. Rampant fraud destroys trust.

Failure to Fully Disclose

In 1999, the Federal Drug Administration (FDA) approved Vioxx to treat arthritis and pain. Five years later, after millions of people were taking it, Vioxx was recalled. New clinical trials indicated Vioxx could increase the risk of a heart attack or stroke.

Thousands of lawsuits were filed against the drug's manufacturer, Merck & Co. One jury awarded $253 million based on evidence presented at trial that Merck may have known about these potentially dangerous side effects, but *failed to disclose* this information to Vioxx patients. In 2007, Merck agreed to pay $4.85 billion to settle an estimated 50,000 lawsuits.[13]

Failing to disclose all relevant and important information is failing "to tell the truth" under ethics-based American Rule of Law. Information is important if it would have changed the outcome of a decision, had it been known.

Telling the truth means full and complete disclosure of all important and relevant (material) information. Failing to do so damages trust.

> *Half a truth is often a great lie.*
>
> **– Benjamin Franklin (1706–1790)**
> American Founding Father

Claims about Products and Services

The Dannon Company, Inc., a large national food retailer, claimed in national ads that *one* daily serving of Activia yogurt relieved bowel irregularity and that DanActive dairy drink helped people avoid catching colds or the flu.

When the company could not provide scientific proof that these claims were true, the Federal Trade Commission (FTC) fined Dannon $21 million for *deceptive advertising.* The FTC also required Dannon to correct its advertising to say it takes *three* servings a day of Activia yogurt to promote bowel regularity. It also said the company is prohibited from saying DanActive reduces the likelihood of getting a cold or flu, unless the claim is approved by the Food and Drug Administration.[14]

Advertisements for products, services, and nutritional claims about food must be truthful, accurate, and capable of being scientifically confirmed.[15] This is especially true for products and services that could be harmful or deadly, such as narcotics or counterfeit drugs.[16]

In recent years, eleven of the largest pharmaceutical companies have paid over $6 billion in civil and criminal fines in the United States for improperly marketing and advertising drugs.[17]

Failing to tell the truth about something important that damages our culture of trust matters. Without truth, we cannot keep and maintain our essential culture of trust.

Commandment #1: Tell the Truth	
Ethics Principle:	Do not lie *about something important* under oath, whether orally or in writing, destroy evidence, or tamper with witnesses in judicial proceedings. Remember the original oath: "I swear to tell the truth, the whole truth, and nothing but the truth, so help me God." Do not lie to a federal official in an official federal investigation, whether directly or indirectly. Be honest and do not intentionally deceive others. Be careful not to mislead others reasonably relying on your statements about something important that would change the outcome of a decision. Fully disclose all important and relevant information. Claims about products and services must be accurate, verifiable, and when required, capable of scientific proof.
Sample Law:	E.g., civil and criminal fraud, misrepresentation, perjury, obstruction of justice, fiduciary duty to inform, wire fraud, mail fraud, securities fraud, bank fraud, conspiracy, False Claims Act, international money laundering, deceptive trade practices, false advertising, racketeering under the Racketeer Influenced and Corrupt Organizations (RICO) Act, theft by deception, making a false statement to law enforcement, fiduciary duty of candor, Freedom of Information Act, falsifying records of a broker dealer and an investment advisor; defamation, libel, slander; lying to a federal official, a *qui tam* (whistleblower) lawsuit.

Chapter 13

Commandment of Trust #2: Fair
Forget This at Your Peril

#2. Be Fair

Unfair behavior acts like an acid, eating away the bonds of trust required for people to live and work peacefully together in a free, civil society. It saps morale in any individual institution, association, or organization, robbing it of its full productive potential. At a societal level, unfairness can lead to social unrest, political instability, crime, violence, and a breakdown in support for Rule of Law. *Unfair treatment destroys trust.*

Fairness is a key ingredient for stable and harmonious organizations, institutions, associations, and free societies under effective Rule of Law. It is therefore a bedrock ethical principle of our self-organizing American culture of trust. The hallmark of *ethics-based* American law is justice. *The essence of justice is fairness.*

The word "fair" shows up regularly in the titles of our statutes: *Fair* Labor Standards Act, *Fair* Employment and Housing Act, *Fair* Credit Reporting Act, *Fair* Packaging and Labeling Act, Public Employees' *Fair* Employment Act, *Fair* Debt Collection and Practices Act, and Lilly Ledbetter *Fair* Pay Act are just a few examples. *However, just saying something is fair doesn't make it fair. It must actually* be *fair.*

> *Though force can protect in an emergency, only justice, fairness, and cooperation can finally lead men to the dawn of eternal peace.*
>
> **– Dwight D. Eisenhower (1890–1969)**
> Supreme Allied commander, WWII
> 34th U.S. president, 1953–1961

What's Fair?

Fairness, like beauty, is in the eye of the beholder, but standards of beauty around the world are remarkably similar. The common denominator appears to be having symmetrical features, thought to be a biological indication of a healthy mate.

Standards of fairness, like beauty, may also have a biological connection. Scientists say that chimpanzees, primates living in large social groups like humans, have rudimentary "rules" of behavior like human concepts of "fairness."[1] We certainly know that fairness is hard-wired in humans at an early age. Almost as soon as young children can talk, one of their favorite complaints is: "That's not fair!"

Fairness means using an objective standard of behavior to eliminate prejudice or favoritism. It does not mean equal results.

The Essence of Fairness = Justice

Workers clearing debris after the 2001 World Trade Center terrorist attack developed serious health problems and sued the city of New York. After years of litigation, the attorneys on both sides agreed to a $657.5 million settlement, but the presiding judge refused to approve it, saying it was unfair to the workers.

The judge said attorneys' fees should be charged to the city, not the workers, and the terms of the settlement agreement needed to be simplified so workers would know what they were entitled to receive. To make sure this was done, the judge said he would supervise the settlement process.[2]

Fairness can only be determined through the *objective* lens of neutral, independent third parties, such as a judge or a jury, not the interested parties. Humans can easily persuade themselves something is fair when it isn't, especially if they benefit from the unfair treatment of others.

Of course, those on the receiving end of unfair treatment instantly recognize when they are being treated unfairly. Unfairness builds resentments and destructive tensions in any organization, community, or country. *If allowed to fester, unfairness inevitably leads to painful and harmful consequences.*

If we are to keep democracy, there must be a commandment: Thou shalt not ration justice.

– Learned Hand (1872–1961)
Judge U.S. Second Court of Appeals,
often quoted by the U.S. Supreme Court

Fair Competition

Archer Daniels Midland Company (ADM), a giant American agricultural company that makes agricultural additives, was accused of price-fixing on products, including lysine (a popular livestock feed additive). A former vice-chairman of the board and two other executives were indicted for price-fixing.

Two executives were sentenced to 2 years in prison and fined $350,000. The third one received a 2½ year prison sentence for price-fixing. ADM paid a $100 million fine and $100 million to settle lawsuits brought by customers and investors.[3]

The goal of American *antitrust law* is to ensure that we have the best quality products and services at the lowest prices.[4] Fair competition means not engaging in practices that restrain or stifle free and open competition for goods and services.

Business competitors must not agree among themselves to set prices (*price-fixing*). They cannot establish *exclusive territories* with competitors or use their dominant market power (*monopoly power*) in predatory ways to hurt competitors. *Tying* one product to another or supporting a *boycott* of a competitor's products may also be antitrust violations.

Antitrust law is enforced by the U.S. Department of Justice (DOJ) and the Federal Trade Commission (FTC):

- **DOJ:** In 1998, the U.S. Department of Justice and 20 states sued Microsoft Corporation for bundling (*tying*) its popular operating system to its web browser. This meant that buyers who wanted to use Microsoft's operating system could not use the browser of a competitior (e.g., Netscape). A consent decree, effective from 2002 through 2011, prohibited Microsoft from engaging in such anticompetitive behavior.[5]

- **FTC:** The FTC regulates anticompetitive business practices, including *mergers and acquisitions*.[6] Companies are prohibited from combining their businesses if it would create an unreasonable concentration of economic power that would prevent fair and open competition.

According to the U.S. Supreme Court: "Antitrust laws...are...as important to the preservation of economic freedom and our free-enterprise system as the Bill of Rights is to the protection of our fundamental personal freedoms."[7]

Government Competing with Private Business: Under ethics-based American Rule of Law, fair competition standards would apply when the government is competing with private enterprise.[8] Unfortunately, this ethics principle was not applied to "government-sponsored entities" (GSEs) like Fannie Mae and Freddie Mac.

GSEs and their highly paid executives benefitted financially from an implied federal government guarantee that their competitors did not have. So far, American taxpayers have paid more than $100 billion to bail out these two GSEs, and the final tab could be much higher. Allowing unfair competition in these two huge GSEs has been a painful and expensive mistake for American taxpayers.

Competitive Bidding: To get the best products and services at the best prices, our businesses, governments, nonprofits, charities, etc., must require multiple independent bids from different sources, based on the same information.

Bid-rigging (e.g., agreeing in advance with competitors which bidder will win or letting one competitor see the bids of others before submitting their own bid) is a definite no-no. Wells Fargo & Co. agreed to pay $148 million to settle criminal and civil *conspiracy* allegations that Wachovia Bank (which it had purchased) had rigged bids in the municipal bond market.[9]

Fair Investing

> The founder of Galleon Group created an "expert" network of consultants at various high technology companies and financial institutions for his $7 billion hedge fund. These "experts" gave him material, confidential, nonpublic corporate information that he used to buy and sell stocks and other securities.
>
> He was convicted and sentenced to 11 years in prison for insider trading and required to pay a criminal fine and forfeiture of $63 million. In addition, he was ordered to pay a civil penalty of $92.8 million. The Galleon hedge fund closed down in 2009, just days after the criminal investigation was announced.[10]

Insider trading involves using, or passing along important confidential information, not yet publicly available, to buy or sell a corporation's stock or other securities. In one recent 18-month period, the U.S. Attorney for Manhattan obtained 35 convictions for insider trading.[11]

Allowing one group of investors to have such an unfair advantage over other investors would destroy trust in American capital markets. Without vibrant and trusted stock markets, American businesses would no longer have access to the large amounts of capital needed to fund the growth and expansion of businesses over the long term.

Public Companies: The Securities and Exchange Commission (SEC) regularly enforces insider trading laws against corporate officers, directors, employees, their friends, business associates, family members and other "tippees," and others who have misappropriated and taken advantage of confidential information from their employers.[12]

For example, a psychiatrist was found guilty of insider trading for using confidential nonpublic corporate information to purchase company stock. He had obtained that nonpublic confidential information in a counseling session with the wife of the company's chairman of the board.[13]

Government Employees: Government employees are guilty of insider trading if they trade on corporate securities using confidential nonpublic information obtained through their jobs.[14]

U.S. Congress and Congressional Staff: *Congressional staffers and members of Congress* who trade in corporate securities after receiving nonpublic confidential information through their duties in the U.S. Congress have an unfair advantage over other investors. This not only damages trust in our stock markets, it damages the public's trust in Congress as well.[15]

Under *ethics-based* American Rule of Law, such behavior is wrong. If we do not enforce what is right, American public cynicism toward the U.S. Congress, already at an all-time high, will continue to grow.

Private Companies: The ethics principle of fair investing *does not only apply to publicly traded companies.* The Securities and Exchange Commission (SEC) sued the head of a *privately owned* family business for *securities fraud.* Before he sold his company to a giant corporation in 2009 for $2.9 billion, the SEC alleged he bought his employees' stock back at a price much lower than its actual value. The SEC alleged he cheated his former employees out of $110 million.[16]

Fair Process

> A former CEO of Brocade Communications Systems, a software services company, was convicted of backdating executive stock options. His conviction was overturned on appeal because the judge said the prosecutor had misled the jury by saying something to the jury he either knew or had reason to know was not true.
>
> The prosecutor had told the jury that the company's finance employees did not know stock options were being backdated, even though there was evidence that they did know. In a second trial, the former CEO was again convicted. The second conviction was upheld on appeal.[17]

A key feature of American justice is *due process*, guaranteed under the U.S. Constitution. Over the centuries, American Rule of Law has developed clear standards of fair treatment by federal, state, and local governments. Criminal convictions in the United States will be overturned if fair processes and procedures are not followed.

Those accused of a crime have the right to be represented by an attorney, the right to know what crimes they are accused of, the right to face witnesses and cross-examine them, the right to provide evidence in their defense, the right to a jury trial, and the right to a public trial where judges follow established fair procedures. Statements by government prosecutors to juries must be fair and accurate.

In broad terms, due process means *reasonable notice* and a *just hearing* in which *fair procedures* are applied equally and fairly to all. Borrowing concepts used in a criminal trial, in general, "due process" means the right to know what you are accused of, the right to have adequate time to prepare a defense, and the right to a fair and open hearing before a neutral, independent person or group.

If serious consequences could result, a person accused of wrongdoing should have the right to be assisted by an attorney, the right to face his accusers and cross-examine witnesses, the right to see all of the evidence against him, and the right to present his own evidence and witnesses to refute the accusations.[18]

Decisions should only be based on the evidence presented at the hearing, not outside evidence that the "accused" has not had an opportunity to review or refute. There should also be an appeal process to a neutral, independent person or group not connected with those involved in the first hearing, or subject to influence by those who participated in the first hearing.

To ensure justice, fair processes should be applied in all our businesses, governments, nonprofits, charities, unions, associations, etc., before punitive action is taken against any individual or entity. A fair and open process is the only way to ensure that *all* relevant and important information is discovered, presented, and fairly analyzed before an important adverse decision is taken against another.

> *The history of liberty has largely been the history of the observance of procedural safeguards.*
>
> **– Felix Frankfurter (1882–1965)**
> U.S. Supreme Court justice, 1939–1962

Fair Play

Because a chairman of the board of Hewlett Packard Company, Inc. (HP) suspected board members of leaking confidential company information to the media, the company hired outside private investigators. At least one of the investigators used *pretexting* to obtain the personal private phone records of board members and journalists without their permission. Pretexting is "the practice of presenting oneself as someone else in order to obtain private information."

When the pretexting scandal became public, the board chairman was required to testify in a Congressional hearing. HP paid $14.5 million to the California attorney general's office. The chairman of the board and HP's general counsel both resigned. One investigator pled guilty to two felony charges for pretexting. He was sentenced to three months in jail.[19]

Fairness means abiding by *standards of fair play and decency.* Certain behaviors are deemed repugnant because they offend community standards about what is reasonable and acceptable behavior. Our self-governing institutions and associations have an obligation to observe and uphold these standards.

Facebook, Inc., the giant social network site, promised its users that information placed on its site would be private. When this wasn't true, the Federal Trade Commission (FTC) charged the company with *"unfair and deceptive" behavior.*[20] To settle the case, Facebook agreed to respect the privacy of its users and be independently audited for 20 years.[21]

Fairness is the lynchpin of America's culture of trust.

Commandment #2: Fair	
Ethics Principle:	The essence of justice is fairness, but *fairness does not mean equal results.* It means using *objective standards of behavior* to eliminate prejudice or favoritism. Being fair means not engaging in practices that stifle free and open competition in the marketplace. It also means not divulging confidential, non-public information obtained in a position of trust and confidence that is used to buy or sell stocks and other securities. Fairness means due process; that is, fair notice of any alleged wrong behavior, and a fair hearing and process with fair procedures that apply equally to all. Fairness also means following community standards of fair play and decency.
Sample Law:	E.g., antitrust, fair competition laws, insider trading, fair use in intellectual property laws, securities fraud, conspiracy, unfair lending practices, unfair business practices, bid-rigging, Racketeer Influenced and Corrupt Organizations Act, conspiracy (e.g., conspiracy to defraud, conspiracy to make false entries in bank records), obstruction of justice, wire fraud, mail fraud, deceptive trade practices, price-fixing, predatory business practices, identity theft, pretexting.

Chapter 14

Commandment of Trust #3: Loyalty
Two Masters Is One Too Many

#3. Be Loyal

"You cannot serve two masters." So says a Biblical admonition in the New Testament.[1] When acting on behalf of another in a position of trust and confidence, you must *always* put the interests of the person you are representing *ahead* of your own interests, or the interests of anyone else.

Thus, the trustee of a trust account must make investment decisions solely for the financial benefit of the trust, not because he receives higher commissions for purchasing certain funds. A doctor must only prescribe drugs that are best for her patients, not because a drug company has given the doctor an all-expense-paid trip to a seminar at an expensive resort. A partner in a partnership may not secretly profit at the expense of another partner. Union leaders must never accept bribes to allow companies to hire illegal workers.

Corporate directors and officers have a fiduciary duty of loyalty to the corporation itself, *a separate legal person* under both American and British Rule of Law dating back to the 19th century. Therefore, under *ethics-based* American Rule of Law, when awarding pay, perks, and benefits to officers or executives, directors *must always act in the best interests of the corporation*, above all other interests, at all times.

State and federal politicians have a responsibility to represent all of their constituents, not just special interests contributing to their campaigns or free-spending lobbyists. They are ethically bound to do what is best for all Americans and for the country, not what's good for themselves, their families, their friends, and those they favor. Politicians must not personally profit from actions they take in their representative capacity. To do otherwise is wrong. It destroys trust in our governments.

A *fiduciary duty of loyalty* applies automatically. Nothing need be agreed to or signed. It automatically applies as soon as one is placed in a position of trust and confidence to act on the behalf of another. Trustees, agents, corporate officers and directors, and partners in a partnership are just a few examples of those who owe a fiduciary duty of loyalty to those on whose behalf they are acting.

The amount of money involved in any breach of this fiduciary duty is irrelevant. Disloyalty harms our culture of trust. Thus, under *ethics-based* American Rule of Law, disloyalty alone can trigger serious legal repercussions (e.g., punitive damages), regardless of the amount of money involved. *Divided loyalties destroy trust.*

Conflicts of Interest

The New York state workers' pension fund is managed by the New York comptroller. However, one former comptroller, instead of managing the $129 billion fund in the best interests of state workers, invested the fund's money if firms gave money to his re-election campaign or paid millions of dollars in consulting fees to his political consultant (called "pay to play").

Six people pled guilty. The former comptroller was sentenced to 1 to 4 years in prison. His political consultant was sentenced to 16 months to 4 years in prison and ordered to return $19 million to the state retirement fund. Several financial firms have paid $120 million in settlements.[2]

A *conflict of interest* generally arises when a person in a position of trust and confidence uses his or her position for personal benefit (e.g., financial gain). This damages trust.

Appearances Matter: However, even the *appearance of a conflict of interest* can damage trust. Therefore, a conflict of interest can also arise when "a person has a private or personal interest sufficient to *appear to influence* the objective exercise of his or her official duties as, say, a public official, an employee, or a professional."[3]

Avoiding a conflict of interest (or the appearance of a conflict of interest) requires individuals to *act at arm's length* with other parties. Picture two people standing side by side but far enough apart that they cannot touch each other. One party cannot physically make the other party move in any particular direction.

Thus, parties acting at arm's length from one another are acting freely and independently of each other. They are not related to one another and do not have any special relationship or control over one another either. *Conflicts of interest or the appearance of conflicts of interest damage trust, whether in business, governments, nonprofits and charities, unions, etc.*

The Revolving Door: Americans' lack of trust toward their federal and state governments has not been helped by the constant *revolving door* between government jobs and the private sector.[4] When former government officials are given lucrative jobs in the private sector when they leave government service, it raises questions about decisions they made while working for the government. Did they make their decisions for the benefit of the American public (as they are duty-bound to do) or were their decisions made for the benefit of those who would later employ them?[5]

Here are just two of the many recent examples that raise questions about potential conflicts of interest involving the *revolving door between government and private business*:

- **Democrat:** Robert Rubin (former U.S. Treasury secretary under President Bill Clinton), along with Sandy Weill (former head of Citigroup, Inc.) and Alan Greenspan (former chairman of the U.S. Federal Reserve), were heavily involved in seeking the repeal of the *Glass-Steagall Act*.[6]

Repealing this law enabled Citigroup to complete its purchase of Travelers Insurance Company to create the gargantuan "too big to fail" bank that later had to be bailed out with $45 billion of taxpayers' money. After leaving government service, Robert Rubin became an advisor and board member of Citigroup for which he reportedly received at least $126 million.[7]

- **Republican:** A former chairman of a U.S. House of Representatives committee in charge of regulating the pharmaceutical industry, Billy Tauzin, played a pivotal role in the passage of the *Medicare Prescription Drug, Improvement, and Modernization Act of 2003.*

  The Congressional Budget Office estimated this new prescription benefit would raise only $7 billion in new revenues to cover the $407 billion in additional costs to the taxpayers under this new law (from 2004 to 2013).[8] In 2004, when Billy Tauzin left the House of Representatives, he accepted a job as chairman of the pharmaceutical industry's top lobbying group with a pay package of at least $2 million a year.[9]

Other situations in which conflicts of interest issues have been raised include:

- A federal lawsuit filed against the National Education Association (NEA) (the largest teachers' union in the United States with more than 2.7 million members), alleging the union collected nearly $50 million in royalties in 2004 to endorse financial products with high fees and poor investment returns to their members.[10]

- New York legislators relied on a former city actuary to justify raising unionized government worker pension benefits. After that actuary underestimated costs to the taxpayers by $500 million, it was discovered that he had failed to disclose he was being paid by government employee unions.[11]

- Some university financial aid officers received financial incentives from student loan companies (e.g., company stock, consulting fees, or other financial benefits) to be placed on the university's student loan "preferred provider" lists.

  One prominent university fired its financial aid officer and agreed to pay $1.1 million to educate students about student loans. It also agreed to have its financial aid office monitored by the state for 5 years.[12]

Representing Both Sides

Del Monte Foods, a multi-billion dollar food and pet product company, agreed to be sold for $5 billion. Its investment bank, Barclays Capital, represented both the seller and the buyers in the sale (using a standard industry practice called staple financing). By providing financial advice to the seller and financing for the buyers, Barclays Capital doubled its fees, collecting $24 million each from the seller and the buyers.

Del Monte's shareholders sued Barclays, alleging that because of the bank's dual and conflicting roles, it failed to get the highest and best price for shareholders. To settle the litigation, Barclays agreed to pay the Del Monte shareholders $23.7 million and Del Monte Foods agreed to pay $65.7 million, for a total of $89.4 million.[13]

It is a conflict of interest to represent both sides of the same transaction. Imagine one attorney representing both the husband and wife in a hostile divorce. When one party gets more, the other receives less.

In theory, you could represent both sides of the transaction if both parties agreed after receiving all relevant information. As a practical matter, it is still unwise to do so. If something goes wrong, prior permission may not be much protection.

The board of directors of Enron Corp. gave its former chief financial officer (CFO), Andrew Fastow, permission to waive the corporation's conflict of interest policy. Fastow made millions of dollars personally in side deals with Enron. Nevertheless, when Enron went bankrupt, Fastow went to prison for 6 years for his role in the collapse of Enron Corporation.

> *No man can serve two masters. For either he will hate the one, and love the other: or he will sustain the one, and despise the other.*
>
> **– New Testament, Matthew 6:24, Bible**

Bribes and Kickbacks

The former mayor of New Orleans was convicted of participating in a bribery and kickback scheme over several years after Hurricane Katrina. Evidence produced at trial showed the former mayor had given favorable treatment to those who had given him bribes and kickbacks amounting to more than $200,000, as well as free travel and personal services, etc. In 2014, he was sentenced to 10 years in prison.[14]

A *kickback* is defined as "[t]he seller's return of part of the purchase price of an item to a buyer or buyer's representative for the purpose of inducing a purchase or improperly influencing future purchases."[15] For example, in a case involving a prominent plaintiff's securities law firm (Milberg Weiss), senior attorneys wrongfully promised their clients 10% of their attorneys' fees to act as lead plaintiffs in their securities lawsuits.

A *bribe* is "the offering, giving, receiving, or soliciting of something of value for the purpose of influencing the action of an official in the discharge of his or her public or legal duties."[16] Bribery is a crime at the local, state, and federal levels, and internationally:

- **Local:** Two deadly crane collapses in New York City killed nine people. The former chief crane inspector for the Department of Buildings was sentenced to 2 to 6 years in prison for taking bribes for "falsifying paperwork related to crane inspections and crane-operated exams."[17]

- **State:** A former New York State Assemblyman was convicted of bribery (and other crimes) for taking bribes worth more than $250,000.[18]

- **Federal:** Two former members of the U.S. House of Representatives were sent to prison for bribery: one, a Republican, received a sentence of 8 years and 4 months;[19] the other, a Democrat, was sentenced to 13 years.[20]

- **International:** In May of 2011, two executives of a manufacturing company (including a former president and a former chief financial officer), along with a Mexican intermediary, were convicted under the Foreign Corrupt Practices Act. They were found guilty of paying bribes to Mexican government officials (at a Mexican state-owned utility company) to get multi-million dollar contracts.[21]

  This was the first U.S. criminal trial and conviction for foreign bribery under this 1977 statute. In recent years, 58 businesses have settled foreign bribery charges with payments of nearly $4 billion.[22]

Gifts and Gratuities

In 2004, an Ohio governor pleaded no contest for failing to report more than 50 gifts he received, worth about $6,000 (e.g., golf outings, meals, and tickets to sports events). He was fined $4,000.

Two of the governor's golf outings were paid for by a coin dealer who was given a $50 million contract to invest in rare coins by the Ohio Bureau of Workers' Compensation. After $13 million in rare coins disappeared, the coin dealer was convicted of stealing from the fund and sentenced to 18 years in prison.[23]

Receiving improper gifts and gratuities includes "anything of substantial value," including free or discounted items or services. Examples include restaurant meals, golf outings, hotel and travel expenses, and event tickets.

Keep in mind that what might appear to be in the gray zone of acceptable gifts and gratuities can fast become black and white conflict of interest allegations under the white-hot glare of publicity.

If you are in a position to help or hinder the party giving you gifts and gratuities, you are exposing yourself to allegations of a conflict of interest. At a minimum, all gifts over a certain minimal amount should be publicly disclosed.

Giving gifts and gratuities can also be a problem. A government relations executive of a large healthcare provider resigned. He had spent $250,000 in company funds over a 7-year period for tickets to sports games and other events to "build relationships" with politicians.[24]

Self-Dealing

> A UCLA surgery professor established a charity nonprofit foundation. He funded it almost entirely with a $3 million donation from himself; only about $130,000 came from donations from others. The California attorney general sued the professor for *self-dealing,* alleging the professor had used the charity's money to benefit companies the professor owned (e.g., $120,000 to produce an educational DVD and $15,000 to build plastic heart models). A charity's directors and officers cannot personally benefit from a nonprofit's income or assets.
>
> To settle the lawsuit, the professor was required to resign as the charity's CEO. He was required to repay $140,000 to the foundation for items spent for his benefit, not the benefit of the charity.[25]

Those acting on behalf of another may not use their positions instead for personal advantage. You cannot personally benefit directly, or indirectly through relatives, business associates, or organizations in which you have an interest. You must not compete with the person, entity, or organization you are representing (e.g., soliciting customers for a competing enterprise while still employed at your current organization).

Confidential Information

> While still employed at Navigant, a consulting firm, two former employees gave confidential information about Navigant and its customers to a competing consulting firm hoping to buy Navigant.
>
> When negotiations broke down for the sale of Navigant, the two former employees resigned and went to work for the competing firm, taking other Navigant employees with them. For disclosing confidential information, Navigant won a $4.1 million verdict against these two former employees.[26]

When acting on behalf of another, you may not use or communicate *confidential information* acquired by you in your representative capacity. Confidential information obtained while you are representing another may not be used, even after your representation of another has been terminated.

Confidential information generally includes information not readily or publicly available that gives an individual, organization, or entity a competitive advantage. For information to be confidential, an individual, organization, or entity generally must have taken reasonable steps to ensure that the information is kept confidential (e.g., requiring check-in and security badges before being admitted into a business).

Loyalty is a key ingredient of trust. We do not trust people or organizations that do not put the interests first of those they are representing above all other interests (including their own interests).

Commandment #3: Be Loyal	
Ethics Principle:	When acting on behalf of others, always put their interests first above your own self-interest or the interests of those you favor (e.g., your family, friends, associates, etc.). Avoid conflicts of interest or the appearance of a conflict of interest by acting *at arm's length* with others. Do not accept kickbacks or bribes. Also, be careful about accepting gifts and gratuities from those in a position to benefit from your decisions or actions, or giving gifts and gratuities to those from whom you can benefit. Do not self-deal. Keep confidential information confidential.
Sample Law:	E.g., breach of fiduciary duty of loyalty, Foreign Corrupt Practices Act, bribery, kickbacks, racketeering, money laundering, conspiracy, wire fraud, mail fraud, bribery of a public official, rewarding official misconduct, False Claims Act, federal and state securities laws, Hobbs Act extortion, fraud, the Anti-Kickback Act, the Stark Law, state conflict of interests statutes.

Chapter 15

Commandment of Trust #4: Care
No Going to Sleep at the Wheel

#4. Be Careful

Being careful is an essential element of our culture of trust. We must trust that our food will not sicken or kill us; that our products will not be dangerously defective and cause us harm; and that those responsible for transporting passengers and goods are properly trained to avoid harming people and property. We must trust that our banks, investment advisors, corporate officers and directors, and professionals are *careful*, *competent*, and *diligent*.

We take being careful for granted until something goes wrong, such as a doctor amputating the wrong leg, an airline pilot overshooting the runway, or a utility company failing to maintain its pipeline and causing a deadly explosion.

The key elements of being careful are being *attentive*, *cautious*, *conscientious*, *competent*, and *diligent*. When acting in a position of trust and confidence on the behalf of another, you have a *fiduciary duty of care*, the highest level of care. *Careless behavior destroys trust.*

> *A little neglect may breed great mischief.*
>
> **– Benjamin Franklin (1706–1790)**
> American Founding Father

Negligence

A diver on a diving excursion with 19 other divers 12 miles off the coast of Long Beach, California, surfaced 400 feet from the diving boat. Although he blew his safety whistle, no one heard him. The diving organizers marked him present, even though he was not onboard, and the boat left without him. When they realized their mistake more than three hours later, they immediately notified the Coast Guard. Eventually, the stranded diver was rescued by a passing ship.

The diver sued the diving excursion company for *negligence*. The jury awarded the diver $1.68 million, deducting $320,000 for the diver's negligence in failing to follow the diving company's instruction to surface closer to the boat.[1]

Being *careful* means paying close attention to potential dangers to avoid making mistakes that could cause harm to people and property. As a general rule, when you can *reasonably foresee* that your actions may cause harm to others, you must conduct yourself as a *reasonably careful person* would under the same or similar circumstances to avoid causing such harm.

Ordinary negligence is a failure to exercise reasonable care. *Gross negligence* is a more extreme lack of care "likely to cause foreseeable grave injury or harm to persons, property, or both."[2] Simply following industry standards of safety is not enough to avoid liability for negligence. Punitive damages may be awarded for failing to take proper care. *Carelessness destroys trust.*

Some individuals and groups, like *common carriers* (e.g., airlines, taxis, railways), *landowners, and others* are held to *higher standards of care.* For example, a common carrier must use the highest care and vigilance of a *very careful* person, not just a reasonably careful person. When a business invites customers onto its property to shop, it must not only repair and correct known dangers, but must also inspect the property to discover and correct unknown hazards.[3]

Reckless Behavior

> Three people at an Arizona retreat died after participating in a sweat-lodge ceremony, in a tent that was extremely hot and airless. The author and self-help guru responsible for the retreat ignored signs that some participants were in serious distress.
>
> Prosecutors argued that the conduct of the self-help guru and author was *reckless.* He was convicted of negligent homicide and sentenced to two years in prison.[4]

Reckless behavior is excessive indifference to the consequences of extremely risky behavior. Driving a car on the freeway at 100 mph, when the maximum speed limit is 65 mph, is an example of reckless conduct. Reckless behavior generally results in much higher monetary damage awards and, if serious enough, can result in criminal charges.

Safe Products

> The drug Phenergan is normally given orally because if injected improperly into an artery, it can lead to gangrene and amputation. The Federal Drug Administration (FDA) approved Phenergan with a warning label that "extreme care" must be used.
>
> A woman being treated for migraine headaches was given Phenergan by injection without first being told that 20 other people had lost limbs from the drug being improperly injected. After part of her arm had to be amputated, she sued the drug maker. A state jury awarded her $7.4 million.[5]

Strict liability applies when handling dangerous animals, such as a vicious dog, or conducting dangerous activities, like handling explosives. No matter how careful you are, you will still be held responsible for injuries to people and/or property damage.

Product liability is a type of strict liability. Those who manufacture, distribute, and sell products (or supply raw materials or parts), are liable for dangerous and defective products that cause injury or harm, even if they use the highest care possible.

Products may be defective or dangerous for different reasons, including: (1) a *manufacturing defect* (e.g., using defective materials), (2) a *design defect* (e.g., failing to provide safeguards like a screen over the whirling blades of a fan), or *failing to warn* (e.g., not disclosing the potentially harmful side effects of drugs).

Data Safety and Security

Retail stores TJ Maxx and Marshalls did not use the upgraded data encryption standards recommended by the banking industry. Therefore, hackers sitting outside of the stores (with only a computer and antenna) could intercept data on the computers, cash registers, and other computerized mobile equipment inside the stores.

Hackers gained access to the database of the parent company, TJX, Co., and stole the private information of 45.7 million of its credit and debit cards from about one year's worth of records, and perhaps as many as 200 million cards over 4 years, although the company says it cannot know for sure. In addition, they stole the driver's licenses, military identification, and Social Security Numbers of about 451,000 customers. TJX paid $40.9 million to settle potential claims of bank *losses caused by this massive data security breach.*[6]

The Privacy Rights Clearinghouse, which maintains a database on security breaches, estimated that between 2005 and 2010, 500 million sensitive records were breached.[7] One giant commercial bank lost computer data tapes containing the personal information of 1.2 million federal employees.[8] The private data of 2.2 million active and reserve military personnel was stolen from the Department of Veterans Affairs.[9]

To prevent identity theft, businesses, governments, universities, and other institutions and associations that collect private data on individuals must take care to protect the security of such data through encryption or other security measures. They must take care to protect personal data from being lost or stolen, exposing individuals to identity theft.

Data breaches must be immediately investigated and reported to law enforcement. Those whose personal information has been compromised must be immediately notified.[10]

Competence

When an Illinois bank, Mutual Bank of Harvey, failed on July 31, 2009, it cost the Federal Deposit Insurance Corporation (FDIC) an estimated $775 million in losses. The FDIC sued eight former bank directors and two former bank officers, as well as the bank's outside general counsel (also a bank director) and his law firm, to recover more than $127 million.

The outside attorney/director and his law firm were sued for *legal malpractice, breach of fiduciary duty* (e.g., a conflict of interest), and *aiding and abetting the director and officer defendants' breaches of fiduciary duties* (e.g., allowing the bank to approve extremely risky loans). The former directors and officers were sued for *gross negligence, negligence,* and *breach of fiduciary duty* for improperly spending the bank's assets (e.g., $250,000 on a wedding, $300,000 for a board of directors meeting in Monte Carlo, and illegally paying $10.5 million in dividends to bank insiders when the bank was failing).[11]

Being careful means being *competent*—that is, having the necessary knowledge, skill, and experience to competently perform the agreed tasks. It means possessing and exercising the necessary degree of care and skill, not just having a degree, title, or certificate.

Failure to carry out responsibilities in accordance with the high standards expected in a profession can result in malpractice claims against licensed professionals, such as doctors, lawyers, and accountants. For example, when Reliance Insurance Co. failed, its outside auditor Deloitte & Touche paid $40 million to settle claims that it breached its fiduciary duty and was professionally negligent in conducting its accounting audit of the insurance company.[12]

Diligence

An individual held investment seminars at which he convinced elderly investors to refinance their home mortgages to invest in what turned out to be a $250 million Ponzi scheme. He touted the safety of this investment, even though he had not independently verified that the investment was legitimate.

Over a five-year period, he raised $74 million from more than 800 investors. He did not tell investors that he received a $2.4 million commission for recommending this investment. The Securities and Exchange Commission (SEC) alleged that this individual breached his fiduciary duty to his clients by *not conducting proper due diligence* on the "product" he was selling before recommending it to investors.[13]

Being careful means that when you agree to do something on behalf of someone else, you must be *diligent*—that is, you must do your homework and be thorough before reaching a decision or taking action.

Eight employees of the Securities and Exchange Commission (SEC) were disciplined for failing to discover Bernie Madoff's $50 billion Ponzi scheme after multiple warnings from whistleblowers.[14] A report by an outside law firm hired by the SEC said that "the agency received six warnings about Mr. Madoff's trading business over 16 years."[15]

Being careful and diligent means *not taking excessive risks* with other people's money and property. When risky bets pay off, no one complains. But taking excessively risky bets often leads to spectacular failures.

Imagine yourself the pilot of a 747 jet. So long as your passengers and property are delivered safely to their destination, no one is likely to ask any questions about whether you were taking too many risks when flying the plane. But if your plane crashes, you will soon face a hostile audience armed with bloody, gory pictures of all those killed and maimed, as well as a tally of the devastating property losses. That's the likely scenario in which any risks you may have taken will be evaluated as to whether they were reasonable or excessive. In addition, if you walk away from the plane crash not only without any injury to yourself or your property, but also extraordinarily wealthy, the level of public scrutiny over how you were flying the plane and for whose benefit you were flying the plane is likely to be extremely intense.

We do not trust those who are not careful, competent, and diligent.

Commandment #4: Be Careful	
Ethics Principle:	Act with care to avoid harm to people and property that is reasonably forseeable. Risks of potential harm must be fully and accurately disclosed. Take care to protect personal data from being lost or stolen, exposing individuals to identity theft. Be competent and diligent. Being competent means having the knowledge, skill, and ability to meet the standard of performance required for the task you have undertaken. Being diligent means doing your homework; that is, researching, investigating, and carefully reviewing all relevant data before making important decisions or taking action, and persevering with tasks until they are properly completed. Do not take excessive risks with other people's money and property. When acting in a position of trust and confidence on behalf of another, you have a fiduciary duty of care, the highest level of care. Manufacturers, distributors, suppliers, and sellers of dangerous or defective products are liable regardless of fault.
Sample Law:	E.g., negligence, product liability, malpractice, recklessness, negligent hiring, negligent supervision, gross negligence, due diligence, shareholders' derivative lawsuit, fiduciary duty of care (and skill), strict liability, international money laundering, securities fraud, unfair trade practices.

Chapter 16

Commandment of Trust #5: Account
The ABCs of Counting the Marbles

#5. Be Accountable

Being accountable means being responsible for results, whether good or bad. Accountable people do not say, "mistakes were made"; they say, "I made a mistake."

Those who receive money and/or property while acting on behalf of another must provide clear, detailed, and accurate records of all money and property received. Being accountable means explaining your actions and decisions in an understandable way. *Not being accountable destroys trust.*

Governments

In 2010, American taxpayers paid an estimated $2.2 trillion to the federal government and more than $700 billion to state governments.[1] Our federal, state, and local governments are accountable to the American taxpayers for the money and property they have received. Where did the money go? Who got it? Why did those parties receive the money? What was it used for? What were the results? Who benefitted?

Our governments must explain what has been done with all of the money and property they have received without accounting tricks, gimmicks, misstatements, or inaccuracies. Governments must use the same precision in reporting to the American public that the Internal Revenue Service (IRS) expects from American taxpayers when we are "accounting" for our incomes to the IRS for tax purposes—meticulous and accurate detail.

In 2011, 51% of Americans polled said they believe the federal government wastes over half of every dollar they collect.[2] *Improper accounting destroys trust.*

Businesses

Investors and lenders must have an accurate accounting of all money and property in a business before lending or investing money. Expenses must be reasonable and necessary. Financial records must be accurate and complete.

Inaccurate or misleading accounting of money and property destroys trust in our businesses. Distrust in business accounting may be why bank stocks fell sharply in 2011, even though banks were reporting very positive financial results.[3]

Others

Trade associations, mutual funds, pension funds, charities, unions, religious institutions, professional sports, educational institutions, etc., handle other people's money and property as well and depend on funding from outside sources. They, too, must give a complete and accurate accounting to their stakeholders of all money and property received.

Nonprofit revenues have grown dramatically—from $678 billion in 1994 to $1.4 trillion in 2004.[4] Distrust has grown as well. The Ethics Resource Center "estimates that charities may lose as much as $40 billion to fraud."[5] In a national survey reported in 2008, about 55% of workers in nonprofits said they have seen fraud, lying to stakeholders, and inaccurate financial records, about the same as for-profit businesses (56%) and the government (57%).[6]

In 2006, a Harris Interactive poll found that "only one in 10 Americans strongly believes charities are 'honest and ethical' in their use of donated funds."[7] *Insiders say that public confidence in charities continues to erode because of "abuse of trust, lack of accountability and, sometimes, a lack of concrete results."[8]*

Duty to Account

Brooke Astor, a New York socialite worth an estimated $185 million, died in 2007 at the age of 105. She had Alzheimer's disease. Prior to her death, her son handled her financial affairs. He was accused of stealing millions of dollars from his mother's estate (e.g., giving himself a $1 million raise for handling his mother's estate and changing her will to inflate his inheritance by tens of millions of dollars).

The 85-year-old son was convicted of *misusing his mother's estate* and sentenced to one to three years in prison. The attorney who helped him change his mother's will and forge his mother's signature was sentenced to one to three years in prison as well.[9]

When acting in a position of trust and confidence and handling money or property on behalf of another, a *fiduciary duty to account* attaches automatically. Nothing needs to be agreed to or signed.

A fiduciary is "an individual in whom another has placed the *utmost* [emphasis added] trust and confidence to manage and protect property or money... wherein one person has an obligation to act for another's benefit."[10] Under the duty to account *any* money or property received while acting on behalf of another—including profits gained through breaching a duty, bribes, kickbacks, or gifts—must be turned over to the one being represented (unless prior permission has been given to do otherwise).

Misusing the money or property of another can sometimes be criminal, especially when the government is involved. A former Santa Fe County sheriff in New Mexico pleaded guilty to criminal charges for selling county government property on eBay. He sold used police body armor and printer cartridges and kept the $75,000 he received from those sales.[11]

Accurate and transparent records of all transactions must be kept. When requested, these records must be made available to those on whose behalf you are acting. As a fiduciary, you must never commingle your money and property with the money or property of others or take money or property from another's account without prior proper authorization.

The best advice when handling other people's money is to handle someone else's money with the same care and concern you would if it were your own money (assuming you handle your own money responsibly). This is especially true when determining what "reasonable and necessary expenses" are.

Ask yourself, "Would I pay the same expenses out of my own pocket for someone else?" If the answer is no, think twice about whether you are "reasonably" spending another's money for "necessary" expenses (whether an individual, a corporation, or other entity).

Reasonable and necessary expenses must be in the best interests of the corporation, government entity, nonprofit, union, charity, etc. (that is, the individual or entity that is being represented by another). Would you pay for the personal multi-million-dollar home of one of your colleagues out of your own pocket? Not likely.

So why would a corporation, nonprofit, charity, etc., pay for the personal home of one of its top executives (who are in control and/or influence the checkbook of the person, entity, organization, or association they are representing and already often extremely well paid)?

Under *ethics-based* American Rule of Law, bear in mind that what are "reasonable and necessary" expenses can look very different to a judge, jury, government investigator, or the public *after* a major crisis (e.g., bankruptcy, crime, or major loss) or national emergency than in times of peace, stability, and prosperity.

Fraud in Accounting

Accounting is defined as "[t]he systematic recording, reporting, and analysis of financial transactions of a business."[12] Accounting standards in the United States over the past several decades have moved away from principle-based accounting (more like *ethics-based* Rule of Law) and moved more toward "rules"-based accounting (more like American Rule of Lawyers and Bureaucrats law on steroids described in Chapter 11).[13]

This appears to have led some corporations and other organizations to falsely believe that technically following the accounting "rules" will protect them from accounting fraud claims. This is not so.

As a former top securities regulator at the Securities and Exchange Commission (SEC) warned in 2002: "corporations strictly following accounting rules still could be accused of securities fraud if the filings don't accurately reflect a company's underlying [financial] condition."[14]

> *When people lie, if they play games, if they take money that doesn't belong to them, they are going to go to jail... if they misstate their financials.*
>
> **– Harvey Pitt (1945–)**
> Chairman, Securities and Exchange
> Commission (SEC), 2001–2003

Whatever accounting methods are used must provide an accurate picture of the *actual* financial health of the individual, business, association, government entity, or other organization.

Business: KPMG, one of the remaining four large accounting firms (there used to be eight), says financial reporting fraud (what is reported to others outside of the company) can include such things as "misstating asset revenue, conceal[ing] liabilities and expenses, improperly recognizing revenue, and improperly omitting or disclosing financial data."[15]

Lawsuits started flying over the more than $600 billion bankruptcy of Lehman Brothers, the largest bankruptcy in American history." One was a class action lawsuit filed by investors against Lehman's officers and directors, underwriters, and its auditor, Ernst & Young. Investors who had suffered huge losses as a result of Lehman's bankruptcy alleged that the officers, directors, underwriters, and auditor had misled them about the true picture of Lehman's finances. In 2011, the underwriters agreed to pay $426.2 million to settle this lawsuit; Lehman's officers and directors agreed to pay another $90 million.[16]

In 2013, Ernst & Young agreed to pay $99 million to settle a class action lawsuit against Lehman's former directors and other financial institutions "for helping Lehman misstate its financial records."[17]

Take-Two Interactive Software, Inc., a company that distributes computer games, allegedly inflated its revenue so top executives could receive huge bonuses.[18] The company shipped out hundreds of thousands of video games to distributors who had no obligation to pay for them, recording them as sales. However, the company accepted returns of the games in subsequent accounting periods.

The company's top executives and the corporation were civilly sued for accounting fraud by the SEC. The company paid a penalty of $7.5 million. The executives agreed to the following penalties and payments: former chairman of the board and CEO: about $3.6 million; former executive vice president and COO: about $1.7 million; former CFO: about $1 million; and the then current CFO: about $100,000.[19]

Government: There can also be fraud in how money is accounted for by our federal, state, and local governments. Here are just a few recent examples:

- **Federal:** An organized crime ring collected $35 million from Medicare by inventing 118 bogus health care clinics in 25 states.[20] Eighteen people were indicted. A U.S. attorney said this was the "single largest Medicare fraud ever perpetrated by a single criminal enterprise."[21]

- **State:** In October 2011, New York City agreed to pay the federal government $70 million for improperly authorizing home care for elderly clients under the federal Medicaid program. The city of New York failed to obtain the required assessments from doctors, nurses, or social workers or the necessary "independent medical review" in disputed cases.[22]

- **Local:** Los Angeles County auditors substantiated 101 instances of fraud during the last six months of 2009.[23] In 2011, the former city administrator for Bell, California, Robert Rizzo, his assistant city manager, and six current and former Bell council members were criminally charged with looting $5.5 million in public money.[24] Although Bell, California, is one of Los Angeles County's poorest cities, Rizzo paid himself a salary package that topped $1.5 million. He and others also received $1.9 million in loans from the county to pay for personal expenses (e.g., purchasing a home and child adoption expenses).[25]

Nonprofit: The American Red Cross, well-known for its disaster assistance, has had recurring problems. Allegations of financial misdeeds in its local chapters have included a Louisiana fundraiser depositing Red Cross donations in her own bank account; a Pennsylvania manager embezzling Red Cross money to support a drug habit; and a Maryland executive forging signatures on Red Cross purchase orders meant for disaster victims.[26] The former CEO of a New Jersey chapter and his bookkeeper were accused by prosecutors of stealing well over $1 million from the Red Cross.[27]

Reasonable and Necessary Expenses

Scandal erupted over allegations of *unreasonable and unnecessary expenses* at the U.S. Government Accountability Office (GAO), the watchdog agency charged with overseeing that federal money is being properly spent. A *Washington Times* Freedom of Information Act request revealed the GAO spent lavishly on its own conferences and awards ceremonies, perhaps as many as 77 of them.

The GAO spent more than $800,000 for a Las Vegas conference that included clowns, a mind reader, and an expensively catered party. It spent more than a quarter of a million dollars for hundreds of employees to attend a one-day conference in Las Vegas.[28]

When you are handling the money and property of another on their behalf, you may only spend money for *reasonable* and *necessary* expenses. Here are some examples of unreasonable and unnecessary "business" expenses that have cost individuals their jobs or led to criminal charges:[29]

- **Nonprofit head:** Taking a limousine short distances between buildings instead of walking or taking a cab; using nonprofit funds to go to a spa and pay for tickets to the Latin Grammy Awards

- **Investment banker:** Running up a $62,000 tab for wine at an expensive restaurant

- **University president:** Charging the university $7,000 for such things as bed sheets and garbage bags for his personal residence

- **Police commissioner:** Using city funds to finance affairs with many different women, including paying for expensive hotels, meals, clothing, and gifts

- **State consumer chief:** Paying for the cost of transportation for the chief and her daughter to attend a Justin Timberlake concert[30]

- **High-ranking U.S. Department of Labor official:** "Coercing" employees to award contracts to a management consultant who was his friend and paying his friend about $700,000 for work that would have cost much less, had there been open competitive bidding[31]

> *Over the past two decades, we have clearly seen an erosion of ethical values.*
>
> **– Arthur Levitt (1931–)**
> Chairman, Securities and Exchange
> Commission (SEC), 1993–2001

Competent Oversight

New York City issued a $73 million contract to Scientific Applications International Corporation (SAIC) for timekeeping software. The contract involved more than 160,000 city employees at different agencies with thousands of job titles and hundreds of union agreements. SAIC hired a subcontractor, TechnoDyne, a certified minority and female-owned company, to perform much of the work.

The contract amount ballooned to $720 million (inflated bills were submitted to the city in a massive kickback scheme). Eleven individuals and TechnoDyne were criminally charged. Two pleaded guilty and cooperated with authorities. To avoid prosecution, SAIC agreed to pay $500 million in restitution and penalties.[32]

Part of fulfilling the responsibility of being accountable means providing competent oversight. This includes watching over the details of a project to ensure it is done right, on time, and without unreasonable cost overruns. Failing to competently oversee how money and property entrusted to you or your organization or entity is handled, while acting on another's behalf, is a breach of your duty to account.

Government Waste and Abuse: Federal, state, and local governments are accountable for competently overseeing the public's money and property. Here are some recent examples indicating serious problems in government accountability:

- The U.S. Department of Energy was faulted for financial mismanagement. It allegedly sold 23 trucks for 17 cents each and a $9,000 copier for a nickel.[33]

- The State of California may have a $500 billion gap between pension and other benefit promises made to state workers and retirees and the money on hand to pay for those promised benefits.[34]

- There may be as much as $100–$200 billion in unnecessary duplication in federal spending. As reported in *The Wall Street Journal*, 15 different agencies oversee food safety laws; there are 20 federal programs to help the homeless; 80 for economic development; 82 to improve teacher quality; 80 to help disadvantaged people with transportation needs; 47 for job training and employment; and 56 to help people understand finances.[35]

- A federal government auditor discovered that the Department of Defense did not have proper documentation for $8.7 billion in reconstruction aid given to Iraq. In fact, for $2.6 billion of that total, the Department of Defense provided no paperwork at all.[36]

- Federal benefit checks worth $180 million were paid to 20,000 dead people over a three-year period.[37]

> *He that is good for making excuses is seldom good for anything else.*
>
> **– Benjamin Franklin (1706–1790)**
> American Founding Father

Misappropriating and Commingling

> An attorney representing a badly injured car accident client settled the claim for $739,043.72 and deposited the money in his client's trust account. The client received $238,507.81.
>
> After deducting his fees, the attorney was supposed to keep $254,188 in that account for future medical expenses. Instead, the attorney left only $9,041. When the client's medical providers could not be paid, the attorney was disbarred from practicing law and ordered to make restitution to his client for the misappropriated funds.[38]

You must maintain a complete record of all transactions and promptly pay or deliver money or property to those entitled to receive it.[39] You may not take money and property from those you are representing without proper authorization.

When handling money and property on behalf of another, you must never commingle these funds or property with your own. All funds and property of another must be kept in a clearly identified separate account. Upon receipt of money or property on behalf of another, you must give prompt notice to that party that you received it.

Without complete, accurate, and transparent accounting of all money and property that one has received while acting on behalf of another, there can be no trust. Accountability also means accepting personal responsibility for results.

Commandment #5: Be Accountable	
Ethics Principle:	When acting on behalf of another in a position of trust and confidence, you have a fiduciary duty to account. Be sure to keep accurate records of all transactions pertaining to money and property entrusted to you. Upon reasonable request, provide a complete and detailed accounting of how the money and property was used, along with receipts and other necessary evidence. Whatever accounting method chosen, it must provide an *accurate and honest picture of the current financial health* of the organization, entity, etc. Do not use accounting tricks or gimmicks to intentionally deceive others. All expenses paid must be reasonable and necessary. Never commingle money and property of others with your own money and property. All money and property received while representing another, including gifts, profits from breaching a fiduciary duty, or illegal bribes and kickbacks, belong to the person you are representing. Being accountable also means providing competent oversight.
Sample Law:	E.g., fiduciary duty to account, securities fraud, fiduciary duty disclose, "aiding and abetting" fraud, fraud and deceit, breach of contract, False Claims Act, money laundering, accounting fraud, Freedom of Information Act, Sarbanes-Oxley Act of 2002, conspiracy.

Chapter 17

Commandment of Trust #6: Property
Protecting Fort Knox

#6. Observe Private Property Rights

Private property rights are the foundation of individual freedom and economic prosperity in the United States. When American colonists first tried collective communal property ownership in the early 1600s, they almost starved.[1] After switching to *individual property rights in Plymouth in 1623,* the colony prospered almost immediately.[2]

American private property rights pre-date the U.S. Constitution. The 1215 Magna Carta placed limitations on the English King's right to take and tax private property.

America's Founding Fathers fervently believed protecting private property rights was essential for liberty. Therefore, private property rights have been protected in the United States since the earliest days of our republic. From the outset, observing private property rights has been a key ingredient of the American culture of trust essential for our self-organizing brand of freedom.

The 5th Amendment in the Bill of Rights of the U.S. Constitution (effective 1791) states: "no person…can be deprived of… property, without due process of law; nor shall private property be taken for public use, without just compensation." This requirement has been interpreted by the U.S. Supreme Court to apply to both the federal and state governments.

> *The moment the idea is admitted into society that property is not as sacred as the laws of God, and that there is not a force of law and public justice to protect it, anarchy and tyranny commence.*
>
> **– John Adams (1735–1826)**
> American Founding Father,
> 2nd U.S. president, 1797–1801

Because private property rights are embedded in the Rule of Law of western countries, private property in western countries can be turned into capital for investments via mortgages and contracts. As discussed earlier in Chapter 9, economist Hernando de Soto pointed out it is not possible to have a modern, prosperous market economy based on private capital without predictable and enforceable legal protection of private property rights.

Throughout most of American history, "title to every house, car, mortgage, bank account, and patent had always been reliably documented."[3] However, in 2009, Hernando de Soto noted that the misuse of credit derivatives has jeopardized the reliability and predictability of America's centuries-old private property rights system.[4] He said that the misuse of credit derivatives in the United States has created incomplete, hidden, and unreliable paper trails of ownership for private property.

> *The personal right to acquire property, which is a natural right, gives to property, when acquired, a right to protection, as a social right... The rights of persons, and the rights of property, are the objects, for the protection of which Government was instituted.*
>
> **– James Madison (1751–1836)**
> American Founding Father,
> 4th U.S. president, 1809–1817

Real and Personal Property

There can be no capitalism without capital. A baseline requirement to create savings that is capable of being turned into wealth (capital) is *clear and predictable title* to privately owned personal property and real estate.

As De Soto observed, billions of people in the world still live in poverty because they live in countries that do not have clear, predictable, and enforceable private property rights. Their homes and businesses exist in an "underground economy" that is outside an effective legal system. Thus, their assets cannot be used as collateral to borrow money for investments (that is, to create capital).

Certainty of ownership under clear, predictable, and enforceable private property rights is an essential ingredient of the culture of trust required for free-market capitalism.

Chain of Title

Two homeowners bought their homes in 2005 with mortgages (loans) from two mortgage companies. By the time the homeowners defaulted on their mortgages in 2007, both mortgages had been re-sold and bundled with a multitude of other mortgages into *mortgage-backed trusts.*

U.S. Bancorp and Wells Fargo & Co., not involved in the original mortgage loan transactions, bought the homeowners' two homes at foreclosure auctions in 2007, claiming they were the "owners" of the mortgages. A judge disagreed. The judge said that title to these mortgages had not been properly assigned (transferred) to the mortgage-backed trusts because the recipients had not been named. Because the banks had foreclosed on the homes months before receiving the necessary legal paperwork ("assignment") required to properly transfer the two mortgage titles to them, the judge refused to recognize the banks as the "owners" of the homes.[5]

Personal property ownership is proven by a contract like a bill of sale or purchase agreement. Motor vehicles are bought and sold with Certificates of Title.

Since the founding of the American republic, *real property ownership* (title to land and improvements) has been *recorded* in the county government records in the *county* where the *land* is *located*.[6]

The county recorder or registrar of deeds is usually an elected official. This neutral, independent party provides "an important democratic check and balance in the preservation of property rights."[7]

For centuries, the United States has had a formal recorded property system that made ownership rights in real estate transparent, accurate, and reliable.

MERS: The proliferation of credit derivatives has damaged our transparent, accurate, and reliable system for recording private property rights in real estate in the United States. In 1997, mortgage companies and banks, with the blessing of Fannie Mae and Freddie Mac (and prodding by federal politicians), developed *a separate private, nontransparent land recording system outside of the county land recording system.*

This alternative database, called *Mortgage Electronic Registration Systems, Inc.* (MERS), was designated the "holder" of the title for pooled mortgage trusts of securitized asset-backed bonds.[8]

The MERS database was created to avoid the expensive and time-consuming task of recording each transfer of title in the county land records for "securitized" pooled mortgages (credit derivatives) that changed hands often. As many as 64 million mortgages (or 60% of all new mortgages) were recorded only in the MERS database—not the county land records as had occurred in the United States for centuries.[9]

When millions of home mortgages defaulted, serious flaws in the MERS recording system became public. Banks had been allowed to *voluntarily* enter and manage their own data, so the data provided was often seriously incomplete. Also, unlike the centuries-old county land recording system, there were no stiff penalties for failure to properly record title in the MERS database. The proper paperwork to legally transfer title (assignments) was often not included in the MERS database.

The determination of who holds title to real property that is only recorded in the MERS database has landed in American courts. Court rulings are divided on whether MERS can be the legal "owner" for the purpose of foreclosing on real estate.[10]

Since millions of home loans have been foreclosed by MERS as the mortgage "owner," we now have uncertainty as to who holds title to millions of pieces of private real property in the United States. *The misuse of credit derivatives has damaged trust in the absolute reliability of title to private real property rights in the United States.*

Robo-Signing: Since MERS is only a database, it has no employees. To process the voluminous amounts of paperwork required to foreclose on private real estate, thousands of low-level employees at mortgage companies, banks, and other financial companies were designated "certifying officers" of MERS.[11]

Although given impressive titles like vice president and assistant secretary, these low-level employees were poorly trained and seriously overworked. They routinely signed affidavits swearing *under oath* that they had reviewed each and every foreclosure file, even when it was physically impossible for them to have done so (e.g., signing affidavits for several thousand foreclosure files in one day).

Certifying officers of MERS were accused of falsely signing affidavits, forging signatures, or improperly notarizing documents in the foreclosure process.[12] *This process, dubbed "robo-signing," further jeopardized clear title to private real estate in the United States.*

At least one state, Nevada, made robo-signing criminal.[13] In November 2011, Nevada's attorney general filed the first criminal cases against employees of Lender Processing Services, one of the organizations used by major banks to handle their foreclosures.[14] In 2012, DocX, one of the largest providers of home foreclosure services to lenders, was indicted on forgery charges.[15]

Also in 2012, the New York attorney general sued Bank of America, Wells Fargo, and JPMorgan Chase alleging that using the MERS database "resulted in deceptive and illegal practices, including false documents in foreclosure proceedings."[16] In 2012, the federal government and 49 states reached a $25 billion settlement with the five largest mortgage services—Bank of America, JPMorgan Chase, Wells Fargo, Citigroup, and Ally Financial (formerly GMAC) for "loan servicing and foreclosure abuses."[17]

Government "Takings"

> The city of New London, Connecticut, approved a development plan that projected it would add jobs and increase tax revenues for the city. When some property owners refused to voluntarily sell their property, the city forcibly took their property under eminent domain. One property owner, Susette Kelo, sued the city.
>
> Up until this time, taking property for a "public purpose" under eminent domain meant taking property to build roads, dams, schools, and such. However, the U.S. Supreme Court ruled that *a city could take private property from one private owner to give to another private owner* (e.g., a private developer), if the city *believed* (without proof) that it would increase tax revenues for the city and create jobs.[18]

The *Kelo* decision sparked an angry backlash. It was viewed by many as a clear violation of sacrosanct American private property rights.[19] Forty-two states adopted eminent domain legislation and ballot measures (permitted under the *Kelo* case) to restore the previously well-established limitations on the government's right to take private property under eminent domain.[20]

Excessive Government Regulation

Excessive restrictions on land use, while not directly interfering with title to private property, do interfere with a landowner's right to use and enjoy his own private property (e.g., new zoning restrictions). Some have suggested that this, too, is a "taking" of private property that requires compensation under the 5th Amendment power of eminent domain.[21]

Intellectual Property

In today's *knowledge-based global economy*, the ability to protect and enforce private intellectual property rights is a critical component of our culture of trust and essential for the success of our free-market capitalist economy.

Intellectual property refers to private property rights for intangible property such as "inventions, literary and artistic works, and symbols, names, images, and designs used in commerce"[22] (*patents, copyrights*, and *trademarks*). Under our American Rule of Law, the term also includes certain types of confidential information (*trade secrets*).[23]

Intellectual property rights in the United States date back to the founding of the republic. Article I, Section 8 of the U.S. Constitution gave Congress the power "[t]o promote the Progress of Science and useful Arts, by securing for limited Times to Authors and Inventors the exclusive Right to their respective Writings and Discoveries." Inventors and authors were given the exclusive right to profit from what they created for a specified period of time.

> *No power on earth has a right to take our property from us without our consent.*
>
> **– John Jay (1745–1829)**
> American Founding Father,
> 1st U.S. Supreme Court Justice, 1789–1795

Patents

> Johnson & Johnson (J&J) was the first to market drug-coated heart stents (tubes that hold arteries open during surgery). When Boston Scientific began selling similar stents using similar technology, numerous patent lawsuits were filed.
>
> After more than 10 years of litigation, Boston Scientific agreed to pay approximately $2.4 billion to settle the lawsuits.[24]

A patent is given to the person who "invents or discovers any new, useful [and nonobvious] process, machine, manufacture, or composition of matter, or any new and useful improvement."[25] The patent holder has a *monopoly* over the invention for a *fixed period of time*.[26] While the patent is in force, no one may make, use, or sell the patented invention without first obtaining a license from the patent holder. In exchange for this right, the patent holder must *publicly disclose* the invention.

Patent litigation and judgments can be very expensive. In 2012, Apple won a $1 billion verdict against Samsung in a lawsuit over smartphone patents.[27] Monsanto won $1 billion from DuPont for violating one of its genetically engineered soybean patents.[28]

In 2011, for the first time, American patents were awarded to *the first person to file for the patent*, not the first person to invent, as in the past. Concerns are being raised that granting a patent to the one who files the patent first (not the first to invent) favors giant businesses and harms smaller start-up companies.[29]

Trademarks

Adidas America, Inc., part of German athletic footwear giant Adidas AG, sold running shoes with three stripes across the side of the shoe. Payless Shoe Source, Inc. sold shoes with two and four stripes similarly placed along the side of their shoes. Both companies sold shoes in the same markets so consumers would likely be confused.

An Oregon jury awarded Adidas America $304.6 million in damages against Payless for *infringing* or *diluting* Adidas's *trademark* or *trade dress*. On appeal, the damage award was reduced to $65.3 million.[30]

A *trademark* is something that identifies the source of goods or services, including both trademarks on goods and marks for services. Trademarks can be words, logos, pictures, slogans, colors, product shapes, or sounds.[31]

Traditionally, trademark infringement required using a mark, symbol, etc., that confused consumers about the source of the goods or services. Today, "famous" trademarks can be "diluted" (e.g., using a mark somewhat similar but unlikely to confuse consumers) or "tarnished" (e.g., using it on goods of lower quality).[32]

There are different levels of trademark protection.[33] The strongest is *fanciful* (e.g., a made-up word like Exxon). The weakest trademark is *descriptive,* which describes the services or goods involved (e.g., Clothes Market to describe a store selling clothes).

Once a product or service loses its unique source identification, it can no longer be trademarked. Aspirin, originally trademarked by a drug company, lost its trademark protection when it became *generic.*

Selling counterfeit items may be criminal. In 2011, two Texas men pleaded guilty to conspiracy for selling counterfeit cellular telephones and wireless devices.[34] Four individuals were sentenced to prison sentences ranging from 2 to 5 years in prison for trafficking in counterfeit movie and music disks.[35]

Counterfeiters take billions of dollars out of the economy and cause the loss of tens of thousands of jobs annually.[36] Counterfeit drugs and fake medical tests can lead to terrible consequences, even death.[37]

Copyrights

Napster, Inc. provided software that enabled others to download and swap copyrighted music files over the Internet. After millions of people had used Napster's software to download copyrighted music without paying for it, the Recording Industry Association of America (RIAA) filed a lawsuit against Napster. Napster was not the *direct* infringer, but the RIAA alleged *contributory* and *vicarious copyright infringement* against Napster.

The court issued an injunction against Napster. Napster filed for bankruptcy, and it was purchased by one of its major investors, German media giant, Bertelsmann AG. Bertelsmann was also sued. It is believed Bertelsmann may have settled one lawsuit for about $60 million and another for an estimated $50–$150 million.[38]

Copyright protects an *original* work of authorship that has been *fixed* in a tangible medium of expression. Thus, an oral speech cannot be protected, but a recording of that speech can be protected by copyright. Original works include literary, musical, dramatic, architectural, movies and audiovisual, pictures, graphics, sculptural, pantomimes, choreographic, and sound recordings.[39]

A copyright holder has the *exclusive right to copy, distribute, and display the work to the public* or to *create derivative works* based on the original. Generally, facts and data cannot be copyrighted.[40]

A *fair use exception* allows copyrighted works to be used for purposes such as "criticism, comment, news reporting, teaching…, scholarship or research."[41] To determine fair use, *four factors* are considered: (1) the nature of the copyrighted work, (2) how much of the work is used, (3) how that use affects the potential market or value of the copyrighted work, and (4) whether the use is for a commercial or nonprofit educational purpose.[42]

Google announced it was creating *Google Books,* a project to scan hundreds of thousands of books to make them available on the Internet, without obtaining permission from all of the copyright owners. The Authors Guild and Association of American Publishers sued Google for copyright violations. In 2013, a U.S. Circuit Court judge said the Google Books project fell under the "fair use" exception because users can only see "snippets" of a book if the copyright holder did not grant permission.[43]

Statutory damages for copyright violations can be expensive. American judges have considerable discretion. The damages range from $750 to $30,000 per violation, and if willful, can go as high as $150,000 per violation.[44] For example, each *song* illegally downloaded in the Napster is considered to be a *separate violation*. With millions of songs downloaded, and the judge assessing damages against Napster at $30,000 per violation (that is, per downloaded song), you can see why Bertelsmann paid tens of millions of dollars to settle Napster's copyright lawsuits.

Violating copyright law can sometimes be a *federal crime.* A first-time offender convicted of conspiracy to commit felony criminal copyright infringement can receive a prison sentence of 5 years and a fine of $250,000, and be required to pay restitution to the victims.

In 2005, two men pleaded guilty to conspiracy to commit criminal copyright infringement.[45] They distributed first-run films and other copyrighted materials on the Internet without authorization. In 2012, they received prison sentences of 30 and 24 months and were required to repay almost $460,000 as restitution.[46]

In a separate case, a Los Angeles police captain with 28 years on the force pleaded no contest to criminal misdemeanor charges for selling counterfeit DVDs of recently released movies.[47]

Trade Secrets

A doll designer for Mattel, Inc.'s Barbie doll line developed the concept for the Bratz doll while still working for Mattel. He left Mattel to develop the Bratz doll for MGA Entertainment, Inc. The Bratz doll became such a huge success, it hurt Mattel's Barbie doll sales. Mattel sued MGA and initially won a $100 million verdict, but that verdict was later overturned. In a second trial, MGA countersued Mattel for *misappropriation of trade secrets,* accusing Mattel of obtaining trade secrets (e.g., MGA's price lists and advertising plans) by using phony credentials to gain access to private showrooms at toy trade fairs.

After almost 8 years of litigation, MGA was awarded $88 million in damages. The judge reduced the award to $85 million, adding $85 million in punitive damages and attorneys' fees and costs. The total award to MGA was $309 million. In addition, Mattel spent $400 million for its own attorneys' fees in these lawsuits.[48]

A *trade secret* refers to information (including a "formula, pattern, compilation, program, device, method, technique, or process") (1) that is *not* generally publicly available that gives an organization a competitive advantage, and (2) that the owner takes *reasonable* measures to keep secret.[49]

Trade secrets are used to protect valuable technical information, such as the formula for Coca-Cola, as well as "business information such as marketing plans, cost and price information and customer lists...."[50] As of December 2011, at least 46 states have adopted some version of the Uniform Trade Secrets Act.

Courts have the power to issue an *injunction* to stop actual or threatened *misappropriation of trade secrets.* For *malicious* or *willful* trade secrets violations, damage awards can be doubled. If a party makes a misappropriation of trade secrets claim in *bad faith,* the court can require that party to pay the attorneys' fees of the party they sued.

Unlike patents, trademarks, and copyrights, a trade secret can last forever, provided it remains secret. Once a trade secret becomes public, however, it no longer has trade secret protection under American law.

The Economic Espionage Act of 1996 makes taking trade secrets for the benefit of a foreign government, foreign instrumentality, or foreign agent a federal crime.[51] In 2012, a former software engineer for Motorola Solutions Inc. received a 4 year prison sentence for stealing Motorola trade secrets for a Chinese company that was developing telecommunications technology for the Chinese military.[52]

Damage to the Environment

A Transocean Deepwater Horizon drilling rig leased to British Petroleum (BP) caught fire and exploded. Eleven crew members died.[53] An estimated 5 million barrels of oil gushed into the Gulf of Mexico. BP set up a $20 billion trust fund to compensate fishermen, local residents, and businesses harmed by the oil spill. It also set aside $40 billion to cover the costs and liabilities for this oil spill, the worst in U.S. history.

In November of 2012, BP agreed to pay $4.5 billion in fines and other penalties. BP has pled guilty to criminal charges. Three BP employees were criminally indicted as well. By 2014, four years after the blowout, BP has already "spent more than $28 billion on damage claims and cleanup costs." It could potentially owe another $18 billion more in civil penalties under the Clean Water Act, after a court ruled in 2014 that BP was grossly negligent.[54]

Observing private property rights in the United States includes responsibility not to damage the environment. There are numerous federal statutes covering environmental hazards such as air, water, and land pollution, nuclear waste and radiation, hazardous materials, and protecting wildlife and endangered species, among many others.[55]

Fines and penalties for environmental damage can be severe. For example, *hazardous waste violations* can carry penalties of up to $32,500 a day for each civil violation and $50,000 a day and/or five years in prison for criminal violations.[56] Criminal fines can range from $25,000 to $250,000 for individuals, as well as 1 to 15 years in prison. A corporation can be fined $1 million.[57]

States can set tougher environmental standards than the federal requirements, never lower. For example, under California state law, civil fines for *air pollution* may be as high as $40,000 a day and as high as $75,000 a day if done *willfully or intentionally*.[58]

Environmental fines can be extremely expensive. For example, if a company has been polluting the air for 10 years, the fine could be 10 (years) x 365 (days in a year) x $40,000 = $146 million. You can easily see why the government has eager takers when it offers to settle a case quickly for a lot less than these fines.

Under ethics-based American Rule of Law, environmental laws must be enforced in the most cost-effective, common sense way. While everyone wants clean air and water and to protect wildlife, there are ongoing fights over how much power should be given to government bureaucrats. A balance must be struck between the need to protect the environment and the rights of citizens to use their land, and the needs of a successful American economy.

A federal judge in Fresno, California, said that "the federal government didn't do a good enough job at considering farmer's water needs while trying to protect threatened salmon."[59] In 2012 the U.S. Supreme Court ruled that before the Environmental Protection Agency (EPA) can enforce the wetland regulations with fines of $37,500 a day, it must provide landowners with due process.[60]

Respect for private property rights, including personal property, real estate, and intellectual property, as well as protecting the environment are key components of the American culture of trust required for a prosperous economy and a stable, peaceful, and secure society.

Commandment #6: Observe Private Property Rights	
Ethics Principle:	Title to cars, mortgages, bank accounts, patents, and other types of private property must be reliably and accurately documented, protected, and enforced. Records of real estate sales must be transparent, reliable, accurate, publicly available, and provide a clear and reliable chain of title that can be insured against defects by a reputable title company (e.g., recording all sales transactions in the county records where the land is located). In case of real estate default, all required steps of the foreclosure processes and procedures that prove chain of title must be followed. A government "taking" of private property should be limited to "public uses" that are clearly governmental, not simply a belief (without proof) that it might result in higher revenue for the government, or more jobs. There must be reasonable, common-sense, and cost-effective laws to prevent environmental pollution, monitor hazardous waste, and protect wildlife.
Sample Law:	E.g., eminent domain, real property law, bailment, conversion, trespass, nuisance, Clean Air Act, Clean Water Act, Endangered Species Act, Resource Conservation and Recovery Act, patents, trade secrets, copyright, trademarks, Lanham Act, Federal Trademark Dilution Act, Digital Millennium Copyright Act, Economic Espionage Act of 1996, civil fraud, criminal fraud, mail fraud, trafficking in counterfeit goods, trademark and trade dress infringement, dilution, unfair competition and deceptive trade practices, copyright and patent infringement, conspiracy, aiding and abetting, false statements to the federal government, mail fraud, wire fraud, and obstruction of justice.

Chapter 18

Commandment of Trust #7: People
Respecting Our Most Important Asset

#7. Respect People

Respecting people is a critical component of our essential self-organizing culture of trust. To survive and succeed in today's knowledge-based global economy, businesses, organizations, governments, and countries must be able to develop, attract, and keep the most creative and talented people.

Peter Drucker, the 20th century management visionary who died in 2005 at the age of 95, foresaw that "knowledge would trump raw material as the essential capital of the New Economy."[1] He understood that people are assets, not liabilities.

In his view, corporations must be human communities based on trust and respect for workers, not just profit-machines.[2] *Respecting people at work in our self-organizing institutions and associations creates trust. Disrespecting people breeds distrust.*

> *Capital is only the fruit of labor, and could never have existed if labor had not first existed. Labor is the superior of capital, and deserves much the higher consideration.*
>
> **– Abraham Lincoln (1809–1865)**
> 16th U.S. president during U.S. Civil War, 1861–1865

Union Law

In the late 19th and early 20th centuries, American courts were hostile toward workers organizing for better wages and working conditions. This attitude changed during the Great Depression when unemployment hit extraordinary levels.

The *Wagner Act* was passed in 1935 to protect the right of American workers to form a union and bargain with employers over their wages and working conditions.[3] *Labor law* in the United States was born.

Employers in private business who unreasonably interfered with their employees' right to form a union could find themselves liable for an *unfair labor practice*. To prevent union abuses, the *Taft-Hartley Act*[4] was passed in 1947 to monitor the power and activities of the unions. In 1959, the *Landrum-Griffin Act*[5] was passed in response to allegations of corruption, racketeering, and other serious misconduct by union management.

After World War II, unions in *private business* flourished, but by the 1990s they had markedly declined in size and power. Union power shifted to *public* employee unions in our *federal, state,* and *local* governments. However, with today's strained government finances, and publicity about outrageously generous pension and medical benefits given to some government workers at taxpayer expense, a backlash against public unions is brewing.

Public government worker unions are now running up against some of the same economic realities that caused union membership in private businesses to drastically decline.

Employment Law

At the height of union power in private businesses in the 1960s, a burgeoning new body of law (that would later become known as *employment law*) was being created. In the 1970s and throughout the 1980s and 1990s, employment law in the United States expanded—first at the federal level, and later in the states.

Effective employment law must balance enough freedom for employers to foster successful businesses with sufficient legal protections for employees to prevent workplace abuses.

Unlike union law, states can make federal employment law standards tougher, and some have. Today, states with overly burdensome employment laws are losing employers, jobs, and taxpayers to states with more business-friendly workplace legal climates.

Like union law, the details of how employment law standards are applied can vary over time. For example, initially sexual harassment claims were almost exclusively filed by women. Today, more men are suing for sexual harassment.[6] African-American plaintiffs were the initial beneficiaries of most race discrimination cases, but Caucasians now sue under discrimination laws for *reverse discrimination.*[7]

Differing college admission standards for protected groups under affirmative action, once considered sacrosanct, are again under review by the U.S. Supreme Court.[8] Like union law, employment law is constantly evolving as workplace conditions and circumstances in the United States change.

Discrimination

Approximately 2,000 salaried African-American employees and managers filed a class action lawsuit against The Coca-Cola Company alleging race discrimination in pay and promotions. They sued under the *disparate impact* theory of discrimination, alleging race discrimination because most of Coca-Cola's African-American employees were only in lower-paying jobs (e.g., human resource and corporate affairs positions), while Caucasians were in the more highly paid jobs (e.g., marketing and finance).

In 2000, Coca-Cola Co. paid $192.5 million to settle this lawsuit, the largest race discrimination settlement in U.S. history. The settlement included $20 million for attorneys' fees and $36 million to establish a mutually acceptable panel to supervise the company's employment practices.[9]

The purpose of anti-discrimination employment law, whether created by statute or judge-made case law, is to ensure that *those hired, paid, rewarded, and terminated in the workplace are* judged by *objective, neutral standards*, free from personal bias. Employers must use *bona fide job-related* and *business necessity* criteria applied fairly and equally to all.

Equal opportunity, however, does not mean equal results. Individual results must still depend on a person's skill, talent, and ability. *To find, attract, and retain the most talented people in all of our workplaces, workers must be evaluated in an objective, fair, nondiscriminatory, and unbiased way.*

The federal 1964 Civil Rights Act[10] prohibits employment discrimination based on *race* (ethnicity, e.g., African-American), *color* (shade of skin color), *creed* (religion), *sex* (gender, generally male and female), and *national origin* (ancestry or place of origin).

Other federal employment discrimination statutes prohibit workplace prejudice based on *age* (over 40 years old), *pregnancy* (must be treated like any other medical disability), *disability* (physical or mental impairments), or *genetic makeup* (genetic information).[11]

Some states, like California, have significantly expanded the categories of protected groups, and the amount of money claimants can recover for discrimination, under state law.[12]

Both *intentional* discrimination (*disparate treatment*) and *unintentional* discrimination (on-its-face neutral employment practices that have an adverse *disparate impact* on protected groups) are prohibited. The disparate treatment theory of discrimination was created by federal statute. The disparate impact theory of discrimination was created by judge-made common law in a 1971 U.S. Supreme Court case.[13] Both forms of discrimination are subject to being applied differently as circumstances in the United States change.

For example, in 2009, the U.S. Supreme Court ruled that a *disparate impact* claim could *not* invalidate a bona fide, vetted, nondiscriminatory promotion test for firefighters. The Court said that just because no African-American firefighters scored high enough to be immediately promoted, the promotion test could not be invalidated; that is, white and Hispanic firefighters with the highest test scores could not be prevented from being promoted.[14]

Eventually, "favorable" discrimination to right past wrongs will run up against the constitutional requirement of *"equal protection" under the law* mandated in the U.S. Constitution.[15]

> *The individual is the central, rarest, most precious capital resource of our society.*
>
> **– Peter F. Drucker (1909–2005)**
> 20th century management consultant

Harassment

Mitsubishi Motors was sued by the Equal Employment Opportunity Commission (EEOC) for creating a *hostile working environment* for its female employees at one of its plants. The EEOC alleged pervasive and repetitive harassment of female employees (e.g., men groping women and squirting women's breasts and buttocks with water).

Mitsubishi agreed to pay $34 million to settle the EEOC's lawsuit. It also agreed to establish a "zero tolerance" sexual harassment policy, revise its complaint procedures, and allow monitors to oversee the company's compliance.[16]

Sexual harassment means either requesting sex in exchange for job-related benefits at work (*quid pro quo*) or using demeaning words or behavior based on sex to create *a hostile work environment*. Both types of harassment are disrespectful and destroy trust.

In 2012, a top male officer in charge of the Immigration and Customs Enforcement office in New York filed a lawsuit against Homeland Security Secretary Janet Napolitano, alleging female supervisors in that government agency were allowed to torment male employees.[17]

Making derogatory and demeaning comments—whether based on sex, race, national origin, age, or other protected class—can create a hostile working environment. A rude, discourteous, and unprofessional work environment not only harms the individuals targeted, it harms the entire organization.

Such behavior destroys the ability of people to work voluntarily, cooperatively, and automatically together as a group without central direction and control to adapt quickly to constant change. *Harassing behavior at work that creates a hostile work environment destroys trust.*

Examples of unacceptable harassing behaviors that have triggered legal action include: providing a secret room with sex magazines for male employees; calling a female employee a "fat bitch"; rubbing an employee's shoulders at work; climbing into an employee's hotel bed while on a business trip; putting a noose around the neck of an African-American employee; grabbing an employee's private parts and suggesting they have sex; and calling employees of Lebanese descent "camel jockeys" and "terrorists."

Such improper conduct interferes with the ability of the targeted workers to perform their jobs at peak levels of performance. Such abusive behaviors are stressful for the individual targeted and can make those targeted physically sick.

Retaliation

A Puerto Rican physician worked nine years for the Cook County, Illinois, pathology department. She filed a sex and national origin discrimination claim in 2003. Within three months, she was suspended, and the following year, she was fired.

The doctor claimed *retaliation* for being outspoken about alleged "misdiagnosis, negligence, acts of concealment and other wrongdoing" that affected patients. She provided evidence in court that refuted the county's claims she had misdiagnosed patients with cancer. A federal jury awarded her a $7.6 million retaliation verdict against Cook County and its former chairman of pathology.[18]

Those who file discrimination claims are protected from retaliation by their employer against themselves, their family, and their friends.[19] Retaliation can include such adverse employment actions such as being suspended, demoted, or terminated, taking a pay cut, or being given less favorable hours. It can also include an employer making negative comments about an employee to the press.

Bullying

A group of students at a Massachusetts high school targeted a 15-year-old female classmate, subjecting her to "relentless" bullying over the Internet (e.g., hurtful derogatory comments and even threats of physical harm).

After the targeted girl committed suicide, nine teenagers were criminally charged. Five pled guilty to lesser misdemeanor charges to avoid more serious felony charges.[20]

A rash of suicides of bullied high school and college students has focused the public's attention on the devastating effects of bullying. In Iowa, a 14-year-old male student committed suicide when he was bullied over the phone and the Internet after admitting he was gay.[21]

A gay Rutgers University student committed suicide when his roommate secretly filmed him in a romantic encounter with another man and posted it on the Internet. The roommate was convicted of a hate crime.[22]

Most states have laws against bullying, cyber-bullying, and related behaviors at our educational institutions.[23] In 2010, Massachusetts outlawed bullying in school and online. Schools were required to develop bullying prevention and intervention plans. Of course, like all American statutes, these new laws against bullying are subject to constitutional challenges in the courts.

Bullying is prevalent in many of our civic institutions and voluntary associations. Unlike harassment under existing discrimination laws, bullying applies to everyone, not just members of a protected class.

Employers in today's modern workplaces must be particularly vigilant in ridding their organizations of bullying. Bullies deliberately target the "best" people in an organization—those who are the most competent, talented, hard-working, and dedicated. Bullying at work destroys trust and robs our self-organizing organizations, institutions, and associations of their most competent, capable, and talented people.

Some bullies are easy to spot because they scream, throw things, and publicly make intimidating and unprofessional comments about a targeted person.

Other bullies are much more subtle. They mask their deliberate and vicious attacks on the targeted person by exhibiting pretend politeness, civility, and "collegiality" in public. However, behind the scenes, these "hidden" bullies actively engage in a deliberate campaign of sabotage that includes vicious, underhanded, and untrue attacks on those they have targeted.

This hidden type of bully is a master at making belittling, demeaning, derogatory, and untrue comments to coworkers, colleagues, superiors, customers, and others behind the targeted person's back—especially about the individual's competence or integrity.[24] These "hidden" bullies exclude targeted people from important meetings and information, and subject them to constant petty humiliations.

An individual targeted by a bully may have no idea that he or she has been singled out for deliberate destructive treatment. A targeted person may even try to reconcile with a bully to try to stop the antagonism, but reconciling with a bully is impossible. A bully's cruel and destructive behavior is *never* the result of miscommunication.

A bully intends to deliberately hurt the targeted person, no matter how "nice" a bully appears to be on the surface. The goal of a bully is to make the targeted person mentally and/or physically sick, and if possible, drive that targeted individual out of the organization. When bullies enlist others in their bullying tactics, whether they participate knowingly or unknowingly, it is called *mobbing.*[25]

Bullies do great damage at any level of an organization, whether they are subordinates, coworkers, or superiors, but they are especially destructive when they are at the top of an organization.

Leaders who are bullies surround themselves with "yes-people." They value personal loyalty over competence and do not tolerate disagreement. *Leaders who are bullies are not trusted.*

Safety and Health

In 2010, 29 miners were killed by an explosion in a West Virginia mine in the deadliest mine disaster in 40 years. The mine was owned by Massey Energy Co. (later acquired by Alpha Natural Resources). The federal Mine Safety and Health Administration's report detailed "flagrant" safety violations (e.g., inadequate safety training, a dangerous build-up of coal dust in the mines, and advance warnings of safety inspections).

Massey was fined a record amount of $10.8 million. Alpha Natural Resources later paid $209 million to settle claims stemming from the explosion. In November 2014, the former CEO of Massey Energy was indicted for conspiracy to violate federal safety and health standards.[26]

Treating people with respect at work means employers must provide their workers with a workplace safe from injury, violence, and harm to their health.

At the federal level, workplace safety standards are enforced by the Occupational Safety and Health Administration (OSHA). When improper safeguards at a BP refinery in Texas City, Texas, led to a massive explosion that killed 15 people and injured 170 people in 2005, BP was fined $21 million. When BP failed to correct the hazardous conditions it promised to correct, OSHA proposed penalties of $87.5 million (which would be the largest OSHA fine in U.S. history).[27]

Many states have their own state agencies that also enforce workplace safety standards. Like employment law, those state safety standards can only be higher than the federal safety standards, never lower.

Employers are required to protect employees from violent coworkers. When a fired employee at a Union Butterfield warehouse came back two days later and shot and killed two employees, their widows recovered over $9 million, including a $7.9 million jury verdict. This is believed to be the highest workplace violence jury verdict in the United States.[28]

Fair Treatment

> Wal-Mart Stores, Inc. was sued in state and federal courts in 42 states for failing to pay overtime and not allowing lunch or other breaks (either promised by the company or required by state law).
>
> In 2008, Wal-Mart agreed to settle 63 cases (involving thousands of former and current hourly workers) for at least $352 million (it could be much higher depending on the final number of claims submitted by current and former employees).[29]

Employers must treat workers fairly when it comes to the terms and conditions of their employment. If they give departing workers unfair and inaccurate references, employers can be sued for defamation. Noncompetition agreements restricting employees from going to work for a competitor, if allowed by state law, must be reasonably limited in time (e.g., two years) and in geographic scope (must be reasonable, depending on the business).

Federal or state law may require that employers give advance notice to employees in the case of certain plant closings.[30] Federal law also protects the rights of employees who are absent from work due to military service.[31]

Respecting people at work in our self-organizing institutions and associations is a critical factor of our essential culture of trust.

Commandment #7: Respect People	
Ethics Principle:	A worker's right to form a union to bargain with employers over their wages and working conditions, when applicable, must be respected. Hire, promote, pay, and reward the best-qualified person for the job using *objective, job-related criteria*. Do not allow intimidating, offensive, or hostile words or behavior to demean, humiliate, or intimidate others, or bullying words or behavior to deliberately sabotage another's performance. Do not retaliate against those who bring bona fide claims of inappropriate behavior to the attention of the proper authorities. Provide a safe working environment that includes physical safety as well as protection from serious health hazards. Treat employees fairly with respect to pay, working conditions, and benefits.
Sample Law:	E.g., Civil Rights Act of 1964, Civil Rights Act of 1991, the Age Discrimination in Employment Act of 1967, the Americans with Disabilities Act of 1990, the Fair Labor Standards Act of 1938, the Family and Medical Leave Act of 1993, the Occupational Safety and Health Act of 1970, the Rehabilitation Act of 1973, Worker Adjustment and Retraining Notification Act (W.A.R.N.), Genetic Information Nondiscrimination Act of 2008, criminal harassment, civil rights violations resulting in bodily harm, negligent hiring.

Chapter 19

Commandment of Trust #8: Promises

Your Word Is Your Bond

#8. Keep Promises

Keeping promises is a core principle of our culture of trust. A promise is "a declaration assuring that one will or will not do something."[1] When someone makes a promise to you *about something important,* and does not keep it, you will not believe him (or her) the next time he makes a promise.

We must be able to depend on an insurance company's promise to pay claims covered by the policy. We must be able to count on a car company honoring its warranty promises. Charities must keep their promises to donors that the money is going to the stated charitable purpose, and not for excessive administrative expenses (e.g., huge compensation packages for their executives). Politicians who fail to keep their promises made during the election campaign will not be trusted either.

Promises under our American Rule of Law can be enforced in a variety of ways, such as lawsuits, losing elections, bad publicity, donors withdrawing their time or money, and many other ways.

> *Rarely promise, but, if lawful, constantly perform.*
>
> **- William Penn (1644–1718)**
> Founder of Pennsylvania

Binding Contracts

ICO Global Communications Holdings, Ltd. (ICO) signed a $2 billion fixed price contract with Hughes Electronics Corp. (HEC) to build and launch 12 communications satellites for ICO. With 10 satellites remaining to be launched, a Boeing company bought Hughes and charged ICO $400 million more to complete the Hughes contract. Boeing was ordered to pay ICO $606.6 million: $370.6 million in compensatory damages and $236 million in punitive damages.

However, on appeal, the $606.6 million verdict was overturned. The appellate court said the undisputed evidence showed that ICO had waived its breach of contract claim for the satellite contracts. Further, the court said that ICO had failed to produce sufficient evidence to prove that Boeing's alleged misrepresentation had caused it harm, an essential element for proving fraud.[2]

A contract involves *promises that can and will be enforced in a court of law.* American contract law is based on British common law contract principles.

From the beginning, contracts have been held in high regard in the United States. Article I, Section 10, clause 1 of the 1789 U.S. Constitution states, "No State shall... pass any Law impairing the Obligation of Contracts." *The ability to rely on another's promise means predictability and certainty regarding future events.*

Contracts have specific legal requirements. They include *offer, acceptance,* and *consideration.* An offer must have definite terms that have been communicated to and accepted by the other party.

The promises made in a contract must be backed by something of value called consideration—which is, either agreeing to do something you do not already have a legal obligation to do or refraining from doing something you have a legal right to do.

As an example, a promise by a business to pay a police officer $100 a week to protect it from crime would be unenforceable, if protecting that business was already part of the police officer's regular duties.

Only those of *legal age* (e.g., 18 years old) and of *sound mind* (e.g., not mentally deficient or intoxicated) can enter into a contract.

The contract must also *not be illegal* (e.g., a contract to kill someone). Most contracts do not require a writing to be enforceable. Some must be evidenced by a writing to be enforceable (e.g., contracts for the sale of land).

Parties are entitled to the *benefit of the bargain* under a contract. For example, a seller who breaches a contract to sell a car may have to pay the buyer the difference between the agreed-upon sales price and the cost of the buyer purchasing a replacement vehicle.

If a contract involves *unique* property, such as land or an original Picasso painting, a court may order the equitable remedy of *specific performance* to force a breaching seller to sell the property as originally promised.

A promise must never be broken.

– Alexander Hamilton (1755 or 1757–1804)
American Founding Father,
1st U.S. secretary of the Treasury, 1789–1795

Interfering with Another's Contract

Pennzoil Company signed a short Memorandum of Agreement to purchase 43% of Getty Oil for $5.3 billion. It issued a press release announcing the merger, but before a formal, detailed written agreement was signed, Texaco Inc. offered to buy Getty Oil for $10.1 billion.

Getty accepted Texaco's offer, but required Texaco to sign an indemnity agreement protecting Getty from any liability to Pennzoil. Pennzoil sued for *tortious interference with a contract*. The court ordered Texaco to pay $10.5 billion. Texaco declared bankruptcy. Eventually, Texaco paid $3 billion to Pennzoil to settle the lawsuit.[3]

Generally punitive damages (damages intended to punish the defendant, not compensate the plaintiff) are not allowed in contract cases. However, punitive damages are allowed for *tortious conduct*, like interfering with another's contractual relationship.

> *Promises may fit the friends, but non-performance will turn them into enemies.*
>
> **– Benjamin Franklin (1706–1790)**
> American Founding Father

Undoing a Contract

When a homeowner was unable to make his mortgage payments because his business declined, the bank seized the property and foreclosed on his $469,000 home.

Three years after the foreclosure, the homeowner was shocked to discover that he was still responsible for repaying $115,000 plus interest, while the balance remained unpaid. His bank had obtained a *deficiency judgment* against him, which was the difference between what he owed on the original mortgage and the price the bank received in the resale of the house to another buyer.[4]

Once agreed to, contracts cannot be easily undone. Otherwise, trust in contracts in the United States would be destroyed. To undo a contract, you must have a legally recognizable reason such as *fraud, mistake, duress,* or *undue influence*. These *equitable* remedies are applied to prevent injustice. Each of these legal causes of action has specific legal requirements.

About a million Americans who could afford to pay their mortgages have defaulted on their mortgages.[5] A mortgage is a binding enforceable contract, which means failing to pay a mortgage may lead to a deficiency judgment.

According to a *Wall Street Journal* article, the District of Columbia and 41 states permit lenders to sue borrowers for deficiency judgments.[6] In many states, judgments remain in force automatically for 10 to 20 years. Also, in many states these judgments are easily renewed.[7]

Not keeping your promises in the United States can be both painful and expensive.

When There Is No Contract

Under judge-made common law, American courts have created additional theories of recovery to enforce promises even when there is no contract. Two of these remedies to prevent injustice are *promissory estoppel* and *unjust enrichment*.

Promissory Estoppel

> A bakery owner wanted to buy a supermarket franchise from Red Owl Stores, Inc. (Red Owl). He was told by Red Owl he could buy one of their franchised stores for $18,000. Relying on this promise, the bakery owner sold his bakery.
>
> When Red Owl refused to sell him the promised supermarket franchise, the former bakery owner sued Red Owl to *recover his out-of-pocket expenses incurred by relying on Red Owl's promise*. The court awarded the former bakery owner his reasonable expenses.[8]

The elements of promissory estoppel are (1) making a promise, (2) on which another party reasonably relies, (3) to his or her detriment. If all three elements are present, a judge may order the party who made the promise to pay any out-of-pocket expenses reasonably incurred by the other party who relied on that promise, even though there is no contract.

Thus, a husband-to-be can change his mind on the day of the wedding. Since a court cannot force him to marry his bride-to-be, there is no enforceable contract. However, a court can require him to pay for expenses reasonably incurred by his former bride-to-be, in reasonable reliance on his promise of marriage (e.g., wedding invitations, the wedding dress, catering expenses of the wedding reception).[9]

Unjust Enrichment

> Richard Scrushy, former chairman and chief executive officer of HealthSouth, received tens of millions of dollars in executive compensation. After a massive multi-billion dollar accounting scandal at HealthSouth was uncovered, Scrushy was sued for unjust enrichment to recover incentive bonuses he received from 1996 through 2002.
>
> The final judgment against him for *unjust enrichment* was approximately $47.8 million.[10]

The general requirements for unjust enrichment are (1) one party receives a *benefit* from the other party, (2) that he (or she) *knowingly accepts* and *retains*, (3) under circumstances that would be *unjust enrichment* to allow that party to keep that benefit.

It is impossible to trust another—whether an individual or organization, politician, or professional—if you cannot rely on the other person or organization to keep their promises.

Commandment #8: Keep Promises	
Ethics Principle:	A contract is a legally binding promise a court will enforce. For breach of contract, the non-breaching party is entitled to the benefit of the bargain. The technical requirements for a contract include an *offer* with definite terms that has been communicated and *accepted*. The *mutual promises* must be backed by *consideration* (e.g., agreeing to do something you already do not have a legal obligation to do, or refraining from doing something you have a legal right to do). Parties to the contract must be of *legal age* and the contract must be for a *lawful purpose*. It is a civil wrong (tort) to interfere with another's contract. Contracts can only be undone, and the parties restored to their original positions as though there was no contract, in certain specific circumstances such as *fraud, mistake, duress,* or *undue influence* (as defined under American law). Even if there is no legally binding contract, you may be liable for out-of-pocket expenses of another who reasonably relied on your promise to his or her detriment (*promissory estoppel*), or where one party confers a benefit on another party, which the other party knowingly accepts and retains, under circumstances that would be *unjust enrichment.*
Sample Law:	E.g., judge-made American common law contract law (derived from British common law contract law), Uniform Commercial Code, tortious interference with a contract, promissory estoppel, unjust enrichment, fraud, undue influence, mistake, duress.

Chapter 20

Commandment of Trust #9: Leadership
Animal Farm Ethics Don't Work

#9. Be a *REAL* Leader

In recent decades, American businesses, governments, and other civic institutions and voluntary associations have spent billions of dollars on leadership training.[1] *In spite of all this money and effort, confidence in American leaders in most of our key institutions and associations has dropped to disturbingly low levels. Why?*

Too many American leaders are missing the one absolutely essential ingredient that all *REAL* leaders must have: *TRUST. REAL* leaders are trusted because they *act—not talk*—in a trustworthy manner. *REAL (authentic) leadership cannot be faked.*

Harvard's Kennedy School conducts an annual nationwide poll on American attitudes toward leaders in a wide cross-section of American institutions, including military, medical, nonprofit and charity, local government, religious, U.S. Supreme Court, education, state government, business, the executive branch (office of the president), news media, U.S. Congress, and Wall Street.[2] In its *2011 Leadership Index*, the Kennedy School reported that trust and confidence in American leaders is at an all-time low:

> Not only in politics but across the board in eight different sectors of national life, Americans have lost confidence in their leaders over the past year. Overall some 77% say that the country now has a crisis in leadership, and confidence levels have fallen to the lowest levels recorded in recent times.[3]

That 2011 Leadership Index said: "[a]bove all, leaders must be *trustworthy...* [which includes] *competence, working for the greater good,* and *achieving results.*"[4] It also said, "Americans' unhappiness with their leaders is approaching the point where it threatens the country's stability and coherence."[5]

Too many American leaders today are not trusted because they are not *REAL leaders and do not act in a trustworthy manner.*

Because power corrupts, society's demands for moral authority and character increases as the importance of the position increases.

– John Adams (1735–1826)
American Founding Father
2nd U.S. president, 1797–1801

REAL American Military Leaders

To determine the essential behaviors of a *REAL* American leader, let's take a closer look at our *REAL* American military leaders who successfully led the country through major wars, and later became president. They include General (later President) *George Washington* (American Revolutionary War); General (later President) *Andrew Jackson* (War of 1812); General (later President) *Ulysses S. Grant* (Civil War); General (later President) *Dwight D. Eisenhower* (World War II).

Only *REAL* military leaders can inspire others to risk serious bodily injury and death to do impossible feats of self-sacrifice, bravery, heroism, and courage necessary to win a war. The United States has been a free nation for more than two centuries only because *ordinary* Americans, under *extraordinary REAL* American military leaders, were able to do what many thought impossible at the time.

Our *REAL* military American leaders were always tough on performance, *but they inspired fierce loyalty in their troops* because their troops *trusted* them.

U.S. Revolutionary War: *George Washington* and his ill-equipped band of citizen soldiers, after eight long years of war, defeated the mightiest military in the world. While commanding general during the Revolutionary War, Washington (who was married to one of the richest women in Virginia) refused to be paid for his services. He only asked to be reimbursed for his expenses.[6]

Washington remained with his troops throughout the war, even during the bitterly cold winters, when British generals generally retreated to the warmth and comfort of the cities. Washington was with his men during the terrible winter at Valley Forge, when his troops were close to starving, and many only had bloody rags for shoes. He was often seen riding his horse in front of his troops, risking his own life to urge his men forward.

When the war ended, Washington refused more power, declining the invitation to become a monarch. After his second presidential term ended, he did something rarely seen in history, *he voluntarily relinquished power. George Washington was a REAL servant leader for his troops, for the American people, and for the country.*

> *Gentlemen, you will permit me to put on my spectacles, for I have grown not only gray, but almost blind in the service of my country.*
>
> **– George Washington (1732–1799)**
> American Founding Father,
> 1st U.S. president, 1789–1797

War of 1812: *Andrew Jackson's* troops loved him. Marching back from a battle, Jackson got off his horse and walked, even though he was not well himself, so soldiers in worse condition could ride.[7] His troops called him "Old Hickory."

Jackson's "army" was only a ragtag band of militia men, pirates, freed slaves, Choctaw Indians, frontiersmen, as well as some regular army recruits. Nevertheless, he defeated the much larger, well-equipped, professional British troops that had just defeated Emperor Napoleon at Waterloo. At the Battle of New Orleans in 1815, Jackson lost only about 100 men (killed or wounded). British casualties were estimated at about 2,000.

U.S. Civil War: *Ulysses S. Grant* could quickly transform unruly farm boys into a disciplined fighting force.[8] Although viciously criticized as a "drunkard," "butcher," and "incompetent," he remained calm under pressure. Grant was a brilliant military strategist, able to fight an entire battle in his head. Like Washington, Grant was often seen riding his horse in front of his troops, risking his own life to lead them forward.

One of his generals, *William Tecumseh Sherman*, marched 62,000 men across Georgia in record time, traveling an unheard of 650 miles in less than 100 days. Sherman and his troops survived only on the food and provisions they could find in the surrounding countryside. His troops called him "Uncle Billy." They knew Sherman would only ask them to fight when it was absolutely necessary. They also knew he would never use them as cannon fodder to further his own career or for personal glory. Sherman's troops did the "impossible" because they *trusted* him.

> *Grant stood by me when I was crazy, and I stood by him when he was drunk, and now we stand by each other.*[9]
>
> **– William Tecumseh Sherman (1820–1891)**
> General under General Ulysses S. Grant during
> U.S. Civil War, 1861–1865

World War II: *Dwight D. Eisenhower* did not make excuses or seek to blame anyone else if he did not get results. A formerly "unknown" soldier before the war, he oversaw the largest military invasion force ever assembled in history—the Normandy invasion of Europe during World War II.

Before the Normandy invasion was launched, Dwight D. Eisenhower wrote a note that would be made public if the invasion failed, stating that the failure was his and his alone.[10] When the invasion succeeded, Eisenhower gave all the credit for its success to his troops, not himself.

These *REAL* American military leaders fiercely believed in our uniquely American brand of freedom. They never wavered. Without question, they believed that our American freedom was worth preserving, no matter what the cost or personal sacrifice. They fought for the cause of freedom and the survival of the nation, not for their own personal gain.

REAL leaders not only say *the right things, they **do** the right things. Because they are trusted, REAL leaders can accomplish extraordinary feats with ordinary people.*

Leaders, Not Saints

Added to this list of *REAL* American military *leaders* are our *REAL* "crisis of survival" American presidents: President George Washington, President Abraham Lincoln, and President Franklin D. Roosevelt.

These *REAL* American crisis and military leaders were human beings, not saints. They had human foibles and weaknesses, just as we all do. They made mistakes and their conduct, at times, was far from perfect.

George Washington and Andrew Jackson owned slaves. Ulysses S. Grant was rumored to sometimes drink too much. Abraham Lincoln and William Tecumseh Sherman suffered bouts of severe depression. There were whispers that Franklin D. Roosevelt and Dwight D. Eisenhower, both married, had mistresses during World War II.

> *Tell me what brand of whiskey that Grant drinks. I would like to send a barrel of it to my other generals.*
>
> **– Abraham Lincoln (1809–1865)**
> 16th U.S. president during the
> U.S. Civil War, 1861–1865

When considering what *REAL* leadership qualities matter in a time of extraordinary crisis, imagine yourself a passenger on a jet flying over New York, when the jet engines suddenly fail because of a flock of birds. The only thing standing between you and certain death is the pilot's ability to land the plane safely on the nearby frigid Hudson River (which is exactly what US Airways pilot Chesley B. "Sully" Sullenberger, III, did in January 2009[11]).

In such a life-and-death crisis situation, do you care whether the pilot is a flawed human being with foibles that have nothing to do with his ability to fly? Or, is it more important to you whether or not the pilot is super-skilled at flying, cares deeply about the safety of *all* on board (not just himself or those he favors), and is courageous, competent, and calm enough under pressure to be able to land the plane safely on the water?

If we wish to find *REAL* crisis leaders to survive the next Fourth Turning generational crisis of survival, we must stop using Utopian standards of personal behavior, perfection, and goodness, and instead look for the absolutely essential quality in a *REAL* leader in a major crisis or national emergency—*TRUST*.

> *Every saint has a past and every sinner has a future.*
>
> **– Oscar Wilde (1854–1900)**
> 19th century English poet and playwright

Animal Farm Ethics

George Orwell wrote *Animal Farm* in 1946 as an indictment of the Soviet Union's Communist "top-down" central government under the ruthless dictatorship of Josef Stalin. In this fable, the pigs persuade the other farm animals to overthrow their human masters who are mistreating the animals.

The pigs promised the farm animals that their lives would be much better in an "all animals are equal" animal-run farm. Being the smartest animals, the pigs quickly took charge. They lulled the farm animals into complacency by *saying* all the right things, such as writing "all animals are equal" rules on the barnyard door.

However, behind the scenes the behavior of the pigs *was anything but equal.* The pigs pushed the farm animals to work harder and harder "for the good of the animal community," while they worked less and less. As soon as farm animals became too old or weak to work, they were immediately shipped off the farm to die, no matter how many sacrifices those animals had made for the benefit of the farm.

They eliminated any animal challenging their authority. Newborn animals were separated from their parents to be indoctrinated with the pigs' real philosophy—"some animals (namely, the pigs) are more equal than others." The pigs commandeered the highly prized milk and apples for themselves. Like their former human masters, only pigs were permitted to drink alcohol.

Over time, the "all animals are equal" rules initially placed on the barnyard door were replaced with pig-centric "some animals are more equal than others" rules. *In the end, the lives of the farm animals were just as miserable under their new pig masters as they had been under their former human masters.*[12]

> *If the American dream is to come true and abide with us, it will, at bottom, depend on the people themselves.* [13]
>
> **– James Truslow Adams (1878–1949)**
> American historian, author of
> *The Epic of America*, 1931

Sadly, many American leaders today are not trusted because they have Animal Farm *ethics.*

REAL American Leadership

REAL American leaders inspire trust under ethics-based American Rule of Law because they (1) *set the example* and (2) *take care of the troops first.*

Today, many fake leaders are running our civic institutions and voluntary associations. They take care of themselves and those they favor, even at the expense of those they are supposed to be representing or leading. *This is not just occurring in our big businesses and on Wall Street. It is occurring across a broad spectrum of our essential self-organizing institutions and associations.*

Many of today's "leaders" are more interested in amassing personal wealth and power for themselves than working on the behalf of the well-being of others in their organizations, their communities, and the country as a whole. Many of our current "leaders" have demonstrated time and time again that they cannot be trusted, because they do not *act* in a trustworthy manner.

Only *REAL* leaders are trusted. *Leaders with* Animal Farm *ethics are never trusted.*

1. Set the Example

REAL leaders set the example *by following the 10 Commandments of Trust* in the institutions and associations they are leading. Under *ethics-based* American Rule of Law, there are consequences when they don't.

Although the following examples are from business, the same basic ethics principles of right and wrong behavior apply to leaders in any of our civic institutions and voluntary associations (although these standards may be enforced in different ways):[14]

Title and Organization	Commandment of Trust	Consequences
Former CEO, *Taylor, Bean & Whitaker Mortgage Corp.*	**TRUTH** (fraud)	30 years in prison[15]
Former CEO, *Comcast Corp.*	**FAIR** (antitrust)	Fined $500,000[16]
Former CEO, *Kellogg, Brown & Root*	**LOYALTY** (bribery)	30 months in prison[17]
Former CEO, former president, former head of the bank loan division, *Washington Mutual Bank*	**CARE** (negligence)	Must return $64 million in retirement, bonus, and golden parachute benefits[18]
Former CEO, *WorldCom*	**ACCOUNTABILITY** (accounting fraud)	25 years in prison[19]
Former CEO, *British Petroleum (BP), Inc.*	**PROPERTY** (environmental damage)	Resigned[20]
Former CEO, *The Boeing Company*	**PEOPLE** (improper relationship with employee)	Resigned[21]
Former CEO, *HealthSouth*	**PROMISES** (unjust enrichment)	Ordered to return $47.8 million in incentive bonuses[22]
Former CEO, *Best Buy*	**LEADERSHIP** (violating company policy)	Resigned[23]
Former Head, *Bernard L. Madoff Securities, LLC*	**ENFORCEMENT** (Ponzi scheme)	150 years in prison[24]

Here are some additional examples of criminal fines, penalties, and restitution awards given to top business leaders who violated one or more of the *10 Commandments of Trust* (e.g., securities fraud and accounting fraud, Commandments of Trust Nos. 1 and 6):

Title and Organization	Prison Sentence	Penalties, Fines, etc.
Former CEO, *American Tissue*, 2006	15 years in prison	$65 million restitution[25]
Former CEO, *Enron*, 2006	24 years prison (later reduced to 14 years)	$60 million forfeiture[26]
Former CEO, *QWEST*, 2007	6 years prison	$44 million forfeiture $19 million fine[27]
Former CEO, *Cendant Corp*, 2007	12 years prison	$3.3 billion fine[28]
Former CEO, *Sweezy Construction*, 2010	7 years in prison	$40 million restitution[29]
Founder, *Galleon* (Hedge Fund), 2011	11 years in prison	$156.6 million[30]

2. Take Care of the Troops First

REAL military leaders in a time of war take care of their troops first. Officers do not eat until after their troops are fed first. Officers do not sleep until they have taken care of the sleeping arrangements of their troops first. This makes sense. After all, the troops are the ones doing the fighting. *REAL* leaders consider the well-being of those they are representing first—*before* taking care of themselves.

A country with only a small number of extremely wealthy people at the top, while the rest of the population suffers serious economic and financial hardships, is unstable. Left unaddressed, wide disparities in wealth and income will eventually weaken one or more of the essential pillars of a successful country: a successful economy, a harmonious peaceful society, a stable political system, and its ability to protect itself from internal and external threats.

Pay, Perks, and Benefits of Big Corporation CEOs

Over the past 40 years, disparities between CEO compensation and the average employee's wages at some of our large public corporations have grown at an alarming rate. Here's how Graef Crystal, a compensation expert, described this disparity in a 2002 TV interview:[31]

- **1973:** CEO compensation = *45 times* average employee's wages
- **1991:** CEO compensation = *140 times*
- **2002**: CEO compensation = *almost 500 times*

"Arm's Length" Transactions: Sometimes this huge jump in CEO compensation packages is "justified" by comparing CEO pay packages to the enormous growth in salaries for sports stars, media stars, and entertainers.

In 2011, golfer Tiger Woods earned $75 million in one year. Star basketball players Kobe Bryant and LeBron James earned $53 million and $48 million respectively.[32] However, paying too much money for just a few players can damage trust between team members and eventually hurt team performance. As a result, some teams are beginning to look at overall pay fairness for everyone on the team.[33]

In 2012, the earnings of top celebrities and media people were reported to be between $18 million and $165 million in one year.[34] Judge Judy, whose daytime TV show had the highest ratings, was paid $45 million.[35]

Certainly, these huge pay packages do say something about the state of America's value system today (as compared to years past), but this compensation comparison ignores a very important difference. Compensation packages for sports and media stars and entertainers are negotiated by independent parties in *arm's length transactions.*

An arm's length transaction under American law means that the parties are acting *freely* and *independently* of each other. It means that party is not in a position to influence or control the other in a way that could create a *conflict of interest.*

Not "Arm's Length" Transactions: In contrast, the compensation *packages of CEOs have not always been negotiated in arm's length transactions.* Over the past three decades, CEOs at many of America's largest corporations have taken on the additional role of acting as the chairman of the board of directors at the same time.

This trend appears to have begun around 1979, when Gordon E. Moore, the cofounder and CEO of Intel Corporation, a giant manufacturer of microprocessors, took on the role of the company's chairman of the board of directors while still acting as its CEO.[36] It didn't take long for other CEOs of giant corporations to follow his example.[37]

Here's the problem. Taking on both the CEO *and* chairman of the board of directors roles at the same time creates a classic *conflict of interest* situation under *ethics-based* American Rule of Law. It is no coincidence that this trend of CEOs taking on both roles coincides with skyrocketing CEO compensation. This is the natural and inevitable result of allowing one person to take on these dual and conflicting roles, which is why ethics-based American Rule of Law calls taking on both roles simultaneously a conflict of interest in the first place.

Separation of Powers: Like our constitutional *separation of powers* concept (judicial, legislative, and executive) inherent in our federal and state governments, a corporation also has separate powers and responsibilities for the board of directors and its executive officers. When one person is both the CEO and the chairman of the board, an essential impartial check on corporate decisions or actions is eliminated. *Allowing the same person to be the CEO and chairman of the board concentrates too much power in the hands of just one person.*

Conflicts of Interest: A long-standing principle of American corporation law for more than 100 years is that a corporation is a separate *legal person.* Under American corporate law, a corporation's *board of directors* is *legally responsible* for *overseeing the activities of the corporation*, which *includes monitoring and evaluating the CEO's performance and setting the CEO's pay.*

When the same person is both the CEO and the chairman of the board, the CEO is, in essence, evaluating and monitoring himself (or herself). Regardless of any protections a corporate board may attempt to put in place, the practical reality is that a CEO, who is also acting as the chairman of the board, is in a position to influence, whether directly or indirectly, the board of directors' decisions about what he (or she) is paid—a classic *conflict of interest* situation under *ethics-based* American Rule of Law.

In the late 1990s, for the first time, *nonowner, nonfounder CEOs* of giant American public companies received a total of more than $1 billion each in compensation, mostly through stock options. The former Disney *CEO and chairman* received over $1 billion that included $680 million in stock options.[38] The former Coca-Cola *CEO and chairman* received about $1 billion that included 16 million shares of Coca-Cola stock.[39] In 2006, stock options given to former CEO and chairman of United Healthcare Group were valued at $1.6 billion.[40]

> *Management is doing things right; leadership is doing the right things.*
>
> **– Peter F. Drucker (1909–2005)**
> 20th century management consultant

Fiduciary Duties: Under *ethics-based* American Rule of Law, officers and directors of a corporation have fiduciary duties *to the corporation itself*, a separate "legal person" under American corporate law. Three of the most important fiduciary duties owed *to the corporation itself* are

- the fiduciary duty of *care* (to be careful, competent, and diligent),

- the fiduciary duty of *loyalty* (to put the corporation's interests ahead of all other interests, including one's own interests), and

- the fiduciary duty to *account* (to use the corporation's money and assets only for what clearly benefits the corporation, not for the personal benefit of officers and directors).

For example, breaching fiduciary duties contributed to a $2.9 billion personal judgment against a former CEO and chairman of the board of HealthSouth.[41]

Corporate directors too often sat on multiple corporate boards at the same time (interlocking directorates). This brought into question whether corporate boards were actually acting independently of each other when making executive compensation decisions.[42] Appointing retired politicians and former lobbyists to corporate boards exposed boards to the possibility of inappropriate political influence.[43]

Pay for Performance? In recent decades, instead of promoting from within, boards of directors began hiring outside "celebrity CEOs" who demanded and received outsized "celebrity" compensation packages.[44] As companies awarded their executives huge compensation packages, other giant corporations scrambled to follow suit to keep and attract top executive talent.

"Pay for performance" became the new mantra of the day. Gone was the "old-fashioned" depression and war American notion that CEOs were expected to bring their top performance to work every day for well-paid, but reasonable compensation and benefits; those who didn't perform were fired.

Executive "pay for performance" targets have skewed financial incentives. Some executives began using dishonest accounting and mass employee layoffs to meet the financial targets required for their bonuses.[45]

> *Mirror, mirror on the wall, who's the highest paid of all?*
>
> **– Graef Crystal**
> Compensation expert, author of
> *In Search of Excess*, 1991

High Pay, Poor Performance: Between 2000 and 2008, before Lehman Brothers suddenly declared bankruptcy, its former CEO and chairman of the board was awarded $484 million in salary, bonuses, and stock options.[46] In 2004, a $9 billion accounting scandal was uncovered at Fannie Mae. Its former CEO and chairman of the board had been paid $91.1 million from 1998–2004, including some $52.6 million in bonuses.[47]

CEOs have been rewarded millions of dollars in severance pay, even after performing poorly. A former president of the Walt Disney Company, terminated after only 14 months, was paid approximately $130 million in severance pay.[48] A former CEO of Hewlett-Packard, terminated after only 11 months on the job, left with $23.2 million in cash and stock in severance pay that included a $10 million sign-on bonus.[49] A former CEO at "troubled" Yahoo, Inc. received $10 million in severance.[50]

Backlash Brewing? Excessive executive pay, perks, and benefits damage the public's trust in our giant American businesses and free-market capitalism. Paying huge amounts of money to top executives in an era when millions of Americans are unemployed and under-employed, and American taxpayers have paid hundreds of billions of dollars to bail out multiple giant corporations, is like waving a red flag in front of an angry bull.

Pay, perks, and benefits tolerated in good economic times can quickly spark a nasty backlash in an era of financial and economic hardship. A major backlash against huge executive compensation awards can take many forms. It could come from the courts and the legal system directly through huge personal liability judgments against officers and directors personally (e.g., civil lawsuits or enforcing clawback clauses) and their corporations.

It could also come through bad publicity that causes the company customers and investors to no longer buy their products and services or invest in their stock. It could also come through a deluge of new government regulations and/or increased taxes as outraged voters, citizens, and consumers register their anger through elections.

A recent 2012 *Wall Street Journal* headline highlights the type of media coverage likely to inflame public opinion against excessive executive compensation: *"For Retiring GE Executive, $89,000 a Month Not to Work."*[51]

GE agreed to pay a 50-year-old retiring GE vice chairman (who had worked for GE for 29 years) $89,000 a month until 2022 as part of an early retirement severance deal with GE, worth at least $28.4 million. He agreed not to work for a GE competitor for 3 years. He could cash in his stock options early and was still eligible to receive a GE supplemental pension at age 60. GE Capital received a $132 billion taxpayer bailout after the Financial Crisis of 2008.[52]

"Maximizing Shareholder Value": Officers and directors who are *REAL* leaders always consider the impact of their decisions on *all facets* of the corporation: *employees, suppliers, creditors, shareholders, customers, and the communities* in which they operate, NOT just the flawed recently popularized "maximizing shareholder value" standard. This is especially true when setting pay, perks, and benefits for top executives.[53]

Depression and war American corporate officers and directors understood this. Many baby-boomer and later generations of American corporate directors and officers have not. Early on, "[Peter] Drucker was sickened by the excessive riches awarded to mediocre executives even as they slashed the ranks of ordinary workers."[54]

Top 1% Highest Paid *Not* Just in Big Business

According to a 2012 *Wall Street Journal* article, those paid an annual salary of $506,000 are in the top 1% of income earners in the United States.[55] Members of the top 1% income earners are now found in American federal and state governments, nonprofits and charities, unions, and other essential institutions and associations. This has created public distrust in leaders of some of our other essential self-organizing civic institutions and voluntary associations too.

Federal and State Governments: While the federal government has been wildly overspending (e.g., $1 trillion deficit a year for four years) and raising fees and taxes, federal administrators are exceedingly well paid, enjoying perks and benefits not available to workers in the private sector.

In 2010, the president of the Atlanta Housing Authority (part of the U.S. Department of Housing and Urban Development) received a total of $644,241 in one year. In addition to her annual salary of $312,500, she received a $135,000 bonus, $126,000 for accrued vacation, $11,250 for unused vacation, and $4,100 for unused paid sick leave.[56]

When California was under severe budget pressure and raising taxes and fees, the highest paid state employee in 2010 was a California prison surgeon who was paid $777,423. According to the *Los Angeles Times*, he "...has a history of mental illness, was fired once for alleged incompetence and has not been allowed to treat an inmate for six years because medical supervisors don't trust his clinical skills."[57]

Charities and Nonprofits: Despite the fact that nonprofits and charities get special tax breaks, the top executives of some of these voluntary associations have been given some eye-popping compensation packages.

The CEO of the Boys and Girls Club in 2008 was paid $988,591.[58] The annual compensation of the CEO of the March of Dimes was $627,104.[59] The president of the American Museum of Natural History was paid $877,000 a year, and the museum also bought a $5 million New York apartment for the CEO where she lived rent-free.[60]

The CEO of the U.S. Chamber of Commerce was paid $1.8 million in compensation in 2005–2006, one of the highest paid association executives in the United States.[61] In 2007, the CEO of the Smithsonian Institute was paid $915,698, a dramatic increase from his 2000 compensation of $536,100.[62]

The 2009 compensation of the interim U.S. Olympic Committee chief was $1,006,336. The May/June 2013 issue of the *Charity Rating Guide & Watchdog Report* reported the CEO of United Way Worldwide was paid $999,574, and the CEO of Easter Seals received $796,501.[63]

Universities: In an era of rapidly escalating university tuition, when students and their parents have borrowed more than $1 trillion from the American taxpayers for their education, some top university officials are very highly paid.

In 2011, total compensation (pay, perks, and benefits) of the 10 highest paid *public* university presidents ranged from a high of $1,992,221 to a low of $738,603.[64] In 2009, the pay, perks, and benefits of the top-10 highest paid presidents of *private* universities ranged from a high of $4,912,127 to a low of $1,542,270.[65] In the 2012–2013 school year, the number of public university presidents making more than $1 million a year doubled to nine.[66]

Unions: The union boss of United Food Commercial Workers Local 464A was paid $528,000 a year to represent mostly minimum wage grocery store workers.[67] The Chief of the Plumbers and Pipefitters Union was paid $1.3 million in 2005.[68] The president of the International Brotherhood of Boilermakers was paid a total of $607,022 a year (base pay: $307,134 and nearly $300,000 in benefits).[69]

At a time when the average pay for teachers is $44,000, the president of the American Federation of Teachers was paid $493,859 and the president of the National Education Association $460,060 (close to the top 1%)[70]

Pastors: One church pastor in 2004 was paid nearly $1 million a year.[71] Another pastor earned $900,000 a year and owned a 10,000-square-foot mansion in Beverly Hills.[72] Could this be why regular church attendance in the United States has been declining?[73]

U.S. Military: There are signs of *Animal Farm* ethics in the U.S. military. A recent *USA Today* article revealed that "without much public scrutiny or oversight" about 158 retired generals and admirals became "senior mentors" who were paid (at taxpayers' expense) about $200–$340 an hour, plus expenses—much more than they were paid while on active duty.

They received this additional pay despite having active ties to the U.S. defense industry—29 of them worked full-time as executives for defense contractors.[74] In 2013, hospital workers at military hospitals were furloughed because of budget cuts.[75]

Extraordinary pay, perks, and benefits for those at the top, while those they are supposed to be leading have stagnant wages for decades, are losing their jobs, and are seriously under-employed (working fewer hours not by choice), is a recipe for trouble.

Only *REAL* American Leaders Can Restore Trust

Only *REAL* American leaders can restore trust in our essential civic institutions and voluntary associations—our business, governments, nonprofits and charities, etc. *REAL* leaders are *competent, interested in the greater good*, and *accountable for results*.

They *set the example* by following the *10 Commandments of Trust* in carrying out their responsibilities in the civic institution or voluntary association they are leading. When making decisions, *REAL* leaders *take care of the troops first.* They take into account the well-being of those they are representing and leading *before* their own self-interest.

A free self-organizing country with institutions and associations run by fake leaders with Animal Farm ethics will not be free for long. That's what history warns us.

Commandment #9: Be a *REAL* Leader	
Ethics Principle:	*REAL* leaders do *not* have *Animal Farm ethics*. *REAL* leaders *set the example* by following the *10 Commandments of Trust.* They *take care of the troops first*, remembering that military officers don't eat until after their troops are fed first, and don't sleep until after they have taken care of the sleeping arrangements for their troops first.
Sample Law:	E.g., civil lawsuits, criminal trials, regulatory actions, Congressional hearings, compensatory and punitive damages, equitable remedies such as restitution to disgorge improper payments, negative publicity that damages reputation, termination or resignation, clawback provisions.

Chapter 21

Commandment of Trust #10: Enforcement

Today's Loophole, Tomorrow's Noose

#10. Enforce Commandments 1–9

To keep and maintain our culture of trust, ethical standards *must be enforced.* In the United States, it is not whether painful enforcement will occur for violating our essential ethical standards; it *must* occur to keep the essential culture of trust on which our freedom, prosperity, peace, stability, and security rests.

> *Government implies the power of making laws. It is essential to the idea of law, that it be attended with a sanction; or in other words, a penalty or punishment for disobedience.*
>
> **– Alexander Hamilton (1755 or 1757–1804)**
> American Founding Father,
> 1st U.S. secretary of the Treasury, 1789–1795

To restore trust quickly, enforcement under *ethics-based* American Rule of Law can become very painful seemingly overnight. Individuals and organizations are often surprised by how swiftly and painfully stepped-up ethics enforcement can occur in the United States.

In response to the savings and loan crisis of the late 1980s, enforcement power under *ethics-based* American Rule of Law greatly expanded.[1] The federal government collected millions of dollars from giant accounting firms and large law firms for "aiding and abetting" savings and loan fraud and for improper audits.[2]

Once the worst of the savings and loan crisis passed, legal limits were placed on the liability of third parties like accountants and attorneys.[3] In today's era of rampant unethical conduct, statutory protections limiting liability for these third parties may not provide much protection in another major financial crisis like the Financial Crisis of 2008.

Power of the Press

Public ethics scandals in the United States often begin with investigative journalists, news organizations, or other individuals and groups taking advantage of our American constitutional guarantees of free press and free speech.

When an ethics scandal becomes public, enforcement of ethical standards can take many forms. Here are just a few possibilities: civil lawsuits for money damages; criminal indictments; Congressional hearings and/or other government investigations and enforcement actions; revocation of favorable tax status and/or favorable tax rates; or politicians voted out of office.

In 2010, *The Los Angeles Times* published a series of articles that uncovered outrageously high salaries and other financial scandals in the small working-class town of Bell, California.[4] Criminal charges were filed against eight current and former city officials, the pensions of former Bell officials were cut, and the accounting firm responsible for auditing the city of Bell's books was fined. Bell's citizens began showing up at government meetings "demanding public documents, asking tough questions and pushing for change."[5]

In 2010, Toyota Motor Corporation was rocked by media reports alleging its cars were suddenly accelerating and causing deaths. Publicity led to the recall of 10 million vehicles, a Congressional investigation and hearings, and hundreds of lawsuits. In 2012, Toyota agreed to pay $1.1 billion to settle a class-action lawsuit.[6]

Information about public ethics topics in the United States is readily available. For example, an Internet database lists all of the California government retirees who receive a yearly pension in excess of $100,000—by name and the exact amount the retiree receives.[7] Almost half of the states use Internet lists showing the names of their top tax delinquents (e.g., the Rhode Island Division of Taxation publishes a list of its top 100 Tax Delinquents[8]).

The American Legal Dragon[10]

Here is an imaginary illustration of how enforcement under *ethics-based* American Rule of Law works. Imagine a dragon living in a very dark cave. Its purpose is to make sure those playing in the sunlight in front of its cave are "playing by the rules" and not cheating and harming others. Those playing in the bright sunlight in front of the cave cannot see or hear the dragon. The cave is pitch black and the dragon stays dead-still, not making a sound. It is awake 24/7; it never sleeps.

During periods of peace and prosperity, the dragon remains in the cave silently watching. If players are "playing by the rules," no one is getting injured, so there are few complaints.

Over time, some players begin to doubt that the dragon exists. They convince themselves that their unethical (wrong conduct) is "legal," especially when they make oodles of money by being unethical. They start to cheat. When nothing happens, they cheat some more. Eventually their cheating causes serious harm to fellow players, who begin to scream and yowl.

In the blink of an eye, out comes the ferocious fire-breathing dragon, lightning-quick, from the cave, snapping off the heads of wrongdoers and leaving a trail of blood and gore. Those playing in front of the cave are once again vividly reminded that, indeed, the dragon is real and very "deadly".

Another generation of players is painfully reminded that "playing by the rules" in front of the dragon's cave is mandatory, not optional, and that breaking the "rules" can have very painful consequences.

Wrong conduct destroys trust and when trust in our self-organizing institutions and associations withers, the economy, society, and country become unstable. To survive a financial crisis or national emergency, the American legal dragon *must* swiftly re-appear to restore trust "overnight."

IRS Lessons in Pain

Another way to understand how enforcement works under *ethics-based* American Rule of Law is to take a look at how the U.S. government collects taxes. Over many decades, the IRS (Internal Revenue Service) has studiously cultivated its public image of being an extremely painful tax enforcer for a very good reason—it works.

Americans know the IRS has tremendous power to sock them with huge penalties, fines, and/or prison sentences and that it is not afraid to use that power *against anyone*. In the United States, no one is safe from the reach of the IRS. Also, American citizens and legal residents must pay U.S. tax on their worldwide income.

A famous country singer who owed over $6.5 million in back taxes ended up owing the IRS $16.7 million after penalties and interest were added. The U.S. government seized and sold most of his possessions.[11] A well-known actor was sent to prison for 3 years for failing to pay his taxes.[12]

A billionaire former president of Helmsley Hotels was sent to prison for 4 years for claiming personal luxuries as business expenses. She paid a $7 million fine and $2 million in restitution.[13] Las Vegas casino workers were sent to prison for conspiracy to provide false information on the amount of their income received as tips.[14] A large prominent Texas law firm, Jenkens & Gilchrist, was forced to close its doors and pay a $76 million fine to the IRS for creating questionable tax shelters.[15] Even a former IRS tax commissioner was sent to prison for 5 years for tax evasion.[16]

Like the enforcement power of the IRS over taxes, enforcement power under ethics-based American Rule of Law can be broad, far reaching, and at times exceedingly painful.

Whistleblowers Welcome

Whistleblowers in the United States are richly rewarded. A federal statute rewards whistleblowers with 30% of the money the government recovers for fraud.[17] In 2012, the University of Phoenix agreed to pay $78.5 million (including $11 million for attorneys' fees)[18] to settle a lawsuit alleging it had improperly rewarded recruiters with incentives (e.g., commissions and bonuses) to enroll students. Two former university counselors, who filed the lawsuit under this federal statute, could receive $22 million.[19]

In 2006, the IRS instituted an enhanced whistleblower program to catch tax cheats. If the IRS recovers $2 million or more, a whistleblower is now paid 15% to 30% of the money recovered. For smaller amounts, a tax whistleblower is paid 10% of the monies recovered.

Whistleblowers are protected under certain circumstances in the military and in our financial institutions.[20] Under the Sarbanes-Oxley Act of 2002 ("SOX"), retaliation against a corporate whistleblower is now criminal.

In recent years, the Securities and Exchange Commission and the Department of Justice have settled securities and corruption cases ranging from $75 million to $550 million.[21] Under the Dodd-Frank Wall Street Reform and Consumer Protection Act, whistleblowers who report violations of securities laws, corruption, or commodities violations to the proper government authorities can receive between 10% and 30% of what the government recovers.[22]

> *All tyranny needs to gain a foothold is for people of good conscience to remain silent.* [23]
>
> **– Thomas Jefferson (1743–1829)**
> American Founding Father,
> 3rd U.S. president, 1801–1809

Unethical Conduct Is Hazardous to Your Wealth

Unethical conduct in the United States can be expensive:

Organization and Individual	10 Commandments of Trust	Settlements, Verdicts, Fines, Penalties, Restitution, etc.
Enron Corp.	**TRUTH** (securities fraud)	$7.12 billion[24]
Bank of America (Countrywide)	**FAIR** (unfair lending practices)	$335 million[25]
Siemens	**LOYALTY** (bribery)	$800 million[26]
American Home Products	**CARE** (safe products)	$3.7 billion[27]
KPMG	**ACCOUNTABILITY** (fraudulent tax shelters)	$456 million[28]
British Petroleum (BP)	**PROPERTY** (environmental damage)	$20 billion[29]
Coca-Cola, Inc.	**PEOPLE** (race discrimination)	$192 million[30]
Texaco, Inc.	**PROMISES** (breach of contract, tortious interference with a contract)	$3 billion[31]
Former CEO, HealthSouth	**LEADERSHIP** (accounting fraud)	$2.9 billion[32]
Google, Inc.	**ENFORCEMENT** (ads for illegal importation of prescription drugs)	$500 million[33]

Unethical Conduct Can Land You in Jail

Unethical conduct in the United States may also be criminal:

Name, Title, and Organization	10 Commandments of Trust	Prison Sentence
Former CEO, *Enron Corp.*	**TRUTH** (securities fraud)	24 years[34]
Former head of hedge fund, *Galleon Group*	**FAIR** (insider trading)	11 years[35]
Former president, *Terra Telecommunications, Inc.*	**LOYALTY** (bribery)	15 years[36]
Former nursing assistant, *Leewood Healthcare Center*	**CARE** (criminal negligence)	6 months[37]
Former CEO, *WorldCom*	**ACCOUNTABILITY** (accounting fraud)	25 years[38]
Former scientist, *Dow Chemical Co.*	**PROPERTY** (theft of trade secrets)	7 years[39]
Former plant manager, *Atlantic States Cast Iron Pipe Co.*	**PEOPLE** (safety and health)	5 years, 11 months[40]
Former chief of staff, *NASA*	**PROMISES** (conspiracy)	3 years, 5 months[41]
Former CEO, *Adelphia Communications, Inc.*	**LEADERSHIP** (looting)	15 years[42]

Pain at the Top

Those at the top of our businesses (and other civic institutions and voluntary associations) may be held *personally responsible* for unethical conduct:

- Former CEO: 15 years in prison, ordered to pay $65 million in restitution (2005)[43]

- Former CEO: 7 years in prison, ordered to pay $40 million in restitution (2010)[44]

- Hedge Fund Founder: 11 years in prison, ordered to pay $156.6 million in penalties, fines, and forfeitures (2011)[45]

- Former CEO: 6 years in prison, ordered to pay $7.1 million in forfeitures and fines (2007)[46]

Pain Down Below

Anyone who participated in the wrongdoing could face stiff enforcement actions:

- Former COO, former head of human resources, and two other former executives: $5.8 million[47]

- Former real estate attorney: 30 years in prison, $12 million[48]

- Former telemarketer: 29 years and two months in prison, ordered to pay $35 million[49]

- Former COO: 25 years in prison[50]

- Former finance executive: 8 years in prison, ordered to pay $1.4 million[51]

Ratcheting Up the Pain

The more unethical behavior permeates our institutions and associations, threatening our essential culture of trust, the stiffer the penalties are likely to become:

- Former CEO: 50 years in prison[52]

- Founder: 330 years in prison[53]

- Former banker: 30 years[54]

- Founder: 150 years in prison, $170 billion[55]

- Former CEO: 12 years and 7 months in prison, $3.3 billion[56]

- Former CEO: Almost 7-year prison term for bribery, $2.9 billion (so far about $100 million of his personal property has been confiscated)[57]

Pain Has Many Faces

- GlaxoSmithKline PLC pleaded guilty to criminal charges of illegally marketing drugs and agreed to pay the government $3 billion. This was one of the largest health-care fraud settlements in U.S. history.[58]

- A former attorney was given a 12-year prison sentence—the longest sentence for insider trading at the time—for divulging confidential, priviledged information to others over a 17-year period.[59]

- A former county commissioner was sentenced to 28 years in prison for "accepting bribes and overseeing a pervasive pay-to-play culture in county government."[60] The judge issued a sentence six years longer than the prosecutors requested because of the damage done to the public trust. So far, 50 contractors and public officials have been convicted in this scandal, including the county assessor and two judges.

To restore trust in our businesses, governments, and other essential self-organizing civic institutions and voluntary associations, serious enforcement actions *must* be brought against those responsible for the unethical conduct that has damaged our essential culture of trust. If "crime" (serious unethical conduct) "pays," expect more of it.

Not enforcing ethical standards against wrongdoers destroys trust.

Commandment #10: Enforce Commandments 1–9	
Ethics Principle:	Because of our constitutional free speech and free press protections, it is much easier for scandals to be revealed in the United States than in other countries. Whistleblowers are not only encouraged, they are often extremely well rewarded. Under *ethics-based* American Rule of Law, there are many creative, flexible, innovative, and "deadly" (painful) ways to enforce ethics standards in our self-organizing civic institutions and voluntary associations. Unethical conduct may be hazardous to your wealth and can land you in jail.
Sample Law:	E.g., whistleblower lawsuits, civil and criminal trials, punitive damages, clawback provisions, Racketeering Influenced and Corrupt Organizations Act, environmental laws, employment laws, insider trading, antitrust, obstruction of justice, lying to a federal official, breach of fiduciary duties, real property laws, intellectual property laws, the Economic Espionage Act of 1996, Foreign Corrupt Practices Act, criminal restitution, accounting fraud, bribes and kickbacks, negligence, recklessness, union law, employment law, contract law, promissory estoppel, unjust enrichment.

Appendix A

10 Commandments of Trust
in the United States

Commandment #1: Tell the Truth	
Ethics Principle:	Do not lie *about something important* under oath, whether orally or in writing, destroy evidence, or tamper with witnesses in judicial proceedings. Remember the original oath: "I swear to tell the truth, the whole truth, and nothing but the truth, so help me God." Do not lie to a federal official in an official federal investigation, whether directly or indirectly. Be honest and do not intentionally deceive others. Be careful not to mislead others reasonably relying on your statements about something important that would change the outcome of a decision. Fully disclose all important and relevant information. Claims about products and services must be accurate, verifiable, and when required, capable of scientific proof.
Sample Law:	E.g., civil and criminal fraud, misrepresentation, perjury, obstruction of justice, fiduciary duty to inform, wire fraud, mail fraud, securities fraud, bank fraud, conspiracy, False Claims Act, international money laundering, deceptive trade practices, false advertising, racketeering under the Racketeer Influenced and Corrupt Organizations (RICO) Act, theft by deception, making a false statement to law enforcement, fiduciary duty of candor, Freedom of Information Act, falsifying records of a broker dealer and an investment advisor; defamation, libel, slander; lying to a federal official, a *qui tam* (whistleblower) lawsuit.

Commandment #2: Fair	
Ethics Principle:	The essence of justice is fairness, but *fairness does not mean equal results.* It means using *objective standards of behavior* to eliminate prejudice or favoritism. Being fair means not engaging in practices that stifle free and open competition in the market-place. It also means not divulging confidential, non-public information obtained in a position of trust and confidence that is used to buy or sell stocks and other securities. Fairness means due process; that is, fair notice of any alleged wrong behavior, and a fair hearing and process with fair procedures that apply equally to all. Fairness also means following community stand-ards of fair play and decency.
Sample Law:	E.g., antitrust, fair competition laws, insider trading, fair use in intellectual property laws, securities fraud, conspiracy, unfair lending practices, unfair business practices, bid-rigging, Racket-eer Influenced and Corrupt Organizations Act, conspiracy (e.g., conspiracy to defraud, conspiracy to make false entries in bank records), obstruction of justice, wire fraud, mail fraud, decep-tive trade practices, price-fixing, predatory business practices, identity theft, pretexting.

Commandment #3: Be Loyal	
Ethics Principle:	When acting on behalf of others, always put their interests first above your own self-interest or the interests of those you favor (e.g., your family, friends, associates, etc.). Avoid conflicts of interest or the appearance of a conflict of interest by acting *at arm's length* with others. Do not accept kickbacks or bribes. Also, be careful about accepting gifts and gratuities from those in a position to benefit from your decisions or actions, or giving gifts and gratuities to those from whom you can benefit. Do not self-deal. Keep confidential information confidential.
Sample Law:	E.g., breach of fiduciary duty of loyalty, Foreign Corrupt Practices Act, bribery, kickbacks, racketeering, money laundering, conspiracy, wire fraud, mail fraud, bribery of a public official, rewarding official misconduct, False Claims Act, federal and state securities laws, Hobbs Act extortion, fraud, the Anti-Kickback Act, the Stark Law, state conflict of interests statutes.

Commandment #4: Be Careful	
Ethics Principle:	Act with care to avoid harm to people and property that is reasonably forseeable. Manufacturers, distributors, suppliers, and sellers of dangerous or defective products are liable regardless of fault. Risks of potential harm must be fully and accurately disclosed. Take care to protect personal data from being lost or stolen, exposing individuals to identity theft. Be competent and diligent. Being competent means having the knowledge, skill, and ability to meet the standard of performance required for the task you have undertaken. Being diligent means doing your homework; that is, researching, investigating, and carefully reviewing all relevant data before making important decisions or taking action, and persevering with tasks until they are properly completed. Do not take excessive risks with other people's money and property. When acting in a position of trust and confidence on behalf of another, you have a fiduciary duty of care, the highest level of care.
Sample Law:	E.g., negligence, product liability, malpractice, recklessness, negligent hiring, negligent supervision, gross negligence, due diligence, shareholders' derivative lawsuit, fiduciary duty of care (and skill), strict liability, international money laundering, securities fraud, unfair trade practices.

Commandment #5: Be Accountable	
Ethics Principle:	When acting on behalf of another in a position of trust and confidence, you have a fiduciary duty to account. Be sure to keep accurate records of all transactions pertaining to money and property entrusted to you. Upon reasonable request, provide a complete and detailed accounting of how the money and property was used, along with receipts and other necessary evidence. Whatever accounting method chosen, it must provide an *accurate and honest picture of the current financial health* of the organization, entity, etc. Do not use accounting tricks or gimmicks to intentionally deceive others. All expenses paid must be reasonable and necessary. Never commingle money and property of others with your own money and property. All money and property received while representing another, including gifts, profits from breaching a fiduciary duty, or illegal bribes and kickbacks, belong to the person you are representing. Being accountable also means providing competent oversight.
Sample Law:	E.g., fiduciary duty to account, securities fraud, fiduciary duty disclose, "aiding and abetting" fraud, fraud and deceit, breach of contract, False Claims Act, money laundering, accounting fraud, Freedom of Information Act, Sarbanes-Oxley Act of 2002, conspiracy.

Commandment #6: Observe Private Property Rights	
Ethics Principle:	Title to cars, mortgages, bank accounts, patents, and other types of private property must be reliably and accurately documented, protected, and enforced. Records of real estate sales must be transparent, reliable, accurate, publicly available, and provide a clear and reliable chain of title that can be insured against defects by a reputable title company (e.g., recording all sales transactions in the county records where the land is located). In case of real estate default, all required steps of the foreclosure processes and procedures that prove chain of title must be followed. A government "taking" of private property should be limited to "public uses" that are clearly governmental, not simply a belief (without proof) that it might result in higher revenue for the government, or more jobs. There must be reasonable, common-sense, and cost-effective laws to prevent environmental pollution, monitor hazardous waste, and protect wildlife.
Sample Law:	E.g., eminent domain, real property law, bailment, conversion, trespass, nuisance, Clean Air Act, Clean Water Act, Endangered Species Act, Resource Conservation and Recovery Act, patents, trade secrets, copyright, trademarks, Lanham Act, Federal Trademark Dilution Act, Digital Millennium Copyright Act, Economic Espionage Act of 1996, civil fraud, criminal fraud, mail fraud, trafficking in counterfeit goods, trademark and trade dress infringement, dilution, unfair competition and deceptive trade practices, copyright and patent infringement, conspiracy, aiding and abetting, false statements to the federal government, mail fraud, wire fraud, and obstruction of justice.

Commandment #7: Respect People	
Ethics Principle:	A worker's right to form a union to bargain with employers over their wages and working conditions, when applicable, must be respected. Hire, promote, pay, and reward the best-qualified person for the job using *objective, job-related criteria*. Do not allow intimidating, offensive, or hostile words or behavior to demean, humiliate, or intimidate others, or bullying words or behavior to deliberately sabotage another's performance. Do not retaliate against those who bring bona fide claims of inappropriate behavior to the attention of the proper authorities. Provide a safe working environment that includes physical safety as well as protection from serious health hazards. Treat employees fairly with respect to pay, working conditions, and benefits.
Sample Law:	E.g., Civil Rights Act of 1964, Civil Rights Act of 1991, the Age Discrimination in Employment Act of 1967, the Americans with Disabilities Act of 1990, the Fair Labor Standards Act of 1938, the Family and Medical Leave Act of 1993, the Occupational Safety and Health Act of 1970, the Rehabilitation Act of 1973, Worker Adjustment and Retraining Notification Act (W.A.R.N.), Genetic Information Nondiscrimination Act of 2008, criminal harassment, civil rights violations resulting in bodily harm, negligent hiring.

Commandment #8: Keep Promises	
Ethics Principle:	A contract is a legally binding promise a court will enforce. For breach of contract, the non-breaching party is entitled to the benefit of the bargain. The technical requirements for a contract include an *offer* with definite terms that has been communicated and *accepted.* The *mutual promises* must be backed by *consideration* (e.g., agreeing to do something you already do not have a legal obligation to do, or refraining from doing something you have a legal right to do). Parties to the contract must be of *legal age* and the contract must be for a *lawful purpose.* It is a civil wrong (tort) to interfere with another's contract. Contracts can only be undone, and the parties restored to their original positions as though there was no contract, in certain specific circumstances such as *fraud, mistake, duress,* or *undue influence* (as defined under American law). Even if there is no legally binding contract, you may be liable for out-of-pocket expenses of another who reasonably relied on your promise to his or her detriment (*promissory estoppel*), or where one party confers a benefit on another party, which the other party knowingly accepts and retains, under circumstances that would be *unjust enrichment.*
Sample Law:	E.g., judge-made American common law contract law (derived from British common law contract law), Uniform Commercial Code, tortious interference with a contract, promissory estoppel, unjust enrichment, fraud, undue influence, mistake, duress.

Commandment #9: Be a *REAL* Leader	
Ethics Principle:	*REAL* leaders do *not* have *Animal Farm ethics*. *REAL* leaders *set the example* by following the *10 Commandments of Trust.* They *take care of the troops first*, remembering that military officers don't eat until after their troops are fed first, and don't sleep until after they have taken care of the sleeping arrangements for their troops first.
Sample Law:	E.g., civil lawsuits, criminal trials, regulatory actions, Congressional hearings, compensatory and punitive damages, equitable remedies such as restitution to disgorge improper payments, negative publicity that damages reputation, termination or resignation, clawback provisions.

Commandment #10: Enforce Commandments 1–9	
Ethics Principle:	Because of our constitutional free speech and free press protections, it is much easier for scandals to be revealed in the United States than in other countries. Whistleblowers are not only encouraged, they are often extremely well rewarded. Under *ethics-based* American Rule of Law, there are many creative, flexible, innovative, and "deadly" (painful) ways to enforce ethics standards in our self-organizing civic institutions and voluntary associations. Unethical conduct may be hazardous to your wealth and can land you in jail.
Sample Law:	E.g., whistleblower lawsuits, civil and criminal trials, punitive damages, clawback provisions, Racketeering Influenced and Corrupt Organizations Act, environmental laws, employment laws, insider trading, antitrust, obstruction of justice, lying to a federal official, breach of fiduciary duties, real property laws, intellectual property laws, the Economic Espionage Act of 1996, Foreign Corrupt Practices Act, criminal restitution, accounting fraud, bribes and kickbacks, negligence, recklessness, union law, employment law, contract law, promissory estoppel, unjust enrichment.

Appendix B

10 Commandments of Trust
"Go Global"

10 Commandments of Trust "Go Global"

The following chart gives you a snapshot picture of instances of the *10 Commandments of Trust* popping up in other countries:

Individual or Organization and Country	Commandment of Trust	Settlements, Verdicts, Fines, Penalties, Scandals, etc.
Former CEO *Deutsche Bank AG* GERMANY	**TRUTH** (fraud)	$456,000 settlement[1]
Toronto Attorney CANADA	**FAIR** (insider trading)	Prison term: 3 years, 3 months[2]
Former President of TAIWAN	**LOYALTY** (bribery)	Prison term: 17 years, 6 months[3]
Seven Former Employees *Union Carbide India Ltd.* INDIA	**CARE** (fatal gas leak)	Prison term: maximum of 2 years[4]
Former CEO *Livedoor Holdings Co.* JAPAN	**ACCOUNT** (accounting fraud)	Prison term: 2 years, 6 months[5]
Chevron Corp, Transocean BRAZIL	**PROPERTY** (environmental damage)	Lawsuit asking for $10.6 billion in damages[6]
Cotswold Geotechnical BRITAIN	**PEOPLE** (safety and health violations)	Approx. $604,339 fine[7] (£385,000)
Swissport Singapore SINGAPORE	**PROMISES** (breach of contract)	$4.7 million judgment[8]
Former President of FRANCE	**LEADERSHIP** (corruption)	Prison term: 2-year suspended sentence[9]
Microsoft, Inc. EUROPEAN COMMISSION	**ENFORCEMENT** (antitrust)	$600 million fine[10]

Appendix C

10 Commandments of Trust in China

10 Commandments of Trust in China

The following chart gives you a snapshot picture of instances of the *10 Commandments of Trust* popping up in China:

Individual or Organization	Commandment of Trust	Settlements, Verdicts, Fines, Penalties, Scandals, etc.
Alibaba Group, China's leading e-commerce platform	**TRUTH** (fraud)	CEO and CFO resigned, 100 sales representatives fired, $1.7 million paid out so far to 2,249 buyers[1]
National People's Congress	**FAIR** (anti-trust)	Adopted the Anti-Monopoly Law of the People's Republic of China, effective Aug. 1, 2008[2]
Former Branch Manager, Bank of China	**LOYALTY** (bribery)	13 years in prison for accepting bribes[3]
Chinese Government	**CARE** (sale of tainted food, drugs, and agricultural products)	774 people arrested over a two-month period as part of a nationwide crackdown[4]
Chairman of the Board, Zhengzhou Baiwen Co. Ltd.	**ACCOUNT** (accounting fraud)	Indicted, facing possible prison sentence[5]
National People's Congress	**PROPERTY** (private property rights)	Amended the 1982 Chinese Constitution to protect private property for the first time since the 1949 Communist revolution[6]
National People's Congress	**PEOPLE** (unfair treatment of workers)	New Labor Contract Law effective Jan. 1, 2008, passed to curb abusive employment practices[7]
National People's Congress	**PROMISES** (contract law)	People's Republic of China Contract Law, effective May 13, 2009[8]
Former Chairwoman, Sanlu Group	**LEADERSHIP** (producing and selling adulterated or substandard milk)	Life in prison[9]
Former Head, State Food and Drug Administration	**ENFORCEMENT** (bribes, unsafe products)	Executed[10]

Chapter Endnotes

Endnotes

Chapter 1: *The Secret Power of Trust*

[1] For a discussion of self-organization in biological systems, *see generally*, Scott Camazine, et al., *Self-Organization in Biological Systems* (Princeton: Princeton University Press, 2001); for a discussion of ants, *see generally,* Deborah M. Gordon, *Ants at Work: How an Insect Society Is Organized* (New York: W.W. Norton & Co., 1999); John H. Sudd, *An Introduction to the Behavior of Ants* (London: Edward Arnold Publishers Ltd., 1967); William Morton Wheeler, *Ants: Their Structure, Development and Behavior* (New York: Columbia University Press, 1910)

[2] News Release, *Collective Intelligence: Ants and Brain's Neurons*, Stanford News Service (Online), Nov. 15, 1993

[3] L. Thomas, *The Lives of a Cell* (New York: Bantam Books, 1974), 12

[4] *See, e.g.*, Mico Tatalovic, *Simple Rules Smooth Traffic on Ant Highways*, Cosmos (Online), Aug. 14, 2008

[5] *History of the Monarchy, Kings and Queens of England, the Anglo-Saxon Kings, Anglo-Saxons, Overview*, The Official Website of the British Monarchy (Online), (last visited Dec. 14, 2014)

[6] A. Groner, *The American Heritage History of American Business & Industry*, (New York: American Heritage Publishing, Co., Inc., 1972), 263

[7] Paul Johnson, *A History of the American People* (New York: HarperCollins Publishers, Inc., 1997)

[8] Thomas A. Stewart, *Whom Can You Trust? It's Not So Easy to Tell*, Fortune, June 12, 2000, 332

[9] Sherman Stafford, *Are You as Good as the Best in the World?*, Fortune, Dec. 13, 1993, 95

[10] *Ibid.*; Keith H. Hammonds, *The New Face of Global Competition*, Fast Company (Online), Jan. 2003; Pete Engardio, *A New World Economy*, Bloomberg Businessweek (Online), Aug. 21, 2005

[11] Joann Muller, *GM Hasn't Been This Popular Since the 1950s*, Forbes (Online), Nov. 17, 2010

[12] Christopher Jensen and Hiroko Tabuchi, *Toyota to Recall 6.4 Million Vehicles*, N.Y. Times (Online), Apr. 9, 2014

[13] Bill Vlasic, *With Sonic, GM Stands Automaking on Its Head,* N.Y. Times (Online), July 12, 2011

[14] Henry Foy and Anurag Kotoky, *Insight: Deadly India Car Factory Rio Sounds Alarm Bells for Industry,* Reuters (Online), Aug. 5, 2012

[15] Emmanuel V. Pitsilis, et al., *Checking China's Vital Signs,* The McKinsey Quarterly (Online), Dec. 2004; reprinted in Forbes (Online), Nov. 4, 2004

[16] Kris Maher, *Next on the Outsourcing List*, Wall St. Journal, Mar. 23, 2004, B1; Stephanie Armour and Michelle Kessler, *USA's New Money-Saving Export: White Collar Jobs*, USA Today, Aug. 5, 2003, 1B

[17] *Ibid.*; Pete Engardio, *A New World Economy: The Balance of Power Will Shift to the East as China and India Evolve*, Businessweek, Aug. 22-29, 2005, 54

[18] Don Lee, *Worries Grow as Health Jobs Go Offshore*, L.A. Times, Jul. 25, 2012, A1

[19] Don Lee, *Research Follows Factories to China*, L.A. Times, Jan. 14, 2007, C1

[20] *Reverse Outsourcing: Indian IT Firms Moving Jobs Back to the US as Outsourcing Comes Full Circle,* FaaDooEngineers.com (Online), May 27, 2011

[21] Schumpeter, *The Trouble with Outsourcing*, The Economist (Online), Jul. 30, 2011

[22] Nin-Hai Tseng, *Made (Again) in the USA*, Fortune (Online), Jun. 29, 2011

[23]Joshua Cooper Ramo, *Globalism Goes Backward*, Fortune, Dec. 3, 2012, 135

[24] Niall Ferguson, *Sinking Globalization*, Foreign Affairs, Mar./Apr. 2005, 64

[25] Lane Jennings, *The Coming of a Molecular Economy*, The Futurist, Jan.–Feb. 2004, 55

[26] David Stipp, *Biotech's Billion Dollar Breakthrough*, Fortune, May 26, 2003, 96–101; *Jobs of the Future*, Newsweek, Apr. 30, 2001, 54–56; Gautam Naik, *Study in Chicken Shows a Method to Regrow Limbs*, Wall St. Journal, Nov. 18, 2006, A5

[27] Glenn McDonald, *Let's Get Small*, Business 2.0, Feb. 1999, 91

[28] Stephen Baker and Adam Aston, *The Business of Nanotech,* Bloomberg Businessweek, Feb. 14, 2005, 64–71

[29] Mike Treder, *Molecular Nanotech: Benefits and Risks*, The Futurist, Jan.–Feb. 2004, 42

[30] *Ibid.; Is That Really Just a Fly?*, Daily Mail U.K. (Online), Jun. 19, 2012

[31] Jennifer Couzin, *Gene Machines*, Industry Standard, Jun. 18, 2001, 38

[32] *A Nano Nail in Silicon's Coffin?,* Bloomberg Businessweek, May 12, 2003 10; Jason Palmer, *Carbon Nanotubes Fit by the Thousands Onto a Chip*, BBC (U.K, Online), Oct. 29, 2012

[33] Don Clark, *IBM, Cray Win Pentagon Funds to Develop Next Supercomputer*s, Wall St. Journal, Nov. 22, 2006, B2

[34] Robert Guy Matthews, *Steel's Latest Hot Spot: The U.S.*, Wall St. Journal, Aug. 14, 2007, 10

[35] John Ferguson and John P.V. Dacre Balsdon, ed, *Marcus Tullius Cicero*, Britannica Academic Edition (Online)

[36] *See, e.g., How Ants Find Food*, Mute (Online), (last visited Dec. 14, 2014)

[37] Thomas, *Lives of a Cell*, *supra* note 3, at 13; *Ants! Nature's Secret Power*, Channel 216 ANIPW, Nov. 17, 2007

Chapter 2: *Through a Different Lens*

[1] Peter Drucker and Brent Schlender, *Peter Drucker Sets Us Straight. The 94-Year-Old Guru Says That Most People Are Thinking All Wrong About Jobs, Debt, Globalization, and Recession*, Fortune, Jan. 12, 2004, 115

[2] Peter Drucker, *Adventures of a Bystander* (New York: Harper & Row, 1978), 1

[3] *Ibid.*

[4] *Ibid.* at 6

[5] *Ibid.*

[6] After the fall of the Shah in Iran, the succeeding Islamic theocracy also has a very active secret police (with a new name). *Iran's Secret Police Raids Homes of Striking Bus Drivers,* Iran Focus News & Analysis (Online), Feb. 2, 2006

[7] Islamic fundamentalists, who overthrew the Shah of Iran, immediately executed 5,000 political prisoners; Reuters, *UN Experts Decry Iran Executions of Arab Minority*, Thomson Reuters Foundation (Online), Jun. 28, 2012

[8] *UK Author to be Jailed in Singapore after Losing Appeal*, Reuters (Online), May 27, 2011

[9] *Newton's Law of Gravitation,* The Free Dictionary by Farlex (Online)

[10] *What is a Black Hole?* NASA (Online), Sept. 30, 2008, (last visited Dec. 14, 2014)

[11] *See,* Appendices A, B & C

[12] *See,* Drucker, *supra* notes 3 and 4

Chapter 3: *Freedom at Risk*

1 Stephanie Banchero, *Students Stumble Again on the Basics of History*, Wall St. Journal (Online), Jun. 15, 2001; George Nethercutt, *Back to School, Back to U.S. History Basics (Education Special Report)*, Real Clear Politics (Online), Sept. 20, 2011

2 Dennis Cauchon, *Government's Mountain of Debt*, USA Today (Online), Jun. 7, 2011

3 Eric Scjeiner, *Conyers: Obamacare is a "Very Small and Modest Bill"*, CNS News (Online), Oct. 21, 2013

4 For a further discussion of law on steroids, *see*, Chapter 11

5 Associated Press, *Former Enron Exec Speaks to College Students on Ethics*, L.A. Times, Mar. 21, 2012, B3

6 Michael C. Dorf, *Can the Legal Profession Improve Its Image?* Find Law (Online), Apr. 17, 2002

7 For further discussion, *see*, Chapter 8

8 *Ibid.*

9 *Ibid.*

10 For further discussion, *see*, Chapter 20

11 William Strauss and Neil Howe, *The Fourth Turning: What the Cycles of History Tell Us About America's Next Rendezvous with Destiny* (New York: Broadway Books, 1997)

12 *Ibid.* at 330

13 Laura Standers, *People Say They Won't Shock Others for Cash, But Do*, Science News, Wired Magazine (Online), Apr. 7, 2011

14 *See*, Appendices B & C

15 For further discussion, *see*, Chapter 6

16 *See*, Appendix C

17 For further discussion, *see*, Chapter 6 and Appendices A, B & C; *see also*, Daron Acemoglu and James A. Robinson, *10 Reasons Countries Fall Apart*, *Failed States 2012 Edition*, Foreign Policy (Online)

18 *Confidence in Institutions*, Gallup (Online), Jun 13, 2013

19 *Ibid.*

20 *Key Data Points, Trust in Government*, Pew Research Center (Online), Mar. 9, 2013

21 *Ibid.*

22 Charles Murray, *Why Capitalism Has an Image Problem*, Wall St. Journal, Jul. 28-29, 2012, C1

23 *See generally*, Gideon Rachman, *Europe and the U.S. are Sinking Together*, Financial Times (U.K., Online), Jul. 4, 2011; *Moody's Warns China Over Bad Debt*, BBC (U.K., Online), Jul 5. 2011; Minxin Pei, *China's Ticking Debt Bomb*, The Diplomat (Online), Jul. 5, 2011; Banyan Asia, *The Trouble With Democracy—and Dictatorship*, The Economist (Online), Aug. 1, 2011

24 Jeff Cox, *US Finances Rank Near Worst in the World: Study*, CNBC (Online), Mar. 24, 2011

25 Jon Rosen, *Review: 'Reckoning' is Chilling Glimpse of a U.S. in Decline*, USA Today (Online), May 21, 2012

26 Andrew Osborn, *As If Things Weren't Bad Enough, Russian Professor Predicts End of U.S.*, Wall St. Journal (Online), Dec. 29, 2008

27 Tony Karon, *Why China Does Capitalism Better than the U.S.*, Time (Online), Jan. 20, 2011

28 *China 'To Overtake US and Dominate Trade by 2030'*, BBC (U.K., Online), Mar. 24, 2011

29 Brett Arends, *IMF Bombshell: Age of America Nears End: China's Economy Will Surpass the U.S. in 2016*, Marketwatch (Online), Apr. 25, 2011

30 *See, e.g.*, Robert Samuelson, *Unhappy Birthday*, Newsweek (Online), Jul. 4, 2011; Toby Harnden, *Down on the 4th of July: The United States of Doom*, The Telegraph (U.K., Online), Jul 3, 2011; Joe Wiesenthal, *A Huge Number Of Americans Believe The Economy Has Now*

Entered "Permanent Decline", Business Insider (Online), Jun. 29, 2011; Shai Ahmed, *U.S. Default Inevitable: Fund Manager*, CNBC (Online), Jul. 13, 2011

[31] Walter Brandimart and Daniel Bases, *United States Loses Prized AAA Credit Rating from S & P*, Reuters (Online), Aug. 6, 2011

[32] For a more detailed discussion, *see, Data, Information, Knowledge, and Wisdom*, The Personality Café (Online), Sept. 24, 2009

Chapter 4: *It's All about Trust*

[1] Mark Pittman and Bob Ivry, *Financial Rescue Nears GDP as Pledges Top $12.8 Trillion (Update 1)*, Bloomberg (Online), Mar. 31, 2009

[2] David Barboza, *China Unveils $586 Billion Stimulus Plan*, N.Y. Times (Online), Nov. 10, 2008

[3] Mark Landler, *World Bank Expects Pain Worldwide*, N.Y. Times, Dec. 10, 2008, B1

[4] Barbara Kiviat, *How to Understand a Trillion-Dollar Deficit*, Time, Jan. 11, 2009

[5] For further discussion, *see*, T.S. Weidler, *Just How Much is 16 Trillion?*, American Thinker (Online), Oct. 17, 2012

[6] *See generally, Fannie Mae and Freddie Mac—End of Illusions*, The Economist (U.K., Online), Jul. 17, 2008

[7] Matthew Karnitschnig, et al., *U.S. to Take Over AIG in $85 Billion Bailout; Central Banks Inject Cash as Credit Dries Up*, Wall St. Journal (Online), Sept. 16, 2008; *see also*, William Greider, *The AIG Bailout Scandal*, The Nation (Online), Aug. 6, 2010

[8] *Buffett Warns on Investment 'Time Bomb'*, BBC News (U.K., Online), Mar. 4, 2003

[9] *Warren Buffet on Derivatives: Edited Excerpts from the Berkshire Hathaway Annual Report for 2002*, Financial Tools (Online), (last visited Dec. 14, 2014)

[10] Michael Sivy, *Why Derivatives May Be the Biggest Risk for the Global Economy*, Time (Online), Mar. 27, 2013

[11] Peter Cohan, *Big Risk: $1.2 Quadrillion Derivatives Market Dwarfs World GDP*, Business Insider (Online), Jun. 9, 2010

[12] Ben Protess, *4 Wall Street Banks Still Dominate Derivatives Trade*, N.Y. Times (Online), Mar. 22, 2011

[13] *See., e.g., Europe After World War II (Mr. Burns' U.S. History Class)* Fast Track Teaching Materials (Online), (last visited Dec. 14, 2014)

[14] Alexander Neubacher and Michael Sauga, *How the East Was Lost: Germany's Disappointing Reunification*, Spiegel International (Online), Jul. 1, 2010

[15] *See, generally*, Theodore Roszak, *The Making of a Counter Culture* (New York: Doubleday & Company, 1968)

[16] For a good description of situation ethics, *see, About Situation Ethics*, BBC Ethics Guide, BBC (U.K., Online), (last visited Dec. 14, 2014)

[17] *See., e.g.*, Manuel Velasquez, et al., *Ethical Relativism*, Markkula Center for Applied Ethics, Santa Clara University (Online), (last visited Dec. 14, 2014)

[18] *See, e.g.*, Dinesh, D'Souza, *Illiberal Education: The Politics of Race and Sex on Campus*, (New York: Random House, Inc., 1992)

[19] *"Barbarians" Revisited*, BloombergBusinessweek (Online), Apr. 2, 1995

[20] Experts differ on how much money was lost; *see, e.g.*, Bert Ely, *Savings and Loan Crisis*, Library of Economics and Liberty (Online), (last visited Dec. 14, 2014); K. Calavita, et al., *The Savings and Loan Debacle, Financial Crime and the State*, Annual Review of Sociology (Online), Aug. 1997, 23:19-38, (last visited Dec. 14, 2014)

[21] Kurt Eichenwald, *Milken Set to Pay a $600 Million Fine in Wall St. Fraud*, N.Y. Times (Online), Apr. 21, 1980

[22] *See,* Commandment of Trust #9 in Chapter 20

[23] *Free Speech Codes on Campus: Political Correctness Run Amok?* Fox News (Online), Jul. 21, 2012

[24] *Abraham Lincoln Quotes,* BrainyQuote (Online)

[25] Steven A. Sass, *Getting Down to Business: The Development of the Commercial Curriculum at the Wharton School in 1910,* The Business History Conference Publications (Online), thebhc.org, (last visited Dec. 14, 2014)

[26] *John Adams Quotes,* John Adams Historical Society (Online)

[27] *Brandeis and the History of Transparency,* Sunlight Foundation (Online), May 26, 2009

[28] *The Indictment of Michael Milken: The Racketeering Charges,* L.A. Times (Online), Mar. 30, 1989; *The Collapse of Drexel Burnham Lambert; Key Events for Drexel Burnham Lambert,* N.Y. Times (Online), Feb. 14, 1990

[29] Bill Mears, *High Court Allows Siegelman, Scrushy Corruption Convictions to Stand,* CNN (Online), Jun. 4, 2012

[30] Carol J. Loomis, *Walter Forbes Goes Down,* CNN Money (Online), Nov. 22, 2006

[31] *See., e.g., Attorney General's Tobacco Enforcement Unit: The Tobacco Master Settlement Agreement (MSA), Model Escrow Statute, and the Nevada Tobacco Directory,* Nevada Attorney General (Online), (last visited Dec. 14, 2014)

[32] Press Release, *Scientists Use MRI to Catch Test Subjects in the Act of Trusting One Another,* California Institute of Technology (Caltech) (Online), Mar. 31, 2005

Chapter 5: *Complacency about Trust Is Dangerous*

[1] Geoff Tibballs, *The Titanic: The Extraordinary Story of the "Unsinkable" Ship* (New York: The Reader's Digest Association, Inc., 1997), 7

[2] *See generally,* Webb Garrison, *A Treasury of Titanic Tales* (Nashville: Rutledge Hill Press, 1998); Lawrence Beesley, et al., with Jack Winocour, ed., *The Story of the Titanic as Told by Its Survivors* (New York: Dover Publications, Inc., 1960); Daniel Allen Butler, *Unsinkable: The Full Story of the RMS Titanic* (Mechanicsburg: Stackpole Books, 1998)

[3] *Disaster At Last Befalls Capt. Smith,* N.Y. Times, Apr. 16, 1912, Encyclopedia Titanica (Online), (last visited Dec. 14, 2014)

[4] Nick Collins, *Titanic Disaster Blamed on Moon,* Telegraph (U.K. Online), Mar. 6, 2012

[5] William J. Broad, *Faulty Rivets Emerge as Clues to Titanic Disaster,* N.Y. Times (Online), Jan. 27, 1998

[6] *Seconds from Disaster: Titanic* (2006), National Geographic Channel (Online), Jan. 17, 2007; News Release, *Metal Detectives: New Book Details Titanic Investigation,* National Institute of Standards and Technology (NIST) (Online), Apr. 15, 2008

[7] William Straus and Neil Howe, *The Fourth Turning: An American Prophecy, What the Cycles of History Tell Us About America's Next Rendezvous with Destiny* (New York: Broadway Books, 1997), 3

[8] *Ibid.* at 6

[9] *Ibid.* at 256

[10] *Ibid.* at 282

[11] Nathan Miller, *New World Coming: The 1920s and the Making of Modern America* (New York: Scribner, 2003), 373

[12] *See, e.g., Stock Market Optimists Need to Read a History of the Great Depression,* The Telegraph (U.K., Online), May 12, 2009

[13] For a full discussion of the 1920s and the Great Depression, *see,* H. Paul Jeffers, *The Complete Idiot's Guide to The Great Depression* (Indianapolis: Alpha, a Pearson Education Company, 2002); John Kenneth Galbraith, *The Great Crash 1929* (Boston: Houghton

Mifflin Company, 1954, 1988); Scott Ingram, *The Stock Market Crash of 1929* (Milwaukee: World Almanac Library, 2005); Robert S. McElvaine, *The Great Depression: America, 1929–41* (New York: New York Times Books, 1984); Robert S. McElvaine, *The Depression and New Deal* (New York: Oxford University Press, 2000); David E. Kyvig, *Daily Life in the United States, 1920-1940* (Chicago: Ivan R. Dee, 2002); Frederick Lewis Allen, *Only Yesterday: An Informal History of the 1920s* (New York: Harper & Row, 1931); Nathan Miller, *New World Coming, supra* note 11; Garet Garrett, *A Bubble That Broke the World* (Boston: Little Brown & Co., 1932)

[14] Tom Brokaw, *The Greatest Generation* (New York: Random House, 1998)

[15] *Ibid.* at xx

[16] *Famous Last Words*, Massachusetts Institute of Technology (Online), http://web.mit.edu/randy/www/words.html, (last visited Dec. 14, 2014)

[17] *Modern History Sourcebook: Neville Chamberlain: "Peace in Our Time,"* 1938, Fordham University (Online), (last visited Dec. 14, 2014)

[18] *See, e.g.,* Edward Chancellor, *Devil Take the Hindmost: A History of Financial Speculation* (New York: Farrar, Straus, Giroux, 1999); Carmen M. Reinhart and Kenneth Rogoff, *This Time is Different: Eight Centuries of Financial Folly* (Princeton, New Jersey: Princeton University Press, 2009); Charles Mackay, *Memoirs of Extraordinary Popular Delusions* (London: Richard Bentley, New Burlington Street, 1932, 1956); Richard Dale, *The First Crash: Lessons from the South Sea Bubble* (Princeton, New Jersey: Princeton University Press, 2004)

[19] Harry S. Dent, Jr., *The Roaring 2000s* (New York: Simon & Schuster, 1998)

[20] Nathan Miller, *New World Coming, supra* note 11 at 152

[21] Joe Richter, *U.S. Consumer Credit Rose Most in 10 Months in April (Update 3),* Bloomberg (Online), Jun. 7, 2006

[22] Dean Baker, *The Economy*, Harper's Magazine (Online), June, 2007

[23] Laurie Cohen, *Citigroup Feels Heat to Modify Mortgages: Nonprofit Groups Press for Subprime Relief; Deciding Who Gets Help*, Wall St. Journal (Online), Nov. 26, 2007

[24] John Kenneth Galbraith, *The Great Crash 1929* (Boston: Houghton Mifflin Company, 1954, 1988), 4; Nathan Miller, *New World Coming, supra* note 11 at 285

[25] Barbara Hagenbaugh, *Consumer Debt Loads at Record*, USA Today (Online), Mar. 17, 2004

[26] *Americans See Biggest Home Equity Jump in 60 Years*, North Carolina Association of Realtors (Online), Jun. 15, 2012

[27] Nathan Miller, *New World Coming, supra* note 11 at 366

[28] *Hedge Fund Information for Investors, Federal Bureau of Investigation* (FBI) (Online), (last visited Dec. 14, 2014)

[29] *Hedge Fund Managers Set New Payout Records in 2007,* Reuters (Online), Apr. 16, 2008

[30] Nelson D. Schwartz & Louise Story, *Pay of Hedge Fund Managers Roared Back Last Year,* N.Y. Times (Online), Mar. 31, 2010

[31] Nathan Vardi, *The 40 Highest Earning Hedge Fund Manager*, Forbes (Online), Mar. 1, 2012

[32] *Rich Managers, Poor Clients*, The Economist, Dec. 22, 2012, 14

[33] *Ibid.*

[34] *The Warning*, Frontline, Public Broadcasting Service (PBS) (Online), posted Oct. 20, 2009, (last visited Dec. 14, 2014)

[35] John Kenneth Galbraith, *The 1929 Parallel*, The Atlantic (Online), Jan. 1987; John Kenneth Galbraith, *The Great Crash 1929* (Boston: Houghton Mifflin Co, 1954, 1988), 58–59

[36] Paul Johnson, *Rothbard Revises the History of the Great Depression,* Ludwig von Mises Institute (Online), Oct. 14, 2011

[37] *What's Behind the Buyout Binge*, Bloomberg Businessweek (Online), Dec. 3, 2006

[38] Shanny Basar, *Billionaires from the World of Finance*, Financial News (Online), Mar. 11, 2011

[39] *See., e.g.,* Mike Sunnucks, *Big Executive Pay, Golden Parachutes at Freeport McMoran,* Phoenix Business Journal (Online), Jun. 3, 2012 (The Chairman of the Board and the CEO would potentially make $61 million each if the company is acquired and they are replaced; they are due to receive $38 million each if they are replaced without a merger. *Ibid.*)

[40] Michael J. de la Merced, *An I.P.O. Glut Just Waiting to Happen,* N.Y. Times, Jul. 15, 2007, 6

[41] Nathan Miller, *New World Coming, supra* note 11 at 366

[42] Daniel H Weinberg, *A Brief Look at Postwar U.S. Income Inequality,* Census Bureau (Online), June 1996

[43] *See, e.g.,* David Leonhardt, *Two Candidates, Two Fortunes, Two Distinct Views of Wealth,* N.Y. Times, Dec. 23, 2007, 26

[44] *It Didn't End Well Last Time,* N.Y. Times, April 4, 2007, A18; Greg Ip and John D. McKinnon, *Bush Reorients Rhetoric, Acknowledges Income Gap,* Wall St. Journal, Mar. 26, 2007, A2

[45] Mark Trumbull, *America's Big Wealth Gap, Is it Good, Bad, or Irrelevant,* Christian Science Monitor (Online), Feb. 14, 2012

[46] Thomas F. Cooley, *A Reasoned Approach to Executive Compensation,* Forbes (Online), Apr. 14, 2010

[47] *Ibid.*

[48] *See generally, The Rise of Financial Fraud,* Center for Retirement Research at Boston College (Online), Feb. 2012, Number 12-5; *Securities/Investment Fraud,* National White Collar Crime Center (Online), January 2007

[49] For further discussion, *see,* Commandment #9 in Chapter 20

[50] H. Paul Jeffers, *The Complete Idiot's Guide to the Great Depression* (Indianapolis: Alpha, a Pearson Education Company, 2002), 39–40; Scott Ingram, *The Stock Market Crash of 1929: Landmark Events in American History* (Milwaukee: World Almanac Library, 2005), 22

[51] Colin J. Seymour, *Pompous Prognosticators,* June, 2001, Gold Eagle (Online)

[52] For a full discussion of the 2008 Financial Crisis, *see, Wall Street and the Financial Crisis: Anatomy of a Financial Collapse,* Report from US Senate Permanent Subcommittee on Investigations (Online), Apr. 13, 2011, www.hsgac.senate.gov, (last visited Dec. 14, 2014)

[53] Ben Protess, *Tallying the Costs of Bank of America's Countrywide Nightmare,* N.Y. Times (Online), Oct. 25, 2012 (up from $30 billion the year before); *see, e.g.,* Jean Eaglesham, et al., *Banks Haunted by Houses,* Wall St. Journal, Jun. 30, 2011, C1

[54] Nelson D. Schwartz and Kevin Roose, *Regulators Sue Big Banks Over Mortgages,* N.Y. Times (Online), Sept. 2, 2011

[55] Jessica Silver-Greenberg, *Mortgage Crisis Presents a New Reckoning to Banks,* N.Y. Times (Online), Dec. 9, 2012

[56] Suzanne Kapner, *Banks Looking at $100 Billion Legal Tab,* Wall St. Journal, Mar. 27, 2013, C1

[57] Christina Rexrode and Devlin Barrett, *B of A Sets Record $17 Billion Settlement,* Wall St. Journal, Aug. 21, 2014, A1

[58] Noah Rayman, *Here's How Much Banks Have Paid Out Since the Financial Crisis,* Time (Online), Aug. 21, 2014, (last visited Dec. 14, 2014)

[59] Spencer Jakab, *Boomer Effect: Gloomy Forecasts,* Wall St. Journal, Mar. 28, 2007, B3A

[60] Associated Press, *U.S. Debt: $30,000 Per American,* USA Today (Online), Dec. 4, 2007

[61] Martin Crutsinger, *Savings Lowest Since Depression: Complacency Over Home Prices Cited,* L.A. Daily News, Jan. 31, 2006, Bus-1

[62] Hugh Carnegy, et al., *IMF Chief Warns Over 1930s-Style Threats,* Financial Times (Online), Dec. 15, 2011

[63] Colin Barr, *Lost Decade? We've Already Had One,* Fortune (Online), April 20, 2011

[64] *The 11 Largest Bankruptcies in American History,* Business Insider (Online), Nov. 29, 2011

Chapter 6: *Why Trust Matters*

[1] *Americans' Trust in Banks Hit Record Low as Financial Scandals Continue*, Public Radio International (Online), Jul. 14, 2012

[2] *See e.g.,* Nien Cheng, *Life and Death in Shanghai* (New York: Penguin Books USA, Inc., 1988); Victor Kravchenko, *I Chose Freedom,* (Piscataway, New Jersey: Transaction Publishers, 1988); *see also, The Great [Russian] Famine,* The American Experience, Public Broadcasting Service (PBS) (Online); Beth Duff-Brown, Associated Press, *Scholars Continue to Reveal Mao's Monstrosities*, L.A. Times (Online), Nov. 20, 1994; *China: Millennial Madness, A Shocking Chinese Account of Chairman Mao's Great Famine*, The Economist (Online), Oct 27, 2012

[3] Sam Staley, *The Rise and Fall of Indian Socialism*, Reason (Online), June 2006

[4] Steve Gutterman and Thomas Grove, *Russian Mass Protests Over Alleged Election Fraud*, The Independent (U.K., Online), Dec. 10, 2011

[5] *See, e.g., Brave New World: A Chronology of China's Ongoing Effort to Transform Itself From a Communist Society to a Global Market Economy*, Frontline (PBS) (Online), (last visited Dec. 14, 2014)

[6] Carl Minzner, *Rule of Law in China: Past, Present, and Future*, The Diplomat (Online), Sept. 7, 2012

[7] *Freedom in the World 2008: Global Freedom in Retreat*, Freedom House (Online), Jan. 16, 2008

[8] Arch Puddington, *2008: Freedom in Retreat: Is the Tide Turning? (Freedom in the World 2008, Essay)*, Freedom House (Online), 2008 edition, Jan. 16, 2008

[9] Jason Groves, *Nightmare Vision for Europe and EU Chief Warns 'Democracy Could Disappear ' in Greece, Spain and Portugal*, Daily Mail (U.K., Online), Jun. 15, 2010

[10] Andrew Cawthorne and Eyanir Chinea, *Chavez's Decree Move Enrages Venezuela Opposition*, Reuters (Online), Dec. 14, 2010

[11] Phyllis Tickle, *Greed: The Mother of All Sins*, Beliefnet (Online), 2002

[12] Mark Frank, *Cuba Announces Mass Layoffs in Bid to Spur the Private Sector*, Reuters (Online), Sept. 10, 2010

[13] Michael Novak, *Business as a Calling* (New York: Simon & Shuster, 1996), 143

[14] *Mission Statement*, Rockefeller Foundation (Online), (last visited Dec. 14, 2014)

[15] *Goals,* Ford Foundation (Online), (last visited Dec. 14, 2014)

[16] *Andrew Carnegie Quotes*, Brainy Quotes (Online), (last visited Dec. 14, 2014)

[17] *Warren Buffett, Bill Gates Giving Pledge Gets 12 More Billionaires to Commit Over Half of Their Fortunes*, Huffington Post (Online), Apr. 21, 2012

[18] *Oprah Winfrey Tops List of Most Generous Stars*, Reuters (Online), Sept. 12, 2008

[19] *Top Funders: 50 Largest Corporation Foundations by Total Giving*, Foundation Center (Online), May 4, 2103

[20] Rich Karlgaard, *Digital Rules: Wonderful Wealth*, Forbes, Oct. 10, 2005, 43

[21] Helen O'Neill, *Hurricane Sandy "Miracle" for Long Island Family Who Lost Home Brings Holiday Smiles*, Huffington Post (Online), Dec. 24, 2012

[22] Jim Puzzanghera, *85 Richest People Own As Much As Bottom Half of Population, Report Says*, L.A. Times (Online), January 20, 2014

[23] E. Scott Reckard, *Judge Approves Deal with WaMu Creditors*, L. A. Times, Feb. 18, 2012, B3

[24] Allison Klein, et al., *Shooting at Pentagon Entrance Leaves 2 Police Officers Hurt, Lone Gunman Dead*, Washington Post (Online), March 5, 2010

[25] Michael Brick, *Man Crashes Plane into Texas I.R.S. Office*, N.Y. Times (Online), Feb. 18, 2012

[26] David Zucchino, *Professor Gets Life in Prison for Killing 3*, L. A. Times, Sept. 25, 2012, A8

[27] Darlena Taylor-Bonds, *Murder-Suicide on the Rise Nationwide*, Examiner (Online), Jul. 19, 2010

[28] Ryan Jaslow, *Suicide Rates Increase Dramatically Among Middle-Aged Americans*, CBS News (Online), May 2, 2013

[29] *See, e.g., Hemet: 37-Year-Old Man Busted for Stealing Copper Wire From Street Lights*, Southwest Riverside News Network (Online), Apr. 2, 2013

[30] *See, e.g.,* Melissa Santos, *Bill Would Penalize Shoplifter "Flash Robs"*, The News Tribune (Online), Feb. 2, 2013

[31] *See, e.g.,* David Stern, *Economic Woes in Latvia Fuel Public's Anger at Government*, N.Y. Times, Mar. 4, 2009, A6

[32] Heather Timmons, *Protesters Sweep India in a Season of Unrest*, N.Y. Times, June 29, 2008, 9

[33] *China "Faces Massive Social Unrest,"* BBC News (U.K., Online), Dec. 5, 2008

[34] *Kenyan MPs Vote to Join World's Best Paid Lawmakers*, BBC News (U.K., Online), Jul. 1, 2010

[35] Jeffrey Gettleman, *Mob Sets Kenya Church on Fire, Killing Dozens*, N.Y. Times (Online), Jan. 2, 2008

[36] Patrick Barta and Wilawan Watcharasakwet, *Thailand Declares State of Emergency*, Wall St. Journal, Apr. 8, 2010, A11

[37] Pracha Hariraksapitak, *Thai Government Declares State of Emergency As Protests Drag On*, Reuters (Online), Jan 21, 2014

[38] Keith Johnson, *Who's a Pirate? U.S. Court Sees Duel over Definition*, Wall St. Journal, Aug. 14-15, 2010, A1

[39] Tracy Wilkinson, *Cartels Push Drug Violence to New Depths*, L.A. Times, May 28, 2012, A1

[40] David Luhnow, *To Root Out Dirty Police, Mexico Sends in a General*, Wall St. Journal, Dec. 23, 2010, A1

[41] *Expert Says Beheadings in U.S. Look Like Work of Cartels*, Channel 5 News KRGV (Online), Jan. 10, 2012

[42] Terry Miller and Kim R. Holmes, *Highlights of the 2011 Index of Economic Freedom*, Heritage Foundation (Online), (last visited Dec. 14, 2014)

[43] Simon Romero, *Blackouts Plague Energy-Rich Venezuela*, N.Y. Times (Online), Nov. 10, 2009

[44] *Hyperinflation in Zimbabwe*, Globalization and Monetary Policy Institute 2011 Annual Report, Federal Reserve Bank of Dallas (Online), (last visited Dec. 14, 2014)

[45] Jerome A. Cohen, *Struggling for Justice: China's Courts and the Challenge of Reform*, World Politics Review (Online), Jan. 14, 2014

[46] John Bussey, *Inside China, Getting Rich Isn't Always So Glorious*, Wall St. Journal, Aug. 17, 2012, B1

Chapter 7: *Trust Is Fragile*

[1] Pascal Fletcher, *Corruption Threatens "Soul and Fabric" of U.S.: FBI*, Reuters (Online), Dec. 8, 2009

[2] Alexis de Tocqueville, *Quotes,* Good Reads (Online)

[3] *See, e.g.,* Josh Friedman, *Bank Settles Enron Lawsuit*, L.A. Times, Jun. 11, 2005, A1; *J.P. Morgan Settles Enron Lawsuit*, Wall St. Journal, Jun. 15, 2005, A3; *Newby v. Enron et al.*, Corporate Counsel, Sept. 2005, 44; David Ho, *Citigroup to Settle Enron Lawsuit*, Jun. 11, 2005, Bus-1; *CIBC to Pay $2.4 Billion in Enron Suit*, L.A. Times, Aug. 3, 2005, C1

[4] Bloomberg News, *Witness Tells of Adelphia Paying Rigas' Golf Fees*, L.A. Times (Online), Mar. 18, 2004

[5] *New Charges Filed Against Ex-Tyco Execs*, Fox News (Online), Sept. 13, 2011

[6] Jonathan Sidener, *Former Peregrine CEO Gets 8 Years in Prison,* Union Tribune San Diego (Online), Dec. 11, 2008

[7] Press Release, *SEC Charges Qwest Communications International Inc. with Multi-Faceted Accounting and Financial Reporting Fraud*, U.S. Securities and Exchange Commission (SEC) (Online), Oct. 21, 2004

[8] Michael J. de la Merced, *Ex-Leader of Computer Associates Gets 12-Year Sentence and Fine*, N.Y. Times (Online), Nov. 3, 2006

[9] Bloomberg News, *Ex-Homestore Exec Pleads Guilty to Securities Fraud*, L.A. Times (Online), Mar. 3, 2006; *Homestore Ex-CEO Sentenced to 15 Years*, L.A. Times (Online), Oct. 13, 2006

[10] Scott Conroy, Associated Press, *Former Cendant Boss Sentenced for Fraud*, CBS News (Online), Jan. 17, 2007

[11] *Waste Management Settles*, CNN Money (Online), Nov. 7, 2001

[12] Jeff Clabaugh, *Time Warner Settles AOL Investigations for $510 Million*, Washington Business Journal (Online), Dec. 15, 2004; *Time Warner Settles AOL Suit for $2.4 Billion*, The Street.com (Online), Aug. 3, 2005

[13] Associated Press, *Freddie Mac Settles Accounting-Fraud Charges: Home-Loan Giant to Pay $50 Million Fine*, NBC News (Online), Sept. 28, 2007

[14] *Ibid.*

[15] Associated Press, *Fannie Mae to Pay Fine of $400 Million*, L.A. Times (Online), May 24, 2006

[16] Don Michak, *A Billion Dollars Paid*, Connecticut Journal Inquirer (Online), Nov. 12, 2013; Press Release, *Largest Health Care Fraud Case in U.S. History Settled, HCA Investigation Nets a Record Total of $1.7 Billion*, U.S. Department of Justice (Online), Jun. 26, 2003

[17] Mark Maremon, *Lawsuit Details Rite Aid's Accounting Woes*, Wall St. Journal, Feb. 8, 2001, C1

[18] *Ex-Rite Aid Chief Pleads Guilty in Billion-Dollar Fraud Scandal*, Baltimore Sun (Online), June 18, 2003; *8 Year Sentence for Rite-Aid Exec*, CBS News (Online), May 7, 2009

[19] Jacob Goldstein, *Merck to Take a $670 Million Hit for Medicaid*, Wall St. Journal (Online), Dec. 4, 2007

[20] David Teather, *Marsh Pays Out $850 Million to Settle Kickback Scandal*, The Guardian (U.K., Online), Jan. 31, 2005

[21] Kevin LaCroix, *Marsh Settles "Contingent Commission" Securities Suit for $400 Million*, The D & O Diary (Online), Nov. 16, 2009

[22] Vikas Bajaj, *AIG to Pay $1.6 Billion in Settlement of Fraud Charges*, N.Y. Times (Online), Feb. 9, 2006

[23] Press Release, *Chevron to Pay $30 Million to Settle Charges for Improper Payments to Iraq under U.N. Oil for Food Program*, U.S. Securities and Exchange Commission, (SEC) (Online), Nov. 14, 2007

[24] Thomas S. Mulligan, *Waksal Pleads Guilty to Six Charges*, L.A. Times, Oct. 16, 2002, C3

[25] Peter Pae, *Another Boeing Employee Charged*, L.A. Times (Online), May 12, 2004; Peter Pae, *Charges Filed Against Ex-Boeing Engineers*, L.A. Times (Online), Jun. 26, 2003

[26] Andy Pasztor, *Boeing to Settle Federal Probes for $615 Million*, Wall St. Journal, May 15, 2006, A1

[27] Udith Rehak, *Tylenol Made a Hero of Johnson & Johnson: The Recall That Started Them All*, N.Y. Times (Online), Mar. 23, 2002

[28] Michael L. Diamond, *Woes for Johnson & Johnson*, USA Today (Online), Nov. 20, 2011

[29] Chuck Bartels, Associated Press, *Arkansas Judge Fines J & J $1.1Billion in Risperdal Case*, USA Today (Online), Apr. 11, 2012

[30] *Spotlight on Stock Options Backdating*, U.S. Securities and Exchange Commission (SEC) (Online); *see also*, Mark Maremont, *Backdating Likely More Widespread*, Wall St. Journal, Aug. 18, 2009, C1

[31] Lewis Krauskopf and Martha Graybow, *Ex-UnitedHealth CEO McGuire to Forfeit Over $400 Million*, Reuters (Online), Dec. 6, 2007

[32] Associated Press, *Broadcom to Settle Backdating Suit for $160 Million*, N.Y. Times, Dec. 30, 2009, B2; *see also*, Amanda Bronstad, *Broadcom Settles Stock Options Backdating Claims for $118 Million*, National Law Journal (Online), Aug. 31, 2009

[33] Stephen Taub, *First Prison Term in Backdating Scandal: Former Comverse General Counsel Wasn't 'The Grand Wizard of Oz', Says the Sentencing Judge, But Still Deserves a Year Behind Bars*, CFO (Online), May 14, 2007

[34] *Report to the President Corporate Fraud Task Force, 2008,* U.S. Department of Justice (Online), (last visited Dec. 14, 2014)

[35] Mary Kreiner Ramirez, *Prioritizing Justice: Combating Corporate Crime from Task Force to Top Priority*, Marquette Law Review (Online), Vol. 93, No. 3, 2010, 990, (last visited Dec. 14, 2014)

[36] Neil Lipschutz, *Ten Years Later, Enron Pales in Comparison*, Wall St. Journal (Online), Nov. 30, 2011

[37] Michael Gormley, *Spitzer Settles IPO Insider Suit*, Washington Post (Online), Jul. 31, 2006

[38] Randall Smith, *NASD Penalizes Wall Street Firms for IPO Deals*, Wall St. Journal, May 19, 2004, C4

[39] *Salomon IPO Deals Provoke Congress*, Wall St. Journal, Aug. 29, 2002, C1; *CSFB Settles IPO Kickback Charges: SEC Says Investigation Continues,* L.A. Times, Jan. 23, 2002, C4; Jathon Sapsford, et al., *Firms Close in on Settlement of IPO Inquiry*, Wall St. Journal, Jun. 22, 2004, C1

[40] *Goldman, Morgan Stanley to Pay to Settle IPO Charges*, (Reuters), Boston Globe (Online), Jan. 26, 2005

[41] Adam Geller, *Brokerages to Pay $1.4 Billion*, L.A. Daily News, Dec. 21, 2002, Business-3; Walter Hamilton and Thomas S. Mulligan, *Wall Street Will Pay $1.4 Billion*, L.A. Times,Apr. 29, 2003, A1; Marcia Vickers, *The Myth of Independenc*e, Businessweek, Sept. 8, 2003, 86

[42] Stephen Choi and Marcel Kahan, *The Market Penalty for Mutual Fund Scandals*, Boston University Law Review (Online), Vol. 87, 2007; *see also, Special Report: Mutual Funds: Perils in the Savings Pool*, The Economist, Nov. 8, 2003, 65; Mortimer B. Zuckerman, *Making Scam Artists Pay*, U.S. News & World Report, Oct. 27, 2003, 76

[43] *See, e.g.,* Josh Friedman, *Morgan Stanley Fined for Incentives*, L.A. Times, Sept. 17, 2003, C1; Julie Creswell, *Dirty Little Secrets*, Fortune, Sept. 1, 2003, 136; Robert Frank, *Now, Mutual Funds Under Fire*, Wall St. Journal, Sept. 4, 2003, C1; Luisa Beltran, *Ex-Prudential Securities Broker Convicted of Fraud*, Wall St. Journal Marketwatch (Online), Sept. 19, 2005; Julie Creswell and John Hechinger, *Putnam to Face State Civil Case In Funds Probe*, Wall St. Journal, Oct. 22, 2003, C1; Josh Friedman, et al., *For the Fund Business, What Went Wrong?* L.A. Times, Nov. 2, 2003, C1; Tom Lauricella, *Alliance Capital Set Up Market-Timing Deals*, Wall St. Journal, Nov. 6, 2003, C1; Tom Lauricella, P*ilgrim and Baxter Face Charges*, Wall St. Journal, Nov. 21, 2003, C1; Walter Hamilton, *Financial Firm Ordered to Close,* L.A. Times, Nov. 26, 2003, C1; Tom Lauricella and Susan Pulliam, *Invesco Charged in Scandal as Strong Quits*, Wall St. Journal, Dec. 3, 2003, C1; Kara Scannell and Tom Lauricella, *In Fund Scandal: Criminal Charges*, Wall St. Journal, Mar. 16, 2004, D9; John Hechinger and Laura Johannes, *MFS to Pay $50 Million In SEC Case*, Wall St. Journal, Mar. 31, 2004, C1; Laura Johannes and John Hechinger, *Why a Brokerage Giant Pushes Some Mediocre Mutual Funds*, Wall St. Journal, Jan. 9, 2004, A1; Deborah Soloman and Tom Lauricella, *Regulators Are Seen Settling With Firms Accused of Overcharges*, Wall St. Journal, Feb. 12, 2004, C6; *15 Brokerages Close to Deal on Fund Discounts*, L.A. Times, Feb. 13, 2004, C4; Tom Lauricella and Aaron Lucchetti, *Scandal Tags Pimco Funds Run by Gross*, Wall St. Journal, Feb. 19, 2004, C1

[44] Press Release, *Former Trader Pleads Guilty in Mutual Fund Case*, Office of the New York Attorney General (Online), Jan. 25, 2006

[45] Michael Flaherty, *Private Equity Regulation May Be Next*, Reuters (Online), Apr. 6, 2006

[46] Reuters, *Bayou Founder Gets 20 Years for Bilking Investors*, N.Y. Times (Online), Apr. 14, 2008

[47] Jonathan Weil, et al., *Scrutiny of Refco Accelerates*, Wall St. Journal, Oct. 12, 2005, C1; Emily Thornton, *Refco: The Reckoning*, Businessweek, Nov. 7, 2005, 114

[48] Peter Lattman, *A Crucial Witness in Rajaratnam Trial Receives Probation*, DealBook, N.Y. Times (Online), Sept. 24, 2012

[49] Chad Bray, *Rajaratnam and Chiesi Are Charged*, Wall St. Journal, Dec. 16, 2009, C3; Jonathan Stempel and Rachelle Younglai, *SEC Sees Evolution in Insider Trading*, Reuters (Online), Nov. 6, 2009

[50] Press Release, *Former Morgan Stanley Financial Analyst and Her Husband, Former Hedge Fund Analyst, Sentenced to 18 Months in Prison for Insider Trading Scheme*, U.S. Attorney, Southern District of New York (Online), Dec. 4, 2007

[51] *Ex-Merrill Lynch Analyst Sentenced for Insider Trading*, Associated Press (Online), Jan. 6, 2007

[52] *Ibid.*

[53] *Raj Rajaratnam–Galleon Group Founder Convicted of Insider Trading Case*, N.Y. Times (Online), Nov. 20, 2012

[54] *Enforcement and Legal Activity*, Auction Rate Securities Information Center, North American Securities Administrators Association (NASAA), (Online), (last visited Dec. 14, 2014)

[55] *State Securities Regulators Announce Settlement with TD Ameritrade in Auction Rate Securities Investigations*, North American Securities Administrators Association (NASAA, Online), Jul. 20, 2009

[56] *Wrapup1–Schwab Faces ARS Fraud Charge, TD Ameritrade Settles*, Reuters (Online), Jul. 20, 2009; Chad Bray, *Ex-Broker Pleads in Auction-Rate Case*, Wall St. Journal, Jul. 23, 2009, C3; Bloomberg News, *Former Broker at Credit Suisse Is Found Guilty*, N.Y. Times, Aug. 18, 2009, B2

[57] Robert Lenzner, *$1.7 Billion Customers' Money Missing from MF Global*, Forbes (Online), Nov. 22, 2011

[58] Lindsay A. Owens, *40-Year Low in America's View of Wall Street*, CNN (Online), Oct. 7, 2011

[59] Curt Anderson, *AP: Ponzi Collapses Nearly Quadrupled in 2009*, Boston Globe (Online), Dec. 28, 2009

[60] Del Quentin Wilber, *Economic Downturn Speeds Collapse of Ponzi Schemes*, Washington Post (Online), Jun. 12, 2009

[61] *See, e.g.,* Steve Stecklow, *Hard Sell Drove Stanford's Rise and Fall*, Wall St. Journal, Apr. 3, 2009, A1; Del Quentin Wilber, *Economic Downturn Accelerates Collapse of Ponzi Schemes*, Washington Post (Online), Jun. 12, 2009; Steve Stecklow, *In Echoes of Madoff, Ponzi Cases Proliferate*, Wall St. Journal, Jan. 28, 2009, A1; Marcia Vickers, *A Scandal Rocks the Polo Set*, Fortune, Nov. 23, 2009, 55; Leslie Wayne, *The Mini-Madoffs: Troubling Times Are Bringing More Ponzi Inquiries to Light*, N.Y. Times, Jan. 28, 2009, B1; Steve Stecklow, et al., *Pair Lived Large on Fraud, U.S. Says*, Wall St. Journal, Feb. 26, 2009, A1

[62] Diana B. Henriques, *Claims Tally Tops 15,400 in Fraud by Madoff*, N.Y. Times, Jul. 10, 2009, B5; Diana B. Henriques, *Trustee May Win Billions for Investors in Madoff*, N.Y. Times, Nov. 10, 2009, B1

[63] Juan A. Lozano, Associated Press, *Stanford Gets 110 Years for Role in $7 Billion Swindle*, Daily Tribune (Online), Jun. 14, 2012

[64] Press Release, *SEC Charges 26 Defendants in $428 Million Securities Fraud That Targeted Senior Citizens and Retirement Savings*, U.S. Securities and Exchange Commission (SEC) (Online), Sept. 5, 2007

[65] Associated Press, *Ex-Mormon Bishop Charged in $20 Million Ponzi Scheme*, Fox News, Apr. 8, 2009; Greg Griffin, *Ponzi-Schemer Merriman Gets 12 and ½ Years in Prison*, Denver Post (Online), Sept. 15, 2010

[66] Thom Weidlich, *Nicholas Cosmo Receives 25 Years in Prison for $413 Million Ponzi Scheme*, Bloomberg (Online), Oct. 14, 2011

[67] Peter Lewis, *Finance Company Agrees to Pay $484 Million in Lending Case*, Seattle Times (Online), Oct. 11, 2012

[68] Press Advisory, *Attorney General Baker Finalizes Predatory Lending Settlement in Nation's Largest Consumer Restitution Case*, Attorney General's Office of the State of Georgia (Online), Aug. 8, 2002

[69] Annys Shin, et al., *The Checkout: Ameriquest Settlement,* Washington Post (Online), Jan. 23, 2006

[70] News Release, *Attorney General Brown Announces Landmark $8.68 Billion Settlement with Countrywide,* Office of the California Attorney General (Online), Oct. 8, 2008

[71] Terry Frieden, *FBI Warns of Mortgage Fraud 'Epidemic'*, CNN (Online), Sept. 17, 2004

[72] Don Thompson, Associated Press, *Mortgage Fraud Is Booming Business for Prosecutors*, Fox News (Online), Dec. 10, 2008

[73] *8 Plead Guilty to Rigging Foreclosure Auction Bids*, San Francisco Chronicle (Online), Oct. 28, 2011

[74] Ianthe Jeanne Dugan, *Did You Hear the One About the Accountant? It's Not Very Funny*, Wall St. Journal, Mar. 14, 2002, A1

[75] *Ibid.*

[76] *Deloitte Pays $210 Million to Settle Adelphia Case: 45% of Total Sum*, Big 4 Blog (Online), Dec. 10, 2006

[77] Jonathan D. Glater, *Auditor to Pay $217 Million to Settle Suits*, N.Y. Times (Online), Mar. 2, 2002

[78] Ashby Jones, *PWC Reaches $225 Million Settlement in Tyco Case*, Wall St. Journal (Online), Jul. 6, 2007

[79] Stephen Taub, *Xerox, KPMG Settle Investor Suit*, CFO (Online), Mar. 27, 2008

[80] *Former Partner at BDO Seidman LLP Sentenced to Prison for Tax Crimes*, Accounting Web (Online), Apr. 25, 2012

[81] Bob Van Voris and David Glovin, *BDO Seidman to Pay $50 Million in Deferred Prosecution*, BloombergBusinessweek (Online), Jun. 14, 2012

[82] Press Release, *Four Current or Former Ernst & Young Partners Found Guilty on Criminal Tax Shelter Charges*, U.S. Department of Justice (Online), May 7, 2009

[83] Lynnley Browning, *3 Convicted in KPMG Tax Shelter Case*, N.Y. Times, Dec. 16, 2008, B11

[84] Ashby Jones, *Gone But Not Forgotten: Jenkens & Gilchrist Trio Indicted for Tax Fraud*, Wall St. Journal (Online), June 9, 2009

[85] Bob Van Voris, *Lawyer Daugerdas Seeks New Trial Based on Juror Misconduct*, Bloomberg (Online), Aug. 15, 2011

[86] Bloomberg News, *Milberg Lawyers Sued by Ex-Partners*, L.A. Times (Online), Jun. 18, 2008; *see also*, Edward Pettersson, *Weiss Sentenced to 2½ Years for Kickback Scheme,* Bloomberg (Online), June 2, 2008; Peter Elkind, *The Fall of America's Meanest Law Firm*, CNN Money (Online), Nov. 3, 2006

[87] Peter Lattman, *Dickie Scruggs Indicted on Federal Bribery Charges*, Wall St. Journal (Online), Nov. 28, 2007; Jenny Jarvie, *For a Legal Legend, a Stiff Dose of Justice*, L.A. Times (Online), Jun. 28, 2008

[88] Chad Bray, *Dreier Is Sentenced to 20 Years for Fraud*, Wall St. Journal, Jul. 15, 2009, A3

[89] Nathan Koppel and Mike Esterl, *Lawyer Crashes After a Life in the Fast Lane*, Wall St. Journal, Nov. 14-15, 2009, A1

[90] Benjamin Weiser, *Lawyer Gets 20 Years in $700 Million Fraud*, N.Y. Times (Online), Jul. 13, 2009

[91] Ian Urbina and Sean D. Hamill, *Judges Guilty in Scheme to Jail Youths for Profit*, N.Y. Times, Feb. 13, 2009, A1

[92] Holbrook Mohr, Associated Press, *Famed Mississippi Judge to Report to Federal Prison*, Fox News (Online), Jan. 4, 2010

[93] William Glaberson, *Ex-Brooklyn Judge to Serve at Least 3 Years for Bribe* , N.Y. Times (Online), Oct. 29, 2002

[94] Tony Perry, *Rep. Cunningham Pleads Guilty to Bribery, Resigns*, L.A. Times, Nov. 29, 2005, A1

[95] Greg Miller, *Ex-CIA No. 3 Pleads Guilty in Fraud Case*, L.A. Times (Online), Sept. 29, 2008

[96] David Stout, *Ex-Louisiana Congressman Sentenced to 13 Years,* N.Y. Times, Nov. 14, 2009, A14

[97] Neil A. Lewis, *Abramoff Gets Four Years in Prison for Corruption*, N.Y. Times (Online), Sept. 4, 2008

[98] Press Release, *Former U.S. Army Officer Sentenced to 42 Months in Prison for Bribery and Weapons Conspiracy*, U.S. Department of Justice (Online), Jan. 22, 2010

[99] Joel Millman, *Major Gets 17½ Years in Iraq Contract Case*, Wall St. Journal, Dec. 4, 2009, A4; Joel Millman, *Third Officer to Plead Guilty in Troop-Supply Plot*, Wall St. Journal, Aug. 13, 2008, A3; Mike Esterl, *Top Food Supplier to Military Indicted*, Wall St. Journal, Nov. 17, 2009, A5; Robbie Brown, *U.S. Says Kuwait Company Overbilled It by Millions for Troops' Food*, N.Y. Times, Nov. 17, 2009, A10

[100] Kim Murphy, *U.S. Goes After Reconstruction Theft, Bribery*, Baltimore Sun (Online), Apr. 12, 2009

[101] Ralph Vartabedian, et al., *Rise in Bribery Tests Integrity of U.S. Border: From California to Texas, 200 Officials Indicted Since 2004*, L.A. Times, Oct. 23, 2006, A1

[102] *Ibid.*

[103] Rick Jervis, *Arrests of Border Agents on the Rise*, USA Today, Apr. 24, 2009, 3A

[104] *Ex-Border Patrol Officer Sentenced in Bribery Case*, L.A. Times, Mar. 27, 2007, B4

[105] Rick Newman, *Trust in Government and Other Institutions Hits New Lows*, US News & World Report (Online), Jun. 20, 2012

[106] *Cajun-Country Era Ends, Prison Term Begins; Former Gov. Edwin Edwards, after Years of Investigations, Goes to Prison for Racketeering*, Christian Science Monitor, Highbeam.com (Online), Oct. 23, 2002

[107] Elizabeth Mehren, *Connecticut's Ex-Governor Gets a Year in Prison*, L.A. Times, Mar. 19, 2005, A19

[108] Adam Nossiter, *Ex-Governor of Alabama Ordered Released*, N.Y. Times (Online), Mar. 28, 2008

[109] Catrin Einhorn, *Ex-Gov. Ryan of Illinois Reports to Prison*, N.Y. Times (Online), Nov. 8, 2007

[110] Press Release, *Former State Senator Thomas Bromwell Sentenced to 7 Years on Charges of Racketeering, Conspiracy and Filing a False Tax Return*, U.S. Department of Justice (Online), Nov. 16, 2007

[111] Associated Press, *Former State Senator Convicted*, N.Y. Times (Online), June 9, 2006

[112] Press Release, *Former Oklahoma State Senator Gene Stipe Sentenced for Perjury, Conspiracy, and Federal Elections Violations*, U.S. Department of Justice (Online), Jan. 30, 2004

[113] *National Briefing, South: Florida: Ex-State Senator Convicted of Bribery,* N.Y. Times (Online), Apr. 11, 2003

[114] Liz Krueger, *Former Senator Guy Velella: Convicted Felon, $80,000-a-Year Public Pensioner*, Gotham Gazette (Citizens Union Foundation) (Online), Oct. 25, 2004

[115] *National Briefing, Midwest: Wisconsin: Former State Senator Sentenced in Corruption Case*, N.Y. Times (Online), Dec. 1, 2005

[116] Gary D. Robertson, *Ex-NC Lawmaker Guilty of Fraud Charges*, USA Today (Online), Apr. 7, 2008

[117] *Ibid.*

[118] News Release, *Former Kickapoo Tribe Casino Employees, Texas State Representative Sentenced for Scheming to Steal More than $2 Million*, U.S. Immigration and Customs Enforcement (Online), Feb. 14, 2008

[119] *Alaska: Ex-Lawmaker Sentenced*, N.Y. Times, Dec. 8, 2007, A14

[120] Press Release, *Alaska State Senator Pleads Guilty to Public Corruption Charges*, U.S. Department of Justice (Online), Dec. 19, 2008

[121] Kareem Fahim, *Seeking Free Home, Ex-Legislator Will Get a Prison Cell Instead*, N.Y. Times (Online), June 13, 2008 ; Susan Saulny, *Metro Briefing, New York, Manhattan: Assemblywoman Pleads Guilty*, N.Y. Times (Online), Jan. 8, 2003; Press Release, *Former New York State Assemblyman and Labor Leader Brian McLaughlin Pleads Guilty to Racketeering*, U.S. Department of Justice (Online), Mar. 7, 2008; Anemona Hartocollis, *Former Democratic Leader in Brooklyn in Convicted*, N.Y. Times, Feb. 24, 2007, A13

[122] Stephen Taub, *Ex–New Mexico Treasurer Sentenced to Prison*, Chief Financial Officer (CFO, Online), Sept. 27, 2007

[123] Craig Karmin, *Plea Cooperation from a Key Figure*, Wall St. Journal, Mar. 11, 2010, C1; Jennifer Peltz, Associated Press, *Ex-NY Comptroller Faces Sentence in Pension Probe*, Seattle Times (Online), Apr. 14, 2011

[124] Gina Chon, *Cuomo Probes Pension "Spiking,"* Wall St. Journal, Mar. 19, 2010, A6

[125] Jimmy DeButts, *Former Birmingham Mayor Larry Landford Gets 15 Years in Prison*, Birmingham Business Journal (Online), Mar. 5, 2010

[126] Kate Linebaugh, *Detroit Mayor Is Released, Faces New Charges*, Wall St. Journal, Aug. 9–10, 2008, A4; David Bailey, *Detroit Mayor Pleads Guilty, To Leave Office*, Reuters (Online), Sept. 4, 2008

[127] Cynthia Daniels, *Former Mayor Gets 3 Years*, L.A. Times, Jul. 14, 2005, B1

[128] Tresa Baldas and Jim Schaefer, *Former Detroit Mayor Sentenced to 28 Years in Prison,* USA Today (Online), Oct. 10, 2013

[129] William M. Welch, *Mayor Guilty in San Diego Bribery Scandal*, USA Today (Online), Jul. 19, 2005

[130] Associated Press, *Baltimore Mayor Convicted on Fraud Charge*, Boston Globe (Online), Dec. 2, 2009

[131] Del Quentin Wilber, *Tax Scam Leader Gets More than 17 Years*, Washington Post (Online), July 1, 2009

[132] FBI Probes, *City Hall Pay-to-Play Trial,* Philadelphia Inquirer (Online), Oct. 8, 2012; Associated Press, *Ex-City Official is Convicted in Philadelphia Corruption Case,* N.Y. Times (Online), May 10, 2005

[133] Associated Press, *Election Workers Sentenced in Ohio Recount*, L.A. Times (Online), Mar. 14, 2007

[134] Ted Rohrlich, *City Hall Insider Accused of Bribery*, L.A. Times, Aug. 24, 2006, A1; Garrett Therolf, *Wong Guilty on 14 Counts*, L.A. Times (Online), Jul. 25, 2008; David Zahniser, *Wong Gets 5 Years for Corruption*, L.A. Times (Online), Oct. 11, 2008

[135] Press Release, *Former Treasurer of South Gate Sentenced to 10 Years in Federal Prison in Corruption Case That Cost City Tens of Millions of Dollars*, U.S. Department of Justice

(Online), Nov. 28, 2006; Hector Becerra, *Robles Sentenced to 10 Years*, L.A. Times, Nov. 29, 2006, B1

[136] Libby Sander, *National Briefing, Midwest: Illinois: Ex-Aide Sentenced in Hiring Scheme*, N.Y. Times, Nov. 21, 2006, A18; Gretchen Ruethling, *4 Chicago Officials Are Found Guilty in Patronage Scheme*, N.Y. Times, Jul. 7, 2006, A13; Matt O'Connor and Dan Mihalopoulos, *Key Figure Pleads Guilty to Hired Truck Charges*, Baltimore Sun (Online), July 29, 2005

[137] Barbara Novovitch, *Major F.B.I. Inquiry in El Paso Results in Second Guilty Plea*, N.Y. Times, Jul. 9, 2007, A13

[138] Randy James, *2 Minute Bio: Bernard Kerik*, Time (Online), Nov. 6, 2009

[139] Christine Hanley, et al., *Carona Loses His National Security Clearance*, L.A. Times, Nov. 17, 2007, B3; Christine Hanley, *Scolding and a Stiff Sentence for Carona*, L.A. Times (Online), Apr. 28, 2009

[140] H.G. Reza, *Jaramillo Begins His Jail Sentence*, L.A. Times, Apr. 3, 2007, B7

[141] Scott Glover, *Ex-Cop Gets 102 Years for Theft-Ring Role*, L.A. Times, May 20, 2008, B3

[142] Associated Press, *Delaware Catholic Diocese Files Bankruptcy Before Sex-Abuse Trial*, N.Y. Daily News, Oct. 19, 2009, 14; Tony Perry, *San Diego Diocese Files for Bankruptcy*, L.A. Times, Feb. 28, 2007, A1

[143] *Los Angeles Catholic Church in Record Abuse Deal*, Reuters (Online), Jul. 15, 2007

[144] Mike Sunnucks, *Baptist Foundation of Arizona Execs' Fraud Convictions Upheld*, Phoenix Bus. Journal (Online), June 10, 2009

[145] Associated Press, *Oral Roberts President Faces Corruption Lawsuit*, MSNBC (Online), Oct. 5, 2007; *Oral Roberts President Exits Amid Scandal*, CBS (Online), Oct. 17, 2007

[146] Chuck Fager, *Fraud: Greater Ministries Leaders Get Lengthy Prison Terms*, Christianity Today (Online), Oct. 1, 2011

[147] Ted Rohrlich, *City Hall Insider Accused of Bribery*, L.A. Times, Aug. 24, 2006, A1; Garrett Therolf, *Wong Guilty on 14 Counts*, L.A. Times (Online), Jul. 25, 2008; *2 Maryland Men Sentenced to Prison in Church Bilking Scheme*, Black Christian News (Online), Dec. 23, 2010

[148] Annie Sweeney, *Guilty Plea in Fraud Scheme That Targeted Muslim Community*, Chicago Tribune (Online), Mar. 28, 2011

[149] Victoria Kim, *Rabbi Sentenced to Two Years in Tax Fraud: Naftali Tzi Weisz Help Funnel Money Back to Donors Via a Jewelry District Network*, L.A. Times, Dec. 22, 2009, A4; Sue Doyle, *Rabbi, Others Plead Guilty to Conspiracy*, L.A. Daily News, Aug. 4, 2009, A3

[150] *Brooklyn Rabbi Sentenced in New Jersey to 46 Months in Prison for Money Laundering Conspiracy*, FBI (Online), Jul. 3, 2012; Associated Press, *New York Rabbi Sentenced in New Jersey for Money Laundering Scheme*, N.Y. Post (Online), Jul. 3, 2012

[151] Jerry Markon, *Ex-Chief of Local United Way Sentenced*, Washington Post (Online), May 15, 2004

[152] Douglas Belkin and Carrie Porter, *Two Trustees Quit in Illinois Admissions Scandal*, Wall St. Journal, Aug. 6, 2009, A5

[153] Associated Press, *College Loan Scandal Widens*, MSNBC (Online), Apr. 10, 2007

[154] Karen W. Arenson, *Columbia to Pay $1.1 Million to State Fund in Loan Scandal*, N.Y. Times (Online), Jun. 1, 2007

[155] Paul Pringle, *Union Workers Express Outrage*, L.A. Times, Dec. 27, 2008, B1; Carl Horowitz, *Ex-Los Angeles SEIU Boss Indicted for Theft, Tax Evasion*, National Legal and Political Center (Promoting Ethics in Public Life) (Online), Aug. 6, 2012

[156] Press Release, *Former New York State Assemblyman and Labor Leader Brian McLaughlin Pleads Guilty to Racketeering*, U.S. Department of Justice (Online), Mar. 7, 2008; Press Release, *Former New York State Assemblyman and Labor Leader Brian McLaughlin Sentenced to Ten Years in Prison for Racketeering and False Statement Crimes*, New York FBI (Online) May 20, 2009

[157] Mike Spector, et al., *Examiner: Lehman Torpedoed Lehman*, Wall St. Journal (Online), Mar. 11, 2010

[158] *Ibid.*

[159] *Ibid.*

[160] *See generally,* Joe Nocera, *Financial Scandal Scorecard*, N.Y. Times (Online), Jul. 20, 2012

[161] *The Worst Banking Scandal Yet? Libor*, Bloomberg (Online), Jul. 12, 2012

[162] Alana Semuels and Jim Puzzanghera, *UBS to Settle Libor Case*, L.A. Times, Dec. 20, 2012, B1

[163] Jacob Benge, et al., *Peregrine CEO's Dramatic Confession*, Wall St. Journal, Jul. 7–8, 2012, A1

[164] Robert Burns, Associated Press, *Auditors Say Billions Wasted in Iraq Rebuild*, L.A. Daily News, Jul. 14, 2012, A1

[165] *Calif. Strips 23 Schools of API Rankings for Cheating,* L.A. Times (Online), Oct. 28, 2012

[166] David Callahan, *The Cheating Culture* (Orlando, Florida: Harcourt, Inc., 2004)

[167] Lynnley Browning, *UBS Executives May Face Prosecution in Tax Evasion Inquiry*, Mar. 5, 2009, B3; Lynnley Browning, *14,700 Disclosed Offshore Accounts*, N.Y. Times (Online), Nov. 18, 2009

[168] Sonia Giordani, *LAUSD Grade Scandal: Administrators Fudged Grades, Official Says*, L.A. Daily News, Sept. 28, 2001, 1

[169] Peter Applebome, *Grades Fixed: An Allegation Shocks No One*, N.Y. Times (Online), Mar. 7, 2009

[170] Kate Brumback, Associated Press, *11 Atlanta Educators Convicted in Test Cheating Scandal,* Athens News (Online), Apr. 4, 2015

[171] Jose Martinez, *Ex-Director of Admissions for Touro Is Guilty of Selling College Degrees,* N.Y. Daily News (Online), Jun. 10, 2009

[172] Ben Chapman and Rachel Monahan, *Cheating Scandal Involving over 50 Kids Rocks Stuyvesant High,* N.Y. Daily News (Online), Jun. 25, 2012

[173] Monica Rhor, *Clear Lake Students Involved in Cheating Scandal,* Houston Chronicle (Online), Jan. 5, 2012

[174] Al Baker, *Suspensions for Cheating at Stuyvesant,* N.Y. Times, Sept. 8, 2012, A16

[175] Kris Axtman, *When Tests' Cheaters Are the Teachers,* Christian Science Monitor (Online), Jan. 11, 2005

[176] Alison Go, *84 GMAT Scores Thrown Out,* U.S. News & World Reports (Online), Sept. 10, 2008; John Hechinger, *Schools Cancel GMAT Scores,* Wall St. Journal, Sept. 11, 2008, D6

[177] Dan Frosch, *18 Air Force Cadets Exit Over Cheating,* N.Y. Times, May 2, 2007, A16

[178] Alan Finder, *34 Duke Students Face Discipline for Cheating,* N.Y. Times (Online), May 1, 2007

[179] Anthony Bianco, *The Future of the N.Y. Times*, Businessweek, Jan. 17, 2005, 64

[180] Marc Peyser, *The Ugly Truth*, Newsweek, Jan. 23, 2006, 62; Motoko Rich, *Lies and Consequences: Tracking the Fallout of (Another) Literary Fraud*, Mar. 5, 2008, B1

[181] *Track Star Marion Jones Sentenced to 6 Months*, CNN (Online), Jan. 11, 2008

[182] Associated Press, *Cyclist Tammy Thomas Convicted in Steroids Case*, KTVU (Online), Feb. 20, 2009

[183] Eddie Pells, Associated Press, *Lance Armstrong's Former Teammates Testify Against Him*, Christian Science Monitor (Online), Oct. 10, 2012

[184] *Barry Bonds Found Guilty of Obstruction,* ESPN (Online), Apr. 14, 2011

[185] *Donaghy Sentenced to 15 Months in Prison in Gambling Scandal*, ESPN (Online), Jul 30, 2008

[186] *Apologetic Vic Gets 23-Month Sentence on Dogfighting Charges,* ESPN (Online), Dec. 11, 2007

[187] Paula Parrish, *USOC President Resigns Baldwin Admits to Lying About Education in Bio*, Rocky Mountain News (highbeam.com, Online), May 25, 2002

[188] Marissa Vogt, *Marilee Jones Leaves Behind Complicated Legacy*, The Tech (MIT, Online) Feb. 2008

[189] Associated Press, *O'Leary Out at Notre Dame After One Week*, Sports Illustrated (Online), Dec. 14, 2001

[190] Floyd Norris, *RadioShack Chief Resigns After Lying*, N.Y. Times (Online), Feb. 21, 2008

[191] Michael M. Grynbaum, *Taxi Agency Missed Scope of Cheating*, N.Y. Times, Mar. 18, 2010, A23

[192] James Sterngold, *Journal of a Plague Year: Faith in Markets Cracks Under Losses* , Bloomberg News (Online), Dec. 31, 2008

Chapter 8: *Our Culture of Trust Is Unique*

[1] *Souter: Republic Is Lost Unless Civic Education Improves*, Legal Times (Online), May 20, 2009; *see also,* Harlow Giles Unger, *Noah Webster: The Life and Times of an American Patriot* (John Wiley & Sons, Inc., 1998) (for further discussion of how early Americans were taught to be Americans through the educational system)

[2] Jimmy Carter, *Inaugural Address*, Bartleby.com (Online), Jan. 20, 1977

[3] *McCulloch v. Maryland*, 17 U.S. 316, 405 (S. Ct. 1819), ThisNation.com, American Government & Politics Online, (last visited Dec. 14, 2014)

[4] *Naturalization Oath of Allegiance to the United States of America,* U.S. Citizenship and Immigration Services (Online), June 25, 2014

[5] *See Mayflower Compact, 1620,* Avalon Project, Yale Law School (Online), (covenant with God to follow the law discussed at greater length later in this chapter) (last visited Dec. 14, 2014)

[6] *Nicolas Sarkozy Joins David Cameron and Angela Merkel View That Multiculturalism Has Failed*, Daily Mail (U.K., Online), Feb. 11, 2011

[7] *Rwanda: How Genocide Happened*, BBC News (U.K., Online), Dec. 18, 2008

[8] Rebecca Santana, Associated Press, *Fearful, Iraq's Sunnis Leave Mixed Neighborhoods*, USA Today (Online), Jan. 2, 2012; Dan Murphy, *Iraq's Exiled Vice President Sentenced to Death as Violence Grows,* Christian Science Monitor (Online), Sept. 9, 2012

[9] *Bosnia Buries Hundreds at Srebrenica Massacre Site*, The Telegraph (U.K., Online), Jul. 11, 2012

[10] Harlow Giles Unger, *Noah Webster, supra* note 1 at xii

[11] Matthew Spaulding, ed., *The Ensuring Principles of the American Revolution*, (Wash., D.C.: The Heritage Foundation, 2001), ix

[12] Brion McClanahan, *The Politically Incorrect Guide to The Founding Fathers* (Wash. D.C., Regnery Publishing, Inc., 2009), 32–33

[13] Clinton Rossiter, ed., *The Federalist Papers* (New York: Penguin Group, 1999), 95

[14] Matthew Spaulding, ed., *The Enduring Principles of the American Founding, supra* note 11 at 54

[15] Robert A. Goldwin, *From Parchment to Power: How James Madison Used the Bill of Rights to Save the Constitution* (Wash. D.C.: American Enterprise Institute Press, 1997), 1 and 4

[16] *See, e.g., Latin America: Constitution Crazy*, Latin Business Chronicle (Online), Oct. 6, 2008

[17] *Washington's Farewell Address 1796,* The Avalon Project, Yale Law School (Online) (last visited Dec. 14, 2014)

[18] *Parliamentary Sovereignty,* Parliament (U.K., Online), (last visited Dec. 14, 2014)

[19] Larry Neumeister, *Judge Rejects $285 Million SEC-Citigroup Settlement*, Associated Press (Online), Nov. 28, 2011

[20] Jessica Holzer, *Court Deals Blow to SEC, Activists*, Wall St. Journal, Jul. 23-24, 2011, B3

[21] Claude Belanger, *Comparing Canadian and American Federalism*, Marianopolis College (Online), Nov. 28, 2005

[22] *Five Years After Kelo: The Sweeping Backlash Against One of the Supreme Court's Most-Despised Decisions*, Institute for Justice (Litigating for Liberty), (Online), (last visited Dec. 14, 2014)

[23] Jillian L. Redding, *Proposed Bills on State Sovereignty in the United States*, Office of Legislative Research (OLR) Report (Online), May 27, 2009

[24] Timothy Gardner, *U.S. States Sue EPA to Stop Greenhouse Gas Rules*, Reuters (Online), Mar. 19, 2010

[25] Robert A. Goldwin, *From Parchment to Power*, *supra* note 15 at 8–9

[26] *Ibid.* at 92

[27] *Religion and the Founding of the American Republic: Overview*, Congressional Record Exhibition, Library of Congress, (Online), (last visited on Dec. 14, 2014)

[28] *Religion and the Founding of the American Republic: Introduction*, Library of Congress (Online), (last visited Dec. 14, 2014)

[29] Gary DeMar, *America's Christian Heritage*, (Nashville, Tenn: Broadman & Holman Publishers, 2003), 56 (citing Public Law 97–280, 96 Stat. 1211, approved October 4, 1982)

[30] Gary Langer, *Poll: Most Americans Say They're Christian (Varies Greatly from the World at Large)* ABC News (Online), Jul. 18, 2004; *see also, Among Wealthy, U.S. Stands Alone in its Embrace of Religion*, Pew Research Center, Dec. 19, 2002

[31] *Questions and Answers about Americans' Religion: More than 8 Out of 10 Americans Identify with a Christian Faith*, Gallup (Online), Dec. 24, 2007

[32] *Table 75: Self-Described Religious Identification of Adult Population: 1990, 2001, and 2008*, U.S. Census (Online), (2012), (last visited Dec. 14, 2014)

[33] *Christian Pastor Faces Execution in Iran for Refusing to Renounce His Faith*, Daily Mail (U.K., Online) , Sept. 29, 2011

[34] *Court of Chancery*, Encyclopaedia Britannica, Academic Edition (Online), (last visited Dec. 14, 2014)

[35] Alex Groner, *The American Heritage History of American Business & Industry* (New York: American Heritage Publishing, Co., Inc., 1972), 22; *see also*, Michael Novak, *The Spirit of Democratic Capitalism*, (New York: Simon & Schuster, 1982)

[36] Samuel Chase, BrainyQuote (Online), (last visited Dec. 14, 2014)

[37] *Analysis Wahhabism*, Frontline, Public Broadcasting Service (PBS) (Online) (last visited Dec. 14, 2014)

[38] Toni Johnson and Mohammed Aly Sergie, *Islam: Governing under Sharia*, Council on Foreign Relations (Online), updated Jul. 25, 2014. For further discussion of the Saudi Arabian legal system, *see* Samuel Westrop, *Saudi Arabia's Brutal Tribal Justice*, Real Clear World (Online) (originally published in the Gatestone Institute), May 2, 2013

[39] *Saudi Arabia Executes Woman Convicted of 'Sorcery,'* The Telegraph (U.K., Online), Dec. 12, 2011

[40] *Saudi Arabia: Law of God Versus Law of Man*, The Economist, Oct. 13, 2007, 50

[41] *A Look at the Writings of Saudi Blogger Raif Badawi—Sentenced to 1,000 Lashes*, The Guardian (U.K., Online), Jan. 14, 2015

[42] *See generally*, John Eidsmoe, *Christianity and the Constitution: The Faith of Our Founding Fathers* (Grand Rapids, Michigan: Baker Book House Co., 1987); David L. Holmes, *The Faiths of the Founding Fathers* (New York: Oxford University Press, 2006)

[43] Gordon Lloyd and Margie Lloyd, ed., *The Essential Bill of Rights, Original Arguments and Fundamental Documents* (Lanham, Md.: University Press of America, Inc., 1998), 254; George B. deHuszar, et al., *Basic American Documents* (Ames, Iowa: Littlefield, Adams & Co., 1953), 66

[44] Peter M. Ivanov, *Russian Orthodox Church and Democratic Transition in Russia*, North Atlantic Treaty Organization, (NATO) (Online), (last visited Dec. 14, 2014)

[45] James Reynolds, *China, Communists Turn to Confucius*, BBC News (U.K., Online), Mar. 20, 2009

[46] *See generally*, James H. Hutson, *Religion and the Founding of the American Republic* (Washington, DC: The Library of Congress, 1998); *Under God in the Pledge: Pros and Cons: Religion in the Original 13 Colonies*, ProCon.org (Online), Jan. 6, 2009

[47] *Constitution of Delaware; 1776*, The Avalon Project, Yale Law School (Online), (last visited Dec. 14, 2014)

[48] Gary DeMar, *America's Christian Heritage*, *supra* note 29 at 21

[49] Russ Stevenson, *Forgotten Foundation: How the Great Ideas of the Christian Faith Became the Foundation of the Western World* (Lenoir, North Carolina: Reformation Press, 2009), 81

[50] *Ibid. at* 79-81

[51] *The 50 States Reference God in Their Constitutions—Truth!*, TruthorFiction.com (Online), Oct. 24, 2008

[52] Newt Gingrich, *Rediscovering God in America, Reflections on the Role of Faith in Our Nation's History and Future* (Franklin, Tenn: Integrity Media Inc., 2006)

[53] John Grafton, ed. *The Declaration of Independence and Other Great Documents of American History*, 1775-1865 (Mineola, New York: Dover Publications, 2000), 44

[54] For examples, *see* Stephen McDowell, *In God We Trust: America's Historic Sites Reveal Her Christian Foundations*, Providence Foundation (Online), (last visited Dec. 14, 2014)

[55] *Quotations, Thomas Jefferson Memorial*, U.S. National Park Service (Online), (last visited Dec. 14, 2014)

[56] *See, e.g.,* the U.S. Supreme Court case, *Engel v. Vitale*, 370 U.S. 421 (1962)

[57] *See, e.g.,* David Barton, *Is President Obama Correct: Is America No Longer a Christian Nation?*, Wallbuilders.com (Online), Apr. 2009

[58] Chaplain Patrick McLaughlin, C.D.R., U.S.N., *No Atheists in Foxholes: Prayers and Reflections from the Front* (Nashville, Tenn: Thomas Nelson, 2008)

[59] John Grafton, ed. *The Declaration of Independence and Other Great Documents of American History, 1775-1865, supra* note 54 at 55–56; George Washington's *Farewell Address to the American People*, Sept. 17, 1796, The Avalon Project, Yale Law School (Online), (last visited Dec. 14, 2014)

[60] *Proclamation Appointing a National Fast Day*, March 30, 1863, Abraham Lincoln Online, Speeches & Writings, (last visited Dec. 14, 2014)

[61] *Franklin Delano Roosevelt's D-Day Prayer*, FDR Library (Online), June 6, 1944, (last visited Dec. 14, 2014)

[62] William J. Federer, *America's God and Country Encyclopedia of Quotations*, (Coppell, Texas: FAME Publishing Inc., 1994), 204

[63] *Ibid.* at 205

[64] Alexis de Tocqueville, (J. P. Mayer, ed.), *Democracy in America* (New York: Anchor Books, 1969), 291 (originally published in 1835)

[65] *Perry v. United States*, 294 U.S. 330 (1935) (one of three gold clause cases), Justia U.S. Supreme Court (Online), (last visited Dec. 14, 2014)

[65] Sue Kirchhoff, et al., *Pension Funding Problems Grow*, USA Today, (Online) May 15, 2005

[67] Michael McDonald, et al., *Central Falls Bankruptcy Casts Shadow Over Rhode Island Pensions*, Bloomberg (Online), Aug. 2, 2011

[68] Ted Nesi, *Central Falls Slashes Dozens of Pensions by 55%; One Gets Cut $41,000*, WPRIChannel 12 News (Online), Sept. 2, 2011

[69] Mary Williams Walsh, *Two Rulings Find Cuts in Public Pensions Permissible*, N.Y. Times (Online), June 30, 2011

[70] Michael Cooper and Mary Williams Walsh, *Alabama Town's Failed Pension Is a Warning*, N. Y. Times (Online), Dec. 22, 2010; *Pritchard Pays Pensioners $600,000*, Local15NBC News (Online), Mar. 8, 2012

[71] *The Underfunding of State and Local Pension Plans*, Congressional Budget Office, (CBO) (Online), Publication No. 22042, May 4, 2011

[72] Michael Cooper and Mary Williams Walsh, *Surpluses Help, But Fiscal Woes for States Go On*, N.Y. Times (Online), May 31, 2013

[73] Cornell Barnard, *18,000 State Employees Each Make More than $100,000 in Pension Payments*, ABC News 10 (Online), Jun. 1, 2012

[74] David Crane, *California's $500 Billion Pension Time Bomb*, L.A. Times (Online), Apr. 6, 2010

[75] Steven Greenhut, *Vallejo's Painful Lessons in Municipal Bankruptcy*, Wall St. Journal (Online), Mar. 26, 2010

[76] Alison Vekshin, et al., *Police Chief's $204,000 Pension Shows How Cities Crashed*, Bloomberg (Online), Jul. 31, 2012

[77] Pamela A. MacLean, *In a First, Bankruptcy Judge Rules Calif. City Can Void Union Contracts*, Law.com (Online), Mar. 17, 2009

[78] John Woolfolk, *San Jose, Other Cities, Find It Easier to Cut Retiree Health Perks Than Pensions*, Mercury News (Online), Apr. 3, 2013

[79] Mary Williams Walsh, *Untouchable Pensions May Be Tested in California*, N.Y. Times (Online), Mar. 16, 2012

[80] Phil Wilson, *CalPERS Can't Sue Bankrupt San Bernadino*, L.A. Times, Dec. 22, 2012, AA4

[81] Mary Williams Walsh, *Bankruptcy Judge in California Challenges Sanctity of Pensions*, N.Y. Times (Online), Oct. 1, 2014

[82] Gary DeMar, *America's Christian Heritage, supra* note 29 at 11

[83] Russ Stevenson, *Forgotten Foundation: How the Great Ideas of the Christian Faith Became the Foundation of the Western World, supra* note 50 at 84 (citing Zorach v. Clauson)

[84] Lawrence M. Friedman, *Law in America: A Short History* (New York: Random House, 2002), 3; *see generally*, H. Wayne House, ed., *The Christian and American Law: Christianity's Impact on America's Founding Documents and Future Direction* (Grand Rapids, MI: Kregel Publications, 1998); William J. Federer, *The Ten Commandments & Their Influence on American Law* (St. Louis, Missouri: Amerisearch, Inc., 2003)

[85] *First Premier Bank Card Offers Customers 79.9% APR Bank Card*, American Banking & Market News (Online), Oct. 15, 2009

[86] *Consumers Warned of Online Payday Loan Sites*, U.S. Government Information, About News (Online), (last visited Dec. 14, 2014)

[87] Charles A. Weisman, *A Handbook of Bible Law—Economic and Monetary Laws* 1991, 1992, 1994 (Online), giveshare.org, (last visited Dec. 14, 2014)

[88] Geert De Clercq, *Special Report: Architects of a Currency in Crisis*, Reuters (Online), Dec. 30, 2011

Chapter 9: *Trust Is Not Worldwide*

[1] *Rights of the Accused*, ThisNation.com (American Government & Politics), (Online), (last visited Dec. 14, 2014)

[2] Jeffery K. Taubenberger and David M. Moren, *1918 Influenza: The Mother of All Pandemics*, Center for Disease Control (Online), Jan. 2006

[3] Michael Mandel, *German and French Banks Got $36 Billion from AIG Bailout*, BloombergBusinessweek (Online), Mar. 15, 2009

[4] Chad Bray, et al., *Accounts Raided in Global Bank Hack*, Wall St. Journal, Oct. 1, 2010, A1

[5] *UN Charter of the United Nations, Article 1*, United Nations (Online), (last visited Dec. 14, 2014)

[6] George Russell, *U.S. Diplomats Growing Frustrated at United Nations' Budget Games*, Fox News (Online), Oct. 7, 2011

[7] *Rolling Up the Culprits*, The Economist (Online), Mar. 13, 2008; *see also*, Colum Lynch, *Many Firms Paid Iraq Oil-for-Food Bribes, Report Alleges*, Washington Post (Online), Oct. 27, 2005

[8] *Rolling Up the Culprits*, The Economist, (Online), Mar. 13, 2008; *Timeline: Oil-for-Food Scandal*, BBC (U.K., Online), Sept. 7, 2005; Claudia Rosett, *Annan's Son Took Payments Through 2004*, N.Y. Sun (Online), Nov. 26, 2004

[9] *See, e.g.,* Associated Press, *Conviction in Oil-for-Food Program*, N.Y. Times, Jul 14, 2006, A4 (conviction of Tongsun Park, a South Korean businessman); Colum Lynch, *Oil-Food Official Pleads Guilty; Graft Allegations in U.N. Program Include Ex-Chief,* The Washington Post, Aug. 9, 2005, A1 (guilty plea of Alexander Yakovlev, a former Russian UN procurement officer); Paul Davies, *Texas Tycoon Pleads Guilty to Iraq-Oil Kickback Scheme*, Wall St. Journal, Oct. 2, 2007, A10 (guilty plea of Texas oil man Oscar S. Wyatt, Jr.); Paul Glader and Nathan Becker, *GE Settles Kickback Charges from SEC*, Wall St. Journal, Jul. 28, 2010, B2 ($23.5 million settlement over kickbacks)

[10] Josh Kron and Jeffrey Gettleman, *U.N. Documents Told of Rapes in Congo*, N.Y. Times, Sept 1, 2010, A6; World Briefing, *More Than 500 Rapes Reported*, L.A. Times, Sept. 8, 2010, A7; Jeffrey Gettleman, *Mass Rapes in Congo Reveals U.N. Weaknesses*, N.Y. Times (Online), Oct. 3, 2010

[11] Robyn Dixon, *U.N. Force in Congo Pilloried*, L.A. Times, Dec. 23, 2012, A4

[12] *Constitution of the People's Republic of China*, The National People's Congress of the People's Republic of China (Online), (last visited Dec. 14, 2014)

[13] *Justice System in China: Facts and Details* (Online), (last visited Dec. 14, 2014); Mary Kay Magistad, *Tipping the Scales: New Chinese Directive Requires Lawyers to Pledge Loyalty to the Communist Party*, PRI's The World, (Online), theworld.org, Mar. 21, 2012; Joseph Kahn, *Deep Flaws, and Little Justice, in China's Court System*, N.Y. Times (Online), Sept. 21, 2005

[14] *Freedom in the World 2011*, Freedom House (Online); *Table of Independent Countries*, Freedom House (Online), (last visited Dec. 14, 2014)

[15] *Naturalization Oath of Allegiance to the United States of America*, U.S. Citizenship and Immigration Services (Online), (last visited Dec. 14, 2014)

[16] David Kravets, *UN Report Declares Internet Access a Human Right*, Wired (Online), Jun. 3, 2011

[17] *The World's Worst Dictators: Top 10 of 2011*, Parade Magazine (Online); [in descending order, they are North Korea, Eritrea, Sudan, Uzbekistan, Syria, Myanmar (formerly known as Burma), Turkmenistan, Cuba, Equatorial Guinea (Mbasogo), Venezuela, and Zimbabwe. Only North Korea and Myanmar are not U.N. members]

[18] Joel Brinkley, *UN Human Rights Council Fails to Police Abuses*, Newsday (Online), Jul. 10, 2012

[19] Laura King, *Cruel Justice Grows along with Taliban's Influence*, L.A. Times, Aug. 22, 2010, A1; for further discussion, *see* Robert F. Worth, *Crime (Sex) and Punishment (Stoning)*, N.Y. Times (Online), Aug. 21, 2010

[20] William J. Kehoe, *Conceptualizing a Framework for Global Business Ethics*, published in O.C. Ferrell, ed., Rights, Relationships and Responsibilities: Business Ethics and Social Impact Management, Fall 2003, 131–152

[21] Archie B. Carroll, *Managing Ethically with Global Stakeholders: A Present and Future Challenge*, Academy of Management Executive (Online), Vol. 18, No. 2, 2004

[22] Tom Eggert, *Five Values That Should Be at the Heart of Your Business*, Capital Region Business Journal, May 1, 2006, 8

[23] *China: The Debate Over Universal Values*, The Economist, Oct. 2, 2010, 43

[24] Hernando de Soto, *The Mystery of Capital* (New York: Basic Books, 2000), 1–13

[25] Agrast, M., et al., *The World Justice Project, Rule of Law Index 2010* (Online); an updated version may be found at The WJP Rule of Law Index 2014 (Online), (last visited Dec. 14, 2014)

[26] Michael Freedman, *Judgment Day*, Forbes, June 7, 2004, 97

[27] *Ibid.*

[28] Brett D. Shaefer, *The International Criminal Court: Threatening U.S. Sovereignty and Security*, Heritage Foundation (Online), Jul. 2, 1998

[29] Xan Rice, *Chad Refuses to Arrest Omar al-Bashir on Genocide Charges*, The Guardian (U.K., Online), Jul. 22, 2010; *Kenya Refuses to Arrest Sudanese President Omar Al-Bashir*, Amnesty International (Online), Aug. 27, 2010

[30] For a more detailed discussion of culture, *see*, Lawrence E. Harrison and Samuel P. Huntington, ed., *Culture Matters: How Values Shape Human Progress* (New York: Basic Books, 2000)

[31] *Ibid.*; *see generally*, David S. Landes, *The Wealth and Poverty of Nations* (New York: W.W. Norton & Co. 1999)

[32] Dennis Prager, *Five Questions Non-Muslims Would Like Answered*, L.A. Times (Online), Nov. 13, 2005

[33] Robert Verkaik, *Princess Facing Saudi Death Penalty Given Secret UK Asylum*, The Independent (U.K., Online) Jul. 20, 2009 (because of global pressure, she was later pardoned)

[34] Aryn Baker, *Afghan Women and the Return of the Taliban*, Time (Online), Jul. 29, 2010

[35] Himanshi Shawan, *Honour Killings Not Just a North Indian Phenomenon*, Times of India (Online), Jul. 6, 2010; Geeta Pandey, *Indian Community Torn Apart by 'Honour Killings'*, BBC (U.K., Online), June 16, 2010

[36] Sharon LaFraniere, *Robbed of Files, Young Chinese Lose the Future*, N.Y. Times, Jul. 27, 2009, A1

[37] Emily Dugan, *More Than 70 Countries Make Being Gay a Crime*, The Independent (U.K., Online), Aug. 1, 2010

[38] Sharon LaFraniere, *African Crucible: Cast as Witches, Then Cast Out,* N.Y. Times, Nov. 15, 2007, A1

[39] *South Africa and Polygamy: Swimming Against the Tide*, The Economist, Apr. 28, 2012, 54

[40] Suzanne Daley, *Greeks' Wealth Is Found in Many Places, Just Not on Tax Returns*, N.Y. Times, May 2, 2010, 1

[41] Liz Alderman, *Real Estate Collapse Spells Havoc in Dubai*, N.Y. Times, Oct. 7, 2010, B7

[42] Norimitsu Onishi, *Pressed by Police, Even Innocent Confess in Japan*, N.Y. Times, May 11, 2007, A1; Christopher Johnson, *Wrongful Conviction Puts Spotlight on Japanese Justice*, Asia Times (Online), Jun. 30, 2012

[43] Karla Zabludovsky, *In Mexico, Rehearsing to Inject Drama into the Courtroom*, N.Y. Times (Online), Aug. 28, 2012

[44] Jo Johnson, *How Justice Is Delayed and Denied in India*, Financial Times, Sept. 6, 2007, 9

[45] *Doing Business in South Asia, 2007,* The World Bank Group (Online), 29, (last visited Dec. 14, 2014)

[46] Tariq Engineer, *In the Shadows of India's Loan Boom*, Wall St. Journal, Jan. 8, 2008, B1

[47] Nancy Gibbs, *How Should America Handle Extreme Speech*, Time (Online), Oct. 3, 2010

[48] *Libel-Law Reform: Fairer But Still Costly*, The Economist, Mar. 27, 2010, 62

[49] Declan McCullagh, *U.S. Court Says No to Web Libel Lawsuit*, CNET (Online), Dec. 16, 2002

[50] *Are Foreign Libel Lawsuits Chilling Americans' First Amendment Rights?* Hearing Before the Committee on the Judiciary, United States Senate (Online), Serial No. J-111-73, Feb. 23, 2010, U.S. Government Printing Office, (last visited Dec. 14, 2014)

[51] John Leo, *Stomping on Free Speech*, U.S. News & World Report, Apr. 19, 2004, 14

[52] *After Free Speech Victory in Federal Court, FIRE Sends Warning to Public Universities Violating the First Amendment*, Foundation for Individual Rights in Education (FIRE), (Online), Sept. 30, 2008, (last visited Dec. 14, 2014)

[53] William Yong, *Iran Sentences Voices of Dissent*, N.Y. Times, Sept. 29, 2010, A10

[54] Andrew Jacobs, *Two Chinese Dissidents Freed After Years in Prison*, N.Y. Times (Online), Mar. 13, 2009

[55] Malcolm Moore, *Father of 'Toxic Milk' Child Jailed in China for Protesting*, The Telegraph (U.K., Online), Nov. 10, 2010

[56] For a more detailed discussion of what happens to journalists in many countries around the world, *see*, *Reporters Without Borders* (Online), (last visited Dec. 14, 2014)

[57] Richard Perez-Pena, *Times Co. Settles Claim in Singapore*, N.Y. Times, Mar. 25, 2010, B4

[58] Lindy Kerin, *Channel Shut Down for Not Airing Chavez Speech*, ABC News (Online), Jan. 26, 2010

[59] *Almost 70 Reporters Killed Worldwide in 2011: RSF*, Reuters (Online), Dec. 21, 2011

[60] *UN Human Rights Office Concerned about Killing of Journalists in Mexico*, UN News Center (Online), Sept. 30, 2011

[61] Elena Milashina, *The High Price of Journalism in Putin's Russia*, N.Y. Times, Nov. 12, 2010, A19

[62] Clifford J. Levy, *Inquiry Revived in Beating of Russian Editor*, N.Y. Times, Nov. 12, 2010, A8

[63] William Yong, *Iran Sentences Voices of Dissent*, N.Y. Times, Sept. 29, 2010, A10

[64] Matt Keating, *The Chinese Journalists in Prison*, The Guardian (U.K., Online), Feb. 20, 2006

[65] *Religious Freedom: Too Many Chains*, The Economist, Dec. 19, 2009, 111

[66] Ching-Ching Ni, *Bibles Becoming Big Business in China*, L.A. Times, Jun. 22, 2008, A6

[67] Andrew Jacobs, *After 10 Years and 2,000 Deaths, China Still Presses Its Crusade Against Falun Gong*, N.Y. Times, Apr. 28, 2010, A4

[68] Jeffrey Fleishman, *Dissident Egyptian Blogger Is Freed*, L.A. Times, Nov. 18, 2010, AA2

[69] Rob Crilly and Aoun Sahi, *Christian Woman Sentenced to Death in Pakistan "For Blasphemy,"* The Telegraph (U.K., Online), Nov. 9, 2010

[70] Kate Linthicum and Amber Smith, *For Bahai, Two Nations Are Worlds Apart*, L.A. Times, July 27, 2009, A6

[71] *Christian Pastor Sentenced to Death in Iran for Refusing to Renounce His Faith Could Be Hanged "At Any Time Without Warning,"* Daily Mail (U.K., Online), Feb. 23, 2012

[72] *Embassies Burn in Cartoon Protest*, BBC, (U.K., Online), Feb. 4, 2006; *Danish Cartoonist Hid in "Panic Room" During Attack*, CNN (Online), Jan. 2, 2010

[73] *Freedom of Association Under Threat: The New Authoritarians' Offensive Against a Civil Society*, Freedom House (Online), Nov. 13, 2008

[74] Anthony Kuhn, *Chinese Protest Leaders Get Jail*, L.A. Times, May 10, 2003, A3

[75] Sergei L. Loiko, *Moscow Police Break Up Large Opposition Protest*, L.A. Times, Sept. 1, 2010, A6

[76] Megan K. Stack, *Police Stop Gays in Their Tracks*, L.A. Times, May 17, 2009, A1

[77] Andrew Jacobs, *Seeking Justice, Chinese Land in Secret Jails*, N.Y. Times, Mar. 9, 2009, A1; Megan K. Stack, *"Black Jails" Stir Outrage in China*, L.A. Times, Sept. 30, 2010, A3

[78] Sharon LaFraniere and Dan Levin, *Assertive Chinese Marooned in Mental Wards*, N.Y. Times, Nov. 12, 2010, A1; Barbara Demick, *Dissenters Silenced in Mental Hospitals*, L.A. Times, Mar. 17, 20012, A1

[79]*Police Brutality in Russia: Cops for Hire*, The Economist, Mar. 20, 2010, 58

[80] Tom Cahill, *Deadly Business in Moscow*, Bloomberg Businessweek (Online), Feb. 18, 2010

[81] Alexei Anishchuk, *Russia's Khodorkovsky Sentenced, West Concerned*, Reuters (Online), Dec. 10, 2010

[82] William Browder, as told to Diane Brady, etc. *Hard Choices*, Bloomberg Businessweek, Jan. 10-16, 2011, 80

[83] Michael Schwirtz, *In Russia, Charges Are Dropped in Jail Death*, N.Y. Times, Apr. 9, 2012, A4

[84] David Barboza, *Rio Tinto Trial in China Concludes,* N.Y. Times (online), Mar. 24, 2010

[85] Norimitsu Inishi, *In Indonesia, Middlemen Mold Outcome of Justice*, N.Y. Times (Online), Dec. 19, 2009

Chapter 10: *Trust Is Up to All of U.S.*

[1] *2014 Index of Economic Freedom*, The Heritage Foundation (Online), (last visited Dec. 14, 2014)

[2] Dave Graham, *U.S. Slips to Historic Low in Global Corruption Index,* Reuters (Online), Oct. 26, 2010

[3] *Corruption Perceptions Index 2013*, Transparency International (Online), (last visited Dec. 14, 2014)

[4] Jim Puzzanghera, *U.S.'s Global Competitiveness Keeps Declining*, L.A. Times, Sept. 6, 2012, B4

[5] John F. Kennedy, *Inaugural Address*, 1961, Bartleby.com (Online), (last visited Dec. 14, 2014)

[6] Army Sgt. 1st Class Michael J. Carden, *National Debt Poses Security Threat, Mullen Says*, U.S. Department of Defense (Online), Aug. 27, 2010

[7] *See, e.g., The National Debt Is $17.3 Trillion,* Federal Budget (Online); *see also,* U.S. National Debt Clock in: Real Time (Online)

[8] Romina Boccia, et al., *Federal Spending by the Numbers, 2014,* The Heritage Foundation (Online), Dec. 8, 2014

[9] *Baby Boomers Face Retirement Shortfall*, ABC 13 TV Virginia (Online), Dec. 29, 2010. Of course, nothing is static and these numbers could change in the future. For example, the L.A. Times reported that nearly 1 in 5 Americans aged 65 or older are either working or looking for jobs rather than drawing on their public retirement benefits. As a result, "[t]he share of seniors claiming Social Security benefits fell in 2012 to the lowest level since 1976." Don Lee, *Older Workers Crowd Labor Market*, Sept. 3, 2012, A1

[10] *Social Security Trust Funds*, Congressional Budget Office (CBO) (Online), http://www.cbo.gov/publication/25052, Mar. 31, 2010

[11] Social Security and Medicare Boards of Trustees, *A Summary of the 2013 Annual Reports*, Social Security Administration (SSA) (Online), (last visited Dec. 14, 2014)

[12] Philip Klein, *Trustees Say Long-Run Medicare and Social Security Deficit Is $66 Trillion*, Washington Examiner (Online), Jun. 1, 2013

[13] Stephen Ohlemacher, *Social Security Faces $29 Billion Shortfall in 2010*, Arizona Republic (Online), Mar. 15, 2010; Merrill Matthews, *What Happened to the $2.6 Trillion Social Security Trust Fund?*, Forbes (Online), Jul. 13, 2011

[14] Philip Klein, *Trustees Say Long-Run Medicare and Social Security Deficit is $66 Trillion, supra* note 12

[15] Alan Greenblatt, *The Federal Debt: How to Lose a Trillion Dollars*, National Public Radio (NPR) (Online), Apr. 30, 2010

[16] Roben Farzad, *A Lost Decade for Savers*, BloombergBusinessweek (Online), Sept. 26, 2012

[17] Elisabeth Bumiller and Thom Shanker, *Panetta Warns of Dire Threat of Cyberattack*, N.Y. Times, Oct. 12, 2012, A1

[18] J. Nicholas Hoover, *Attacks Focus DOD on Cybersecurity Partnerships*, Information Week (Online), Jul. 15, 2011

[19] Gopal Ratnam, *Pentagon Accuses China of Cyberspying on U.S. Government*, Bloomberg (Online) May 7, 2013

[20] *China's Military Rise*, The Economist (Online), Apr. 7, 2012

[21] *Hu Jintao Tells China Navy: Prepare for Warfare*, BBC (U.K. Online), Dec. 7, 2011

[22] Daniel Fisher, *The Global Debt Bomb*, Forbes (Online), Jan. 21, 2010

[23] *EBT Card Scam Costing Taxpayers $750 Million Yearly*, ABC News (Online), May 24, 2012

[24] *$2 Million Lottery Winner Still Gets Food Stamps*, MSNBC News (Online), May 19, 2011; Chris Ingalls, *Feds: Seattle Welfare Recipient Lives in Million Dollar Home*, King 5 News (Online), Dec. 2, 2011

[25] *Americans Say Federal Gov't Wastes Over Half of Every Dollar*, Gallup (Online), September 19, 2011

[26] *America's Infrastructure Report Card*, American Society of Civil Engineers (Online), infrastructurereportcard.org, 2009 (last visited Dec. 14, 2014)

[27] Shan Carter and Amanda Cox, *One 9/11 Tally: $3.3 Trillion*, N.Y. Times (Online), Sept. 8, 2011

[28] Seth Borenstein, *Billion-Dollar Weather Disasters Smash U.S. Record*, L.A. Daily News, Dec. 8, 2011, A8. This figure doesn't take into account Hurricane Sandy in 2012, *see e.g.*, Associated Press, *Hurricane Sandy Estimated to Cost $60 Billion*, Time (Online), Oct. 31, 2012

[29] Robert Lenzner, *Europe in 2011 a Worse Crisis Than the U.S. in 2008*, Forbes (Online), Sept. 30, 2011

[30] Associated Press, *Interracial Marriage Hits New High—1 in 12*, CBS News (Online), Feb. 16, 2012

[31] Gerry J. Gilmore, *World War II Flying "Ace" Salute Racial Progress*, U.S. Department of Defense (Online), Feb. 20, 2004

[32] *See, e.g.,* Charles E. Francis, *The Tuskegee Airmen* (Boston: Branden Publishing Co., 1988); Lynn M. Homan and Thomas Reilly, *The Tuskegee Airmen* (Charleston, S.C.: Arcadia Publishing, 1998)

[33] *Tuskegee Airman Goes on to Become First Air Force African-American General*, U.S. Air Force (Online), Feb. 6, 2012

[34] *Navajo Code Talkers: World War II Fact Sheet*, Naval History & Heritage (Online), May 19, 2014

[35] *Fighting for Democracy, Japanese-Americans,* Public Broadcasting Station (PBS), (Online), http://www.pbs.org/thewar/at_war_democracy_japanese_ american.htm, (last visited Dec. 14, 2014)

[36] Michael D. Hull, *Japanese-American 442nd Regimental Combat Team— Jul. '96 World War II Feature,* Wieder History Group, Aug. 19, 1996, http://www.historynet.com/japanese-american-442nd-regimental-combat-team-july-96-world-war-ii-feature.htm; *see also,* Masayo Umezawa Duus, *Unlikely Liberators* (Honolulu: University of Hawaii Press, 1987)

[37] For further information about Audie Murphy, *see America's Most Decorated World War II Combat Soldier*, The Audie L. Murphy Memorial Website, http://www.audiemurphy.com/index.htm (last visited Dec. 14, 2014); *see also,* his autobiography, Audie Murphy, *To Hell and Back* (New York: Henry Holt & Co., 1949); *Audie Murphy: Great American Hero*, Biography DVD 1996, 2005

[38] *See, e.g.,* Penny Colman, *Rosie the Riveter* (New York: Crown Publishers. 1995); Emily Yellin, *Our Mothers' War* (New York: Free Press, 2004)

[39] *Definition of Crisis*, Business Dictionary (Online), (last visited Dec. 14, 2014)

[40] Peter Coy, *Lessons from the Credit-Anstalt Collapse*, Bloomberg Businessweek (Online), Apr. 20, 2011

[41] Clinton Rossiter, *The Federalist Papers* (New York: Penguin Group, 1999), 27

[42] Ben Hirschler and Scott Malone, *Insight: In Euro Zone Crisis, Companies Plan for the Unthinkable*, Reuters (Online), Nov. 29, 2011; *Euro Contingency Planning*, Treasury, Risk and Finance Professionals (Online), treasurers.org, May 16, 2012

[43] Don Lee and Henry Chu, *Europe's Woes Put a Drag on World Growth*, L.A. Times, May 25, 2012, A1

[44] Minxin Pei, *China's Ticking Debt Bomb,* The Diplomat (Online), Jul. 5, 2011

[45] *Chinese Factories Hit by Strike Amid Manufacturing Slowdown*, L.A. Times (Online), Nov. 28, 2011; David Pierson, *Chinese Leaders Fret about Unrest as Economy Worsens*, L.A. Times, Dec. 6, 2011, B1

[46] David Pierson, *Being a Bear on China Gains Favor*, L.A. Times, Nov. 28, 2011, A1

[47] Chris Larono, et al., *China Seeks to Calm Anger over Passports*, Wall St. Journal (Online), Nov. 28, 2012

[48] Chrystia Freeland, *Corruption and India's 1 Percent,* Reuters (Online), Nov. 18, 2011; Gerald Jeffries, *Graft Trial Jolts Brazil's Ruling Party*, Wall St. Journal, Sept. 25, 2012, A14

[49] Michael Patterson & Shiyin Chen*, BRIC Decade Ends with Record Stock Outflows as Goldman Says Growth Peaked*, Bloomberg (Online), Dec. 28, 2011

[50] Andrew E. Kramer, *As Money Flees Russia, Tycoons Find Tough Times*, N.Y. Times, Dec. 11, 2011, 8

[51] Soutik Biswas, *Hundreds of Millions without Power in India*, BBC News, (U.K., Online), Jul. 31, 2012

[52] *Rising Tide of Restrictions on Religion*, Pew Forum (Online), Sept. 20, 2012; Steven Lee Myers, *State Dept. Report Says Countries Have Repressed Religious Freedom with Laws*, N.Y. Times, May 21, 2013, 9

[53] Chris Cillizza and Aaron Blake, *Obama: The Most Polarizing President Ever*, Washington Post (Online), Jan. 20, 2012

[54] Erica Orden, *Hollywood's New Bible Stories*, Wall St. Journal, Sept. 28, 2012, D1

[55] Ellie Genower, *Harvey Weinstein to Produce "Ambitious" Ten Commandments Television Series*, Daily Mail (U.K., Online), Nov. 22, 2013

[56] *Tim Tebow Tops Forbes' 2013 List of America's Most Influential Athletes,* Forbes (Online), May 6, 2013

[57] Jeff Yang, et al., *Jeremy Lin on Kobe Bryant, God and His Fast Break to Fame*, Wall St. Journal (Online), Feb. 11, 2012; *see also*, Luke Leung, *God Is My Audience, Says Jeremy Lin, First Chinese-American Drafted by NBA,* Gospel Herald (Online), Jun. 23, 2010

[58] Adelle M. Banks, *Poll: Nearly 80 Percent of Americans Say They Are Christian*, Houston Chronicle (Online), Jan. 5, 2012

[59] Daisy Grewal, *In Atheists We Distrust*, Scientific American (Online), Jan. 17, 2012

[60] Catalina Camia, *Poll: Record Number of Independents Buck Parties*, USA Today (Online), Jun. 4, 2012

[61] Neil Howe and William Strauss, *Generation Give and Give and Give*, USA Weekend, Apr. 22-24, 2005, 6

[62] Janice Lloyd, *Senior Volunteer Honorees Make Communities Better,* USA Today (Online), Apr. 20, 2012

[63] William Baldwin, *Do You Live in a Death Spiral State?* Forbes (Online), Nov. 25, 2012; Gale Holland and Sam Quinones, *California Demographic Shift: More People Leaving Than Moving In*, L.A. Times (Online), Nov. 27, 2011

[64]*Record High in U.S. Say Big Government Greatest Threat*, Gallup (Online), Dec. 18, 2013

[65] William Straus and Neil Howe, *The Fourth Turning: An American Prophecy* (New York: Broadway Books, 1997), 331

Chapter 11: *Restoring Trust*

[1] *Federal Tax Law Keeps Piling Up*, Wolters, Kluwer, CCH: 2013 (Online), www.cch.com/taxpileup.pdf, (last visited Dec. 14, 2014)

[2] *65 Percent Say Congress Doesn't Read Bill*, United Press International (UPI) (Online), Jan. 18, 2011

[3] Eva Rodriguez, *Post Partisan: Read Before You Vote, Congressman*, Washington Post (Online), Jul. 28, 2009

[4] *Full Text, "The Patient Protection and Affordable Care Act,"* L.A. Daily News (Online), posted June 28, 2012

[5] Paul Bedard, *6 Pages of Obamacare Equals 429 Pages of Regulations*, U.S. News & World Report (Online), Apr. 7, 2011

[6] Jim Angle, *Efforts to Implement ObamaCare Law Raise Concerns of Massive Government Expansion*, Fox News (Online), Jul. 3, 2013

[7] Review and Outlook, *The Uncertainty Principle*, Wall St. Journal (Online), Jul 14, 2010

[8] *Ibid.; see also, Dodd-Frank Act Implementation—Executive Overview*, American Bankers Association (Online), (last visited Dec. 14, 2014)

[9] Perry Skoutelas, *Dodd-Frank 9000 Pages But No Clear Answers*, Fordham Corporate Law Forum, Fordham Corporate Center (Online), Nov. 26, 2012

[10] Legal "gobbledygook" in American laws became so bad, the federal Plain Writing Act was passed in 2010. This statute requires federal agencies to communicate with the public in clear, easy to understand English. Since there is no penalty for not complying, it has had only mixed results. Calvin Woodward, Associated Press, *New Law Gets off to Shaky Beginning*, L.A. Daily News, July 20, 2012, A1; *see also, Plain Writing Act of 2010: Federal Agency Requirements,* (Online), plainlanguage.gov, (last visited Dec. 14, 2014)

[11] Gary Fields and John R. Emshwiller, *As Criminal Laws Proliferate, More Are Ensnared*, Wall St. Journal, Jul. 23-24, 2011

[12] John S. Baker, Jr. and Dale E. Bennett, *Measuring the Explosive Growth of Federal Crime Legislation* (Federal Enactments 1997 through 2003), The Federalist Society for Law and Public Policy Studies, Crime Report (Online), fedsoc.server326.com, (last visited Dec. 14, 2014)

[13] *Ibid.*

Chapter 12: *Commandment of Trust #1: Truth*

[1] *Ex-Detroit Mayor Kilpatrick Is Sentenced to 4 Months*, CNN (Online), Oct. 28, 2008; *Kilpatrick Aide Beatty Gets 120-Day Term*, United Press International (UPI) (Online), Jan. 6, 2009

[2] Press Release, *Former Computer Associates CEO Sanjay Kumar and Former Head of World-Wide Sales Stephen Richards Plead Guilty to All Charges of Securities Fraud and Admit Lying to Federal Investigators to Cover up the Scheme*, Department of Justice (Online), Apr. 24, 2006; Alex Berenson, *Ex-Executive Agrees to Pay $800 Million in Restitution*, N.Y. Times (Online), Apr. 13, 2007; Dow Jones/AP, *2 Years in Prison for Ex-Software Executive*, N.Y. Times (Online), Jan. 17, 2007; China Martens, *Former CA Sales Executive Gets Seven Years in Jail*, InfoWorld (Online), Nov. 15, 2006; Ron Zapata, *Ex-Computer Associates CFO Gets 7-Month Sentence*, Law360 (Online), Jan. 29, 2007

3 Title 18, U.S. Code, Section 1001; *see also,* John R. Emshwiller and Gary Fields, *For Fed, "Lying" Is a Handy Charge*, Wall St. Journal, Apr. 10, 2012, A1

4 *Bernard Kerik's 4-Year Prison Sentence Upheld*, CBS News New York (Online), Mar. 31, 2011

5 Associated Press, *"I Will Be Back," Stewart Vows after Sentencing*, NBC News (Online), Jul. 17, 2004

6 *Judge More Than Doubles Casey Anthony's Bill to over $217,000*, CNN (Online), Sept. 23, 2011

7 Ben Protess, *Mortgage Executive Receives 30-Year Sentence,* N.Y. Times (Online), Jun. 30, 2011; Dana Hedgpeth, *Taylor, Bean & Whitaker Owner Guilty in Fraud Scheme,* Washington Post (Online), Apr. 19, 2011

8 For a more detailed description of some of the many types of fraud, *see, e.g., Welcome to Fight Fraud America!,* Fight Fraud America (Online), (last visited Dec. 14, 2014); *see also, Financial Crimes Report to the Public,* Federal Bureau of Investigation (FBI) (Online), Oct. 1, 2009–Sept. 30, 2011

9 Tracy Ceonen, *Fraud Files: Does a Tough Economy Lead to More Fraud?*, Daily Finance (Online), Feb. 27, 2010

10 *JP Morgan Among 17 Banks Sued by U.S. for $196 Billion,* Bloomberg Businessweek (Online), Sept. 3, 2011

11 *FTC Announces "Operation False Charity" Law Enforcement Sweep,* Federal Trade Commission (FTC) (Online), May 20, 2009

12 Chad Bray and Andrew Grossman, *Prosecutors: $1 Billion Scam Derailed*, Wall St. Journal, Oct. 28, 2011, A6

13 Bruce Japsen, *Jury: Vioxx to Blame*, Chicago Tribune (Online), Aug. 20, 2005; *Merck's Hard Choices*, The Economist (Online), Nov. 25, 2008; *Merck to Fund $4.85 Billion Vioxx Settlement*, CBS News (Online), Jul. 17, 2008

14 News Release, *Dannon Agrees to Drop Exaggerated Health Claims for Activia Yogurt and DanActive Dairy Drink,* Federal Trade Commission (FTC, Online), Dec. 15, 2010; *FTC Approves Final Order Settling Charges thatDannon Made Deceptive Claims for Activia Yogurt and DanActive Drink,* (FTC) (Online), Feb. 4, 2011

15 Ilan Brat and Jared Favole, *Food Makers Warned on Claims*, Wall St. Journal, Mar. 4, 2010, D2; *Advertising, FAQs: A Guide for Small Business*, Bureau of Consumer Protection, Business Center, Federal Trade Commission (FTC) (Online), Apr. 1, 2001

16 Alicia Mundy, *FDA Criminal Office to Boost Prosecutions*, Wall St. Journal, Mar. 4, 2010, D2

17 *Big Pharma Behaving Badly: A Timeline of Settlements*, Fierce Pharma (Online), Oct. 5, 2010

Chapter 13: *Commandment of Trust #2: Fair*

1 *Chimpanzees Prefer Fair Play to Reaping an Unjust Reward* (The Primate Diaries), Science Blogs (Online), Apr. 22, 2010

2 Mireya Navarro, *Judge Rejects Deal on Health Claims of Workers at Ground Zero*, N.Y. Times, Mar. 20, 2010, A12

3 *Archer-Daniels-Midland Company History*, Funding Universe (Online), (last visited Dec. 14, 2014)

4 *See, e.g., Sherman Anti-Trust Act*, The Free Dictionary by Farlex (Online), (last visited Dec. 14, 2014)

5 Sharon Pian Chan, *Long Antitrust Saga Ends for Microsoft*, Seattle Times (Online), May 11, 2011

6 *Competition Counts: How Consumers Win When Businesses Compete*, Federal Trade Commission (FTC) (Online), (last visited Dec. 14, 2014)

7 *Ibid.*, citing U.S. Supreme Court Justice Thurgood Marshall in *United States v. Topco Associates, Inc.*, 405 U.S. 596, 610 (1972)

[8] *Unfair Government Competition: A Threat to the U.S. Economy*, Heritage Foundation (Online), Jun. 03, 2009

[9] Brent Kendall, *Wells Settles Wachovia Bid-Rig Case*, Wall St. Journal, Dec. 9, 2011, C3

[10] Kevin McCoy, *Rajaratnam Settles Civil Insider Trading Case*, USA Today (Online), Dec. 27, 2012; Reuters, *Raj Rajaratnam Ordered to Pay $92.8 Million Fine in SEC Civil Suit*, Huffington Post (Online), Jan. 8, 2012

[11] Timothy Spangler, *Rajaratnam's Conviction and the Future of Hedge Funds*, Forbes (Online), May 11, 2011

[12] *Insider Trading*, U.S. Securities and Exchange Commission (SEC) (Online), (last visited Dec. 14, 2014)

[13] Credit Markets, *Psychiatrist Is Sentenced*, N.Y. Times (Online), Jan. 8, 1992

[14] *Insider Trading*, (SEC) (Online), *supra* note 12

[15] Brody Mullins, et al., *Congressional Staffers Gain from Trading in Stocks*, Wall St. Journal (Online), Oct. 10, 2010; *see also,* Tyler Durden, *Congress Exempts Most Federal Workers from Key Insider Trading Requirement,* Zero Hedge (Online), Apr. 13, 2013

[16] Peter Lattman, *S.E.C. Charges Stiefel Labs and Its Former Chief with Share Buyback Fraud*, N.Y. Times, Dec. 13, 2011, B7

[17] Michael J. de la Merced, *Judges Overturn Backdating Conviction*, N.Y. Times, Aug. 19, 2009, B1

[18] *Due Process: Introduction*, Legal Information Institute (LII), Cornell University Law School (Online), (last visited Dec. 14, 2014)

[19] Bob Sullivan, *HP Investigators Hacked Reporters' Phone Data*, CNBC (Online), Sept. 7, 2006; Latif Lewis Williams, *Feds Delay Sentencing in HP Pretexting Case Due to "Related Matter,"* Daily Finance (Online), Aug. 30, 2011; *Definition of Pretexting*, Merriam-Webster Dictionary (Online), (last visited Dec. 14, 2014); Don Reisinger, *HP "Pretexting" Scandal Ends with Former P.I.'s Sentencing,* C/Net (Online), Dec. 14, 2012

[20] Shayndi Raice and Julia Angwin, *Facebook "Unfair" on Privacy*, Wall St. Journal, Nov. 30, 2011, B1

[21] Somini Sengupta, *F.T.C. Settles Privacy Issue at Facebook*, N.Y. Times (Online), Nov. 29, 2011

Chapter 14: *Commandment of Trust #3: Loyalty*

[1] New Testament, Matthew 6:24, Biblehub (Online), (last visited Dec. 14, 2014)

[2] Danny Hakim, *City Corruption under Ex-Comptroller, Aide Pleads Guilty in Pension Case,* N.Y. Times, Mar. 11, 2010; Danny Hakim, *Former Hevesi Aide Pleads Guilty in Pension Case,* N.Y. Times (Online), Mar. 20, 2010; John Eligon, *Adviser Pleads Guilty in Pay-to-Play Pension Scheme,* N.Y. Times (Online), Nov. 22, 2010; John Eligo, *Hevesi Adviser is Sentenced in Pension Scandal,* N.Y. Times (Online), Feb. 17, 2011

[3] *See, e.g.,* Chris MacDonald, *Definition: Conflict of Interest: A Basic COI Toolkit,* Chris MacDonald CA (Online), citing Chris MacDonald, et al., *Charitable Conflicts of Interest,* Journal of Business Ethics 39:1-2, 67-74, August 2002, 68, (last visited Dec. 14, 2014)

[4] *A Matter of Trust*, Revolving Door Working Group (Online), cleanup washington.org, Oct. 2005, (last visited Dec. 14, 2014)

[5] For further discussion, *see Revolving Door*, Center for Responsive Politics (Online), opensecrets.org, (last visited Dec. 14, 2014)

[6] *The Warning*, Frontline, Public Broadcasting Corp. (PBS) (Online), Oct. 20, 2009

[7] *The Long Demise of Glass-Steagall*, Frontline, Public Broadcasting Corporation (PBS, Online); Eric Dash and Louise Story, *Rubin Leaving Citigroup; Smith Barney for Sale*, N.Y. Times (Online), Jan. 9, 2009

[8] *A Detailed Description of CBO's Cost Estimate for the Medicare Prescription Drug Benefit*, Congressional Budget Office (CBO) (Online), Jul. 1, 2004

[9] William M. Welch, *Tauzin Switches Sides from Drug Industry Overseer to Lobbyist*, USA Today (Online), Dec. 15, 2004

[10] Kathy Kristof, *Unions' Advice Is Failing Teachers*, L.A. Times (Online), Apr. 25, 2006

[11] Danny Hakim, *Union-Paid Actuary Was Off by $500 Million on Pension Costs, Records Show*, N.Y. Times, June 3, 2008, A23

[12] Karen W. Arenson, *Columbia to Pay $1.1 Million to State Fund in Loan Scandal*, N.Y. Times (Online), Jun. 1, 2007

[13] Michael J. de la Merced, *Del Monte and Barclays Settle Lawsuit for $89 Million*, N.Y. Times, Oct. 7, 2011, B7

[14] U.S. Attorney's Office, *C. Ray Nagin, Former New Orleans Mayor, Convicted on Federal Bribery, Honest Services Wire Fraud, Money Laundering, Conspiracy and Tax Charges*, Federal Business of Investigation (FBI) (Online), Feb. 12, 2014; Matt Smith and Deanna Hackney, *Ex-New Orleans Mayor Ray Nagin Guilty After Courtroom "Belly Flop,"* CNN (Online), Feb. 14, 2014; Mark Berman, *Former New Orleans Mayor Ray Nagin Sentenced to 10 Years in Prison,* Washington Post (Online), Jul. 9, 2014

[15] *Definition of Kickback*, Free Dictionary by Farlex (Legal, Online), (last visited Dec. 14, 2014)

[16] *Bribery*, The Free Dictionary by Farlex (Legal, Online), (last visited Dec. 14, 2014)

[17] Chad Bray, *Ex-Chief Crane Inspector Admits Taking Bribes*, Wall St. Journal, Mar. 24, 2010, A8; Colleen Long, Associated Press, *Ex-NYC Crane Inspector Sentenced for Bribery*, NBC News (Online), June 16, 2010

[18] U.S. Attorney's Office, *New York State Assemblyman William F. Boyland, Jr. Convicted on Bribery, Fraud, Extortion, Conspiracy, and Theft Charges*, Federal Bureau of Investigation (FBI, Online) Mar. 6, 2014

[19] *Crooked Congressman Going to Prison*, CNN (Online), Mar. 3, 2006

[20] Associated Press, *Democratic Congressman Jefferson Reporting to Prison in Two Weeks*, Fox News (Online), Apr. 20, 2012

[21] Press Release, *California Company, Its Two Executives and Intermediary Convicted by Federal Jury in Los Angeles on All Counts for Their Involvement in Scheme to Bribe Officials at State-Owned Electrical Utility in Mexico*, Department of Justice (Online), May 10, 2011; Mike Koehler, *The Verdict Is in on Lindsey Manufacturing Company Case,* Corporate Compliance Insights (Online), May 12, 2011

[22] Leslie Wayne, *Hits, and Misses, in a War on Bribery*, N.Y. Times (Online), Mar. 10, 2012

[23] Associated Press, *Tom Noe, Convicted GOP Fundraiser, Appeals Conviction*, Cleveland Plain Dealer (Online), June 8, 2011; James Dao, *Coins Go Missing, and G.O.P. Insider Becomes Outcast*, N.Y. Times (Online), May 28, 2005; John Robinson Block, *State of Turmoil: The Coingate Scandal* (A Note from the Publisher), Toledo Blade (Online), April, 2005

[24] Patrick McGreevey and Noam N. Levey, *Kaiser Puts Ticket Tab at $250,000*, L.A. Times, Feb. 26, 2004, B1

[25] *Update: UCLA Professor to Repay Charity. Under Settlement,* Chronicle of Philanthropy (Online), Dec. 7, 2009; Raja Abdulrahim, *UCLA Surgeon Sued for Benefiting from His Own Charity.* L.A. Times (Online), Sept. 10, 2009

[26] James E. Hall, et al., *$4.1 Million Award for Violating Fiduciary Duty,* Workforce (Online), Dec. 18, 2007

Chapter 15: *Commandment of Trust #4: Care*

[1] Margot Roosevelt, *Man Wins $1.68 Million in Scuba Case*, L.A. Times, Oct. 24, 2010, A43

[2] *What Is Gross Negligence*, The Free Dictionary by Farlex (Legal, Online), (last visited Dec. 14, 2014)

3 *Property Owners' Legal Duty to Prevent Injury*, FindLaw (Online), (last visited Dec. 14, 2014)

4 Alex Tresniowski, *Deaths in the Desert*, People (Online), Nov. 9, 2009; Associated Press, Bob Ortega, *Self-Help Guru Gets Multiple Years in Sweat Lodge Deaths*, The Arizona Republic, USA Today (Online), Nov.18, 2011

5 Jean Bravin, *High Court Eases Way to Liability Lawsuits*, Wall St. Journal, Mar. 5, 2009, A1; David G. Savage, *Right to Sue Drug Makers Is Affirmed*, L.A. Times, Mar. 5, 2009, A1; Jerry Markon, *High Court Case Looms Large for Drugmakers*, Washington Post (Online), Nov. 4, 2008

6 Joseph Pereira, *How Credit-Card Data Went Out Wireless Door*, Wall St. Journal, May 4, 2007, A1; Joseph Pereira and Robin Sidel, *TJX in Security–Breach Deal*, Wall St. Journal, Dec. 3, 2007, A16

7 *500 Million Sensitive Records Breached Since 2005*, Privacy Rights Clearinghouse (Online), Aug. 26, 2010

8 Paul Nowell, Associated Press, *Bank of America Loses Tapes with Federal Workers' Data*, Washington Post (Online), Feb. 26, 2005

9 Hope Yen, *VA Identity Theft Scandal Growing*, L.A. Daily News, Jun 7, 2006, News-8; Associated Press, *DSW Data Theft Much Worse Than Predicted*, USA Today (Online), Apr. 19, 2005; Reuters, *Citigroup Reports Loss of Data*, L.A. Times, Jun. 7, 2005, C3

10 Jonathan T. Rubens, *So Many Privacy Rules!* , Business Law Today, July/Aug. 2009, 55; Nick Akerman, *Protecting Personal Data*, National Law Journal, Dec. 3, 2007, 12

11 Kevin M. LaCroix, *FDIC's Latest Failed Bank Lawsuit Targets Bank's Lawyers*, The D & O Diary (Online), Oct. 28, 2011; Becky Yerak, *Dozen Real Estate Loans at Center of FDIC's $127M Suit in Mutual Bank Failure*, Chicago Tribune (Online), Nov. 1, 2011

12 Daniel Hays, *Deloitte & Touche to Pay $40 M in Reliance Case*, Property Casualty 360 (Online), A National Underwriter Website, Nov. 25, 2008

13 Press Release, *SEC Charges Detroit-Area Stock Broker Who Lured Elderly into $250 Million Ponzi Scheme*, U.S. Securities and Exchange Commission (SEC, Online), Sept. 28, 2009

14 Bloomberg News, *S.E.C. Punishes 8 Workers in Errors Tied to Madoff*, N.Y. Times, Nov. 12, 2011, B6

15 Andrew Ackerman, *SEC Discipline over Madoff*, Wall St. Journal, Nov. 12–13. 2011, B1

Chapter 16: *Commandment of Trust #5: Account*

1 *The Revenue Outlook*, Congressional Budget Office (CBO) (Online); Melissa Braybrooks, Julio Ruiz, Elizabeth Accetta, *State Government Tax Collections Summary Report: 2010* (Online), Mar. 10, 2011

2 Jeffrey M. Jones, *Americans Say Federal Gov't Wastes over Half of Every Dollar*, Gallup (Online), September 19, 2011

3 Floyd Norris, *Distortions in Baffling Financial Statements*, N.Y. Times (Online), Nov. 11, 2011

4 Christopher Farrell, *Do-Gooders Doing Mischief*, BloombergBusinessweek, Apr. 21, 2008, 18

5 *Ibid.*

6 *Ibid.*

7 Sharon Hoffman, *For U.S. Charities, A Crisis of Trust*, MSNBC (Online), Nov. 21, 2006

8 *Ibid.*

9 Jose Martinez and Corky Siemaszko, *Brooke Astor Son Anthony Marshall Sentenced to 1 to 3 Years in Prison for Fleecing Mother out of Estate*, N.Y. Daily News, Dec. 21, 2009; Mallory Simon and Beth Karas, *Brooke Astor's Son Sentenced to Prison*, CNN (Online), Dec. 21, 2009; Jessica Ravitz and Beth Karas, *Brooke Astor's Son, His Lawyer Guilty of Bilking*

Estate, CNN (Online), Oct. 8, 2009; Sean Gardiner, *Astor's Son Imprisoned*, Wall St. Journal (Online), Jun. 21, 2013

[10] *Definition of Fiduciary*, Free Dictionary by Farlex (Online), (last visited Dec. 14, 2014)
[11] Dennis J. Carroll, *New Mexico Sheriff Faces Possible Jail Term over eBay Sales*, Reuters (Online), Jul. 21, 2011
[12] *Definition of Accounting*, Investor Words (Online), (last visited Dec. 14, 2014)
[13] *See, e.g.,* Section 108 (d) of the Sarbanes-Oxley Act of 2002 directing the Securities and Exchange Commission (SEC) to study ways to shift U.S. G.A.A.P. accounting standards from detailed rules back to general principles, *Study Pursuant to Section 108(d) of the Sarbanes-Oxley Act of 2002 on the Adoption by the United States Financial Reporting System of a Principles-Based Accounting System,* U.S. Securities and Exchange Commission (SEC) (Online); *see also,* Jonathan C. Dickey (Gibson, Dunn & Crutcher, LLP), *Litigation Against Accountants and Lawyers: The Year of Living Dangerously*, West Legal Works, 17th Annual Litigation and Resolution of Complex Class Actions Workshop, Gibson, Dunn & Crutcher, LLP (Online), Nov. 1–2, 2007
[14] Steve Leisman, *SEC Accounting Cop's Warning: Playing by Rules May Not Ward Off Fraud Issues*, Wall St. Journal, Feb. 12, 2002, C1
[15] *The High Cost of Fraud*, Corporate Counsel, Feb. 2004, 23
[16] Michael Rapoport, *Ernst & Young Agrees to Pay $99 Million in Lehman Settlement,* Wall St. Journal (Online), Oct. 18, 2013
[17] *Ibid.*
[18] *Litigation Release No. 19260*, U.S. Securities and Exchange Commission, (SEC) (Online), Jun.9, 2005
[19] *Ibid.*
[20] Michael Wilson and William Rashbaum, *Real Patients, Real Doctors, Fake Everything Else*, N.Y. Times, Oct. 13, 2010 (Online); for additional instances of federal fraud, *see, e.g.,* Chris Edwards and Tad DeHaven, *Downsizing the Federal Government*, CATO Institute (Online), downsizinggovernment.org, Aug. 2009
[21] *Ibid.*
[22] Anemona Hartocollis, *City to Pay $70 Million in Medicaid Suit*, N.Y. Times (Online), Oct. 31, 2011
[23] Garrett Therolf, *County Auditors Find Much Fraud*, L.A. Times, May 27, 2010, AA1
[24] *Grand Jury Indicts Bell's Rizzo, Spaccia on New Charges*, KTLA News (Online), Mar. 30, 2011; Jeff Gottlieb, et al., *6 Charged in Bell Corruption Case Reject Plea Deal*, L.A. Times (Online), Feb. 7, 2011
[25] Corina Knoll, *Bell Official Thought Loans Legal*, L.A. Times, Mar. 1, 2011, AA3
[26] Jaime Holguin, *Disaster Strikes in Red Cross Backyard*, CBS News (Online), Feb. 11, 2009
[27] *Ibid.*
[28] Jim McElhatton, *GSA Scandal Widens; Dozens of Conferences Now under Investigation*, Washington Times (Online), Aug. 1, 2012
[29] Brian Satterfield, *5 Tales of Outrageous Expense Account Abuse*, Human Resources World (HRWorld) (Online), May 29, 2008
[30] Michael Rothfeld, *State Consumer Chief Quits Amid Cost Questions*, L.A. Times, Mar. 28, 2009, A3
[31] Steve Vogel, *Obama Appointee at Labor Resigns after Ethics Probe*, Washington Post (Online), Jul. 28, 2011
[32] Jim Dwyer, *Inflated Bills? Kickbacks? Just the Start*, N.Y. Times, Jul. 13, 2011, A20; David W. Chen and William K. Rashbaum, *City Payroll Project Was Riddled with Fraud, U.S. Says,* N.Y. Times, Jun. 21, 2011, A21; Michael M. Grynbaum, *Contractor Strikes $500 Million Deal in City Payroll Scandal,* N.Y. Times (Online), Mar. 14, 2012

[33] Ralph Vartabedian, *Photocopies Cost More Than Copier*, L.A. Times, Mar. 21, 2003, A28

[34] Juliet Williams, Associated Press, *State's Pension Woes Detailed*, L.A. Daily News, Dec. 14, 2011, A4

[35] Damian Paletta, *Billions in Bloat Uncovered in Beltway*, Wall St. Journal, Mar. 1, 2011, A1

[36] Matthew Cole, *$9 Billion in Iraq Reconstruction Funds Missing*, ABC News (Online), Aug. 2, 2010

[37] Associated Press, *Government Checks Sent to Dead People*, New Haven Register (Online), Jun. 19, 2010

[38] *Disbarments, James Friend Jordan*, California Bar Journal (Online), January 2012

[39] *See e.g.*, DR 9-102, *Preserving Identity of Fund and Property of a Client*, ABA Model Code of Professional Responsibility (1983), Legal Information Institution (LII), Cornell University Law School (Online), (last visited Dec. 14, 2014)

Chapter 17: *Commandment of Trust #6: Property*

[1] Peter Voettke, *The Role of Private Property in a Free Society*, The Virginia Institute (Online), Apr. 2005; *see also*, Nicholas Wade, *Girl's Bones Bear Sign of Cannibalism by Starving Virginia Colonists*, N.Y. Times (Online), May 1, 2013

[2] *Ibid.*

[3] Elizabeth Eaves, *Shining a Light on Shadow Economies*, Forbes, Dec. 14, 2009, 21

[4] Hernando de Soto, *Toxic Assets Were Hidden Assets*, Wall St. Journal, Mar. 25, 2009, A13

[5] Thom Weidlich, *Banks Lose Pivotal Foreclosure Case in Massachusetts High Court*, Bloomberg (Online), Jan. 7, 2011

[6] Christopher Lewis Peterson, *Two Faces: Demystifying the Mortgage Electronic Registration System's Land Title Theory*, William & Mary Law Review, Vol. 53, No. 1, 2011, 114, (available at SSRN:http://ssrn.com/ abstract=1684729), (last visited Dec. 14, 2014)

[7] *Ibid.* at 115, citing 76 C.J.S. Registers of Deeds Sec. 4 (2011)

[8] Michael Powell and Gretchen Morgenson, *MERS? It May Have Swallowed Your Loan*, N.Y. Times (Online), Mar. 5, 2011; for a discussion of MERS *see* Thomas Kilpatrick, *Mortgage Electronic Registration System (MERS): A Twenty First Century Creation Navigating an Eighteenth Century Legal System*, National Law Review (Online), Dec. 13, 2011

[9] Stephanie Armour, *Fight Over Who Has Legal Right to Foreclose Makes Mess Worse*, USA Today (Online), Oct. 11, 2010

[10] *Nevada Supreme Court Upholds Two Trial Court Decisions in Favor of MERS*, MERS, mersinc.org, Dec. 21, 2012; Michelle Conlin, *State Court Ruling Deals Blow to U.S. Bank Mortgage System*, Reuters (Online), Sept. 14, 2012

[11] Thomas Kilpatrick, *Mortgage Electronic Registration System (MERS), supra* note 8

[12] Pallavi Gogoi, Associated Press, *Robo-Signing Scandal May Date Back to the Late 1990s*, NBC News (Online), Sept. 1, 2011

[13] Tim Reid, *Insight: Evidence Suggests Anti-Foreclosure Laws May Backfire*, Reuters (Online), Jun. 27, 2012

[14] Jeff Horwitz, *Nevada Files First Criminal Charges, In Robo-Signing Case*, American Banker (Online), Nov. 16, 2011

[15] Gretchen Morgenson, *Company Faces Forgery Charges in Mo. Foreclosures*, N.Y. Times (Online), Feb. 6, 2012

[16] Reuters, *New York Sues 3 Big Banks over Mortgage Database*, N.Y. Times (Online), Feb. 3, 2012

[17] Krista Franks, *Robo-Signing Settlement Finalized*, DS News (Online), Feb. 9, 2012

[18] Linda Greenhouse, *Justices Rule Cities Can Take Property for Private Development*, N.Y. Times (Online), Jun. 23, 2005; *Kelo vs. New Longdon* (04-108) 545 U.S. 469 (2005), 268

Conn. 1,843 A. 2d 500, affirmed, June 23, 2005, Legal Information Institution (LII), Cornell University Law School (Online)

[19] Silla Brush, *Real Angry over Real Estate*, U.S. News & World Report, Oct. 10, 2005, 34; *Property Rights and Eminent Domain: Hands Off Our Homes*, Economist (Online), Aug. 15, 2005

[20] Larry Morandi, *State Eminent Domain Legislation and Ballot Measures*, National Conference of State Legislatures (Online), Jan. 1, 2012

[21] James W. Ely, Jr., *Regulatory Taking*, Answers (Online), Oxford Companion to the US Supreme Court, answers.com, (last visited Dec. 14, 2014)

[22] *What Is Intellectual Property?*, World Intellectual Property Organization (WIPO) (Online), (last visited Dec. 14, 2014)

[23] *The Uniform Trade Secrets Act* (UTSA), NDAs for Free (Online), ndasforfree.com (last visited Dec. 14, 2014), for a sample list of various intellectual property laws in the U.S., *see*, *United States of America: IP Laws and Treaties*, World Intellectual Property Organization (WIPO) (Online), (last visited Dec. 14, 2014)

[24] Ashby Jones, *A Good Day for J & J: Boston Scientific to Pay More in Stent Litigation*, Wall St. Journal (Online), Feb. 1, 2010

[25] *General Information Concerning Patents*, U.S. Patent and Trademark Office (Online), Nov. 2011

[26] *Trademark, Patent, or Copyright?* United States Patent and Trademark Office (Online), (last visited Dec. 14, 2014)

[27] Nick Wingfield, *Jury Awards $1 Billion to Apple in Samsung Patent Case*, N.Y. Times (Online), Aug. 24, 2012

[28] Andrew Pollack, *Monsanto Wins $1 Billion in a Biotech Patent Case*, N.Y. Times, Aug. 2, 2012, B1

[29] Gary Lauder, *New Patent Law Means Trouble for Tech Entrepreneurs*, Forbes (Online), Sept. 20, 2011

[30] Thomas Long, *Adidas Awarded Nearly $305 Million for Retailer's Infringement*, CCH Trademark Law Guide, Newsletter (Online), business.cch.com (last visited Dec. 14, 2014): *Adidas Sues Payless Again*, Portland Business Journal (Online), Apr. 3, 2009; Michael Valek, *Adidas Wins Big Trademark Dispute*, C/Net (Online), May 7, 2008

[31] *Trademark, Patent, or Copyright?*, U.S. Patent and Trademark Office (Online), (last visited Dec. 14, 2014), *Example of Trademark Devices*, BitLaw (Online), (last visited Dec. 14, 2014)

[32] *See, e.g.*, Jessica C. Kaiser, *Victor's Not So Little Secret: Trademark Dilution Is Difficult But Not Impossible to Prove Following Moseley v. V. Secret Catalogue, Inc.*, Chicago-Kent Law Review (Online), Feb. 23, 2005

[33] *Strength of Trademarks*, BitLaw (Online), (last visited Dec. 14, 2014)

[34] *Two Texas Men Guilty of Trafficking Counterfeit Goods at Mall Kiosks*, Federal Bureau of Investigation (FBI) (Online), Sept. 9, 2011

[35] News Releases, *Fifth Member of CD and DVD Counterfeiting Ring in Atlanta Sentenced to Prison*, Federal Bureau of Investigation (FBI) (Online), June 17, 2011

[36] C. J. Lin, *Suspects, Fake Goods Nabbed*, L.A. Daily News (Online), Dec. 7, 2011

[37] Kathy Chu, *Growing Problem of Fake Drugs Hurting Patients, Companies*, USA Today (Online), Sept. 13, 2010; Peter Loftus, *U.S. Probes Alleged Seller of Fake J & J Diabetes Monitors*, Wall St. Journal Apr. 8, 2010, B4

[38] Joseph Menn, *Napster Lawsuits Near Resolution*, L.A. Times, Mar. 27, 2007, C2; *The Napster Decision: Excerpts from Ruling by the 9th Circuit Court*, N.Y. Times (Online), Feb. 13, 2001

[39] For further discussion of copyrights, *see generally*, U.S. Patent and Trademark Office (Online); Richard, Stim, *Patent, Copyright & Trademark: An Intellectual Property Desk Reference*, 12th ed. (Berkeley: Nolo Press, 2012)

[40] Mitchell Zimmerman, *Copyright Basics for Non-Experts*, California Bar Journal, Feb. 2006, 14

[41] Richard, Stim, *Patent, Copyright & Trademark: An Intellectual Property Desk Reference*, 9th ed. (Berkeley: Nolo Press , 2007) 186, 324

[42] *Ibid.* at 190

[43] Cade Metz, *8 Years Later, Google's Book Scanning Crusade Rule "Fair Use,"* Wired (Online), Nov. 14, 2013

[44] *Copyright Law of the United States of America and Related Laws Contained in Title 17 of the United States Code (Chapter 5),* The U.S. Copyright Office (Online), (last visited Dec. 14, 2014)

[45] Press Release, *Final Guilty Plea in Operation Digital Gridlock, First Federal Peer-to-Peer Copyright Piracy Crackdown*, U.S. Department of Justice (Online), May 31, 2005 (in violation of Title 17, United States Code, Section 506, and Title 18, United States Code, Sections 371 and 2319); *U.S. Peer-to-Peer Pirates Convicted*, BBC (U.K., Online), Jan. 20, 2005; Press Release, *Leader of Internet Piracy Group "IMAGINE" Pleads Guilty to Copyright Infringement Conspiracy*, U.S. Department of Justice (Online), Aug. 29, 2012

[46] Press Release, *Two Members of Internet Piracy Group "IMAGiNE" Sentenced in Virginia for Criminal Copyright Conspiracy,* U.S. Department of Justice (Online), Nov. 2, 2012

[47] David Reyes, *Police Captain Pleads No Contest in DVD Piracy Case*, L.A. Times, Aug. 21, 2002, B3

[48] Ann Zimmerman, *Mattel Loses to Rival in Bratz Spat*, Wall St. Journal, Apr. 22, 2011, B1; Ann Zimmerman, *MGA Wins $309 Million in Bratz Spat with Mattel*, Wall St. Journal, Aug. 5, 2011, B3; Andrea Chang, *MGA Wins Big in Bratz Doll Trial*, L.A. Times, April 22, 2011, B1

[49] *Trade Secret: Definition*, Legal Information Institution (LII), Cornell University Law School (Online), (last visited Dec. 14, 2014)

[50] *Trade Secret Basics FAQ*, Nolo Press (Online), (last visited Dec. 14, 2014)

[51] *Protection of Trade Secrets,* United States Code, Title 18, Part II, Chapter 90, Sections 1831–1839, Legal Information Institute (LII), Cornell University Law School, (Online), (last visited Dec. 14, 2014)

[52] Andrew Harris, *Ex-Motorola Worker Gets 4 Years for Trade Secret "Raid,"* Bloomberg (Online), Aug. 29, 2012

[53] Cain Burdeau and Holbrook Mohr, Associated Press, *Choppy Seas Thwarting Efforts to Halt Relentless Spread of Crude*, L.A. Daily News, May 1, 2010, A1

[54] Julia Werdigier, *Moex, a Partner of BP, Is to Pay $1.1 Billion to Cover Some Damage from Oil Spill*, N.Y. Times, May 21, 2011, B3; Clifford Krauss, *BP Will Plead Guilty and Pay Over $4 Billion*, N.Y. Times (Online), Nov. 15, 2012; for a full description of the potential fines and penalties, *see*, Robert Meltz, *Federal Civil and Criminal Penalties Possibly Applicable to Parties Responsible for the Gulf of Mexico Oil Spill*, Congressional Research Service (Online), fas.org, Dec. 16, 2010; Campbell Robertson and Clifford Krauss, *BP May Be Fined for Spill in Gulf*, N.Y. Times, Sept. 5, 2014, A1

[55] For a more detailed list, *see, Laws and Executive Orders*, U.S. Environmental Protection Agency (EPA), (Online), (last visited Dec. 14, 2014)

[56] *Enforcement of Hazardous Waste Regulations*, U.S. Environmental Protection Agency (EPA) (Online), http://www.epa.gov/wastes/ inforesources/pubs/training/enforc.pdf, (last visited Dec. 14, 2014)

[57] Nicholas J. Nastasi and Jennifer A. DeRose, Saul Ewing LLP, *Federal Environmental Law: Criminal Enforcement*, Association of Corporation Counsel (Online), Feb. 1, 2012

[58] *AQMD's Enforcement Authority*, South Coast Air Quality Management District (Online), http://www.aqmd.gov/home/about/authority/ enforcement#8, (last visited Dec. 14, 2014)

[59] *Water Ruling: People Matter as Much as Fish*, ABC News (Online), May 18, 2010

[60] Bill Mears, *"Little Guy" Wins High Court Fight over Property Rights*, CNN (Online), Mar. 21, 2012

Chapter 18: *Commandment of Trust #7: People*

[1] *The Man Who Invented Management*, BloombergBusinessweek (Online), Nov. 28, 2005

[2] *Ibid.*

[3] *The 1935 Passage of the Wagner Act,* National Labor Relations Board (NLRB) (Online), (last visited Dec. 14, 2014)

[4] *1947 Taft-Hartley Act,* National Labor Relations Board (NLRB) (Online), (last visited Dec. 14, 2014)

[5] *1959 Landrum-Griffin Act*, National Labor Relations Board (NLRB) (Online), (last visited Dec. 14, 2014)

[6] *See., e.g., Man Suing City for Sexual Harassment, Wrongful Termination*, WFTV Channel 9 (Online), Jun. 1, 2007

[7] *See, e.g.,* Claire Gordon, *White Male Worker, Doug Carl, Wins $300,000 in "Reverse Discrimination" Suit*, AOL (Online), Aug. 31, 2012; Sophia Hall, *White Police Lieutenant Files Reverse Discrimination Lawsuit Against Mayor of Freeport*, CBS News New York (Online), Jan. 27, 2012

[8] Wyatt Andrews, *Supreme Court Hears Case on Affirmative Action*, CBS Evening News (Online), Oct. 10, 2012

[9] *Coca-Cola to Pay $192.5M to Settle Racial Discrimination Suit,* Insurance Journal (Online), Nov. 17, 2000; Davan Maharaj, *Coca-Cola to Settle Racial Bias Lawsuit*, L.A. Times (Online), Nov. 17, 2000

[10] *Civil Rights Act (1964),* Our Documents (Online), ourdocuments. gov, (last visited Dec. 14, 2014)

[11] For a general description of federal discrimination laws, *see, e.g., Federal Equal Employment Opportunity (EEO) Laws: Federal Laws Prohibiting Job Discrimination Questions and Answers,* U.S. Equal Employment Opportunity Commission (EEOC) (Online), (last visited Dec. 14, 2014)

[12] *Brochures and Posters*, California Department of Fair Employment and Housing (Online); dfeh.ca.gov; *Employment FAQ*, California Department of Fair Employment and Housing (Online), (last visited Dec. 14, 2014)

[13] This theory of discrimination law was created by the U.S. Supreme Court in the 1971 *Griggs v. Duke Power* case (judge-made American common law); *see, e.g., Griggs v. Duke Power,* North Carolina History Project (Online), (last visited Dec. 14, 2014)

[14] Robert Barnes, *Justices Rule for White Firemen in Bias Lawsuit*, Washington Post (Online), June 30, 2009; *Court Rules for White Firefighters in Discrimination Case*, Fox News (Online), Jun. 29, 2009; *Ricci v. DeStefano,* U.S. Supreme Court, Legal Information Institute (LII), Cornell University Law School (Online), Jun. 29, 2009

[15] *Equal Protection: An Overview,* Legal Information Institute (LII), Cornell University Law School (Online), (last visited Dec. 14, 2014)

[16] Kathy Bergen and Carol Kleiman, *Mitsubishi Will Pay $34 Million*, Chicago Tribune (Online), Jun 12, 1998; *Mitsuibishi Settles for $34 Million*, CNN (Online), Jun. 11, 1998; Stephen Braun, *Mitsubishi to Pay $34 Million in Sex Harassment Case*, L.A. Times (Online), Jun. 12, 1998

[17] Eyder Peralta, *Top New York ICE Officer Sues Napolitano for Discrimination Against Men*, National Public Radio (NPR) (Online), Aug. 10, 2012

[18] Erika Slife, *Cook County Told to Pay $7.6 Million in Hospital Retaliation Lawsuit*, Chicago Tribune (Online), Dec. 14, 2011

[19] This comes from judge-made American common law: *Robinson v. Shell Oil Co.* (1996), Findlaw (Online), (last visited Dec. 14, 2014)

[20] Wire Staff, *Prosecutor: 9 Teens Charged in Bullying That Led to Girl's Suicide*, CNN (Online), Mar. 29, 2010; *More Mass. Teens Plead in Bully-Suicide Case*, Gainsville Sun (Online), May 5, 2011; Russell Goldman, *Teens Indicted After Allegedly Taunting Girl Who Hanged Herself*, ABC News (Online), Mar. 29, 2010

[21] *Iowa Paper Devotes Front Page to Fighting Bullying*, Fox News (Online), Apr. 22, 2012

[22] *Dharun Ravi*, N.Y. Times (Online), Dec. 30, 2012

[23] *Policies & Laws*, Stop Bullying (Online), stop bullying.gov, (last visited Dec. 14, 2014)

[24] John E. Richardson, and Linnea B. McCord, *Are Workplace Bullies Sabotaging Your Ability to Compete*, Graziadio Business Report (Online), Fall 2001, citing, Dr. Harvey Hornstein, *Brutal Bosses and Their Prey: How to Identify and Overcome Abuse in the Workplace* , and Gary and Ruth Namie, *The Bully at Work: What You Can Do to Stop the Hurt and Reclaim Your Dignity on the Job*

[25] *Ibid.*, citing Noa Davenport, Ruth Schwartz, and Gail Pursell Elliott, *Mobbing: Emotional Abuse in the American Workplace* (Ames, Iowa: Civil Society Publishing, 1999) at 5

[26] Kris Maher, *Feds Blame Owner of the Mine*, Wall St. Journal, Dec. 7, 2011, A3; Cliff Weathers, *CEO of Coal Mine Where 29 Workers Died Is Indicted,* Alternet (Online), Nov. 14, 2014

[27] News Release, *U.S. Department of Labor's OSHA Issues Record-Breaking Fines to BP*, U.S. Department of Labor, Occupational Safety and Health Administration (OSHA, Online), Oct. 30, 2009

[28] *Significant Workers' Compensation Settlements, Allman v. Union Butterfield (2000)*, Ganly & Ramer, PLLC (Online), (last visited Dec. 14, 2014)

[29] Steven Greenhouse and Stephanie Rosenbloom, *Wal-Mart to Settle Suits Over Pay for $352 Million*, N.Y. Times, Dec. 24, 2008, B1; Andrea Chang, *Wal-Mart Settles Suits by Workers*, L.A. Times, Dec. 24, 2008, C1

[30] Steve Lohr, *Quiet Layoffs Sting Workers without Notice*, N.Y. Times, Mar. 6, 2009, A1

[31] Toya Cirica Cook Haley, *When Johnny Marches Home,* Corporate Counsel, May 2003, 67

Chapter 19: *Commandment of Trust #8: Promises*

[1] *Definition: Promise*, Free Dictionary by Farlex (Legal, Online), (last visited Dec. 14, 2014)

[2] Edvard Pettersson and Valerie Reitman, *ICO Wins $236 Million Punitive Damages Against Boeing (Update2),* Bloomberg (Online), Oct. 31, 2008; Edvard Pettersson, *Boeing Wins Reversal of $604 Million ICO Global Verdict,* Bloomberg Business (Online), Apr. 13, 2012

[3] Tamar Lewin, *Pennzoil-Texaco Fight Raised Key Questions*, N.Y. Times (Online), Dec. 19, 1987

[4] Kimbriell Kelly, *Lenders Seek Court Actions against Homeowners Years after Foreclosure*, Washington Post (Online), Jun. 16, 2013

[5] Jessica Silver-Greenberg, *House Is Gone but Debt Lives On*, Wall St. Journal, Oct. 1, 2011

[6] *Ibid.*

[7] *See, e.g., Statute of Limitations on Judgments*, Card Report (Online), (last visited Dec. 14, 2014)

[8] *Hoffman v. Red Owl Stores, Inc. (1965)*, Case Briefs, Bloomberg Law (Online), (last visited Dec. 14, 2014)

[9] *Promissory Estoppel Law & Legal Definition*, U.S. Legal Definitions (Online), (last visited Dec. 14, 2014), *Promissory Estoppel*, Contract Law Cases (Online), Nov. 1, 2008

[10] *HealthSouth, Recovery of Amounts Due from Richard M. Scrushy*, Wikinvest (Online), (last visited Dec. 14, 2014)

Chapter 20: *Commandment of Trust #9: Leadership*

[1] *See, e.g.,* Rajeev Peshawaria, *The Great Training Robbery: Why the $60 Billion Investment in Leadership Development Is Not Working,* Forbes (Online), Nov. 1, 2011

[2] *National Leadership Index 2011*, Center for Public Leadership, Harvard Kennedy School (Online), (last visited Dec. 31, 2012); *see also,* John Baldoni, *Americans' Confidence in Leaders Hits a New Low,* CBS Money Watch (Online), (last visited Dec. 14, 2014)

[3] *National Leadership Index 2011, supra,* note 2

[4] *Ibid.*

[5] *Ibid.*

[6] *George Washington's Commission as Commander in Chief,* Primary Documents in American History, Web Guides, The Library of Congress (Virtual Service, Digital Reference Section) (Online), (last visited Dec. 14, 2014)

[7] Alma H. Burton, *Four American Patriots: The Story of Andrew Jackson,* Heritage History (Online), (last visited Dec. 14, 2014)

[8] *Ulysses S. Grant, American President: A Reference Source,* Miller Center, University of Virginia (Online), (last visited Dec. 14, 2014)

[9] *William Tecumseh Sherman Quotes*, Brainy Quote (Online), (last visited Dec. 14, 2014)

[10] Eloise Lee, *The Chilling Letter Eisenhower Drafted in Case the Nazis Won on D-Day*, Daily Finance (Online), Jun. 6, 2012

[11] Alex Altman, *Chesley B. Sullenberger, III*, Time (Online), Jan. 16, 2009; *Sully Sullenberger Performs Miracle on the Hudson*, This Day in History, (Online), history.com, Jan. 15, 2009

[12] George Orwell, *Animal Farm* (New York: Penguin Putnam, Inc., 1946)

[13] Jon Meacham, *Keeping the American Dream Alive*, Time, Jul. 2, 2012, 35

[14] *See,* Chapter 7

[15] Nathan Koppel, *Lee Farkas Gets 30-Year Sentence*, Wall St. Journal, Jul. 2, 2011 (Online)

[16] Joe Flint, *Comcast CEO Fined $500,000 to Settle Antitrust Charges*, L.A. Times, Dec. 17, 2011, B3

[17] Press Release, *Former Chairman and CEO of Kellogg, Brown & Root Inc., Sentenced to 30 Months in Prison for Foreign Bribery and Kickback Schemes*, U.S. Department of Justice (Online), Feb. 23, 2012

[18] Aaron Smith, *Ex-WaMu Execs in $64 Million Settlement*, CNN Money (Online), Dec. 13, 2011

[19] Associated Press, *Ebbers Sentenced to 25 Years in Prison,* NBC News (Online), Jul 13, 2005

[20] Press Release, *BP CEP Tony Hayward to Step Down and Be Succeeded by Robert Dudley,* British Petroleum (BP) (Online), Jul. 27, 2010

[21] Chris Isidore, *Boeing CEO Out in Sex Scandal*, CNN Money (Online), Mar. 7, 2005

[22] *Scrushy Has a Tough Week*, White Collar Crime Prof Blog (Online), lawprofessors. typepad.com, Aug. 28, 2006

[23] Miguel Bustillo, *Best Buy CEO Quits in Probe,* Wall St. Journal (Online), Apr. 10, 2012

[24] Diana B. Henriques, *Madoff Is Sentenced to 150 Years for Ponzi Scheme*, N.Y. Times (Online), Jun. 29, 2009

[25] *Former American Tissue CEO Sent to Prison for 15 Years for $300 Million Fraud,* USA Today (Online), Sept. 25, 2006

[26] Alexei Barrionuevo, *Enron's Skilling Is Sentenced to 24 Years*, N.Y. Times (Online), Oct. 24, 2006

[27] Jeffrey Wolf, *$44 Million Forfeited by Former Qwest CEO Joe Nacchio Distributed to Fraud Victims*, Channel 9 NBC News (Online), May 3, 2012

[28] *Ex-Cendant Chair Forbes Loses Court Appeal*, The Star (Online), Oct. 2, 2007

[29] *Former CEO of Sweezy Construction Inc. Sent to Prison*, My Harlingen News (Online), Nov. 16, 2010

[30] Peter Lattman, *Rajaratnam Ordered to Pay $92.8 Million Penalty*, N.Y. Times (Online), Nov. 8, 2011

[31] *Executive Excess Part 1*, Public Broadcasting Corporation (PBS) (Online) News Hour, Dec. 2, 2002

[32] Kurt Badenhausen, *The World's Highest-Paid Athletes,* Forbes (Online), May 31, 2011; (also, in many cases the yearly compensation of athletes may include lucrative endorsement fees from independent third party companies, not just their salaries from their teams)

[33] Russell Adams, *Leveling the Playing Field,* Wall St. Journal, Apr. 1–2, 2006, 1

[34] Dorothy Pomerantz, ed. *The World's Most Powerful Celebrities,* Forbes (Online), May 16, 2012

[35] Dave Nemetz, *"Judge Judy" Tops Daytime Ratings in First Year Post-Oprah,* Yahoo! TV (Online), Jun. 8, 2012

[36] *Gordon E. Moore,* Encyclopaedia Britannica (Online), (last visited Dec. 14, 2014)

[37] *See. e.g.*, Shelly K. Schwartz, *Tipping Point for Combined Chairman and CEO*, CNBC (Online), Nov. 15, 2012

[38] Seth Lubove, *Disney's Sinergy*, Forbes (Online), Mar. 15, 2004

[39] *Coke CEO Roberto C. Goizueta Dies at 65,* CNN (Online), Oct. 18, 1997

[40] Neal St. Anthony, *McGuire's Payday Is a Shame, If Not a Crime*, Star Tribune (Online), Apr. 21, 2006

[41] Jessica M. Karmasek, *HealthSouth Founder Loses $2.9 Billion Appeal*, Legal Newsline (Online), Jan. 31, 2011

[42] *Interlocking Directorate*, The Free Dictionary by Farlex (Online), (last visited Dec. 14, 2014); for example, Vernon Jordan, attorney and close confidante of President Bill Clinton sat on nine boards, Jeff Gerth, *The First Friend—A Special Report; Being Intimate with Power, Vernon Jordan Can Wield It,* N.Y. Times (Online), Jul 14, 1996

[43] Douglas A. McIntyre and Brian Zajac, *Retirement Plan: The Corporate Boards That Love Ex-Politicans*, MSNBC News (Online), Jun. 13, 2012

[44] Big corporations are discovering common sense solutions: "Chief executives hired internally outlast [and] outperform their rivals." Rachel Emma Silverman and Lauren Weber, *An Inside Job: More Firms Opt to Recruit from Within*, Wall St. Journal, May 30, 2010, B1, B8

[45] Associated Press, *Scandal to Cost Ex-Fannie Mae Officers Millions*, N.Y. Times (Online), Apr. 19, 2008

[46] Brian Ross and Alice Gomstyn, *Lehman Brothers Boss Defends $484 Million in Salary, Bonus*, ABC Nightline (Online), Oct. 6, 2008; *see, also*, Walter Hamilton, et al., *Lehman Bros. Elite Stood to Get $700 Million*, L.A. Times (Online), Apr. 27, 2012

[47] Marcy Gordon, *Franklin Raines to Pay $24.7 Million to Settle Fannie Mae Lawsuit*, Seattle Times (Online), Apr. 18, 2008

[48] Michelle Kessler, *Excessive Executive Pay Lands on Front Burner Again*, USA Today (Online), Mar. 7, 2006

[49] Associated Press, *Embattled Home Depot CEO Nardelli Resigns, To Take $210 Million with Him,* Fox News (Online), Jan. 3, 2007

[50] *Ibid.*

[51] Kate Linebaugh and Joann S. Lublin, *For Retiring GE Executive, $89,000 a Month Not to Work*, Wall St. Journal, Aug. 2, 2012, B1

[52] *F.D.I.C. to Bank $139 Billion in GE Capital Debt*, N.Y. Times (Online), Nov. 12, 2008

[53] *See, e.g.*, Jesse Eisinger, *Challenging the Long-Held Belief in "Shareholder Value,"* N.Y. Times, Jun. 28, 2012, B5, discussing a new book written by Cornell Law School professor, Lynn A. Stout, *The Shareholder Value Myth* (Barrett-Koehler Publishers)

[54] John A. Byrne, with Lindsey Gerdes, *The Man Who Invented Management*, Bloomberg Businessweek (Online) Nov. 27, 2005

[55] Phil Izzo, *What Percent Are You?*, Wall St. Journal (Online), Oct. 19, 2011 (Online)

[56] Jamie Goldberg, *HUD Makes Salary Cap Permanent*, L.A. Times (Online), Jun. 6, 2012

[57] Jack Dolan, *Prison Doctor Gets Paid for Doing Little or Nothing*, L.A. Times (Online), Jul. 13, 2011

[58] Stephanie Strom, *Lawmakers Seeking Cuts Look at Nonprofit Salaries*, N.Y. Times (Online), Jul. 26, 2010

[59] *Ibid.*

[60] Kevin Flynn and Stephanie Strom, *Plum Benefit to Cultural Post: Tax-Free Housing*, N.Y. Times (Online), Aug. 9, 2010

[61] P.B. Gray, *Inside the Chamber*, CFO Magazine, June 2006, 64

[62] Robin Pogrebin, *Smithsonian Ex-Chief Criticized in Report*, N.Y. Times, Jun. 21, 2007, B1

[63] *Top 25 Compensation Packages*, Charity Watch (Online), May/Jun. 2013

[64] Facts and Figures, *Highest-Paid Public-College Presidents, 2011 Fiscal Year*, Chronicle of Higher Education (Online), May 20, 2012; (in descending order: Ohio State, Texas A & M, Pennsylvania State at University Park, University of Kentucky, University of Michigan, Texas Tech, University of Texas, University of Minnesota-Twin Cities, University of Central Florida, Virginia Tech)

[65] Facts and Figures, *Highest-Paid Private College Presidents, 2009 Fiscal Year*, Chronicle of Higher Education (Online), Dec. 5, 2011, http:// chronicle.com/article/Executive-Co (in descending order: Drexel, Johns Hopkins, University of the Pacific, Northwestern, Vanderbilt, Mountain State, Rensselaer Polytechnic Institute, Swarthmore College, Yale, Chapman)

[66] Michael McDonald, *Nine Public College Presidents Paid More Than $1 Million*, Bloomberg (Online), May 19, 2014

[67] Sarah Ryley, *The Daily Exclusive: Minimum Rage: Grocery Workers Stunned by Fat-Cat Union Boss' Salary: $528,000*, The Daily (Online), Apr. 30, 2012

[68] Review & Outlook, *Fun Union Facts*, Wall St. Journal, Sept 19, 2006, A20

[69] Carl Horowitz, *Boilermakers Bosses Receive Excessive Salaries, Benefits*, National Legal and Policy Center (NLPC) (Online), May 25, 2012

[70] Perry Chiaramonte, *Average Teacher Makes $44,000 While Their Top Union Bosses Pull in Nearly $500,000*, Fox News (Online), Jul. 14, 2012

[71] Sarah Posner, *John Hagee's Controversial Gospel*, The American Prospect (Online), Mar. 12, 2008

[72] Preston Lauterbach, *Church of God in Changeover*, Memphis Flyer (Online), Nov. 8, 2007

[73] Rebecca Barnes and Lindy Lowry, *7 Startling Facts: An Up Close Look at Church Attendance in America*, Church Leaders, Schwartz Report (Online), (last visited Dec. 14, 2014); *see also*, *Taxpayers Pay for Televangelists' Lavish Lifestyles*, *Churches Damaged by Lack of Oversight and Disclosures*, Charity Watch (Online), Apr./May 2011

[74] Tom Vanden Brook, et al., *How Some Retired Military Officers Became Well-Paid Consultants*, USA Today (Online), Nov. 18, 2009

[75] *Walter Reed Hospital Workers Receive Furlough Notices*, ABC7 News (Online), May 30, 2013

Chapter 21: *Commandment of Trust #10: Enforcement*

[1] For a further discussion of the savings and loan crisis, *see, e.g.*, K. Calavita, et al., *The Savings and Loan Debacle, Financial Crime and the State,* Annual Review of Sociology, Vol. 23; 19–38, Aug. 1997, Annual Reviews (Online), (last visited Dec. 14, 2014)

[2] *Large Accounting Firm to Pay $186.5 Million in Audit Settlement with AM-Accounting Fines,* Associated Press (Online), Aug. 9, 1994; Robert A. Rosenblatt, *Accounting Firm to Pay U.S. Record Fine Over S & L Failures,* L.A. Times, Tech—Massachusetts Institute of Technology (MIT) (Online), Nov. 24, 1992

[3] Pillsbury Winthrop Shaw Pittman LLP, *The Private Securities Litigation Reform Act of 1995,* Find Law (Online), Mar. 26, 2008

[4] *3 Bell Leaders to Quit in Pay Scandal,* L.A. Times (Online), Jul. 23, 2010

[5] *Ibid.*; Catherine Saillant, *Bell-Style Civic Scrutiny Spreads,* L.A. Times, Feb. 21, 2011, A1

[6] Mike Ramsey, *Toyota in $1.1 Billion Gas-Pedal Settlement,* Wall St. Journal (Online), Dec. 27, 2012

[7] *CalPERS, 9,111 Retired California Government Workers Receive Pensions in Excess of $100,000 (and also for CalSTRS and UC),* California Pension Reform (Online), (last visited Dec. 14, 2014)

[8] *See, e.g., Top 100 Tax Delinquents,* State of Rhode Island, Division of Taxation, Department of Revenue (Online)

[9] *Patrick Henry Quotes,* Brainy Quotes (Online), (last visited Dec. 14, 2014)

[10] Linnea McCord and Michael Magasin, *The American Legal Dragon Awakens: Act Unethically, Expect Serious Pain,* The Clute Institute (Online), Vol. 8, No. 2, 2010

[11] Charles E. Cohen, *The Taxman Is Taking Almost All Willie Nelson Owns; Now It's His Turn for Some Farm Aid,* People (Online), Mar. 4, 1991

[12] Michael Martinez, *Actor Wesley Snipes Reports to Prison to Begin Sentence,* CNN (Online), Dec. 9, 2010

[13] James Barron, *Despite Frantic Appeals, Helmsley Gets Four Years,* N.Y. Times (Online), Mar. 19, 1992

[14] *Casino Workers Sentenced for Tax Fraud,* Casino City Times (Online), Sept. 24, 2002

[15] Lynnley Browning, *Texas Law Firm Will Close and Settle Tax Shelter Case,* N.Y. Times (Online), Mar. 30, 2007

[16] Leslie Haggin Geary, *Tax Troubles of the Rich and Famous,* CNN Money (Online); Feb. 20, 2003

[17] Kaiser Saurborn & Mair, P.C. *The False Claims Act,* Find Law (Online), Mar. 26, 2008

[18] Cary O'Reilly and Daniel Golden, *Apollo Settles University of Phoenix Recruiting Suit (Update 3),* Bloomberg, Dec. 14, 2009

[19] Doug Lederman, *$78.5 Million Settles U. of Phoenix Case,* Inside Higher Education (Online), Dec. 15, 2009

[20] *See., e.g., The Military Whistleblower Protection Act,* United States Coast Guard, U.S. Department of Homeland Security (Online), Apr. 15, 2014; Ben Kerschberg, *The Dodd-Frank Act's Robust Whistleblowing Incentives,* Forbes (Online), Apr. 14, 2011

[21] Ben Kerschberg, *The Dodd-Frank Act's Robust Whistleblowing Incentives,* Forbes (Online), Apr. 14, 2011

[22] *Ibid.*

[23] *Thomas Jefferson Quotes,* Brainy Quotes (Online), (last visited Dec. 14, 2014)

[24] Stephen Taub, *Enron Settlements Hit Record $7 Billion,* CFO (Online), Aug. 3, 2005

[25] *B of A in Record Settlement with U.S. Over Bias Case,* MSNBC News (Online), Dec. 21, 2011

[26] David Gow, *Record U.S. Fine Ends Siemens Bribery Scandal,* The Guardian (U.K., Online), Dec. 15, 2008

27 N.Y. Times News Service, *Judge OKs a Settlement of $3.7 Billion on Fen-Phen*, Deseret News (Online), Aug. 29, 2000

28 Jonathan D. Glater, *8 Former Partners of KPMG Are Indicted*, N.Y. Times, (Online), Aug. 30, 2005

29 Associated Press, *BP OKs $20 Billion Escrow Fund, Halts Dividend*, MSNBC News (Online), Jun. 16, 2012

30 *Coca-Cola Settles Race Suit*, CNN Money (Online), Nov. 16, 2000

31 Michael Arndt, *Texaco to Pay Pennzoil $3 Billion*, Chicago Tribune News (Online), Dec. 20, 1987

32 Associated Press, *Richard Scrushy's Final Appeal of $2.9 Billion Verdict Rejected by Alabama Supreme Court*, Alabama Wire (Online), Apr. 15, 2011

33 Nathan Koppel, *Google Shells Out $500 Million to Settle Criminal Investigation*, Wall St. Journal (Online), Aug. 24, 2011

34 Shaheen Pasha, *Skilling Gets 24 Years*, CNN Money (Online), Oct. 24, 2006

35 Peter Lattman, *Galleon Chief Sentenced to 11-Year Term in Insider Case*, N.Y. Times (Online), Oct. 13, 2011

36 Samuel Rubenfeld, *Telecoms Exec Receives Longest FCPA Sentence Ever*, Wall St. Journal (Online), Oct. 26, 2011

37 Press Release, *Certified Nursing Assistant Sentenced to Jail Term for Criminal Negligence*, U.S. Department of Justice (Online), Feb. 7, 2011

38 Associated Press, *Ebbers Sentenced to 25 Years in Prison*, MSNBC News (Online), Jul. 13, 2005

39 *7 Year Prison Sentence in Dow AgroSciences Economic Espionage Case*, Womble Carlyle, Innovators at Law, Womble Carlyle Trade Secrets Blog (Online), Dec. 23, 2011

40 Press Release, *Cast Iron Pipe Manufacturer Sentenced for Environmental Crimes and Worker Safety Violations*, U.S. Department of Justice (Online), Apr. 24, 2009

41 *Ex-NASA Aide Sentenced in Contracts Conspiracy*, MSNBC News (Online), Nov. 18, 2012

42 *Adelphia Founder Sentenced to 15 Years*, CNN Money (Online), Jun. 20, 2005

43 Associated Press, *Former American Tissue CEO Sent to Prison for 15 Years for $300 Million Fraud*, USA Today (Online), Sept. 25, 2006

44 *Former CEO of Sweezy Construction Inc. Sent to Prison*, My Harlingen News (Online), Nov. 16, 2010

45 Peter Latman, *Rajaratnam Ordered to Pay $92.8 Million Penalty*, N.Y. Times (Online), Nov. 8, 2011

46 Dionne Searcey, *Qwest Ex-Chief Gets 6 Years in Prison for Insider Trading*, Wall St. Journal (Online), Jul. 28, 2007

47 Ed Stych, *List: 30 Ex-Petters Employees Agree to Pay Back $8.5 Million*, Minneapolis/St. Paul (Twin Cities) Business Journal (Online), Nov. 30, 2011

48 Investopedia, *Sentences for White-Collar Criminals: Too Harsh or Too Lenient?*, Forbes (Online), Jun. 8, 2012

49 Liz Moyer, *In Pictures: The Longest White-Collar Prison Sentences*, Forbes (Online), Jun. 24, 2009

50 Gregg Blesch, *Poulsen Sentenced to 30 Years, Parrett Gets 25*, Modern Healthcare (Online), Mar. 27, 2009

51 Stephen Taub, *Crumpler Appeal Doesn't Stand Up*, CFO (Online), Apr. 13, 2007

52 Andrew M. Harris, *Ex-National Lampoon CEO Tim Durham Gets 50 Years in Prison*, Bloomberg Business (Online), Nov. 30, 2012

53 Liz Moyer, *In Pictures: The Longest White-Collar Prison Sentences*, Forbes (Online), Jun. 24, 2009

54 *Ibid.*

[55] Diana B. Henriques, *Madoff Is Sentenced to 150 Years for Ponzi Scheme*, N.Y. Times (Online), Jun. 29, 2009; Associated Press, *Madoff Ordered to Forfeit More Than $170 Billion*, Fox News (Online), Jun. 27, 2009

[56] Zachary Howard, Reuters, *Ex-Cendant Chairman Gets Over 12 Years in Prison*, Washington Post (Online), Jan. 17, 2007

[57] Associated Press, *Richard Scrushy's Final Appeal of $2.9 Billion Verdict Rejected by Alabama Supreme Court*, Alabama Wire (Online), Apr. 15, 2011

[58] Jeanne Whalen, et al., *Glaxo Sets Guilty Plea, $3 Billion Settlement*, Wall St. Journal, Jul. 3, 2012, B1

[59] David Porter, Associated Press, *Lawyer Gets Longest-Ever Insider Trading Sentence*, Boston Globe (Online), Jun. 4, 2012

[60] Douglas Belkin, *Ohio Official Sentenced to 28 Years*, Wall St. Journal, Aug. 1, 2012, A3

Appendix B

[1] Karin Matussek, *Ex-Deutsche Bank CEO Brauer to Pay $456,000 to End Trial Over Kirch Case*, Bloomberg (Online), Dec. 19, 2011

[2] *Toronto Lawyer Sentenced to 39 Months for Insider Trading*, The Star (Online), Jan. 7, 2010

[3] *Taiwan Makes Bribe—Paying Illegal*, NDTV (Online), Jun. 8, 2011

[4] Rama Lakshmi, *7 Former Union Carbide Officials Sentenced to 2 Years for Bhopal Gas Tragedy*, Washington Post (Online), Jun 8, 2010

[5] *Japan's Ex-Livedoor CEO Found Guilty of Accounting Fraud*, Voice of America (Online), Nov. 1, 2009

[6] Samantha Pearson, *Brazil Sues Over Oil Spill*, Financial Times (Online), Dec. 14, 2011

[7] *Cotswold Geotechnical Fined £385,000 in First Corporate Manslaughter Conviction*, The Telegraph (U.K., Online), Feb. 17, 2011

[8] Aviation Daily, *Tiger Airways Awarded Damages of $4.7 Million in Suit Against Swissport*, Aviation Daily (Aviation Week) (Online), May 24, 2010, 6

[9] *Former French President Convicted of Corruption*, Dec. 14, 2011, Voice of America (Online), Dec. 14, 2011, Jan. 22, 2009

[10] Matt Hines, *Microsoft Pays EU in Full*, CNET News (Online), Jul. 2, 2004

Appendix C

[1] *Alibaba and the 2,236 Thieves*, The Economist, Feb. 26, 2011, 73

[2] Jun Wei and Janet L. McDavid, *China's Anti-Monopoly Law*, for abstract, *see* National Law Journal (Online), Oct. 15, 2007, 12 (last visited Dec. 14, 2014)

[3] Didi Tang, *China Official in Sex Case Gets Prison for Bribery*, Yahoo News (Online), Jun. 28, 2013

[4] David Barboza, *774 Arrests in China over Safety*, N.Y. Times, Oct. 30, 2007, C1

[5] Karby Leggett, *Charges Are Filed in Landmark Chinese Fraud Case*, Aug. 7, 2002, Wall St. Journal, A12

[6] *China Endorses Private Property*, BBC News (U.K., Online), Mar. 15, 2004

[7] Ira Phillips, *China's New Labor Law: A View from Foreign Business*, China Research Center (Online), Aug. 18, 2008

[8] Dan Harris, *China Contract Law: Going All Clear on Us Now*, China Law Blog (Online), Jun. 4, 2009

[9] Cui Xiaohuo, *Sanlu Ex-Boss Gets Life for Milk Scandal*, China Daily (Online), Jan. 22, 2009

[10] Alexa Olesen, *China Ex-Food and Drug Chief Executed*, Washington Post (Online), July 10, 2007

References and Resources

Frederick Lewis Allen, *Only Yesterday: An Informal History of the 1920s* (New York: Harper & Row, 1931)

W.B. Allen and Gordon Lloyd, ed. *The Essential Antifederalist*, 2nd ed. (Lanhan, Maryland, Rowman & Littlefield Publishers, Inc., 2002)

David Barton, *Original Intent: The Courts, the Constitution & Religion* (Aledo, Texas: Wallbuilders, 1996, 2010)

Jacques Barzun, *From Dawn to Decadence, 1500 to the Present: 500 Years of Western Cultural Life* (New York: HarperCollins Publishers, 2000)

Janine M. Benyus, *Biomimicry* (New York: Quill, William Morrow, 1997)

Adolf A. Berle & Gardiner C. Means, *The Modern Corporation & Private Property* (New Brunswick, USA: Transaction Publishers, 2007; originally published in 1932)

Richard Berstein and Ross H. Munro, *The Coming Conflict with China* (New York: Alfred A. Knopf, 1997)

William J. Berstein, *The Birth of Plenty: How the Prosperity of the Modern World Was Created* (New York: McGraw-Hill, 2004)

Bob Blaisdell, *The Wit and Wisdom of Abraham Lincoln, A Book of Quotations* (Mineola, New York: Dover Publications, Inc., 2005)

Louis E. Boone, *Quotable Business: Over 2,500 Funny, Irreverent, and Insightful Quotations about Corporate Life* (New York: Random House, 1992)

Gerard V. Bradley, *Religious Liberty in the American Republic* (Wash., D.C.: The Heritage Foundation, 2008)

H.W. Brands, *Andrew Jackson: His Life and Times* (New York: Random House, Inc., 2006)

H.W. Brands, *The First American: The Life and Times of Benjamin Franklin* (New York: Random House, Inc., 2000)

Tom Brokaw, *The Greatest Generation* (New York: Random House, 1998)

Richard Brookhiser, *George Washington on Leadership* (New York: Perseus Books Group, 2008)

Brian Brown, ed., *The Wisdom of the Chinese: Their Philosophy in Sayings and Proverbs* (New York: Garden City Publishing Co., Inc., 1938)

Tammy Bruce, *The Death of Right and Wrong* (New York: Random House, Inc., 2003)

Robert Bryce, *Pipe Dreams: Greed, Ego and the Death of Enron* (New York: Public Affairs, 2002)

Thomas Bulfinch, *Bulfinch's Mythology* (New York: The Modern Library, 2004)

Daniel Burstein and Arne de Keijzer, *Big Dragon: China's Future: What it Means for Business, the Economy and the Global Order* (New York: Simon & Schuster 1998)

Daniel Allen Butler, *"Unsinkable": The Full Story of the RMS Titanic* (Mechanicsburg, Pennsylvania, Stackpole Books, 1998)

David Callahan, *The Cheating Culture, Why More Americans are Doing Wrong to Get Ahead* (New York: Harcourt, Inc., 2004)

Scott Camazine, Jean-Louis Deneubourg, Nigel R. Franks, James, Sneyd, Guy Theraulaz, Eric Bonabeau, *Self-Organization in Biological Systems,* (Princeton: Princeton University Press, 2001)

Fritjof Capra, *The Web of Life: New Scientific Understanding of Living Systems* (New York: Doubleday, 1996)

Dan Carrison & Rod Walsh, *Semper Fi: Business Leadership the Marine Corps Way* (New York: American Management Association, 1999)

Gorton Carruth and Eugene Ehrlich, *The Harper Book of American Quotations* (New York: Wings Books, 1988)

Edward Chancellor, *Devil Take the Hindmost: A History of Financial Speculation* (New York: Farrar, Straus, Giroux, 1999)

Penny Colman, *Rosie the Riveter: Women Working on the Home Front in World War II* (New York: Random House Inc., 1995)

Joseph R. Conlin, *The Morrow Book of Quotations in American History* (New York: William Morrow & Co., 1984)

Michael L. Cooper, *Fighting for Honor: Japanese Americans and World War II* (New York: Houghton Mifflin Co., 2000)

Michael J. Crozier, Samuel P. Huntingon, Joji Watanuki, *The Crisis of Democracy* (New York: New York University Press, 1975)

Richard Dale, *The First Crash: Lesson From the South Sea Bubble* (Princeton: Princeton University Press, 2004)

Nonie Darwish, *Cruel and Unusual Punishment: The Terrifying Global Implications of Islamic Law* (Nashville: Thomas Nelson, 2008)

Noa Davenport, Ruth Schwartz, and Gail Pursell Elliott, *Emotional Abuse in the American Workplace* (Ames, Iowa: Civil Society Publishing, 1999)

Hernando de Soto, *The Mystery of Capital: Why Capitalism Triumphs in the West and Fails Everywhere Else* (New York: Perseus Books Group, 2000)

Gary Demar, *America's Christian Heritage*, (Nashville, Tenn: Broadman & Holman Publishers, 2003)

Harry S. Dent, Jr., *The Roaring 2000s* (New York: Simon & Schuster, 1998)

Peter F. Drucker, *The Age of Discontinuity: Guidelines to Our Changing Society* (New Brunswick: Transaction Publishers, 1969)

Peter F. Drucker, *Adventures of a Bystander* (New York: Harper & Row, 1978)

Peter F. Drucker, *Managing in the Next Society* (New York: St. Martin's Press, 2002)

Dinesh D'Souza, *What's So Great about America*? (Wash., D.C.: Regnery Publishing, 2002)

Dinesh D'Souza, *Illiberal Education: The Politics of Race and Sex on Campus* (New York: Random House, Inc. 1991)

Masayo Umezawa Duus, *Unlikely Liberators: The Men of the 100th and 442nd* (Honolulu: University of Hawaii Press, 1987)

John Eidsmoe, *Christianity and the Constitution: The Faith of Our Founding Fathers* (Grand Rapids, Michigan: Baker Book House Co., 1987)

Joseph J. Ellis, *Founding Brothers: The Revolutionary Generation* (New York: Vintage Books, 2000)

Joseph J. Ellis, *His Excellency: George Washington* (New York: Random House, Inc., 2004)

Marshall Everett, ed. *Wreck and Sinking of the Titanic: The Ocean's Greatest Disaster* (L.H. Walter, 1912)

William J. Federer, *America's God and Country: Encyclopedia of Quotations* (Coppell, Texas: Fame Publishing, Inc., 1994)

William J. Federer, *The Ten Commandments & Their Influence on American Law* (St. Louis, Missouri: Amerisearch, Inc., 2003)

Jay M. Feinman, *Law 101: Everything You Need to Know About the American Legal System* (New York: Oxford University Press, 2000)

Joseph Fletcher, *Moral Responsibility: Situation Ethics at Work* (Philadelphia, Pennsylvania: The Westminster Press, 1967)

Joseph Fletcher, *Situation Ethics: The New Morality* (Philadelphia, Pennsylvania: The Westminster Press, 1966)

Robert Flood, *Up With America: Rediscovering Our Christian Heritage* (Denver, Colorado: Accent Publications, Inc., 1984)

Robert William Fogel, *The Fourth Great Awakening* (Chicago: University of Chicago Press, 2002)

Jere Bishop Franco, *Crossing the Point: The Native American Effort in World War II* (Denton, Texas: University of North Texas Press, 1999)

Milton Friedman, *Capitalism and Freedom* (Chicago: University of Chicago Press, 2002)

Lawrence M. Friedman, *American Law: An Introduction*, 3rd ed. (New York: W.W. Norton & Co., 2005)

Lawrence Friedman, *Law in America: A Short History* (New York: Random House, 2002)

Lawrence M. Friedman, *American Law in the 20th Century* (New Haven: Yale University Press, 2002)

Thomas L. Friedman, *The World Is Flat: A Brief History of the Twenty-First Century* (New York: Farrar, Straus and Giroux, 2005)

Francis Fukuyama, *The End of History and the Last Man* (New York: Avon Books, 1992)

Francis Fukuyama, *Trust: The Social Virtues and the Creation of Prosperity* (New York: Simon & Schuster, 1995)

Mark A. Gabriel, *Islam and Terrorism: What the Quran Really Teaches About Christianity, Violence and the Goals of the Islamic Jihad* (Lake Mary, Florida: Front Line, A Strang Co., 2002)

John Kenneth Galbraith, *The Great Crash 1929* (Boston: Houghton Mifflin Company, 1954, 1988)

Charles B. Galloway, *Christianity and the American Commonwealth* (Powder-Springs, Georgia: American Vision, Inc., 2005)

John W. Gardner, *Living, Leading and the American Dream* (San Francisco: Jossey-Bass, 2003)

John W. Gardner, *In Common Cause: Citizen Action and How It Works* (New York, W.W. Norton & Co., 1973)

John W. Gardner, *On Leadership* (New York: Free Press, 1990)

Garet Garrett, *A Bubble That Broke The World* (Boston: Little, Brown, and Co., 1932)

Webb Garrison, *A Treasury of Titanic Tales* (Tennessee: Rutledge Hill Press, 1998)

Charles Gasparino, *Blood on the Street: The Sensational Inside Story of How Wall Street Analysts Duped a Generation of Investors* (New York: Free Press, 2005)

Newt Gingrich, *Rediscovering God in America: Reflections on the Role of Faith in Our Nation's History and Future* (Nashville, Tenn: Integrity House, 2006)

Robert A. Goldwin, *The Parchment to Power: How James Madison Used the Bill of Rights to Save the Constitution*, (Wash., D.C.: AEI Press, 1997)

Deborah Gordon, *Ants at Work* (New York: W.W. Norton & Co., 1999)

John Grafton ed., *The Declaration of Independence and Other Great Documents of American History 1775–1865* (Mineola, New York: Dover Publications, Inc., 2000)

Robert Graves, *The Greek Myths* (New York: Penguin Books, 1955)

Kenneth R. Gray, Larry A. Frieder, George W. Clark, Jr., *Corporate Scandals: The Many Faces of Greed, The Great Heist, Financial Bubbles, and the Absence of Virtue* (St. Paul, Minnesota: Paragon House, 2005)

Barbara Greenman, *A Treasury of American Quotations* (London: CRW Publishing Ltd., 2004)

George S. Grossman, ed., *The Spirit of American Law*, (Boulder, Colorado: Perseus Books Group, 2000)

Allen C. Guelzo, *Lincoln: A Very Short Introduction* (New York: Oxford University Press, 2009)

David Halberstam, *The Reckoning* (New York: Avon Books, The Hearst Corp., 1986)

Gary Hamel, *Leading the Revolution* (Boston: Harvard Business Press, 2000)

Lawrence E. Harrison and Samuel P. Huntington, ed. *Culture Matters: How Values Shape Human Progress* (New York: Perseus Books Group, 2000)

Timothy Harper, *The Complete Idiot's Guide to the U.S. Constitution* (New York: Penguin Group USA, Inc., 2007)

Robert L. Heilbroner, *The World Philosophers: The Lives, Times and Ideas of the Great Economic Thinkers* (New York: Simon & Shuster, 1953)

Eugene W. Hickok, *Why States? The Challenge of Federalism* (Wash., D.C.: The Heritage Foundation, 2007)

E.D. Hirsch, Jr., *Cultural Literacy: What Every American Needs to Know* (New York: Random House, Inc. 1988)

Richard Hofstadter, *The American Political Tradition & the Men Who Made It* (New York: Random House, Inc., 1973)

David L. Holmes, *The Faiths of the Founding Fathers* (New York: Oxford University Press, 2006)

Harvey A. Hornstein, *Brutal Bosses and Their Prey* (New York: The Berkley Publishing Group, 1996)

H. Wayne House, ed., *The Christian and American Law: Christianity's Impact on America's Founding Documents and Future Direction* (Grand Rapids, MI: Kregel Publications, 1998)

Philip K. Howard, *The Death of Common Sense: How Law is Suffocating America* (New York: Warner Books, Inc., 1994)

Philip K. Howard, *The Collapse of the Common Good: How America's Lawsuit Culture Undermines Our Freedom* (New York: Ballantine Publishing Group, 2001)

Samuel Huntington, *The Clash of Civilizations and the Remaking of the World Order* (New York: Touchstone Books, 1997)

Samuel Huntington, *Who Are We? The Challenges to America's National Identity* (New York: Simon & Schuster, 2004)

Charles Hurd, *A Treasury of Great American Quotations* (New York: Hawthorn Books, Inc., 1964)

James H. Hutson, *Religion and the Founding of the American Republic* (Washington, DC; The Library of Congress, 1998)

George B. deHuszar, Henry W. Littlefield, Arthur W. Littlefield, *Basic American Documents* (Ames, Iowa: Littlefield, Adams & Co., 1953)

Scott Ingram, *The Stock Market Crash of 1929: Landmark Events in American History* (Milwaukee: World Almanac Library, 2005)

H. Paul Jeffers, *The Complete Idiot's Guide to the Great Depression* (Indianapolis: Alpha, a Pearson Education Company, 2002)

Lynne W. Jeter, *Disconnected: Deceit and Betrayal at WorldCom* (Hoboken, New Jersey, John Wiley & Sons, Inc., 2003)

Paul Johnson, *George Washington: The Founding Father* (New York: HarperCollins Publisher, 2005)

Paul Johnson, *A History of the American People* (New York: HarperCollins Publishers, 1997)

Peter Krass, ed., *The Book of Leadership Wisdom: Classic Writings by Legendary Business Leaders* (New York: John Wiley & Sons, 1998)

Frederick Kershner, Jr., *Tocqueville's America: The Great Quotations* (Athens, Ohio: Ohio University Press, 1983)

Shoshanna Kirk, *Greek Myths: Tales of Passion, Heroism, and Betrayal* (San Francisco: Chronicle Books, 2005)

John P. Kotter, *Leading Change* (Boston: Harvard Business Press, 1996)

Ray Kurzweil, *The Singularity is Near: When Humans Transcend Biology* (New York: Viking, Penguin Publishing, 2005)

David E. Kyvig, *Daily Life in the United States, 1920-1940: How Americans Lived Through the "Roaring Twenties" and the Great Depression* (Chicago: Ivan R. Dee, 2002)

Frank Lambert, *The Founding Fathers and the Place of Religion in America* (Princeton, New Jersey: Princeton University Press, 2003)

David S. Landes, *The Wealth and Poverty of Nations: Why Some Are So Rich and Some So Poor* (New York: Norton, 1998, 1999)

Robert Lawson, *Watchwords of Liberty: A Pageant of American Quotations* (Boston, Mass: Little, Brown & Co., 1945)

Gabriel Richardson Lear, *Happy Lives and the Highest Good: An Essay on Aristotle's Nicomachean Ethics* (Princeton, New Jersey: Princeton University Press, 2004)

Arthur Levitt, with Paula Dwyer, *Take On the Street* (New York: Pantheon Books, 2002)

Michael Lewis, *Liar's Poker: Rising through the Wreckage of Wall Street* (New York: Penguin Books, 1989)

Michael Lewis, *The Big Short: Inside the Doomsday Machine* (New York: W.W. Norton & Co., Inc., 2010)

Seth Lipsky, *The Citizen's Constitution: Annotated Guide* (New York: Perseus Books Group, 2009)

Gordon Lloyd and Margie Lloyd, *The Essential Bill of Rights: Original Arguments and Fundamental Documents* (Lanham, MD: University Press of America, Inc., 1998)

Walter Lord, *A Night To Remember* (New York: Henry Holt and Co. 1955)

Charles Mackay, *Extraordinary Popular Delusions and the Madness of Crowds* (London: L.C. Page & Co., 1841)

J. P. Mayer, ed., in Alexis de Tocqueville's *Democracy in America* (New York: HarperCollins, 1969) (Originally published in 1835)

Michael J. Mazarr, *Global Trends 2005: An Owner's Manual for the Next Decade* (New York: St. Martin's Press, 1999)

Brion McClanahan, *The Politically Incorrect Guide to The Founding Fathers* (Wash. D.C., Regnery Publishing, Inc., 2009)

Robert S. McElvaine, ed., *Down & Out in the Great Depression: Letters from the "Forgotten Man"* (Chapel Hill, The University of North Carolina Press, 25th Anniversary, 2008)

Robert S. McElvaine, *The Great Depression: America, 1929-41* (New York: New York Times Books, 1984)

Robert S. McElvaine, *The Depression and New Deal: A History in Documents* (New York: Oxford University Press, 2000)

Richard McKeon, ed., *Introduction to Aristotle* (New York: The Modern Library, 1992)

Patricia and Fredrick McKissack, *Red-Tail Angels: The Story of the Tuskegee Airmen of World War II* (USA: Walker Publishing Co., Inc., 1995)

Chaplain Patrick McLaughlin, CDR, USN, *No Atheists in Foxholes: Prayers and Reflections from the Front* (Nashville, Tennessee: Thomas Nelson, 2008)

Bethany McLean and Peter Elkind, *The Smartest Guys in the Room: The Amazing Rise and Scandalous Fall of Enron* (New York: Penguin, 2003)

William G. McLoughlin, *Revivals, Awakenings, and Reform* (Chicago: University of Chicago Press, 1978)

James M. McPherson, *Abraham Lincoln and the Second American Revolution* (New York: Oxford University Press, 1991)

Hamish McRae, *The World in 2020: Power, Culture and Prosperity* (Boston: Harvard Business School Press, 1994)

Richard L. Means, *The Ethical Imperative: The Crisis in American Values* (Garden City, New York: Doubleday & Co., 1970)

Buckner F. Melton, Jr., ed., *The Quotable Founding Fathers* (New York: Fall River Press, 2008)

Nathan Miller, *New World Coming: The 1920s and the Making of Modern America* (New York: Scribner, 2003)

Margaret Miner and Hugh Rawson, *American Heritage Dictionary of American Quotations* (New York: Penguin Books, USA, 1997)

Margaret Miner and Hugh Rawson, *A Dictionary of Quotations From the Bible* (New York: Kensington Publishing Co., 1988)

Baron de Montesquieu, *The Spirit of the Laws* (New York: Hafner Publishing Company, 1949)

Randall K. Morck, ed., *A History of Corporate Governance Around the World*, National Bureau of Economic Research (Chicago: University of Chicago Press: 2007)

Audie Murphy, *To Hell and Back*, (New York: Henry Holt & Co., 2002)

Gary Namie and Ruth Namie, *The Bully at Work* (Naperville, Illinois: Sourcebooks, Inc., 2000)

Jacob Needleman, *The American Soul: Rediscovering the Wisdom of the Founders* (New York: Penguin Putnam, Inc., 2002)

Andrew Nikiforuk, *Pandemonium: How Globalization and Trade are Putting the World at Risk* (St. Lucia, Queensland, Australia: University of Queensland Press, 2006)

Michael Novak, *Business as a Calling: Work and the Examined Life* (New York: The Free Press, Simon & Schuster, 1996)

Michael Novak, *The Spirit of Democratic Capitalism* (New York: Simon and Schuster, 1982)

Walter K. Olson, *The Litigation Explosion: What Happened When America Unleashed the Lawsuit* (New York: Penguin Books U.S.A., Inc., 1991)

Walter K. Olson, *The Rule of Lawyers: How the New Litigation Elite Threatens America's Rule of Law* (New York: St. Martin's Press, 2003)

George Orwell, *Animal Farm: A Fairy Story* (New York: Penguin Putnam, Inc., 1946, 1996)

The Oxford Dictionary of Quotations: 3rd Edition, (Oxford: Oxford University Press, 1979)

Jay A. Parry, Andrew M. Allison, W. Cleon Skousen, *The Real George Washington* (National Center for Constitutional Studies, 1991, 2009)

Suzy Platt, *Respectfully Quoted, A Dictionary of Quotations: The Essential Reference Guide for Writers and Speechmakers* (New York: Barnes & Noble, 1993)

Jack N. Rakove ed., *The Annotated U.S. Constitution and Declaration of Independence*, (Cambridge, Mass: Harvard University Press, 2009)

Nancy B. Rapoport & Bala G. Dharan, *Enron: Corporate Fiascos and Their Implications* (New York: Foundation Press, 2004)

Robert V. Remini, *Andrew Jackson: A Biography* (New York: St. Martin's Press, 2008)

Clinton Rossiter, *The Federalist Papers* (New York: Penguin Group USA Inc., 2003)

Theodore Roszak, *The Making of a Counter Culture: Reflections on the Technocratic Society and its Youthful Opposition* (New York: Doubleday & Co., Inc., 1968)

Vincent Ryan Ruggiero, *Becoming a Critical Thinker*, 7th ed. (Boston: Wadsworth Cengage Learning, 2009)

Joseph Schumpeter, *Capitalism, Socialism and Democracy* (New York: HarperPerennial, 1976)

Les R. Scorba, *Trust: The One Thing That Makes or Breaks a Leader* (Nashville: Thomas Nelson, Inc. 2004)

Amity Shales, *The Forgotten Man: A New History of the Great Depression* (New York: Harper Pernennial, 2007)

Fred R. Shapiro, *The Oxford Dictionary of American Legal Quotations* (New York: Oxford University Press, 1993)

Robert J. Shiller, *Irrational Exuberance*, 2nd ed. (Princeton, New Jersey: Princeton University Press, 2005)

W. Cleon Skousen, *The 5000 Year Leap: The 28 Great Ideas That Changed the World* (Malta, ID: National Center for Constitutional Studies, 1981)

Thomas Sowell, *Basic Ecoonomics: A Common Sense Guide to the Economy* (New York: Basic Books, 2011)

Thomas Sowell, *Race and Culture: A World View* (New York: Basic Books, 1994)

Matthew Spalding, ed., *The Enduring Principles of the American Founding* (Wash., D.C.: The Heritage Foundation, 2001)

Matthew Spalding ed., *The Founders' Almanac: A Practical Guide to the Notable Events, Greatest Leaders & Most Eloquent Words of the American Founding* (Wash. D.C., The Heritage Foundation, 2002)

Matthew Spalding, *We Still Hold These Truths: Rediscovering Our Principles, Reclaiming Our Future* (Wilmington, Delaware: The Heritage Foundation, 2009)

Robert Spencer, ed., *The Myth of Islamic Tolerance: How Islamic Law Treats Non-Muslims* (Amherst, New York: Prometheus Books, 2005)

Rick Stephens & Elane V. Scott, *The System: Seeking the Soul of Commerce: Creating the Next Generation of Capable People* (Whittier, California: Preparation Press, 2006)

Mark Stevens, *The Big Eight: An Incisive Look Behind the Pinstripe Curtain of the Eight Accounting Firms Whose Practices Affect the Lives and Pocketbooks of Every American* (New York: Macmillan Publishing Co., 1981)

Mark Stevens, *The Big Six: A Behind-The-Scenes Look at the Scandals, Power Plays, and Plays, and Professional Lapses at the Nation's Top Accounting Firms* (New York: Simon and Schuster, 1991)

Russ Stevenson, *Forgotten Foundation: How the Great Ideas of the Christian Faith Became the Foundation of the Western World* (Lenoir, North Carolina: Reformation Press, 2009)

John Stossel: *Give Me a Break: How I Exposed Hucksters, Cheats, and Scam Artists and Became the Scourge of the Liberal Media...* (New York: HarperCollins Publishers, 2004)

William Strauss and Neil Howe, *The Fourth Turning: What the Cycles of History Tell Us about America's Next Rendezvous with Destiny* (New York: Bantam Doubleday Dell Publishing Group, Inc., 1997)

Joe Studwell, *The China Dream: The Quest for the Last Great Untapped Market on Earth* (New York: Atlantic Monthly Press, 2002)

John H. Sudd, *An Introduction to the Behaviour of Ants* (London: Edward Arnold Publishers, 1967)

Roger J. Sullivan, *Morality and the Good Life: A Commentary on Aristotle's Nicomachean Ethics* (Memphis: Memphis State University Press, 1977)

James Surowiecki, *The Wisdom of Crowds: Why the Many Are Smarter than the Few and How Collective Wisdom Shapes Business, Economies, Societies and Nations* (New York: Doubleday, Random House, Inc., 2004)

Mimi Swartz with Sherron Watkins, *Power Failure: The Inside Story of the Collapse of Enron* (New York: Random House, Inc., 2003)

Olivia and Robert Temple, *The Complete Fables: Aesop* (New York: Penguin Books, 1998)

Geoff Tibballs, *The Titanic* (New York: Reader's Digest, 1998)

Lewis Thomas, *The Lives of a Cell: Notes of a Biology Watcher*

(New York: Bantam Books, 1974)

Mel Thompson, *The Wisdom of the Ancient Greeks* (Oxford: Oneworld, 2002)

Lester C. Thurow, *The Future of Capitalism: How Today's Economic Forces Shape Tomorrow's World* (New York: William Morrow & Co, 1996)

Alexis de Tocqueville, *Democracy in America Vols. 1 & 2* (New York: Vintage Books, 1990)

Barbara Ley Toffler, *Final Accounting: Ambition, Greed, and the Fall of Arthur Andersen* (New York: Random House, Inc., 2003)

Harlow Giles Unger, *The Life and Times of Noah Webster, An American Patriot* (New York, John Wiley & Sons 1998)

M. Mitchell Waldrop, *Complexity: The Emerging Science at the Edge of Order and Chaos* (New York: Simon & Schuster, 1992)

Peter Warburton, *Debt & Delusion: Central Bank Follies That Threaten Economic Disaster* (Princeton, N.J.: Worldmetaview Press, 1999, 2005)

Doris Weatherford, *American Women and World War II* (Edison, New Jersey, Book Sales, Inc., 1990)

Max Weber, *The Protestant Ethic: The Spirit of Capitalism* (Los Angeles, California: Roxbury Publishing Co., 2002)

Margaret J. Wheatley, *Leadership and the New Science* (San Francisco: Berrett-Koehler Publishers, 1999)

William Morton Wheeler, *Ants: Their Structure, Development, and Behavior* (New York: Columbia University Press, 1910)

Jack Winocour, ed., *The Story of the Titanic As Told By Its Survivors* (New York: Dover Publications, Inc., 1960)

Art Wolfe, Steven Dow, Tracy Dobson, Jeffrey Nesteruk, *Understanding the Law: Principles, Problems and Potentials of the American Legal System* (St. Paul, Minnestota, West Publishing Co. 1995)

Gordon S. Wood, *The Creation of the American Republic*, 1776–1787 (Chapel Hill, NC: The University of North Carolina Press 1969, 1998)

Gordon S. Wood, *The American Revolution*: *A History* (New York: The Modern Library, 2002)

Emily Yellin, *Our Mothers' War: American Women at Home and At the Front During World War II* (New York: Free Press, 2004)

Some Additional Selected Websites:

www.bartleby.com/quotations/
www.brainyquote.com/
www.quotationspage.com/
www.foundingfatherquotes.com/
www.marksquotes.com/Founding-Fathers/

Index

accountability, financial (Commandment #5). *See also* accounting fraud
  areas of potential misconduct, 217–223
  business accountability, 217
  and competent oversight, 222
  and fiduciary duty to account, 218, 258
  government accountability, 217
  misappropriating and comingling funds, 223
  by nonprofit organizations/charities, 218
  and principle-based *vs.* rules-based accounting, 219
  reasonable and necessary expenses, 221
  relationship to trust, 217, 223
  sample laws related to, 224, 277
  underlying ethics principles, 224, 277
accountants
  competency expectations, 214
  legal limits on, 263
  as watchdogs, 106–7
accounting, defined, 219
accounting fraud
  definition and examples, 100, 219–221
  penalties for, 267, 285, 289
  and principle-based *vs.* rules-based accounting, 219
Ackoff, Russell, 42
Acton, Lord, 126
Adams, John
  on facts as unarguable, 53
  on fulfilling the American dream, 253
  on the importance of fairness, 128
  on moral authority in leaders, 249
  on property rights as sacred, 225
  on public virtue, 54
  on relationship between freedom and moral/religious principles, 134–35
Adelphia Communications Co., 99–100, 106, 268
adolescents, misconduct by, 164
The Adventures of a Bystander (Drucker), 17
advertising, deceptive, 189, 193
Aesop's Fables, 15, 39
affirmative action, 236
Affordable Care Act, 166, 185
Afghanistan, suppression of religious expression in, 156
Africa, culture-specific ethical standards, 153

age discrimination, 237

air pollution violations, 233

Alabama, scandals involving elected officials, 109, 111

Alaska, scandals involving elected officials, 110

all-force cultures, 78, 81–82

all-trust cultures, 78–80

Ally Financial, 228

America. *See* ethics-based American Rule of Law; freedom, American; United States of America

America (song), 136

American Civil War, 33, 80, 251. *See also* Grant, Ulysses S.; Lincoln, Abraham; Sherman, William Tecumseh

American dream, 86

American exceptionalism, 120–21

American Home Products, 267

American International Group (AIG)

 bailout, 45, 146

 credit default swaps, 44

 ethical breaches, 101

The American Lawyer, on levels of corporate fraud, 102

American Museum of Natural History, compensation complaints, 260

American Red Cross, accounting fraud scandals, 221

American Revolutionary War

 as conflict based on moral imperatives, 124

 as first major American national emergency, 33

 Washington's leadership, 250

American Rule of Law. *See* ethics-based American Rule of Law

American Rule of Lawyers and Bureaucrats

 ascendency of, features, 31–32

 and dependence on "experts," 34, 184–86

 and the destruction of trust, 34, 36, 175

 and emphasis on the legal over what is right, iii, 183

 and top-down governance models, 34

America the Beautiful (song), 136

Ameriquest Capital Corp., predatory lending practices, 105–6

Animal Farm (Orwell), as model of top-down leadership approach, 253

antitrust laws

 purpose, 196

 violating, penalties, 285, 289

ants, ant communities

 Argentine ants, 4, 14

 bottom-up organizing principles, 4

 physical strengths and weakness of individuals, 3

 resemblance to human communities, 4

self-organizing capacity, 3, 13–14
task specialization among, 4
wisdom of, summary, 6
AOL/Time Warner, accounting fraud, 100
Apple, patent lawsuit with Samsung, 229
Arcesilaus, 186
Archer Daniels Midland (ADM), price fixing convictions, 196
Aristotle
importance of a strong middle class, 89, 169
on relationship of law and justice, 75
Arizona sweat lodge deaths, as reckless, 212
arm's length transactions, 256
Arthur Andersen
accounting fraud scandal, 106
legal punishment, 142
Articles of Confederation, 129–130
Astor, Brooke, 218
atheists, 135, 177
Atlanta Housing Authority, excessive compensation at, 260
Atlantic States Cast Iron Pipe Co., safety and health violations, 268
attorneys, ethical misconduct among, 108
auction rate securities, scandals related to, 104–5
Australia
author's education and experience in, 18–21
Constitution, 20–21
defamation lawsuit against *Barron's*, 155
automatic action, 6

Babson, Robert W., 70
baby-boomers
and catastrophic increase in national debt, 60–61
erroneous distrust of earlier generations, 41
as the "Me" Generation, 47
Banking Act of 1933 (Glass-Steagall Act), 63
Bank of America (Countrywide)
financial penalties, 267
predatory lending practices, 105–6
settlement of lawsuits and claims, 72
banks, Americans' distrust of, 75–76
Baptist Foundation of Arizona bankruptcy scandal, 106, 113
Barclay's Capital, double dealing lawsuit, 205–6
The Battle Hymn of the Republic (song), 136
Bayou Management hedge fund collapse, 104
BDO Seidman, accounting fraud scandal, 107

Bell, California, financial mismanagement, 112, 220, 264

benefit of bargain remedy, 244

Bennis, Warren, 6

Bertelsmann AG, and Napster copyright infringement, 230

the Bible. *See also* Judeo-Christian values

    admonitions regarding loyalty, 203, 206

    resurgence as theme in mainstream culture, 177

bid-rigging, 197

billionaire's, numbers of in the United States, 89

Bill of Rights. *See* U.S. Constitution

biotechnology, biotech revolution, 9–10

Boeing Corporation

    contract dispute with ICO, 243

    ethics scandals, 101

Born, Brooksley, 68

borrowed money, misuse of, 68

bottom-up organizing principle

    as basis for American Rule of Law, 4, 34

    and capacity to adapt to change, 6

    and the American dream, 253

    and the American freedom model, 76

    as key to all-trust success, 80

    and the Protestant Christian heritage, 133

boycotting competitors, 197

Boys and Girls Club, compensation complaints, 260

Brazil

    economic challenges, corruption, 176

    newness as a country, 176

    penalties for ethical misconduct in, 285

breach of contract, 267, 285

breach of fiduciary duty, 214

bribery

    as crime, 206

    defined, 207

    as form of conflict of interest, 206–7

    involving public employees, 111

    penalties for, 267–69, 285, 289

British Petroleum (BP), Transocean Deepwater Horizon fire and oil spill, 233, 267

British Rule of Law, common law legal system, 14, 20–21, 82, 92, 94, 124, 127, 132, 154–55. *See also* United Kingdom/Britain

Broadcom Corp., backdated stock options, 102

Brocade Communications Systems, CEO conviction, 199

Brown v. the Board of Education, 140

Bryant, Kobe, 256

Buffet, Warren
    on credit derivatives, 45
    philanthropy, 88
bullying, defined and examples, 239–240
businesses/corporations. *See also* accounting fraud; CEOs/executives *and specific*
    examples
    and CEO compensation, 256
    ethical misconduct, 99–101, 220
    ethics training, ineffectiveness, 23–24
    fiduciary responsibilities, 257–58
    and financial accountability, 217
    financial reporting requirements, 217
    public, insider trading rules, 198
    revolving door with government, 204–5
    separation of powers built in to, 256–57
bystander role/perspective
    Drucker's definition, 17–18
    and experiencing multiple perspectives, 18–20
    and the stating of unpopular truths, 27

cab drivers, overcharging by, 116–17
California
    anti-employment discrimination statutes, 237
    excessive compensation complaints, 260
    scandals involving public school cheating, 115
    scandals involving city officials, 112
    scandals involving law enforcement, 113
    scandals involving mayors, 111
    workers' pensions, misconduct related to, 141, 178, 222
CalPERS, 141
Canada
    Charter of Rights and Freedoms, 129
    federalism in, 128
    penalties for ethical misconduct in, 285
capitalist free-market economy
    and capital, 226
    dependence on culture of trust and law, 51, 151
    and the drive to excel and succeed, 86–87
    and importance of property titles, 226
    and investor trust, 79–80
    and private *vs.* government decision-making, 79
Capitol Dome, Washington, D.C., Christian inscription on, 137
care, fiduciary duty of, 214, 257

carefulness, being careful (Commandment #4)
   areas of potential misconduct, 212–14
   characteristics and behaviors, 211–12
   and competence, 214
   and data safety and security, 213–14
   and diligence, 214
   and negligence, 211–12
   and product safety, 212–13
   and reckless behavior, 212
   relationship to trust, 211, 214
   sample laws related to, 215, 276
   standards for, variability in, 212
   underlying ethics principle, 215, 276
Carnegie, Andrew, 88
Cater, Jimmy, 120–21
Cathcart, Jim, 15
Catholic Church
   child abuse scandals, 113
   top-down governance model, 5
celebrity salaries, arm's length transactions, 256
Cendant Corporation accounting fraud, 100
Central Falls, Rhode Island, pension cuts, 140–41
centrally planned and controlled economies
   India, post-independence, 82–83
   Soviet Russia and post-revolutionary China, 81–82
CEOs/executives. *See also* businesses/corporations
   celebrity CEOs and pay for performance, 258
   as chairman of the board, inherent conflict, 256–57
   interlocking directorships, 258
   penalties for unethical conduct, 268
   salaries/compensation, 48, 69–70, 256–59
Ceran, C. W., 15
chain of title, misconduct associated with, 226–27
chairman of the board, CEO's as, 256–57
Chamberlain, Neville, 62
Chancery courts, religion-based, in England, 132
change, adaptation
   constancy of, 11
   as key to long-term survival, 6
   rapid, as one key to American exceptionalism, 120
change-of-control clauses in employment contracts, 69
character, defined, 50
Chase, Samuel, 133

Chavez, Hugo
    control over Venezuela's media, 156
    economic failures, 94
    use of freedom as mask for force, 85
cheating, as epidemic, 65, 69–70, 114–15
The Cheating Culture (Callahan), 115
checks and balances systems, 126–27
Chevron Corporation
    environmental damage charges, 285
    ethical misconduct, 101
China
    constitutional rights, limits on, 149
    and culture-specific ethical standards, 153
    economic reforms and adoption of a "freer" cultural model, 83
    enforcement of 10 Commandments of Trust in, 150, 289
    expanding territorial claims, 176
    global economic dominance, 7–8, 37
    hybrid force (government)/"trust" (economy) culture, 94–95
    imprisonment of journalists in, 156
    Internet censorship, 155
    judiciary as extension of the Communist government, 158–59
    military spending, 168
    newness as a country, 176
    offshoring of jobs to, 8
    population, United States population *vs.*, 39
    proscriptions against assembly, protests, 157
    protests and social disharmony in, 92
    religious expression in, 156
    renewed teaching of Confucianism in, 135
    slowing of economic growth in, 175
Chinese Revolution, 1949, 81–82, 124
Christian heritage and identity, 130–32. *See also* Judeo-Christian values
Churchill, Winston, 82–83
Cicero, 12–13
citizenship, United States
    Oath of Allegiance, 148–49
    requirements, 122–23
    responsibilities associated with, 165
city bankruptcies, and unfunded pensions and medical benefit payments, 141
civic institutions, erosion of ethical integrity within, 22
civics education, importance, 40, 120
Civil Rights Act of 1964, 165, 237
Civil Rights Act of 1991, 127
Clean Water Act, penalties under, 233

Clinton, Bill, 97, 129
Coca-Cola Company race discrimination lawsuit, 236, 267
codes of conduct, voluntary, ethics as, 51
Coleridge, Samuel Taylor, 24
collateralized debt obligations, 71
collective action, and the self-organizing capacity of ants, 3–4
Colorado, pension cuts/restrictions, 140–41
comingling funds, 223
Commandment #1: Tell the Truth
    areas of potential misconduct, 189–193
    relationship to trust, 187, 193
    sample laws related to, 194, 273
    underlying ethics principles, 194, 273
Commandment #2: Fairness
    areas of potential misconduct, 196–200
    relationship to justice, 196
    relationship to trust, 195–96, 200
    sample laws related to, 201, 274
    underling ethics principle, 201, 274
Commandment #3: Loyalty
    areas of potential misconduct, 203–8
    relationship to trust, 203, 208
    sample laws related to, 209, 275
    underlying ethics principle, 209, 275
Commandment #4: Care
    areas of potential misconduct, 212–14
    relationship to trust, 211, 214
    sample laws related to, 215, 276
    underlying ethics principle, 215, 276
Commandment #5:Accountability
    areas of potential misconduct, 217–223
    relationship to trust, 217, 223
    sample laws related to, 224, 277
    underlying ethics principles, 224, 277
Commandment #6: Property Rights
    areas of potential misconduct, 226–233
    respecting, as component of trust, 225–26, 233
    sample laws related to, 234, 278
    underlying ethics principles, 234, 278
Commandment #7: Respecting People in the Workplace
    areas of potential misconduct, 235–241
    employment law, 236–37
    relationship to trust, 235, 241
    sample laws related to, 241, 279

underlying ethics principles, 241, 279
unions/union law, 235–36
Commandment #8: Keeping Promises. *See also* contracts, contract law
  areas of potential misconduct, 243–46
  relationship to trust, 243, 246
  sample laws related to, 247, 280
  underlying ethics principles, 247, 280
Commandment #9: Real Leadership
  areas of potential misconduct, 252–261
  essential behaviors of real leaders, 250–52
  relationship to trust, 249, 261
  sample laws related to, 262, 281
  underlying ethics principles, 262, 281
Commandment #10: Enforcing Standards
  relationship to trust, 263, 270
  sample laws related to, 270, 282
  tools for enforcement, 264–270
  underlying ethics principles, 270, 282
Commodities Futures Modernization Act (2000), 63–64, 68
common carriers, standards of care, 212
common law legal systems
  free speech rights, 155
  and promises made without contracts, 245–46
common sense. *See also* ordinary people; wisdom
  and being smart, 41
  as a component of wisdom, 12–13
competence
  as aspect of accountability, 222
  as aspect of carefulness, 214
competition, fair, 196–97
complacency
  about ethics and trust, dangers, 59, 75
  about risk, dangers, 65, 70
  and *hubris*, 61–62
Computer Associates (CA) International, accounting fraud, 100, 190
computers, and bioinformatics, 10
confidentiality, laws related to, 208
conflicts of interest
  and appearance of a conflict, 204
  bribes and kickbacks, 207
  and CEOs as chairman of the board, 256–57
  defined, 204
  fraudulent endorsements, 205

gifts and gratuities, 207
  and the revolving door between government and private industry, 204–5
Confucianism, 135
Congo, ineffectiveness of the UN in, 148
Connecticut, scandals involving governors, 109
considerations, defined, 244
conspiracy charges, penalties for, 268
constitutions, written, numbers of, 84. *See also* U.S. Constitution
consumer debt boom, 64–66
contracts, contract law
  areas of potential misconduct, 243–44
  in China, legal protections, 289
  and contract enforcement in India, 154
  deficiency judgements, 245
  effective, as key ingredient for success of capitalism, 151
  importance of in U.S. Constitution, 244
  and remedies for contract breaches, 244
  rules governing, 244
  tortious interference rules, 244–45
  undoing, 244–45
Cook County, Illinois, retaliation-related lawsuit, 238–39
cooperative action, as component of the wisdom of ants, 4, 6
copyrights, copyright protections, 229–231
corporate directors. *See* CEOs/executives
corporations/businesses. *See* businesses/corporations
corruption
  crippling nature of, 98
  increasing levels of in the United States, 98, 161–62
  penalties for, 285
Corruption Perceptions Index (Transparency International), 161–62
Corzine, Jon, 105
Cotswold Geotechnical, safety and health violations, 285
counterfeit goods, 230–31
Countrywide Home Loans. *See* Bank of America (Countrywide)
"covenant-lite" credit terms, 69
creativity, as skill needed for success, 11
credit cards, 66
credit default swaps/derivatives
  and the AIG bailout, 44–45
  Buffet's view of, 45
  in global financial economy, 45–46
  and MERS, 227–28
  risks associated with, 67–68, 226

Credit Suisse First Boston, stock spinning by, 103
Credit Suisse Group, auction rate securities fraud, 104
crimes, federal, expanding numbers of, 186
criminal accusation, and promise of due process, 199
criminal negligence, penalties for, 268
crisis, as both danger and opportunity, 172–73
critical thinking
    characteristics, 49–50
    and the maintenance of freedom, 40, 50
    need to relearn as Americans, 164
    political thinking vs., 49
    and the Protestant Christian heritage, 133
Crystal, Graef, 256
Cuba, move towards open-market economy in, 87
culture
    "cultural sensitivity," 48
    damaged, challenges of repairing, 47
    importance and changeability, 46–47
culture of trust. See trust, culture of
Cunningham, Randy "Duke," 108
cyberattacks, defending against, 167

Dannon Company, Inc., deceptive advertising charges, 193
Darwin, Charles, 6, 15
data analysis and evaluation, 49–50
data safety and security, 213–14
Davis, Benjamin O. Jr., 172
Davis, Benjamin O. Sr., 171–72
debt, global
    expanding levels of, 168
    threats of default, 175
debt, personal
    during the 1920s, 64
    and usurious interest rates, 142–43
debt, United States national
    catastrophic increases, 44, 60–61, 72
    comparison of the 1920s and the 2000s, 64–65
    as danger to stability, 37–38, 73, 168
    and federal expenditure, 166
    increase in following 2008 financial crisis, 43
    interest payments on, 166
    and Social Security benefits, 166
Declaration of Independence
    references to God in, 135–36

as uniquely American document, 122

defamation lawsuits under common law system, 155

defense spending

    cutting, cautions, 167

    and ethics scandals, 101

deficiency judgements, 245

degrees, academic, lying about on résumés, 116

Del Monte Foods, stockholder lawsuit, 205–6

Deloitte & Touche, accounting fraud scandal, 106, 214

democracy. *See also* ethics-based American Rule of Law; freedom, American; United
  States of America

    ballet analogy, 84

    defense spending, 84

    and importance of trust, 35

    numbers of, globally, 84

    representative republic *vs.*, 125

Democracy in America (de Tocqueville), 5

denial, dangers of, 57

Denmark, efforts to limit free speech in, 157

Department of Defense (DOD), lack of competent oversight, 222

Department of Justice (DOJ), enforcement of antitrust laws, 197

Department of Veterans Affairs (VA), data breaches, 213

descriptive trademark protection, 230

design defects, and product liability, 213

De Soto, Hernando, 151, 225–26

de Tocqueville, Alexis

    and the ability to correct mistakes, 40

    on American propensity for self-organization, 5

    Democracy in America, 120–21

    on democracy *vs.* socialism, 86

    on destructive force of focus on self-gratification, 99

    on fiscally irresponsible government, 166

    on relationship of liberty and morality, 131

    on religion in America, 139–140

Deutsche Bank AG, fraud charges, 285

dictatorships

    and breakdowns in trust, 35

    and economic success in China, 37

    as failure of self-governance, 37

    and force, 24

diligence, as aspect of carefulness, 214

direct democracy, 125

disability

    disability fraud, 192

and employment discrimination, 237

disclosure, full, 192–93

discrimination
and anti-discrimination employment law, 236
disparate treatment theory, 237
intentional *vs.* unintentional, 237

dishonesty. *See* lying/dishonesty

disloyalty, repercussions, 203

District of Columbia, scandals involving public officials, 112

distrust, culture of. *See also* ethics-based American Rule of Law; trust, culture of
approaches to restoring, 117
carbon monoxide simile for, 75
dangers associated with, 25–26, 35–36
and economic failure/pain, 90–91
and the Financial Crisis of 2008, 44–45
and greediness/wrongful acquisition of wealth, 87–88
and social disharmony, 91–92

diversity, and unity as Americans, importance, 170–72

DocX, forgery indictment, 228

Dodd-Frank Wall Street Reform and Consumer Protection Act, whistleblower protections, 266

Dow Chemical Co., theft of trade secrets, 268

Drexel, Burnham Lambert, 48

Drucker, Peter
on excessive compensation paid mediocre executives, 259
forecasting abilities, 17–18
on management *vs.* leadership, 257
on people as assets, 235, 237
predictions of Japan's economic boom, 17
on the role of the bystander, 27

drug-related/gang crime, and insecurity, 93

Dubai, real estate market crash, 154

due diligences, as fiduciary duty, 214

due process, 199–200

Eastern European countries, changes following fall of Soviet Union, 84

Easter Seals, compensation complaints, 260

East Germany, "top-down" dictatorship model, 46–47

Ebbers, Bernie, 99

Economic Espionage Act of 1996, 232

economic success
and erroneous predictions about, 62
and the importance of respecting private property rights, 225–26
national, defined, 79

and responsibility, 150

The Economist, on hedge-fund manager performance, 67–68

educational system, United States

    ethical misconduct in, 115–16

    failure to teach history, civics or critical thinking, 40

    importance to ability to compete, 6–7

    moral education, 50, 135

    and the offshoring of white-collar and professional jobs, 8

    and teaching about meaning of being an American, 120, 123

Egypt

    control of the Muslim Brotherhood in, 169–170

    suppression of religious expression in, 156

Einstein, Albert, 183

Eisenhower, Dwight D.

    importance of fairness in times of peace, 195

    as real leader, 5, 251

    on strength needed to maintain freedom, 93

elected officials. *See* public officials and employees

elections, United States

    electoral college, 125

    fair and transparent, 80

    presidential campaign costs, 129

Ellis, Joseph J., 119

eminent domain, 228

employment law, 236–37

energy companies, ethics scandals, 101

England. *See* United Kingdom/Britain

Enron Corp.

    scandal, as symptomatic of larger ethics problems, 22

    securities fraud, penalties for, 99, 267–68

    waiving of conflict of interest policy, 206

entitlements

    defined, 165

    ending, 168

    as privileges, not rights, 165

environmental damage, fines and penalties for, 233, 267, 285

environmental sustainability, importance, 11

"*e pluribus unum*," 123

Equal Employment Opportunity Commission (EEOC), lawsuit against Mitsubishi Motors, 238

equal opportunity, meaning in employment law, 237

Ernst & Young, accounting fraud, 107, 114, 220

Ethelberht of Kent, 4

ethics, ethical conduct. *See also* ethics-based American Rule of Law; 10

Commandments of Trust; unethical conduct
  as absolute *vs.* culture-specific, 48, 152–54
  as basis for trust and American survival, 5, 14, 22–23, 35–36, 46, 56, 80
  concept of "global ethics," 149–150
  confusion about, 24, 29–30
  defined, 51
  enforcement cycles, 55
  identifying, recognizing, 55–56
  laws governing, 24–25
  loyalty as, 203
  as mandatory/absolute, 24, 26, 53–54
  myths about, 52–53, 148
  political thinking about, dangers, 50
  relationship with morality and the law, 51–52
  and relative ethics, 47
  and responsibility, 150
  similarity to laws of physics, 24–25
  and the 10 Commandments of Trust, 25
  training in, challenges, 23–24, 51
ethics-based American Rule of Law. *See also* American Rule of Lawyers and
  Bureaucrats; ethics, ethical behavior; freedom, American; 10 Commandments of
  Trust; trust, culture of; U.S. Constitution
  and ability to change quickly, 33–34
  and acceptance of court rulings, 92
  vs. the American Rule of Lawyers, 31
  basis in Judeo-Christian values, 51–52, 131–32
  and bottom-up organizing principle, 34
  and the creation of a "land of opportunity," 124
  defined/components, 50, 183
  and enforcement of ethical standards, 32–33, 175, 142, 183, 233, 263, 265
  and fair treatment/due process, 197, 199
  heritage from British Rule of Law, 132
  and the Internal Revenue Service, 265
  the "Just Kidding" clause, 140–41
  and need for simplified laws and regulations, 185
  and the priority of civilian law over God's law, 133
  and public *vs.* private ethics, 53–54
  and requirement of loyalty, 203
  and response to 9/11 terrorist attacks, 119
  and right *vs.* legal behavior, 31
  shared belief system underlying, 121–23
  and the spirit of the law, 142
  trust as key element of, 14, 18, 22–23, 170, 194
  as unique, 21, 120

Ethics Resource Center, on fraud among charities, 218

ethics scandals. *See* unethical conduct

European Union (EU)
 comparison with the United States, 143
 culture-specific ethical standards, 153
 indebtedness within, as challenge to survival, 85
 national "speech codes," 155
 penalties for unethical conduct in, 285
 privacy laws, 154
 threats of debt defaults, 175

exams, cheating on, 116

excellence, desire for, *vs.* greed, 86

experience, as a component of wisdom, 12

experts. *See also* American Rule of Lawyers and Bureaucrats
 and the American Rule of Lawyers and Bureaucrats, 34, 186
 errors, mistakes by, 46, 59, 70, 198
 following blindly, 41–42
 over-reliance on, x, 41, 70, 72–73
 as people with knowledge, expertise, 11
 and political thinking, 145
 and risky investment instruments, 71
 and the wisdom of ordinary people, 13

Facebook, Inc., violations of fair play/decency standards, 200

failing to warn, and product liability, 213

failure to disclose, and conflicts of interest, 205

fairness, fair behavior (Commandment #2)
 areas of potential misconduct, 196–200
 bid-rigging, 197
 defined, 195
 and due process, 199
 and fair competition, 196–97
 and fair investing, 198
 fair play, 200
 "government sponsored entities," 197
 importance, 195
 and justice, 195–96
 relationship to justice, 196
 relationship to trust, 195–96, 200
 sample laws related to, 201
 underling ethics principle, 201
 violation by GSEs, 197

fair play and decency standards, 200

fair procedures, defined, 199

fair treatment laws, 241

fair use exception to copyright protection, 231

fanciful trademark protection, 230

Fannie Mae

    accounting fraud scandal, 100

    as a "government sponsored entity," 197

    and the Mortgage Electronic Registration System, 227

    and salary to CEO despite poor performance, 258

Farewell Address, 1796 (Washington), 138

Fastow, Andrew, 31, 206

federal government, U.S. *See also* debt, United States national

    accounting for spending, 217

    accounting fraud, 220

    examples of excessive compensation, 260

    excessive regulations, 34

    expansion in power and size of, 128

    federal crimes, 186, 190

    growing distrust and fears of, 35–36, 178

    protections against power of in the Bill of Rights, 129–130

    revolving door with private industry, 204–5

    Social Security, Medicare/Medicaid spending, 166

    separation of powers, 127

    tensions with state governments, 128–29

Federal Housing Finance Agency (FHFA), suits related to mortgage securities fraud, 192

federalism, 126, 128

Federal Trade Commission (FTC)

    deceptive advertising charges against Dannon, 193

    enforcement of antitrust laws, 197

    enforcement of fair play and decency standards, 200

    "Operation False Charity," 192

Ferguson, Niall, 9

fiduciary

    defined, 218–19

    fiduciary duty of care, 214, 257

    fiduciary duty of loyalty, 203, 257

    fiduciary duty to account, 218, 258

finance reform laws, 185

financial aid officers, improper receipt of incentives, 205

financial crises, global, and widespread unethical behaviors, 37

Financial Crisis of 2008

    bailouts and other costs, 71–72

    bank bankruptcies and takeovers during, 76

    and complicated financial and investment products, 44

economic failure/pain associated with, 90–91
fear generated by, 43
global impacts, 175
and income of hedge fund managers during, 67
and national debt increases, 43–44
and raising the federal bank deposit guarantee amount, 75–76
and uncovering of numerous ethical violations, 70
financial markets
and complicated financial/investment instruments, 45
expanded riskiness of, 71
scandals related to, 102–5
fiscal responsibility, restoring, 166
Fisher, Irving, 62
Fletcher, Joseph, 47
flexibility, as skill needed for success, 11
Florida, scandals involving elected officials, 110
food stamp fraud, 169
Forbes, Walter, 55
Forbes' 28th Annual World's Billionaire Issue, 89
force
as only alternative to freedom, 76
as result of lack of trust, 24, 35, 75
Foreign Corrupt Practices Act, 207
foreign investment, and effective Rule of Law, 152
foresight, preparation, benefits, 74
Fortune, article of reverse globalization, 9
Founding Fathers. *See also* freedom, American; U.S. Bill of Rights; U.S. Constitution
  and specific individuals
    recognition of test implied by American freedom, 173
    recognition of the importance of religion, 134
The Fourth Turning (Strauss and Howe), 60–61
Fourth Turning generational crisis, 33, 39
Foxworthy, Jeff, 177
France, penalties for ethical misconduct in, 285
Frankfurter, Felix, 200
Franklin, Benjamin
  on America's fight for the liberty, 175
  on carelessness, neglect, 211
  on choice of rulers, 35
  on half-truths, 193
  on hanging together, 171
  on the importance of freedom of thought and speech, 130
  on the importance of keeping promises, 245
  on the importance of religion to good government, 137

on making excuses, 223

on preparation, 57

on role of religion for ordering society, 138, 143

fraud

accounting fraud, 100, 219–221,

defined, 191

fraudulent tax shelters, 267

penalties for, 267, 285, 289

proving, 243

types of fraud, 191

Freddie Mac

accounting fraud scandal, 100

as a "government sponsored entity," 197

and the Mortgage Electronic Registration System, 227

freedom, American. *See also* ethics-based American Rule of Law; U.S. Bill of Rights; U.S. Constitution

the commitment of real leaders to, 250–52

comparisons with other nations, 149

force as only alternative to, 76

freedom of assembly, 157

freedom of religion, 156

freedom of speech, 32, 54, 154–56

freedom of the press, 32, 54

preserving, retaining, 37, 40–41, 84–85, 148–49, 164, 171, 175

price of, 164

and self-governance, 123

taking for granted, as dangerous, 85

trust as essential for, 22–24

uniqueness, recognizing and cherishing, 21, 50, 76, 120, 124, 175

free market economies, need for trust, 35, 175

French Revolution, 1780, 124

Friedman, Thomas, 151

full disclosure provisions

and failing to warn, 213

importance and variability in, 187

Galleon Group, insider trading convictions, 104, 198, 268

Gates, Bill, 88

GE, excessive executive compensation at, 259

Gekko, Gordon (movie character), 48

General Accounting Office (GAO), unreasonable/unnecessary expenses, 221

General Motors, role in auto industry, 7–8

genomics, 10

Germany, penalties for ethical misconduct in, 285

Getty Oil, contract-related lawsuits, 244

gifts and gratuities, improper, 207

GlaxoSmithKline PLC, illegal marketing penalties, 269

global citizenship, as myth, 145, 148

global economies

    changes in, 175

    cyclic globalization, 9

    declining US position, 162

    global Rule of Law, as myth, 146, 151

    hyper-competitive nature of, 6–7

    importance of knowledge, 11–12

    and interconnection of financial markets, 45, 146

    knowledge-based, and intellectual property rights, 229

    an reverse globalization, 8–9

    threats to, 8, 73

global ethics

    lack of common definition for, 150

    as myth, 145, 149

God, American faith in, 135–38. *See also* Judeo-Christian values

"In God We Trust" motto, 137

Goebbels, Joseph, 50

Goldman Sachs, illegal stock schemes, 103–4

Google, Inc.

    financial penalties, 267

    Google Books copyright issues, 231

government officials. *See* public officials and employees

government spending. *See also* U.S. government

    following Financial Crisis of 2008, 175

    and preventing waste and abuse, 222–23

    understanding debt levels, 44

government-sponsored entities (GSE), violations of fairness principles, 197

grade inflation and falsification, 115–16

Grant, Ulysses S.

    on importance of relying on the Bible, 144

    on obligations inherent in citizenship, 165

    as real leader, 251

Great Depression and World War II

    comparisons with current crisis period, 72–73

    and the "Greatest Generation," 61–62

    response to, involvement of all Americans in, 39

    slow onset of crisis, 61, 64

    as third major American national emergency, 33

Greater Ministries International Ponzi scheme, 113

"Greatest Generation," 61–62

Great Seal of the United States, 123
Greece
    challenges of maintaining culture of trust in, 85
    default by, global impacts, 146
    tax evasion in, 153
greed
    definition, 86
    drive to excel *vs.*, 86
    as wrongful acquisition of wealth, 86–88
"Greed Generation," 48
gross negligence, 212
grown-up citizens, behaviors of, 163–64
Gulliver's Travels (Swift), 34

Hamilton, Alexander
    on dangers of government by force, 81
    on enforcement and punishment, 263
    on experiment of creating good government by choice, vii, 173
    on the importance of keeping promises, 244
    on the importance of state governments within the U.S. Constitution, 128
    on willingness to fight for freedom, 177
Hand, Learned, 30, 196
harassment, defined/examples, 238
Havel, Václav, 145
"haves" *vs.* :have nots." See income inequality
Hayes, Bill, 145
hazardous waste violations, 233
HealthSouth accounting fraud, 100–101, 246, 258, 267
hedge fund scandals, 67, 102–3
Henry, Patrick
    on difference between right and wrong as unchangeable, 187
    on the importance of government transparency, 264
    and willingness to fight for freedom, 177
Hewlett Packard Company, Inc.(HP)
    high CEO salary despite poor performance, 258
    violations of principles of fair play, 200
Higher School Certificate (Australia), 19
high school grade inflation and falsification, 115–16
historical cycles ("turnings")
    the Awakening, rebellion against parental constraint, 60
    the Crisis, and the need for action to survive, 60
    the High, optimism following WWII, 60
    the Unraveling, culture wars, 60

history
  as cyclic, repetitive, 60–62
  importance of understanding, 49
  teaching of in American schools, 40
Hitler, Adolf, 62, 85
Holmes, Oliver Wendell Jr., 61
home mortgage and equity loans. *See* mortgages
Homestore.com accounting fraud, 100
honesty. *See* truth telling (Commandment #1)
Hospital Corporation of America, ethical breaches, 101
hostile work environments, 238
Household International, predatory lending practices, 105–6
Howe, Neil, 33, 60–61
hubris and complacency, 58, 63
Hughes Electronic Corp. (HEC), contract dispute, 243
Hu Jintao, 168
Human Genome Project, 10
human nature/behavior
  and the drive to excel, 86–87
  timeless/immutable traits, 57–58
  understanding, importance, 13, 49
"human rights" concept (United Nations), as vague and unenforceable, 146–47
human values, universal, lack of consensus on, 150–51
Hurricane Katrina, lawsuits involving attorney misconduct, 107
hybrid trust (government)/force (economy) culture, 82

ICO Global Communications Holdings, Ltd. (ICO), mishandling of contracts, 243
identity theft, responsibility to protect against, 213
ignorance, and the loss of freedom, 41
illegal actions. *See* ethics-based American Rule of Law; unethical conduct
illegal advertising, penalties for, 267
Illinois, scandals involving elected officials, 109, 112
ImClone Systems, ethical breaches, 101
immigrants, desire to live under the American Rule of Law, 123–24
Immigration and Customs Enforcement office sexual harassment lawsuit, 238
inalienable rights, as an American concept, 20
income inequality/disparities. *See also* CEOs/executives
  comparison of the 1920s and the 2000s, 65, 69
  as destabilizing, 89–90, 143
  and social disharmony, 91–92
Index of Economic Freedom (Heritage Foundation)
  on relationship between freedom and standard of living, 94
  United States' declining ranking, 161

India
    abandonment of top-down governing approach, 83
    common law legal system, backlogs, 154
    culture-specific ethical standards, 153
    economic challenges, corruption, 176
    newness as a country, 176
    offshoring of jobs to, 8
    as part "trust," part force culture, 82
    penalties for ethical misconduct in, 285
    social disharmony in, 91
Indonesia, corrupt law enforcement in, 159
Industrial Revolution, 9
infrastructure decay, 169
innovation, capacity for, as skill needed for success, 11
insecurity, national, sources of, 93
insider trading
    defined, 198
    financial penalties and jail time for, 269
    increasing numbers of scandals related to, 104
    penalties for, 268, 285
insight, as a component of wisdom, 12
installment debt contracts, 65
Institute for Global Ethics, 150–51
insurance companies
    credit default swaps *vs.*, 45
    ethics scandals, 101
    real, regulations governing, 45
integrity, defined, 50
intellectual property rights, 229
intent to deceive, 191
interest-only loans, 66
interest rates, usurious, 142–43
Internal Revenue Service (IRS)
    full disclosure provisions, 187
    image of, as powerful tax enforcer, 265
    on numbers of tax cheats, 115
    whistleblower reward program, 266
International Criminal Court (ICC), 152
International Monetary Fund (IMF)
    on 1930's-style threats to global economy, 73
    on China's emergence as world's largest economy, 37
Internet, as source of information, 264
investigative journalism, 264
investing, fair

and free market economies, 35

and insider trading, 198

and risks taken by investors, 154

IPO process (initial public offerings), scandals related to, 102–3

Iran, imprisoning of bloggers for anti-government speech, 155

Iraq

rebuilding, scandals associated with, 115

social disharmony in, 91

Islam, Islamic Countries

countries based on *vs.* Christian-based countries, 132

culture-specific ethical standards, 154

ISIS, rise to power, 170, 176

religious expression in, 156

Sharia law, 133–34

Israel, lie-detector company defamation lawsuit, 155

Jackson, Andrew

on Bible as foundation of the American Republic, 143

as real leader, 251

on reasons not to ally with other countries, 150

James, LeBron, 256

Japan

civil *vs.* criminal law in, 154

economic boom, Drucker's predicting of, 17

penalties for ethical misconduct in, 285

production of cars in the United States, 7

Japanese-Americans, bravery during World War II, 172

Jay, John, 229

Jefferson, Thomas

on the absoluteness of moral principle, 51

on culture of fear, 162

on the dangers of big government, 34, 129

on force and despotism, 79

on government by the people, 23

on ignorance and freedom, 41

on importance of identifying wrong doers, 266

on paramount importance of honesty, 187

on responsibility of Americans to limit government, 164

on vigilance as the price of freedom, 164

Jefferson, William, 108

Jefferson Memorial, Christian inscription on, 137

Jenkins & Gilchrist, tax fraud by, 107

jobs, employment

continuous shifting in, 9

and reductions in autoworker salaries, 8
    and reverse globalization, 8–9
    uncertainty of, 8
Johnson, F. Ross, 48
Johnson, Paul, 5
Johnson and Johnson (J&J)
    ethics scandals, 101
    patent infringement lawsuit, 229
journalists, the press
    cheating by, 116
    and freedom of the press, 32, 54
    importance of investigative journalism, 264
    international suppression, imprisonment and killing of, 155–56
    role in revealing unethical conduct, 264
JPMorgan
    settlement of lawsuits and claims, 72
    stock spinning by, 103
Judeo-Christian values. *See also* ethics-based American Rule of Law; 10
  Commandments of Trust
    as basis for ethics-based American Rule of Law, 51–52
    resurgence in mainstream American culture, 177
    role in American success, 131, 132
    upholding and recognizing, 175
Judge Judy, 256
judges
    anon-independent, and Rule by Law, 158
    rulings on government actions, 127
    unethical conduct among, 108
junk bonds, 48. *See also* insider trading
just hearings, defined, 199
justice. *See also* fairness
    disparate views on, 145
    and fairness, 195
the "Just Kidding" clause, 140–41

Kant, Immanuel, 12
Kelso lawsuit, 128–29, 228
Kennedy, John F.
    as first Catholic president, 132–33
    on God-given rights of American people, 165
Kenya, 92
Khodorkovsky. Mikhail, 158
kickbacks, 206–7
killing, ethical proscription against, 13

knowledge, value and limits of, 11–12
   as basis for success, insufficiency of, 12
   as one component of wisdom, 12
   temporal nature of, 12
knowledge processing, 10
Kozlowski, Dennis, 100
KPMG, accounting fraud, 107, 267

labor, importance in capitalist society, 235
landowners, standards of care required of, 212
land recording systems, transparent *vs.* nontransparent, 227–28
Landrum-Griffin Act of 1959, 235
law courts, secular, in England, 132
law enforcement
   relationship to ethics and morality, 51–52, 71–72, 183
   scandals involving, 112–13
law of gravity, 24
laws, federal
   and expanding number of federal crimes, 186
   and fairness principles, 195
   writing in understandable language, importance, 185–86
lawyers. *See also* American Rule of Lawyers and Bureaucrats
   and changing definitions of what is legal, 140
   expanded power and authority, 31
   lawyer education, U.S. *vs.* Australia, 21
   legal malpractice, 214
leaders/leadership, real (Commandment #9)
   Animal Farm ethics and fake leadership, 253–55
   areas of potential misconduct and unethical behavior, 252–261
   and CEO compensation, 256–59
   essential behaviors, 250–52
   examples of, 250–52
   fiduciary responsibilities, 257–58
   as human, flawed, 252
   and "maximizing shareholder value" concept, 259
   relationship to trust, 249, 261
   sample laws related to, 262, 281
   setting an example, 254
   taking care of troops first, 255
   underlying ethics principles, 262, 281
Leewood Healthcare Center, criminal negligence penalties, 268
legal system, U.S., and importance of due process, 199–200
Lehman Brothers
   accounting fraud, 114, 220

bankruptcy, 99
    and executive compensation, 258
lending standards, 64
leveraged money, phantom wealth, 64
Levitt, Arthur, 222
Lewis, Sinclair, 179
Li, Jeremy, 177
libel tourism, 155
LIBOR scandal, 115
lies, repeating, Goebbels on, 50
Lincoln, Abraham
    on America as world's hope, 176
    on ethical principles as absolute, 42
    faith in the wisdom of the people, 37
    on the imperative of national unity, 39
    on the importance of education, 49
    on importance of sustaining the Constitution, 125
    proclamation of a day of national prayer, 138–39
    on retaining the Constitution intact, 264
    on the superiority of labor over capital, 235
    on taking responsibility, 168
lines of credit, 66
Liu Xiaobo, 150
Livedoor Holdings, Japan, accounting fraud, 285
Lombardi, Vince, 15
loophole mentality, 62
looting charges, penalties for, 268
Los Angeles County, accounting fraud scandal, 220–21
The Los Angeles Times
    article on disparities in wealth in the United States, 89
    on ethical violations in California schools, 115
    investigation of Bell, California finances, 264
Louisiana, scandals involving elected officials, 108–9
loyalty (Commandment #3)
    areas of potential misconduct, 203–8
    and confidentiality, 208–9
    and conflicts of interest, 204
    fiduciary duty of, 203
    relationship to trust, 203, 208
    and revolving door behaviors, 204
    sample laws related to, 209, 275
    and self-dealing, 208
    underlying ethics principle, 209, 275

lying/dishonesty
   claims about products and services, 193
   as crime with a victim, 189
   and the destruction of trust, 56
   failure to disclose, 192–93
   intent to deceive, 191
   lying to the government, 190
   lying under oath (perjury), 189–190
   obstruction of justice, 190

Madison, James
   on difference between a democracy and a republic, 125
   on the importance of popular respect for the Constitution, 129–130
   on need for distrust of men in power, 126
   on need for understandable laws, 186
Madoff, Bernie
   Ponzi schemes, 105
   punishment, 142
   and SEC's due diligence failures, 214
Magna Carta, 4
manufacturing defects, and product liability, 213
manufacturing jobs, 8–9
Marbury vs. Madison, 127
margin loans, 67–68
Marsh & McLennan, ethical breaches, 101
Maryland, scandals involving elected officials, 110–11
Mattel/MGA, litigation over Bratz dolls, 232
maturity, behaving like a grown-up, 163–64
Mayflower Compact
   as covenant with God, 135
   and Rule of Law, 4
Medicare/Medicaid
   accounting fraud, 101, 220
   government spending on, 166
   increasing costs of, as unsustainable, 73
   as unfunded liabilities, 141
"Me" Generation, 47
Merck & Co., Inc., ethical breaches, 101, 192
mergers and acquisitions boom, 64–65, 68–69
Merrill, Edward, 70
MERS. *See* mortgages
Mexico
   bribery scandals, 207
   civil law system and culture of corruption, 93, 154

insecurity associated with drug cartels, 93

MF Global scandal, 105

MGA/Mattel litigation over Bratz dolls, 232

Michigan
    scandals involving elected officials, 111
    scandals involving religious leaders, 113

Microsoft, Inc.
    antitrust lawsuit, 285
    antityping (bundling) lawsuit, 197

Midas, King, 86

Middle East
    culture-specific ethical standards, 153
    decreasing stability in, 169

Midnight Express (movie), 145

Milberg Weiss, legal system fraud, 107

military personnel, employee rights, 241

Milken, Michael, 48, 55

Minnesota, pension cuts/restrictions, 140–41

misappropriating funds, 223

misconduct. *See* unethical conduct

Mitsubishi Motors, discrimination lawsuit against, 238

molecular economy, 9–10

money, borrowed (leveraged), and "phantom" wealth, 64

monopoly power, proscriptions against, 196–97

moral principles. *See also* ethics, ethical conduct; ethics-based American Rule of Law
    and knowing the difference between right and wrong, 51
    relationship with ethics and the law, 51–52
    religious basis for, 134–35
    and trustworthy leadership, 249–250
    as underlying founding of the United States, 121, 124

Morgan Stanley, insider trading, 103–4

Mormons, Ponzi scheme involving, 105

mortgages
    comparison of the 1920s and the 2000s, 66
    defaulting on, and ongoing contract obligations, 245
    mortgage and foreclosure fraud, 106
    mortgage-backed bonds, 71
    mortgage-backed trusts, 226–27
    Mortgage Electronic Registration Systems, Inc. (MERS), 227–28
    public registries for, 227
    risky, 66–67, 71–72

Motorola Solutions, Inc., trade secrets violations, 232

motor vehicle titles, 227

Mugabe, Robert, 94
multiculturalism *vs.* diverse uniculturalism, 122–24
Murphy, Audie, 172
mutual fund industry scandals, 102
The Mystery of Capital (de Soto), 151

nanotechnology, nanometers, 10
Napster, Inc., copyright infringement lawsuit, 230
NASA, conspiracy charges, 268
National Education Association (NEA), fraudulent endorsements, 205
nations/national cultures
    all force cultures, 78
    all-trust cultures, 78
    culture-specific ethical standards, 152–54
    fragility and changeability of, 46–47, 76–77
    hybrid force (government)/"trust" (economy) culture, 79
    hybrid trust (government)/force (economy) culture, 78–79
natural disasters, increasing costs associated with, 169
Navajo Code Talkers, 172
Navigant, confidentiality breach lawsuit, 208
negligence, 211–12
Nevada, criminalizing of robo-signing, 228
"New Age" ethics, 47–48
New London, CT, *Kelo* lawsuit, 128–29, 228
New Mexico, scandals involving elected officials, 110–11
"new morality," and the "Greed Generation", 48
New Orleans, bribes and kickbacks following Hurricane Katrina, 207
New York City
    accounting fraud, 220
    bribery scandal, 206
    overcharging by cab drivers, 116–17
New York State
    lawsuits involving deceptive mortgage practices, 228
    scandals involving elected officials, 110–11, 206
    scandals involving law enforcement, 112–13
The New York Times
    cheating by a reporter, 116
    on leveraged buyouts in the 2000s, 69
    public apology for anti-Singaporean editorial, 155–56
9/11 terrorist attacks
    response to, among the American people, 119
    settlement with workers, fairness issues, 196
Nixon, Richard, ethics scandal, 97
noncompetition agreements, 208, 241

nonprofit organizations
   accounting fraud, 221
   examples of excessive compensation, 260
   financial accountability, 218
North Carolina, scandals involving elected officials, 110
Northwest Ordinance, 135

Oath of Allegiance of Citizenship, 122–23, 148–49
oaths, legal, importance, 190
obstruction of justice, 189–190
Occupational Safety and Health Administration (OSHA), responsibilities, 240
official religion, proscription against in the U.S. Constitution, 130–31
offshoring, 8–9
Ohio, scandals involving elected officials, 112, 207
Oil-for-Food program (United Nations) scandals, 147–48
Oklahoma, scandals involving elected officials, 110
Once Upon a Car: The Fall and Resurrection of America's Big Three Auto Makers—GM, Ford and Chrysler (Vlasic), 8
"Operation False Charity," 192
optimism, blind, as *hubris*, 57–58
Oral Roberts University, scandal involving misuse of funds, 113
ordinary people, wisdom and courage of, 12–13, 33, 41, 129, 171, 186, 250, 252
Orwell, George, 253
oversight, competent, 222–23
ownership of property, and legal titles, 226

Paine, Thomas
   on absoluteness of moral principle, 192
   on bad government, xi
   on moderation, 163
Pakistan, suppression of religious expression in, 156
partners/partnerships, loyalty required of, 203
pastors, excessive compensation packages, 261
patents, 229–230
Patient Protection and Affordable Care Act, 166, 185
payday loans, 66
pay for performance, 258
"pay to play" scandals, 111
Penn, William
   on absoluteness of moral principle, 18
   on promises, 243
Pennsylvania, scandals involving elected officials, 112
Pennsylvania Act, 136
Pennsylvania Constitution, 136

Pennzoil Company, lawsuit with Texaco, 244

Pension Benefit Guaranty Corporation (PBGC), 140

pensions

and financial misconduct, 68, 71, 103, 112, 204–5

losses associated with, 99, 102

obligations associated with, 169, 222

"pay to play" schemes, 111

reforms, reductions, 178, 236, 264

as unfunded liabilities, 30, 111, 140–41

Peregrine Financial Group, Inc., embezzlement scandal, 100, 115

perjury (lying under oath), 189–190

personal property. *See* property ownership

pharmaceutical companies, ethics scandals, 101

Phenergan lawsuit involving carelessness, 212

philanthropy, 88, 150

phoenix analogy, 178

Pitt, Harvey, 219

Plessy v. Ferguson, 140

police, corrupt, 158

political instability, and loss of trust, 92–93

political stability, defined, 79

political thinking (indoctrination)

critical thinking *vs.*, 49

as destructive, in free societies, 50

and ethical confusion, 50

Ponzi schemes

and due diligence requirements, 214

examples, 105

during the 1920s, 69–70

involving religious institutions/leaders, 113

Portugal, erosion of culture of trust in, 85

positive change, indicators of, 177–78

power, absolute, distrust of, 4, 31, 78, 85–86, 89, 126–30, 135–36, 138

predatory lending practices, 105–6

presidential election campaign costs, 129

pretexting, 200

price-fixing, 196

PricewaterhouseCoopers, 107

principle-based accounting, 219

Pritchard, Alabama, pension cuts, 140–41

Privacy Rights Clearinghouse, on data breaches, 213

private equity funds (leveraged-buyouts), 67–69, 102–3

private ethics *vs.* public ethics, 53–54

private property rights (Commandment #6). *See also* mortgages areas of potential misconduct, 226–233

in China, legal protections, 289

and clear legal titles, 226

and "collective" property in all-force cultures, 81–82

copyrights, copyright protections, 230–31

and environmental protection, 233

and excessive government regulation, 228

and a free market economy, 79, 225–26

and government "takings," 228

patents, 229

and record keeping rules, 227

respecting, as component of trust, 225–26, 233

and the Rule of Law, 151

sample laws related to, 234

trademarks, 229

trade secrets, 232

underlying ethics principles, 234

unethical mortgage practices, 227–28

product liability, 212–13

promise-keeping (Commandment #8). *See also* contracts, contract law

areas of potential misconduct, 243–46

promissory estoppel, 246

relationship to trust, 243, 246

sample laws related to, 247, 280

underlying ethics principles, 247, 280

unjust enrichment, 246

property ownership. *See* private property rights (Commandment #6)

Protestant Christianity. *See also* Judeo-Christian values

in America, de Tocqueville's views on, 139–140

and bottom-up organizing principle, 4–5, 133

impact on English legal system, 132

role in American success, 131–33

Supreme Court recognition of primacy of in the United States, 142

public ethics, 53–55

publicity, and enforcement of ethical standards, 32, 54, 83, 183, 243, 259

public officials and employees

bribery, 207

corruption and bribery charges, 285

employee unions, 236

importance of transparency, 264

and insider trading rules, 198

loyalty to constituents, as ethical requirement, 203

managing public funds, and conflicts of interest, 204

mandatory ethical behaviors, 24

scandals involving, 108–13

"pump and dump" stock schemes, 69–70

punitive damages, 203, 212, 232, 243, 245

Putin, Vladimir, 158

Quran (Koran), 133–34, 170

Qwest Communications International accounting fraud, 100

race discrimination, 267

Racketeer Influenced and Corrupt Organizations (RICO) statute, 55

Rajaratnam, Raj, 104

Ralroad Retirement Board disability fraud, 192

reading, and critical thinking, 49–50

Reagan, Ronald, 173

real estate scandals. *See also* mortgages; private property rights (Commandment
  #6)

    comparison of the 1920s and the 2000s, 64–67

    mortgage and foreclosure fraud, 106

    predatory lending practices, 105–6

reality, confronting, 57

reasonable care, defined, 211–12

reckless behavior/conduct, defined, 212

record keeping, and financial accountability, 223, 227

Red Owl Store, Inc. lawsuit for promissory estoppel, 246

Refco Inc., scandals involving, 104

register of deeds, 227

regulations, U.S. government

    and environmental protection, 233

    excessive, debilitating nature, 34

    as impinging on property rights, 228

    need to reduce, 184–85

relative ethics, 47–48

religion

    freedom of, as Constitutional guarantee, 130–31

    freedom of *vs.* freedom from, 134

    growing intolerance of, global manifestations, 176

    increasing restrictions on, 138

    practice of, in America, 137

    and the priority of civilian law over God's law, 133–34

    religious leaders, scandals involving, 113–14

representative republic *vs.* democracy, 125

resources and supplies, and sustainability, 11

respecting others (Commandment #7)

    areas of potential misconduct, 235–241

employment law, 236–37
relationship to trust, 235, 241
sample laws related to, 241, 279
unethical conduct, 241, 279
unions/union law, 235–36
responsibility, personal, and sustainable freedom, 40–41
résumés, lying on, 116
retaliation, examples, 238–39
reverse discrimination, 236–37
revolving door between government and private business, 204–5
Rhode Island
pension system overhaul, 178
publicizing tax delinquents, 264
Rigas, John and son, 99–100
right behavior. *See also* ethics-based American Rule of Law
and culture of trust, 51
identifying, recognizing, 55–56
and the 10 Commandments of Trust, 184
as underlying ethics, 51, 187
rights in U.S. Constitution. *See* freedom, American; U.S. Constitution
"The Rime of the Ancient Mariner" (Coleridge), 24
Rio Tinto employees in China, imprisonment, 158–59
risks as a nation, complacency about, 44, 58–59, 62, 69–70, 97
Rite Aid Corp., ethical breaches, 101
Rizzo. Robert, 112
"The Roaring 2000s"
comparison with the "Roaring Twenties," 64–65
complacency about risk, 70
consumer debt boom, 65–66
income inequality/disparities, 69
mergers and acquisitions boom, 68–69
rampant cheating during, 70
real estate boom, 66–68
"The Roaring Twenties"
comparison with the "Roaring 2000s," 64–65
complacency about risk, 69–70
consumer debt boom, 65–66
income inequality/disparities, 69
mergers and acquisitions boom, 68
rampant cheating during, 69–70
real estate boom, 66
stock market boom, 67
Rockefeller, John D., 88

Roosevelt, Franklin D.
   on balancing individual and national interests, 170
   on government of and by the people, 38
   internment of Japanese-Americans, 172
   national prayer on D-Day. 1944, 139
   on roots of confidence, 42
Roosevelt, Theodore
   on "get-rich-quick" thinking, 57
   on need for moral education, 98
Rosie the Riveter, 172
Rubin, Robert, 204–5
Rule of Force, 78
rule of law. *See also* American Rule of Lawyers and Bureaucrats; ethics-based
  American Rue of Law
   American *vs.* European, 154
   as country/culture-specific, 151–52, 154
   diversity of global views about, 145, 151
   ethics based, as foundational principle in America, 4–5
   failures of, and political instability, 92
   Rule by Law *vs.*, 157–58
   and successful free market capitalism, 151
   Westernized *vs.* non-Westernized countries, 151–52
   World Justice Project's criteria for, 151
rules-based accounting, 219
the rural poor, bravery among during World War II, 172
Russia, Russian Federation
   adoption of hybrid cultural model, 83
   corrupt law enforcement in, 158
   economic challenges, corruption, 176
   newness as a country, 176
   proscriptions against assembly, protests, 157
   resurgence of Russian Orthodox Church, 135
   violence against journalists in, 156
   wheat shortages, global impacts, 146
Russian Revolution, 124

safety and health violations, penalties for, 268, 285, 289
safety nets, unrealistic expectations about, 73
Samsung, patent lawsuit with Apple, 229
Santa Fe, NM, misconduct by public officials, 218
Santayana, George, 62
Saudi Arabia
   dominance of God's law in, 133–34
   pact with China to receive nuclear weapons technology, 169

savings rates, negative, as warning sign, 73

Schopenhauer, Arthur, iii

Schumacher, E. F., iii

Scientific American, on distrust of atheists, 177

Scientific Applications International Corporation (SAIC), TechnoDyne scandal, 222

scientific laws, and the laws of ethical conduct, 24–25

Scrushy, Richard
    trials and conviction, 55
    unjust enrichment lawsuit, 246

Securities Act of 1933, 102

Securities and Exchange Commission (SEC)
    accounting fraud cases, 107
    charges against Freddie Mac, 100
    charges related to backdated stock options, 101
    due diligence failures, 214
    full disclosure provisions, 187
    insider trading law enforcement, 198
    judicial rejection of rule giving investors more power, 128
    rules governing private companies, 198–99
    securities fraud penalties, 267–68
    settlement with Bank of America, judicial rejection of, 127
    warnings regarding accounting rules, 219
    whistleblower-induced lawsuit, 266

security, national, defined, 79

self-dealing, 208

self-determination, 20

self-organizing. *See also* ethics-based American Rule of Law; trust, culture of
    by Americans, early examples, 4–5
    and the culture of trust, 14
    importance of wisdom to, 13
    as key to surviving crises, 119, 179
    and personal responsibility, 40
    self-governance, 123
    underlying concepts and behaviors, 3, 13–14, 22–26

sexual harassment, 238

shareholder value, maximizing, 259

Sherman, William Tecumseh
    on mutual support among leaders, 251
    as real leader, 251

"ship-of-state," American, potential for sinking, 59

shootings, random, and rising lack of trust, 91

Siemans, bribery scandal, 267

Singapore, penalties for ethical misconduct in, 285

situational ethics, 47–48

Situation Ethics: The New Morality (Fletcher), 47

Skilling, Jeff, 99

skills, 21st century, 10–11

social harmony, 79, 90–91

social media, 83. *See also* journalists, the press

Social Security

    government spending on, 166–67

    increasing payments for as unsustainable, 73

Socrates, 48

Souter, David, 120

Soviet Union

    dissolution, 83

    as example of failed all-force culture, 81–82

Spain, erosion of culture of trust in, 85

specific performance remedy, 244

speculative bubbles, 64–65

speech codes, use of to suppress free speech, 155

spirit of the law, 142

Spitzer, Eliot, 102

sports

    celebrity pay packages, 256

    cheating within, 116

standard of living

    declining, in the United States, 161

    relationship to freedom and trust, 94

standards, enforcing (Commandment #10)

    ethics-based American Rule of Law, 32–33, 175

    power of the press, 264

    relationship to trust, 263, 270

    sample laws related to, 270, 282

    tools for enforcement, 264–270

    underlying ethics principles, 270, 282

    whistleblowers, 266

Stanford, Allen, 105

Star-Spangled Banner (song), 136

state constitutions, references to God in, 136–37

state governments. *See also specific states*

    accounting fraud, 220

    examples of excessive compensation, 260

    rights afforded in the U.S. Constitution, 128

    tensions with federal government, 128–29

steel production, United States, 11

steroids, use of by athletes, 116

stock analyst recommendations, scandals related to, 102

stock market. *See also* Financial Crisis of 2008
  comparison of the 1920s and the 2000s, 64–65, 67
  and slow development of the Great Depression, 61
  stock options, backdated, as ethics violation, 101
Strauss, William, 33, 60–61
strict liability, 212
suicide rates
  and bullying, 239
  rising, in the United States, 91
Sullenberger, Chesley B. "Sully" III, 252
A Summary of the 2014 Annual Reports, 166–67
Sunni-Shiite Muslim tribal war, 170
supercomputers, 10
Supreme Court of the United States. *See* U.S. Supreme Court
sustainability, importance, 11
swarm intelligence, 3, 13–14
Swissport Singapore, breach of contract charges, 285
Syria, civil war in, 176

Taft-Hartley Act of 1947, 235
Taiwan, penalties for ethical misconduct in, 285
Take-Two Interactive Software, Inc., accounting fraud, 220
Tauzin, Billy, 205
taxes
  cheating on, 115
  over-complexity of U.S. tax code, 184
tax enforcement policies and actions, 265–66
taxpayer bailouts, 100
Taylor, Bean & Whitaker (TBW), indictment for criminal fraud, 191
Taylor, Charles, 152
Tebow, Tim, 177
TechnoDyne scandal, 222
technology
  biotechnology, biotech revolution, 9–10
  and global criminal operations, 146
telling the truth. *See* truth, telling the (Commandment #1
10 Commandments of Trust. *See also* trust, culture of *and specific commandments*
  following, and restoring culture of trust, 34–37, 183
  global manifestations, 159
  listing of, 25
  simplicity of, 184
  summary, 14–16, 173–182
  as universal and unchangeable, 24, 26, 32, 53, 187
Tenet Healthcare, ethical breaches, 101

Tennessee, scandals involving state senators, 110
Terra Commination's, Inc., bribery penalties, 268
terrorist threats, and national insecurity, 93
Texaco, Inc.
    contract breaches, penalties, 267
    lawsuit with Pennzoil, 244
Texas
    scandals involving elected officials, 110, 112
    Texas City BP refinery explosion, 240
Thailand, political instability and failure of the Rule of Law, 92–93
Thatcher, Margaret, 121
theft of trade secrets, penalties for, 268
Time magazine, on U.S. free speech protections, 154–55
Titanic, sinking of, 58–59
TJX, data safety breach, lawsuit involving, 213
tobacco companies, lawsuits and settlements, 55
"too big to fail" concept, 58–59
"top-down" governance/dictatorship model, 34, 76, 81, 86–87
tortious interference with a contract, 267
Toyota Motor Co.
    media publicity about car defects, 264
    role in auto industry, 7–8
trademarks, trademark protection, 229, 230
trade secrets, 229, 232
Triple A ratings, 70–71
trust, culture of. *See also* distrust, culture of; ethics, ethical conduct; ethics-based
    American Rule of Law; 10 Commandments of Trust; unethical conduct
    approaches to restoring, 6, 35, 55–56, 117, 174, 179, 183, 261
    and capacity to lead during a crisis, 252
    and care/being careful, 211–12
    and constitutional rights, 32
    creating and sustain, challenges, 35
    erosion of, 89, 218
    as essential for successful free-market economy, 59, 152
    and fairness principles, 195–200
    importance to survival of American freedoms, 5, 7
    laws of as timeless and immutable, 52, 56, 187
    and leadership, 249
    and loyalty, 203, 208
    oxygen metaphor for, 75
    physiological components, 55–56
    and the Rule of Law, 14
    and self-dealing, 22–23
    and self-organizing, 5

signs of stress, rubber band analogy, 162–63
sustaining, as challenging and requiring work, 84–85
and the wrongful acquisition of wealth, 87–88
trustees, loyalty required of, 203
truth, telling the (Commandment #1)
areas of potential misconduct, 189–193
and full disclosure, 192–93
and lying under oath (perjury), 189–190
and paramount importance of honesty, 187
relationship to trust, 187, 193
sample laws related to, 194, 273
underlying ethics principle, 194, 273
tsunami of ethics scandals. *See* unethical conduct
Tuskegee Airmen, 171–72
Twain, Mark
on courage, 173
on reading, 39
2010 Rule of Law Index (World Justice Project), 151–52
2011 Leadership Index (Kennedy School of Government), 249
TXU Corp. (Energy Future Holdings), buy out of, 69
Tyco International, accounting fraud scandal, 100, 106
tying (bundling) products, and unfair competition, 197

unethical conduct. *See also* distrust, culture of; enforcement; ethics, ethical conduct;
ethics-based American Rule of Law; trust, culture of
accelerating prevalence, 23–24, 97–98, 161
among leaders and public officials, 97–98, 108–13, 254–55
as basis for distrust, 39, 46, 97, 114–15, 195–96
as emergency situation, 5, 29–30, 46, 161
financial and legal consequences, 72, 264–69, 285
identifying, recognizing, 55–56
and illegal actions, 54
and inability to think critically, 49
"Me" Generation, 47
and political thinking (indoctrination), 50
Ponzi scandals, 105
rationalizing, denying, 34
reporting in the U.S. *vs.* other countries, 154–55
role of press in revealing, 264
scandals involving businesses/corporations, 22, 99–102
scandals involving religious institutions/leader, 113–14
scandals involving unions, 114
scandals involving "watchdogs" and "gatekeepers," 106–8
scandals related to real estate, 105–6

scandals related to Wall Street firms and financial markets, 101, 102–7, 142–43

and societal decline as gradual process, 30–31, 46

during the 2000s, 70

and "Wrath of God" punishments, 142

and the wrongful acquisition of wealth, 87–88

unfair lending practices, 267

unfair treatment, 195–96

unicultural diversity, 122–24

Uniform Trade Secrets Act, 232

Union Carbide India Ltd., safety and health violations, 285

unions

excessive compensation packages, 260–61

laws related to, 235–36

scandals involving, 114

United Airlines, pension cuts, 140

United Healthcare, backdating claims, 102

United Kingdom/Britain

contracts, 244

corporate entities, 203

free speech in, defamation lawsuits, 155

government model, 129

peace treaty with Hitler, 62

penalties for ethical misconduct in, 285

Protestant heritage, 132, 153

Rule of Law, common law system, 14, 20–21, 82, 92, 94, 124, 127, 132, 154–55

shared heritage with, 19

United Nations

Human Rights Commission/Charter of Human Rights, as unenforceable, 146–47

Human Rights *vs.* Bill of Rights, 149

International Criminal Court (ICC), 152

as weak, unaccountable organization, 146–48

United States Customs and Border Protection, scandals involving, 109

the United States military, scandals involving, 109

United States of America. *See also* ethics-based American Rule of Law; freedom, American; 10 Commandments of Trust; trust, culture of; U.S. Bill of Rights; U.S. Constitution

contributions to the United Nations budget, 146–47

decreased standard of living in, 161

delusion of invincibility, 40

as diversely unicultural, 122–24

economic decline/instability, 37–38, 161

ethical confusion, as emergency situation, 5, 29–30, 38–39, 46, 161

and the Fourth Turning, 60–61

government model, comparison with China, 94–95

government model, comparison with the European Union, 143–44

Judeo-Christian moral values, 124, 131–32

and levels of confidence in key institutions, 35–36

need for unity of purpose, 39, 122–24, 171

population *vs.* China's population, 39

potential for failure, 29–30, 59, 92

relative stability and durability of, 33, 176

return of offshored jobs to, 8–9

unique features, x, 5, 20–26, 32–33, 37, 40, 50, 119–125, 144

wars and military actions, costs of, 72

United Way

excessive compensation lawsuit, 260

local chapter misconduct, 114

unity, as Americans (united we stand), 39, 122–24, 171. *See also* freedom, American

Universal Declaration of Human Rights (United Nations), 149

universities, schools, scandals involving, 114, 116, 205, 221, 260, 266

University of Illinois admissions scandal, 114

University of Pennsylvania, Wharton School of Business, 52

University of Phoenix, whistleblower-induced lawsuit, 266

unjust enrichment, 246

unreasonable/unnecessary expenses, examples, 221

unsafe products, penalties for, 267

U.S. Bancorp, mortgage and foreclosure fraud, 226

U.S. Bill of Rights. *See* freedom, America; U.S. Constitution

U.S. Chamber of Commerce, compensation complaints, 260

U.S. Congress

Budget Office estimates of unfunded state liabilities, 141

employees, insider trading rules, 198

public disapproval levels, 35–36, 184

U.S. Constitution/Bill of Rights. *See also* freedom, American

Article I, Section 10, 244

checks and balances system, 126–27

educating people about, 32

as embodiment of stability and change, 121

federalism, 128

5th Amendment, 225

as fundamental document guiding American self-governance, 125

guarantees of due process, 199

individual rights guaranteed under, 129–130

limitations to federal power, 126

potential for failure, 59

and representative republican government, 125

respecting, importance, 125–26

enforcement of under American Rule of Law, 148–49

right to petition the government, 157
rights under as God-given and irrevocable, 124, 126, 132, 161
succinct language in, 184
as tool for limiting federal power, 126
as uniquely American document, 122, 129–130
U.S. Department of Energy, financial mismanagement, 222
U.S. Department of Justice
Corporate Fraud Task Foci, 102
mortgage fraud cases, 106
U.S. Environmental Protection Agency (EPA), limiting of wetland regulations, 233
U.S. Federal Deposit Insurance Company (FDIC), raising of guarantee amount, 75–76
U.S. military
excessive compensation packages, 261
Navajo Code Talkers, 172
U.S. Olympic Committee, excessive compensation complaints about, 260
U.S. Supreme Court
Brown v. Board of Education, 140
capacity to reverse rulings, 140
and consideration of social, political and economic factors, 140
disparate treatment theory of discrimination, 237
on importance of antitrust laws, 197
Kelso case, 128–29
limits on EPA wetland rules enforcement, 233
Marbury vs. Madison, 127
Plessy v. Ferguson, 140
recognition of the United States as a Christian country, 142
role within system of checks and balances, 126–27

values, identifying, 50
van Gogh, Theo, 157
Virginia Charter, 136
virtue, defined, 50
Vlasic, Bill, 8
Volcker, Paul, report on UN Oil-for-Food program, 146–48
voluntary action, and self-organization, 6
volunteerism, 88

wages. *See also* CEOs/executives
auto workers, reductions in, 8
workers' *vs.* mega-salaries for the few, 48
Wagner Act of 1935, 235
Wahhabism, 133–34
Wall Street (movie), 48

Wall Street/finance industry, scandals related to, 67, 102–5

The Wall Street Journal
    on costs of 2008 financial crisis, 72
    on duplication in federal spending, 222
    on executive compensation, 259
    on post-Enron levels of corporate fraud, 102
    on relationship of freedom and standard of living, 94
    on top 1% of income earners, 259

Wall Street Reform and Consumer Protection Act ("Dodd-Frank Act"), 185

Wal-Mart Stores, Inc., lawsuits involving unfair employee treatment, 241

Walt Disney Company, and excessive CEO compensation, 258

War of 1812, 251

war on terror, costs, 169

Warren, Earl, on the spirit of the law, 142

Washington, George
    on arbitrary power and freedom, 31
    on choosing to be free, 17
    commitment and service, 251
    Farewell Address, 1796, 138
    on force of government, 167
    on God and good government, 132
    on God-given rules of order and right, 161
    on importance of legal oaths, 190
    on the importance of the success of the American experiment, 179
    as real leader, 250
    references to God in first inaugural address, 137
    on the relationship of moral duty to happiness, 42
    on system of checks and balances, 127

Waste Management accounting fraud, 100

watchdogs, "gatekeepers"
    ethical misconduct involving, 106–8
    loss of authority, implication, 22

Watson, Thomas J., 97

wealth, easy riches
    appeal of, 63–64
    and the mergers and acquisition boom, 68–69
    and "phantom" wealth, 64
    and the "Roaring 2000s," 64–65

Webster, Daniel, 165

Wells Fargo & Co.
    bid-rigging penalties, 197
    mortgage and foreclosure rulings against, 226

West Germany
   "bottom-up" freedom model, 47
   cultural differences with East Germany, 46–47
West Point, racism at, 170
Wharton, Joseph, 52
whistleblowers, 238–39, 265
white-collar service jobs, offshoring of, 8
Whitman, Walt, 27
Wilde, Oscar, 253
Wilmott, Paul, 45
Winfrey, Oprah, 88
Wisconsin, scandals involving elected officials, 110
wisdom. *See also* experts; ordinary people
   and common sense, 12–13
   components, 12
   and "experts," 41
   as timeless, 12
women, bravery during World War II, 172
Woods, Tiger, 256
workers/employees
   bullying, 239–240
   in China, legal protections, 289
   employment law, 236–37
   harassment, 238
   relationship to trust, 235
   retaliation, 238–39
   unfair treatment, 241
   unions/union law, 235–36
work ethic, Protestant, 133
workforce participation, United States, declining, 169
workplace violence, compensation for, 240
WorldCom accounting fraud, 99, 268
The World Is Flat (Friedman), 151
World's Largest Debtor Nation, United States as, 72
World War II
   Audie Murphy, 172
   Eisenhower's leadership, 251
   Navajo Code Talkers, 172
   100th/442nd Regimental Combat Teams, 172
   the Tuskegee Airmen, 171–72
"Wrath of God" enforcement, 142
wrong doing, wrong conduct. *See* unethical conduct

Yahoo, Inc., and excessive compensation complaints, 258

Zimbabwe, Mugabe's ruinous policies in, 94
Zuma, Jacob, 153

Acknowledgements

So many people over the years have helped me with information, opinions, support, resources, and encouragement that it would be impossible to thank them all. However, I would like to thank a few of the people who were most instrumental in the completion of this project.

Several people took the time to review an early draft of the book and provide helpful suggestions and insights, including Terry Young, Joetta Forsyth, Steven Ferraro, Steven Orpurt, Douglass Gore, Michael Shay, Rick Stephens, Elane Scott, Kevin Buck, Harvey Cohen, John Dean, and Jon Wilson.

Others who deserve special mention are Jess Rosas, Nelly Kazman, Lori Putnam, Charla Griffy-Brown, Darrol and Carole Stanley, Sandra Moore, John O'Malley, Manon Gosting, Maria Brahme, Bonny Herman, Jim Cathcart, Dan Martin, Dorothy and Allen Greenstein, and Nelli and Felix Rubinstein. Sonia Kradjian, Donna Brown Guillaume, and John Weiss were kind enough to lend me books from their personal libraries.

A very special thank you goes to Joyce Briggs, who spent countless hours editing an earlier version of the book. I would also like to thank Nancy Ellen Dodd who did the same for one of the latest versions. A special thank you goes to Gia Honnen Weisdorn, who edited the last version in a very short period of time. Their editorial comments and suggestions were invaluable.

I would also like to thank the informal group of people who graciously engaged in vigorous debates with me over many years on hot-button controversial issues from different points of view, almost a lost art in America today. These debates helped clarify my thinking about how and why the United States has gone so dangerously off-track over the past 40 years when it comes to morality, ethics, and trust. In particular, John Xenakis, author of the blog generationaldynamics.com, always had wise insights to add to the conversation.

I would be remiss if I did not also thank my publisher, Robert Carkhuff, Jr. This book took many more years to complete than either he or I originally thought. Nevertheless, he stuck with this project, providing much needed encouragement, guidance, and support. His comments and suggestions, although sometimes challenging for me to execute, made this book much better than it would have been without his assistance. Also, a special thank you goes to Jean Miller, who handled the final production phase of this book with great patience, skill, care, and kindness. Working with her was a real pleasure.

Finally, I would like to thank the large numbers of students and audience participants I've had the privilege of meeting in classes and at various speaking venues over many years. It was participants in these classes and speaking events who first encouraged me to write this book. Without them, this book would never have been written.

ABOUT THE AUTHOR

Dr. McCord holds a Bachelor of Arts degree from the University of Sydney, Australia, which included the first year of law school at the University of Sydney Law School (after receiving a government Australian Commonwealth Scholarship for a six-year Arts/Law degree), a Juris Doctor (J.D.) degree from the University of Houston Law Center (where she served as an editor of the Houston Law Review), and a Master of Business Administration (M.B.A.) degree from the University of Texas at Austin.

Dr. McCord practiced law for many years before becoming a full-time business law professor, including acting as a corporate counsel (and later a General Counsel in one of the companies) of Schlumberger Technology Corporation (a subsidiary of Schlumberger Limited, headquartered in New York and Paris).

Prior to joining the law faculty at the Graziadio School of Business and Management at Pepperdine University, she was a member of the law faculty at the business school of California State University, Northridge. She has taught business law, ethics, and critical thinking in undergraduate, graduate, and executive business school programs, as well as corporate executive workshops and seminars. She has also been a keynote speaker at numerous corporate, government, nonprofit, association and university events.

Because of her unusual background, education, and experience, she brings a fresh perspective on the extraordinary gift of America's self-organizing culture of trust and freedom, our secret key to survival and success in the turbulent age of the 21st century.

Dr. McCord may be reached at Linnea.McCord@pepperdine.edu.